U0515752

目录

目录

CONTENTS

中国文化遗产
CHINA CULTURAL HERITAGE

奇迹天工

中国古代发明创造文物展

主编　国家文物局　中国科学技术协会

Exhibition of Ancient Chinese Inventions Artifacts

Compiled By
State Administration of Cultural Heritage
China Association for Science and Technology

文物出版社
Cultural Relics Press

奇迹天工——中国古代发明创造文物展

主办单位

国家文物局　中国科学技术协会

承办单位

中国文物交流中心　中国科学技术馆

协办单位

中国国家博物馆　上海博物馆

中国科学院上海硅酸盐研究所　中国丝绸博物馆

CONTENTS

架起沟通文明的桥梁

中国是一个文明古国，更是一个发现和发明的国度。在绵延长达五千年的华夏文明史上，中华民族不仅发展形成了以“天、算、农、医”为代表的中国古代科学体系，而且取得了造纸术、印刷术、指南针和火药等一系列重大技术成就，为人类社会的文明进步做出了重要贡献。

现代奥林匹克运动发源于2000多年前的古希腊文明，经过近一个多世纪的曲折发展，现代奥林匹克精神已经成为当代普世价值的重要组成部分。奥运会使不同国家、不同民族、不同信仰的人聚在一起，相互交流，加强了解，增进友谊，从而有助于建立一个美好和平的世界。

科学技术是人类文明进步的先声，科学技术历史是人类文明进步的刻度。值此第29届夏季奥运会在北京举办之际，中国科学技术协会和中国国家文物局携手合作，共同努力，从内容丰富、博大精深的中国古代发明创造的大海中，精心撷取了几片浪花，通过《奇迹天工——中国古代发明创造文物展》奉献给世界各国的朋友们，为北京奥运会增添一些色彩，也体现了科技奥运的理念，为世界了解中国提供一个窗口，为沟通东西方文明架起一座桥梁。

奥运连五洲，友谊传四海。衷心希望中国古代发明创造文物展能够为加强沟通、增进理解、促进友谊、加深互信、共创文明和谐的新世界作出积极的贡献。

祝愿人类的明天更美好！

中国科学技术协会常务副主席 邓楠

Construct Bridges Linking the Civilizations

China is a nation with early civilization and abundant discoveries and inventions. In the 5000 years of civilization history, Chinese people established the ancient science system represented by "Astronomy, Mathematics, Agronomy and Medicine", and contributed papermaking, printing, compass and gunpowder to the progress of the human civilizations.

Modern Olympics originated from the ancient Greek civilization over 2000 years ago; through the development for more than one century, the modern Olympic Spirit has become an important component of contemporary Universal Value. Olympics gathers together peoples of different countries, different ethnic groups and different persuasions, improves communications, mutual understandings and friendship, and helps to build a beautiful and peaceful world.

Science and technology are the vanguard for the progress of human civilization, and the history of science and technology is the milestone of these progresses. At the time of the 29th Olympic Games held in Beijing, China association for Science and Technology and State Administration of Cultural Heritage made joint efforts to pick up some flowers from the colorful garden of ancient Chinese inventions and discoveries and arranged this "Exhibition of Ancient Chinese Inventions Artifacts" for our friends at home and from abroad attending this great gathering. We hope that this exhibition will add some luster to the Beijing Olympic Games, provide a window for the world to know more about China and construct a bridge linking the civilizations in the East and West.

We heartily hope our exhibition contributes positively for strengthening communications and understandings, improving friendship and mutual confidence and building a prosperous and harmonious world.

May we have a more beautiful future!

Executive Vice President, China Association for Science and Technology
Deng Nan

天工开物　传承文明

为体现北京奥运会“人文奥运、绿色奥运、科技奥运”主题，集中展示中国文化的博大精深、古代科技的辉煌灿烂，由国家文物局、中国科学技术协会联合主办的《奇迹天工——中国古代发明创造文物展》，在党中央、国务院领导同志，北京奥组委、文化部的高度重视和大力支持下，在中国文物交流中心、中国科学技术馆及全国24个省、市、自治区的78家参展单位的共同努力下，于2008年7月28日，在北京奥运中心区国家奥林匹克公园内的中国科技馆新馆隆重开幕。

本次展览通过三百多件（组）巧夺天工的精品文物，把辉煌灿烂的中国古代科技文明重现于世人眼前。对于来自不同地区、不同国家，有着不同文化和生活背景的海内外朋友，走近华夏文明、了解中国古代科技发展史，增进不同民族与文化间的沟通交流，将起到有力的促进作用。展览通过展示中国古代伟大的发明创造，对于彰显中华民族的伟大智慧和创造力，增强民族自豪感和自信心，弘扬以爱国主义为核心的民族精神具有重要的意义。

中华民族拥有五千年连绵不断的文明史，拥有门类众多、不可胜数的珍贵文物，还拥有撼天朔地、辉煌灿烂的发明创造。中国古代科技文明自远古时代开端并形成原始积累，在春秋战国时期奠定基础，经过两汉、隋唐和宋元时期的持续发展，至明代中期，传统科学技术达到了一个新的高峰。不但为后世留下了指南针、火药、造纸术、活字印刷术四大发明，还有十进位制、赤道坐标系、瓷器、丝绸、二十四节气等重大发明和发现，以及一系列集大成的科技著作。中国古代科技文明，既是中华民族生存和发展的基础，也是中华民族对世界和人类的贡献，更是中国古代文明发展成就的象征。

这些传统科学思想和科学技术的突出成就，是中华民族辛勤耕耘、善于观察、长于思索、勇于探究、注重传承的实证，闪耀着古代先民智慧的光辉。许多发明、发现和创造对于世界科技发展史都有着开天辟地的重要意义。马克思曾经指出：“火药、指南针、印刷术这是预告资产阶级社会到来的三大发明……总的说来是变成科学复兴的手段，变成对精神发展创造必要前提的杠杆。”

文物作为历史和文明的载体，忠实地记录了中华民族祖先们在天文学、地理学、数学、物理学、化学、生物学和医学等方面数量众多的、内容丰富的重要的发现、发明和创造，以实物形态荷载了古代科技文明的精神实质，更是“科技是第一生产力”的物化表现。这些弥足珍贵的文物，充分体现了中华民族祖先们的伟大智慧和创新精神，有力证明了中华文明的发展史就是一部中华民族的持续创新史。

“锦绣华服”、“雄奇宝器”、“典藏文明”、“泱泱瓷国”，《奇迹天工——中国古代发明创造文物展》的四个主题鲜明独特，具有极强的展示功能和教育意义。三百多件（组）文物精品穿越时空铺就的“古代科技文明走廊”，彰往昭来，借2008年北京奥运会这一天赐良机，让全世界在丝绸的华美婉约、青铜器的庄严浑厚、纸张的轻柔朴质和瓷器的光彩流转中，感受中华民族传统的丝绸染织术、青铜铸造术、造纸印刷术和瓷器制作术中蕴藏的浩瀚难穷的中国古代科技文明和中华文化精髓，用物化的历史和文化形态为“科技奥运、人文奥运”理念做出最佳的注脚。

国家文物局局长 单霁翔

The Supernatural Craftsmanship, the Uninterrupted Civilization

To express the themes of "People's Olympics, Green Olympics and High-tech Olympics" of Beijing Olympic Games, and exhibit the sophisticated Chinese culture and the splendid ancient Chinese sciences and technology, Chinese State Administration of Cultural Heritage and China Association for Science and Technology jointly hold this "Exhibition of Ancient Chinese Inventions Artifacts" under the caring of our Central Government and the support of Beijing Organizing Committee of Olympic Games and Ministry of Culture in China Science and Technology Museum located in the Beijing Olympic Green, which is in the Olympic central area, on the eve of the great meeting of the 29th Olympic Games. In total 78 partner museums and other institutions participated in this exhibition.

By more than 300 pieces and sets of carefully selected artifacts, we display the achievements of Chinese ancient science and technology for our friends with various cultural backgrounds and life styles, through which we believe that our friends' understandings to Chinese civilization and science and communications among peoples in different regions all over the world will be improved greatly. Moreover, the exhibition also provides our compatriots an opportunity to get deeper knowledge to our glorious past and have stronger sense of patriotism and self-confidence to create a wonderful future.

Since the remote ancient times, Chinese people have begun to accumulate experiences on science and technology; in the Spring-and-Autumn and Warring-States Periods, the foundations for the future developments have been firmly laid. Through the continuing development from the Han to the Song and Yuan Dynasties, Chinese traditional science and technology reached their climax in the mid-Ming Dynasty. This thousand-year long development endowed us not only the four great inventions: compass, gunpowder, papermaking and printing, but also decimal system, equatorial coordinate system, porcelain, silk textile, the twenty-four solar terms and other significant discoveries and inventions, as well as a series of written works on science and technology. The scientific and technological civilizations of ancient China are not only the bases for the surviving and development of Chinese people, but also Chinese people's contributions to the mankind and symbols of Chinese civilization.

These outstanding achievements of Chinese traditional science and technology are the results and evidence for the hard work, close observation, meticulous thinking and reasoning, brave exploration and diligent studying and instructing of our ancestors; many discoveries and inventions are critically meaningful to the progresses of human civilization. Karl Marx has pointed out that "Gunpowder, the compass, and the printing press were the three great inventions which ushered in bourgeois society. Gunpowder blew up the knightly class, the compass discovered the world market and founded the colonies, and the printing press was the instrument of Protestantism and the regeneration of science in general; the most powerful lever for creating the intellectual prerequisites."

As embodiments of history and civilization, the artifacts loyally noted our ancestors' great discoveries and inventions in the fields of astronomy, geography, mathematics, physics, chemistry, biology and medicine, showed the spiritual nature of ancient science and civilization of China and expressed the thought of "Science and technology are the No. 1 productive force". These invaluable artifacts conserved the significant intelligence and original spirits of ancient Chinese people and proved the development of Chinese civilization to be a history of ceaseless innovation.

The subjects of the four sections: "the Ancient Art of Silk Weaving and Dyeing, Techniques of Ancient Bronze Production, the Traditional Techniques of Papermaking and Printing and The Techniques of Ancient Porcelain Production" of our exhibition are unique, clear, strongly understandable and educationally significant; the "Science, technology and culture gallery" built by the more than three pieces and sets of carefully selected artifacts leads our guests and friends from all over the world to experience Chinese traditional techniques of silk weaving, bronze casting, papermaking and printing and porcelain manufacturing by enjoying the beautiful silks, elegant bronzes and wonderful porcelain wares displayed here at the intervals of the intensive competitions on the playgrounds.

Director of State Administration of Cultural Heritage
Shan Jixiang

前　言

在我们这个古老的国度，曾经有过许多的创造与发明。

中国古代在天文学、地理学、数学、物理学、化学、生物学和医学上都有许多发现、发明与创造。我们有指南针、火药、造纸和印刷术四大发明，还有十进位制、赤道坐标系、瓷器、丝绸、二十四节气等重大发明。

古代的发明与创造，随着历史的脚步慢慢远去，是不断面世的古代文物让我们淡忘的记忆又渐渐清晰起来。

这里展陈的文物是庄重的青铜器和光彩的瓷器，还有华美的丝绸和轻柔的纸张，真切的文物从几个侧面展示着中国发明与创造的历史。

在北京奥运欢腾的节日里，我们走进新落成的中国科学技术馆，凝视这些珍贵的古代文物，呈现在我们面前的是天工创造的一个个奇迹。

PREFACE

In the course of China's long and venerable history, a vast array of inventions, ranging from the basic to the highly complex, have brought changes to the pattern of life in nearly every generation.

In ancient China, innovations were put forth in the fields of astronomy, geography, mathematics, physics, chemistry, biology, and the medical sciences, to name a few.

The four inventions that brought about the greatest historical changes were papermaking, printing, gunpowder, and the compass. Other major Chinese contributions to world culture include the decimal system, the equatorial coordinate system, ceramics, silk production, and the twenty-four solar period system.

This exhibition includes magnificent bronze vessels, elegant ceramics, beautiful silks, and fine examples of early paper. Even though memory has faded with time and these past inventions and achievements have been integrated into our modern existence, it is impossible to overlook our debt to the early Chinese. These artifacts are vivid reminders of the creativity of early inventors and the imagination of early artisans.

On this joyous occasion of Beijing hosting the 2008 Olympic Games, this exhibition in the new hall of the China Science and Technology Museum displays some of China's most amazing treasures of heavenly works.

锦绣华服

古代丝绸染织术

蚕桑丝绸是中国古代重要的发明创造之一，它与中华五千年古老文明同岁。先人们植桑养蚕结茧，取蚕丝巧织经纬，后来发明提花机织出灿烂文锦，还通过印花刺绣锦上添花。

丝绸是中国之珍、东方之宝。丝绸为中国文明写下了光辉的一页，更为世界文化贡献了灿烂的篇章。丝绸搭起了连接中西的桥梁，古代丝绸之路成为中外文化交流的重要通道。

The Ancient Art of Silk Weaving and Dyeing

The production of silk using mulberry silkworms was one of the most significant inventions in ancient China and developed alongside China's 5,000 years of civilization. Ancient Chinese not only cultivated mulberry trees to raise silkworms that were used to produce silk fibers and then woven into textiles, but also developed the technical process of reeling from the cocoon. The silk fabric was then dyed and embroidered to enhance a piece's aesthetic value.

Silk was an extremely valuable commodity for China as well as the rest of Asia and soon spread to other countries where its appeal was instantaneous. As this type of textile was an important trade good it lent its name to the famous Silk Road, the most important conduit for cultural exchanges between China and foreign civilizations.

蚕桑为业
Sericulture

蚕丝是古代中国人最早利用的动物纤维之一。早在新石器时代，植桑和养蚕已成为原始生业的重要内容。在历史时期，衣食以农桑为本，历代劝课农桑，桑蚕业不断有新的发展。

Sericulture represents the earliest Chinese efforts at animal husbandry. Since the Neolithic period, mulberry plant cultivation and silkworm rearing have been central to the subsistence. Sericulture technology developed significantly over the years, as a result of careful attention to these two areas.

新石器时代的蚕茧壳

这是约公元前3500多年山西夏县西阴村出土的仰韶文化时期的蚕茧壳，长约1.36、宽约1.04厘米。茧壳被锐利的刀刃切去了一部分，据美国斯密森学院鉴定确认为蚕茧。

Silkworm Cocoon

Late Neolithic Period (ca. 3500 BCE), Length: 1.36cm, Width: 1.04cm. Excavated at Xiyin Village, Xiaxian County, Shanxi Province. This silk cocoon was cut in half by a sharp blade and has been identified by the Smithsonian Institution of the USA as the species known as bombyx mori, or the domesticated silkworm.

丝带

新石器时代良渚文化（约公元前3200–前2200年）
长2–4、宽0.5cm
浙江湖州钱山漾出土
浙江省博物馆藏

Silk Ribbon

Late Neolithic Period (ca. 3200–2200 BCE)
Length: 2–4cm,Width: 0.5cm
Excavated at Qianshanyang, Huzhou, Zhejiang
Collection of the Zhejiang Provincial Museum

良渚文化钱山漾遗址出土物中有丝线、绸片和用丝线编织而成的丝带。这是迄今为止长江流域发现的最早的丝绸实物。

采桑人物图青铜壶

战国（公元前475–前221年）
高35.5、腹径26cm
山西襄汾出土
山西博物院藏

Bronze Round *Hu* Decorated with Motifs Depicting the Harvesting of Mulberry Leaves

Warring States Period (475–221 BCE)
Height: 35.5cm, Diameter at Widest Point: 26cm
Excavated at Xiangfen, Shanxi
Collection of the Shanxi Museum

战国时期典型的青铜器物，上面铸出的采桑和竞射活动是当时常见的装饰题材。铜壶颈部图案中清晰地表现了桑树品种之一——乔木桑，高大的桑树下有众多女子或头顶或手执篮筐，桑树之上亦有几名女子正在采摘桑叶，脚下的树枝上还挂有篮筐。

采桑人物纹青铜壶纹饰图
Details of Design Depicting People Picking Mulberry Leaves on Bronze *Hu*

忙採葉
大眠
又七八日蠶二分半長寸半帶白色方第四大眠

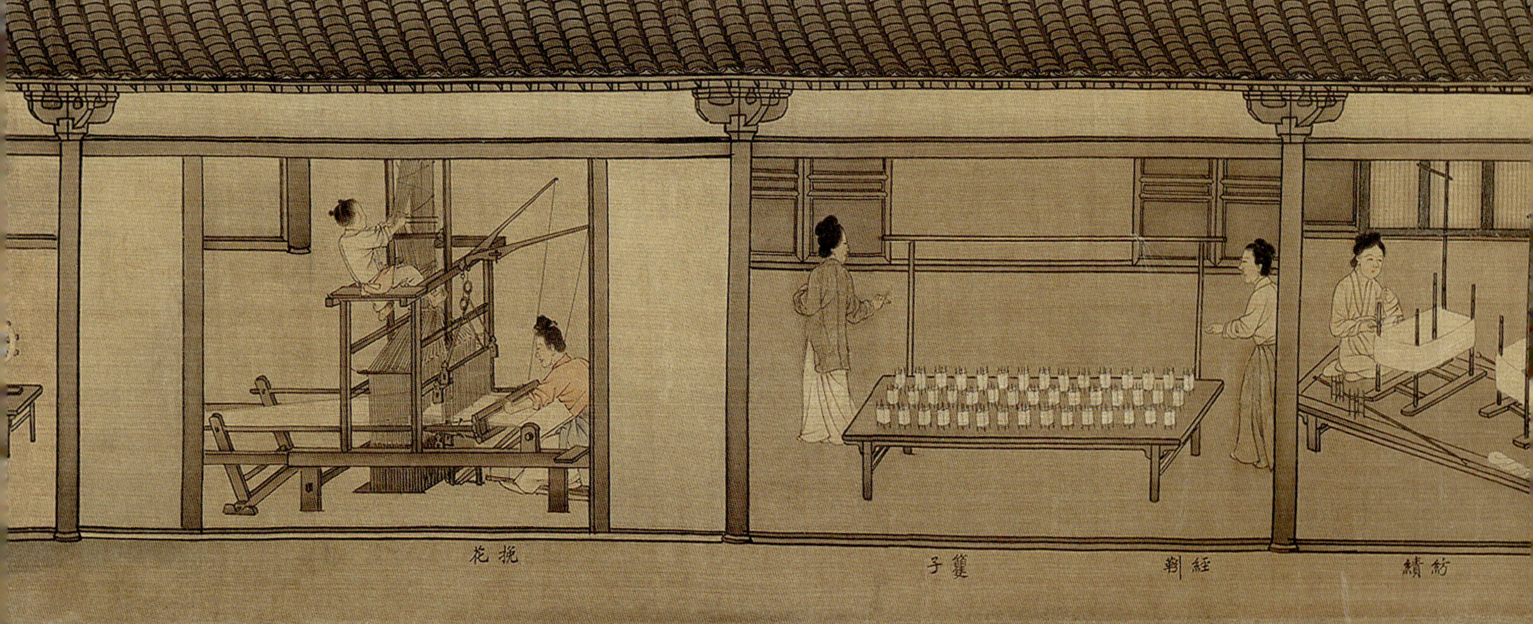
挽花
籰子
經靷
紡績

《蚕织图》

南宋（公元1127–1279年）
吴皇后题注本
纵27.5、横513cm
黑龙江省博物馆藏

Sericulture and Weaving

Painting on silk with subtitles by Empress Wu
Southern Song dynasty (1127–1279CE)
Length: 513cm, Width: 27.5cm
Collection of the Heilongjiang Provincial Museum

《耕织图》是南宋绍兴初年于潜(今临安)县令楼璹首创的两套详细描绘农耕和蚕织生产全过程的配诗连环画，原本今已不存，南宋吴皇后题注本《蚕织图》是至今流存的最早版本。

此图共由24个生产场景组成，每幅画下面均有标有节气和生产周期。《蚕织图》所绘当时蚕桑丝绸生产其工艺完善，设备进步，说明古代蚕桑丝绸生产技术至此已定型，后来并无大变。

蚕的轮回

蚕的一生经历由卵而虫、由虫而蛹、由蛹而蛾的生物变态过程，使古人联想到生死轮回，卵是生命的源头，卵孵化成幼虫犹如生命的诞生，蛹可以看成是生命的一个终结，蛹羽化成蛾就是古人所追想的死后灵魂的去向，所以汉魏以前的古墓中常有金蚕（青铜蚕）、玉蚕、陶蚕之类的模制品作陪葬的现象。

古人从蚕的生命史中看到了它所喻示的永生象征，还产生了对蚕赖以生存的桑树的崇拜。古时男女在桑林中祭祀高媒之神（即生育之神）以求子，或是在桑林中举行祭天求雨活动，蚕与桑不仅给人们带来了美丽的丝绸，还带来了美好的精神追求。

Life Cycle of a Silkworm

The life circle of a silkworm has four steps, an egg, the larva, the pupa (cocoon stage), and finally the moth. This transformation was thought by the ancient Chinese to be a reincarnation, with the egg as the origin of life that then hatches as a larva. The pupa stage resembles the end of the life, while the moth emerging from the cocoon references the rebirth of a soul in a corporeal body. As a result, golden silkworms (made of bronze), jade silkworms, ceramic silkworms and other burial objects in the form of a silkworm were frequently interred in ancient tombs before the Han Dynasty.

As the ancient Chinese thought the life cycle of a silkworm was the perfect embodiment of the concept of immortality, mulberry trees that the silkworms lived on became objects of worship. Ceremonies to the Immortal Matchmaker (God of Procreation) were held under mulberry trees by those who hoped to have children. Other rituals were held in mulberry tree groves in which participants prayed for rain. Thus silkworms and mulberry trees not only produced fine textiles, but also became important icons for religious veneration.

蚕的结构图
The Chart of Silkworm

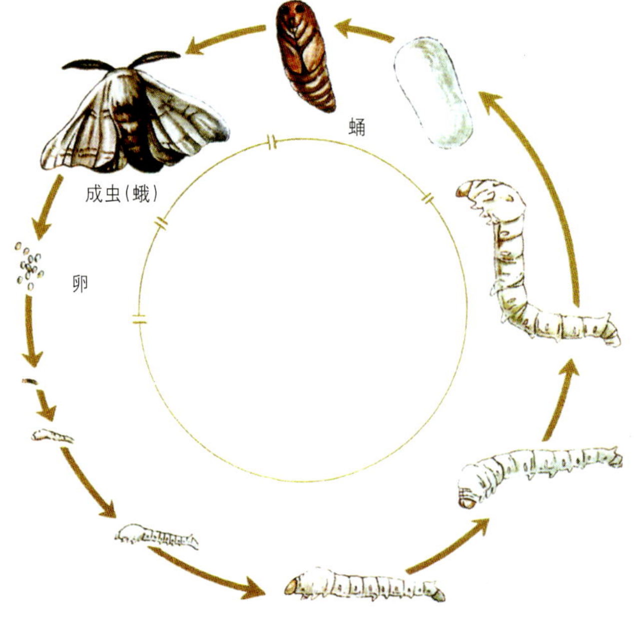

蛾
Moth

丝绸生产

丝绸产品在织造前需进行缫丝、络丝、摇纬、整经等加工过程。先将若干根丝同时抽出，缫成生丝后，将绕在缫丝车上的绞状丝，转绕到丝筒上，再通过摇纬车绕到纡管上，置于梭中作纬线，而后在织机上与整理好的经线相互交织。织机的出现与完善是生产丝织品的重要前提，织机的开口、投梭、打纬三种机构运动是织物织造的基本步骤。

The Manufacturing of Silk

The manufacturing of silk textiles requires reeling, twining the thread, preparing the weft, arranging the warp, and other processes. Multiple fibers are simultaneously reeled from a cocoon and entwined together into raw silk threads; this was done on a reeling wheel. The silk filaments were then rolled onto bobbins and wound to the beam of a loom using a spinning wheel. The spinning wheel was fixed to a shuttle, which carries the silk threads, called weft threads, through the warp that would have been set up on the loom. The invention of looms and their technical developments were an important basis for silk manufacturing. Shedding, shuttling, and beating of weft threads are the three basic mechanical movements required for weaving.

玉蚕

西周（约公元前11世纪-前771年）
长4.8、宽0.9、厚0.5cm
山西侯马出土
山西博物院藏

Jade Plaque in Silkworm Shape

Western Zhou (11th Century-771 BCE)
Length: 4.8cm,Width: 0.9cm,Thickness: 0.5cm
Excavated at Houma, Shanxi Province
Collection of the Shanxi Museum

玉蚕呈半环形，通体雕琢成节褶状。玉蚕晶莹、细腻、润泽，是蚕虫崇拜的体现。

蚕和蚕丝

家蚕属鳞翅目蚕蛾科（Bombyx mori），一生经历卵、幼虫（蚕）、蛹、成虫（蛾）四个阶段。蚕卵孵化出蚁蚕，经过3-4次的蜕皮，约30天后长成熟蚕，吐丝结茧，同时成蛹，一周后化蛾，钻出茧壳，雌雄交配，产卵后死去。丝由蚕茧中抽出，成为织绸的原料。一颗蚕茧可抽出约1000米长的茧丝，若干根茧丝合并成为生丝。

Silkworm and Silk

Domesticated silkworms are the caterpillar of the silk moth bombyx mori, which goes through four stages in its life cycle, egg, larva, pupa, and finally it becomes a moth. After an egg hatches, the caterpillar molts three to four times over the course of roughly 30 days before becoming a mature silkworm ready to spin a cocoon. The silkworm then spins a protective cocoon that encases itself completely so it can then safely transform into a chrysalis, which is the pupa stage. After a week or so, the chrysalis breaks through the cocoon and emerges as a moth. The moths then mate and the female lays eggs. A few days after emerging from the cocoon, the moths die and the life cycle commences again. The silk fibers that are reeled from the cocoons become the basic material for silk production. Each cocoon yields a thousand meters of silk filament and several filaments entwined together make an even, strong thread, which is called raw silk.

桑叶
Mulberry Leaf

臘月浴蠶
切葉
積細
葉餧
清明日暖種
拂烏兒
烏兒出如
頭髮細長
一分來
摘葉

下繭
約繭
剥繭
秤繭
盐繭甕藏

體餧
穀雨前第一眠
第二眠
第三眠
暖蠶

生繰
蠶蛾出種
謝神供絲
絡垛

错综经纬
Warp and Weft

中国丝织技术出现在新石器时代，先秦时期渐趋完善，至汉代有明显进步。汉代以踏板斜织机为代表，形成了缫丝、纺线、织造等较为完备的技术体系。由于充分利用错综变蹑技术，提高了生产效率，丰富了丝绸品种，使丝绸花色更加美轮美奂。

"生自蚕茧，成于机杼"。在声声机杼的撞击中，曼帛轻纱源源流淌出来。

Chinese silk weaving technology was first developed in the Neolithic period, evolved during the pre-Qin period, and dramatically improved in the Han Dynasty when the treadle loom was invented and comprehensive technical systems for reeling, spinning, and weaving appeared. By taking full advantage of these developments, Han Dynasty weavers increased their productivity and variety of textiles they made, as well as enhancing the colors of silk fabrics.

As noted in the Book of the Later Han, "...born with cocoons and accomplished with shuttles..." , along with the click-clack of looms comes graceful silks.

织机之始
Origin of the Loom

最初出现的织机是以手提综开口的腰机，后来发明了脚踏提综的踏板素织机。脚踏提综的采用将织工提综的两只手解放出来，专门从事投梭和打纬，明显提高了织造效率。由于原始腰机以人作支架固定织机及经线，极大地限制了人的运动。用机架取代身体，并用脚踏板来传递动力拉动综片开口，这就是中国对世界纺织技术一大贡献的踏板织机。

踏板织机大约出现在战国时期，但踏板织机的图像较多地出现在东汉时期的墓室画像石上，山东、江苏、四川等地均有出土，描绘的通常是曾母投杼或牛郎织女的故事，反映了当时一般家庭的织造情况。

The earliest looms were hand looms that were tied around a weaver's waist at one end and were known as backstrap looms. Treadle looms were invented later and allowed weavers to raise the warp threads with the threadles. This invention significantly increased the efficiency of weaving, since it kept the weaver's hands free to manipulate the shuttle as well as making it easier to raise and lower warp threads in selected combinations. Early backstrap looms were stationary and stabilized the warp threads, therefore the movements of the weaver were confined within a small limit. By adding a frame to the loom and using a treadle to lift the heddles the treadle loom was invented. This was a great contribution that China made to textile industries across the globe.

Although invented during the Warring States period, images of treadle loom were more frequently found on stone reliefs in Eastern Han Dynasty tombs in Shandong, Jiangsu, and Sichuan provinces. Such carvings depict the ancient stories of "Zeng Mu Tǒu Zhǔ" (lit. Zeng's mother drops the shuttle) and "Níu Láng Zhi Nü" (līt. the Cowherd and the Weaver Girl), reflecting that weaving activities were fairly common during the period.

纺织场景青铜贮贝器

西汉（公元前206－公元8年）
通高21、盖径24.5cm
云南晋宁石寨山出土
中国国家博物馆藏

Bronze Cowry Shell Container Depicting Weaving Activities

Western Han Dynasty (206 BCE－8 CE)
Height: 21cm, Diameter of lid 24.5cm
Excavated at Shizhaishan, Jinning, Yunnan
Collection of the National Museum of China

贮贝器是古代滇人用以盛放贝币的器具，此件贮贝器盖上共铸有18人，均为妇女。其中一人端坐在圆垫上，身上鎏金，可能为监督纺织者。器盖边缘有踞坐者数人，最为引人注目的是使用腰机进行织造的女奴形象，她们席地而坐，将织机用腰带缚在腰上，脚蹬住经轴，依靠两脚及腰脊控制经丝的张力。贮贝器形象地反映了当时云南地区使用原始腰机进行纺织生产的情况，这种织机在现代佤族、独龙族等少数民族中还能看到。

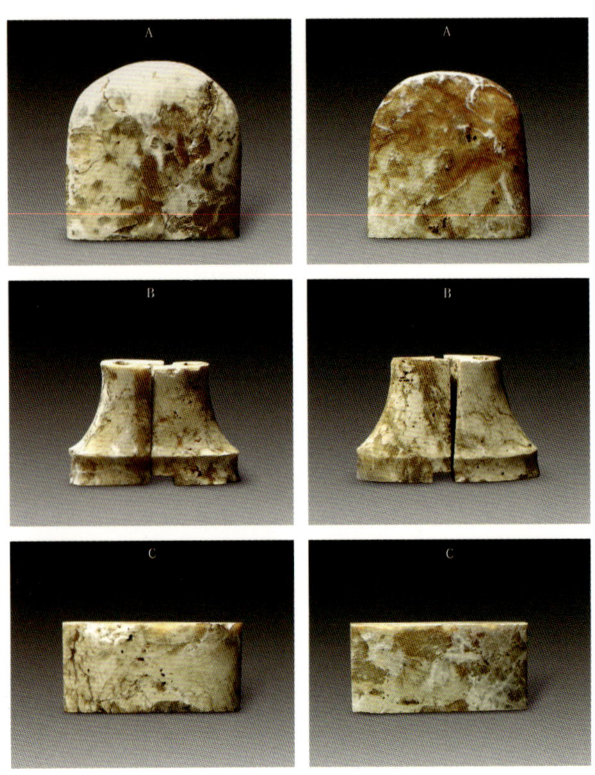

原始腰机的工作原理

良渚出土的织机是最古老的织机机型。它用手提综杆和分经杆结合使经丝分为上下两层以形成梭口，用于织制平纹织物。织机以人的身体作为机架，织轴用腰带缚于织者腰上，故称原始腰机。

Mechanism of a Preliminary Backstrap Loom

The Liangzhu Loom is the oldest known type of loom. By manually raising the harnesses of the loom and inserting a rod to make shed the loom was used for weaving tabby or plain weave fabrics. Since the cloth bean of the loom was fastened around the weaver's waist at one end, it is also known as a waist backstrap loom.

踏板织机的工作原理

踏板织机出现于战国前后。汉代的踏板织机经面倾斜，两块踏板通过中轴控制一片综开口，并与原有的自然开口结合，织成平纹织物。这种织机将织工从手提综片中解放出来，大大提高了生产效率。

The Mechanism of Treadle Looms

Treadle looms first appeared during the Warring States period and Han Dynasty versions held the warp in an oblique position with two treadles connected to an axle through which one heddle is attached. With a natural shed made by a rod and a hew shed made by the heddle, the treadle loom raised and lowered the warp threads, keeping the weaver's hands free and significantly increasing work efficiency.

织机玉饰件

新石器时代良渚文化（公元前3200–前2200年）
A长4、宽3cm；B长2.8、宽3cm；C长4.5、宽2cm
浙江余杭良渚出土
良渚文化博物馆藏

Jade Loom Parts

Neolithic Period, Liangzhu Culture (3200–2200 BCE)
A–Length:4cm, Width: 3cm; B–Length: 2.8cm, Width: 3cm; C–Length: 4.5cm, Width: 2cm;
Excavated at Liangzhu, Yuhang, Zhejiang
Collection of the Liangzhu Culture Museum

织机玉件出土时每对相距约35厘米，中间原应有木质杆棒，可复原出整个原始织机由经轴、开口杆和织轴三部分构成，是目前所知中国发现最早的最为完整的织机构件。

纺织图画像石

东汉（公元25–220年）
高93、宽61cm
江苏泗洪出土
南京博物院藏

Stone Relief Depicting Weaving Activities

Eastern Han Dynasty (25–220 CE)
Height: 93cm, Width: 61cm
Excavated in Sihong County, Jiangsu
Collection of the Nanjing Museum

汉代画像石常用于构筑墓室，画像的主要题材为人物故事。画面上描绘的是“曾母投杼”的故事，可以看到当时织机生产场面及斜织机的型制。这幅纺织图雕工精湛，织机的雕刻精细，其经面倾斜，织机上的踏板和综片的连接方法非常独特，在织机的经面之下、中部偏上处有两根相互垂直的短杆伸出，并通过绳索或木杆分别与两块踏板相连。

巧构经纬
Fabric Weaving

通过织机上穿综的变化，形成不同组织结构，可以织造出不同的丝绸品种。汉代已经有绢、纱、缟、纨等平素织物和提花的绮和锦，唐代之后又出现了缂丝、缎、绒和妆花，织锦的生产从原来的经锦向纬锦发展，色彩更加华美。

By raising loom harnesses in different combinations a variety of weaves could be made that produced different types of fabric. Fabrics with a plain or tabby weave were widely fashioned during the Han Dynasty including gauze, and taffeta. Other fabrics with a patterned weave, such as damask and jin-silk were also made. Tapestries, satin, velvet and brocade textiles were more commonly produced later after the Tang Dynasty. Production of weft-faced fabrics gradually prevailed over that of warp-faced fabrics, and were produced with beautiful color combinations.

对龙对凤纹锦

战国（公元前475–前221年）
长24、宽11cm
中国丝绸博物馆藏

Dragon and Phoenix Patterned Jin-silk

Warring States Period (475–221 BCE)
Length: 24cm, Width: 11cm
Collection of the China National Silk Museum

此锦为战国时期典型的平纹经锦织物，以红、棕、白三色分区交替显花，其中红色由朱砂涂染而成。锦是一种多彩的熟织物，经锦的兴盛时期在战国时出现，一般使用分区换色的办法来表现更多的色彩，即在整个幅宽中将经线分为若干个区，各区中每组经线颜色各不相同。

杯纹绮

西汉（公元前206-公元8年）
长59.5、宽41、幅边宽0.3cm
湖南长沙马王堆出土
湖南省博物馆藏

Damask with a Pattern of Ear Cups

Western Han Dynasty (206 BCE – 8 CE)
Length: 59.5cm, Width: 41cm, Margin width: 0.3cm
Excavated at Mawangdui, Changsha, Hunan
Collection of the Hunan Provincial Museum

两汉时期，平纹地单层暗花织物被称为绮，与锦、绣等被同列为有花纹的高级丝织品。汉代的绮在组织结构形式上主要有两种：一种是在平纹地上以斜纹显花,另一种是在平纹地上隔经显花。马王堆所出杯纹绮以菱形叠加而成的耳杯纹样作表现主题，图案上下左右全部对称，是在平纹地上以斜纹显花的绮织物。

绒圈锦（部分）

西汉（公元前206–公元8年）
长61、宽24cm
湖南长沙马王堆出土
湖南省博物馆藏

Jin-silk with Loops (Part)

Western Han Dynasty (206 BCE–8 CE)
Length: 61cm, With: 24cm
Excavated at Mawangdui, Changsha, Hunan
Collection of the Hunan Provincial Museum

绒圈锦又称起绒锦、起毛锦，是汉代新出现的一个织锦品种。绒圈锦虽有“绒”之名，其表面效果也与后世起绒织物极为相似，然而组织结构依旧是战国秦汉时期常见的平纹经重组织，只是在织造时提起其中部分经线，织入起绒杆，织成后抽去起绒杆，使纬线形成具有浮雕效果的立体花纹。

杯纹罗（部分）

西汉（公元前206–公元8年）
长56、宽49.5、幅边宽0.2cm
湖南长沙马王堆出土
湖南省博物馆藏

Gauze with a Pattern of Cups (Part)

Western Han Dynasty (206 BCE–8 CE)
Length: 56cm, Width: 49.5cm, Margin width 0.2cm
Excavated at Mawangdui, Changsha, Hunan
Collection of the Hunan Provincial Museum

汉代罗织物的主要组织类型是链式罗，其中以四经绞罗最为常见。此件杯纹罗为暗花罗织物，在四经绞地上以二经绞组织显花，形成对比鲜明的特殊效果。罗织物的出现较早，在殷墟妇好墓出土的连体甗和铜小方彝上都有发现罗织物的痕迹，为无固定绞组罗，也称链式罗。自商而唐，纱罗织物的主要组织类型是链式罗，其中又以四经绞罗最为常见。

缂 丝 缂丝也作刻丝或剋丝、克丝等，以通经断纬的方法织成，至迟在唐代就已出现。两宋时期是缂丝工艺的巅峰时期，缂丝技艺有了大的发展，不仅织幅大大增宽，而且图案内容和形式也较唐代丰富。

Silk Tapestr Silk tapestries, also known as kesi, were made by a weft-faced weaving process in which all warp threads are hidden in the completed work that was developed at least by the Tang Dynasty. Silk tapestry production reached its peak in the Song Dynasty when weaving techniques were improved and larger works were created with a greater variety of patterns and designs in comparison with pieces from the Tang Dynasty.

缂丝紫地花卉鸾鹊谱

北宋（公元960–1127年）
长131.6、宽55.6cm
辽宁省博物馆藏

Silk Tapestry with Flower and Legendary Bird Designs on Purple Background

Northern Song Dynasty (960–1127 CE)
Length: 131.6cm, Width: 55.6cm
Collection of the Liaoning Provincial Museum

缂丝在宋代的兴盛离不开当时皇帝对书画的喜好，北宋文思院中就有专门的“克丝作”，生产缂丝用于装裱书画。

缂丝紫地花卉鸾鹊谱局部
Part of Tapestry with Flower and Legendary Bird Designs on Purple Background

缂丝山茶及牡丹

南宋（公元1127–1279年）
长25、宽25cm；长23、宽24cm
辽宁省博物馆藏

Silk Tapestry with Camellias and Peonies

Southern Song Dynasty (1127–1279 CE)
Length: 25cm, Width: 25cm;
Length: 23cm, Width: 24cm
Collection of the Liaoning Provincial Museum

南宋时期缂丝转而向纯艺术品的方向发展，出现了不少能缂织欣赏性花鸟画题材的缂丝名手，朱克柔就是其中的代表人物之一，这两幅缂丝均是她的代表性作品。

妆 花 受唐代的缂丝和织成的影响，唐代开始出现了妆花工艺，如唐代织成袈裟用一根通梭丝作底，结合非通梭显花，就是一件妆花绢。妆花是挖梭工艺的别称，如一种提花织物在花部采用通经断纬的方法显花，这种织物便可以称作是妆花织物，具体又可以根据地部组织而有所不同。

妆花兴盛期在明清两代，明定陵所出的170余匹袍料和匹料中，妆花织物占了一半以上，北京故宫博物院更收藏了不胜枚举的妆花织物。其中妆花缎更是清代最为流行的面料，在宫中御用的提花面料中占据主导地位。

Brocade Inspired by silk tapestries of the Tang Dynasty, the "zhuang hua" (lit. to brocade with patterns) technique emerged, which was specifically used for the weaving of long robes. Brocades were typically woven on a draw loom. Such looms used a supplementary weft technique, that is, the ornamental brocading was produced by a supplementary, non-structural, weft in addition to the standard weft (or foundation weft) that holds the warp threads together. The weave made with this method on any ground is called brocade, which may have various names according to different weaves of the ground. Brocade was popular during the Ming and Qing dynasties. Among the 170 bolts of dress and drapery fabrics found in the Ding Mausoleum of the Ming Dynasty, over half of them are brocade. In addition, numerous brocade fabrics are in the collection of the Palace Museum in Beijing. Brocaded satin was the most popular fabric in the Qing Dynasty and were the dominant textiles provided to the Imperial Palace.

鹧鸪海石榴纹妆花绫

辽（公元916-1125年）
长62、宽45cm
中国丝绸博物馆藏

Twill Brocade with a Partridge and Sea Pomegranate Motif

Liao Dynasty (916-1125 CE)
Length: 62cm, Width: 45cm
Collection of the China National Silk Museum

为契丹东丹国左相耶律羽之墓随葬品，原属于一件左衽长袍的残片。图案按照服装款式的要求设计，使用一组经线和两组纬线交织而成，织成之后按照图案进行裁剪。

明黄彩云金龙妆花纱夹袍

清雍正（公元1723—1735年）
身长144、通袖长190、下摆宽130cm
故宫博物院藏

Lined Bright Yellow Silk Gauze Robe Brocaded with Multi-colored Clouds and Golden Dragons

Yongzheng period, Qing Dynasty, (1723–1735 CE)
Length: 144cm, Sleeves: 190cm, Breadth: 130cm
Collected of the Palace Museum

明黄彩云金龙妆花纱夹袍是皇帝吉服，用于元旦、冬至及万寿节等喜庆吉日。形制是：圆领，大襟右衽，马蹄袖端，直身式袍服。此件衬月白色团龙杂宝暗花纱里，缀铜镀金錾流云纹扣四枚。

此件龙袍的面料是用妆花技法织造，明黄色暗团云龙实地纱地上，织造彩云金龙纹样。金龙用捻金线织制，海水及云纹的勾边用片金织制，织造工艺极为繁复，技法变幻自然流畅，精致匀细。面料构图华丽端庄，极具皇家气派，体现出清代雍正朝江宁织造妆花纱织造工艺水平与纹样装饰的风格。

手编织物
Manual Brading

织成通常是指织而不裁的成品，是一种手编织物，由绕编、斜编、绞编三种方法完成，它直接按照使用的形状进行织制，织成之后可以直接使用，不需裁剪。手编是机织的基础，战国至汉晋，各种手编织物十分丰富，它与机织物一直并存发展。

Manual works were made by hand alone without using any machines. The three basic methods of manual weaving include wrapping, brading and twinning. Fabrics produced using these methods were normally formed into the desired shape during the process so that tailoring was not necessary. Manual brading was the basis for loom weaving and from the Warring States period through the Han to Jin Dynasties there emerged a great variety of manual made textiles that rivaled loom weaves.

几何纹编织绦（部分）

战国（公元前475－前221年）
长36.5、宽4.8cm
湖北江陵马山楚墓出土
荆州博物馆藏

Geometric Patterned Silk Braid (Part)

Warring States Period (475–221 BCE)
Length: 36.5cm, Width: 4.8cm
Excavated from a Chu Tomb at Mashan, Jiangling, Hubei
Collection of the Jinzhou Museum

花纹由小六边形组成，按纬线方向排列，每行九个小六边形，行间夹以小三角形组成的斜向条带，相互连接，形成大三角形。经线和地纬为深棕色，花纬则有红棕色和棕色两种，为了使花纬能较好地遮盖地纬组织，也易于使花纹显出立体效果，采用的花纬较地纬要粗一些。

几何纹编织巾（部分）

约汉晋时期（公元1-3世纪）
长168、宽25cm
新疆民丰尼雅出土
新疆文物考古研究所藏

Geometric Patterned Braded Band (Part)

Ca. Han to Jin Dynasties (1st-3rd century CE)
Length: 168cm, Width: 25cm
Excavated at the Niya Site in Minfeng, Xinjiang
Collection of the Xinjiang Institute of Archaeology

出土时包裹在女墓主头部。以双层表里换层组织斜编而成，编织带呈狭长形，在两端各留有长短不一的流苏，以双层组织表里换层斜编而成，共使用了720根蓝色丝线和240根红色丝线，在织物表面形成蓝红格纹交错的效果。

编织鞋

东晋（公元317-420年）
长19、宽8、高2.5cm
新疆吐鲁番出土
新疆维吾尔自治区博物馆藏

Shoes

Eastern Jin Dynasty (317-420 CE)
Length: 19cm, Width: 8cm, Height: 2.5cm
Excavated at Turfan, Xinjiang
Collection of the Xinjiang Uyghur Auronomous Region Museum

绞编法是一种古老的技法，采用一组平行、一组相互绞转的两个系统的丝线进行编织，后来被广泛地应用到织成履的编织中。纬线采用红、蓝、米白、浅褐等色丝线，采用绞编法编织，在编织时把某一色的丝线展现在织物的一面以显示花纹，而把其余的丝线沉在背后，设色绚丽，制作精细。

天机提花
Mechanical Patterning

为了贮存生产中丝绸花纹的信息，织机上安置了提花装置，这样可以得到重复循环的织纹。在战国和秦汉间，这种方法多被用于生产结构复杂的锦类产品。到了唐初，新发明的新型花本式提花机不仅具有贮存记忆的功能，而且可以织出任意变化的造型，大大拓展了丝绸图案的表现力。

In order to replicate pattern designs, weavers would fix a group of shafts on the loom so that the weaving movements could be repeated. Between the Warring States period, Han and Jin dynasties, this technique was used to produce complex patterns on fabrics, such as jin silk. By the beginning of the Tang dynasty, draw loom had evolved such that, not only were they able to retain and repeat the pattern designs, but complex new variations in patterns were also possible. The results were highly expressive pictorial images that appeared as textile decorations.

多综式提花
Heddle Loom for Patterning

织锦代表了中国丝织技术的最高水平。汉代以前的锦，主要采用平纹重组织，花纹小且多循环重复，可能是通过多综式提花机织成。多综式提花机具有信息贮存和记忆的功能，是世界上最早能控制织物经向图案循环的织机，它多采用以脚踏板控制提花的多综多蹑机，用踏板来控制提花的综框，在织造一个纬向完全循环内一根纹经可以同时穿入数片花综内，花纹的复杂程度决定了使用综框片数的多少，而综框的多少又决定了踏板的数量。

Jin silk represents the high point of weaving techniques in ancient China. Before the Han Dynasty, jin silk was mostly a warp-faced compound tabby weave with small-sized patterns produced on a patterning loom, which had the ability to retain and repeat pattern designs. In fact, it was the earliest loom that controls over the weave to create patterns with repeated pictorial motifs. Mostly probably, more heddles, each connected to one treadle, and more treadles were set up on the loom, so that, the loom was known as multi-heddle a multi-treadle patterning loom.

舞人动物纹锦（局部）

战国（公元前475－前221年）
长74、宽50、幅边宽0.8cm
湖北江陵马山出土
荆州博物馆藏

Jin-silk with a Design of a Ritual Ceremony (Part)

Warring States Period (475－221 BCE)
Length: 74cm, Width: 50cm
Excavated at Mashan, Jiangling, Hubei
Collection of the Jingzhou Museum

舞人动物纹锦无论从色彩图案还是织造技术上来看，都是战国时期织锦的典范。其中最为引人注目的是舞人纹样，织锦表现的或许是楚地的巫舞活动。

塔形纹锦（局部）

战国（公元前475–前221年）
长83、宽24、幅边宽0.4cm
湖北江陵马山出土
荆州博物馆藏

Jin Silk Decorated with a Tower Motif (Part)

Warring States Period (475–221 BCE)
Length: 83cm, Width: 24cm, Margin width 0.4cm
Excavated at Mashan, Jiangling, Hubei
Collection of the Jingzhou Museum

马山一号楚墓出土的塔形纹锦不做衣衾，主要用于制作捆扎衣衾包裹的锦带，还用于木俑所穿绢裙的缘和囊。此件塔形纹锦为一锦带，二色经线交替起花，并采用了分区配色的方法，相邻条带间的塔形纹样也不尽相同。色线的组合有三种：浅棕和土黄；深棕和土黄；朱红和土黄，这三组色线依次顺条带排布，使锦的色彩更显鲜艳多变，光彩夺目。

“元和元年”鹿纹锦

东汉元和元年（公元84年）
长12、宽5.5cm
新疆和田地区博物馆藏

Jin silk Decorated With Deer Patterns and Characters Denoting the Date

First year of Yuanhe of the Eastern Han Dynasty (84 CE)
Length: 12cm, Width: 5.5cm
Collection of the Khotan Museum, Xinjiang

锦囊的主体部分以五种织锦制成，包括囊袋口缘用锦、束带部位“延年益寿长葆子孙”锦、袋身“元和元年”(公元84年)锦、瑞鸟云纹锦和袋底用锦。“元和元年”锦是目前发现的唯一有明确纪年的织锦，锦囊原可能作存纳首饰或印信等贵重物品之敛袋。

大几何纹锦

战国（公元前475–前221年）
长66.5、宽28.5cm
湖北江陵马山出土
荆州博物馆藏

Large Geometric Patterned Jin Silk

Warring States Period (475–221 BCE)
Length: 66.5cm, Width: 28.5cm
Excavated at Mashan, Jiangling, Hubei
Collection of the Jingzhou Museum

织锦主题纹样保留较为完整，由不对称的锯齿形几何骨架构成，填入各种小型几何纹样。这是一种变形的菱形图案，是由早期的小几何形纹样发展而来，在战国时期十分流行。

"王侯合昏千秋万岁宜子孙"锦被

约汉晋时期（公元1-3世纪）
长168、宽94cm
新疆民丰尼雅出土
新疆文物考古研究所藏

Jin Silk Quilt

Ca. Han to Jin Dynasties (1st-3rd century CE)
Length: 168cm, Width: 94cm
Excavated at the Niya site, Minfeng, Xinjiang
Collection of the Xinjiang Institute of Archaeology

锦被由两幅完整的王侯合昏千秋万岁宜子孙锦缝合而成，单层无衬。这件织锦当为中原地区官营丝织作坊专为地方王侯织制的婚礼用锦，一般人不可能得到此类织锦。

“王侯合昏千秋万岁宜子孙”锦枕

约汉晋时期（公元1-3世纪）
长32、宽11.5cm
新疆民丰尼雅出土
新疆文物考古研究所藏

Jin Silk Pillow

Ca. Han to Jin Dynasties (1st-3rd century CE)
Length: 32cm, Width: 11.5cm
Excavated at the Niya site, Minfeng, Xinjiang
Collection of the Xinjiang Institute of Archaeology

锦枕内装干草，与棉被为一套，同为中原地区官营丝织作坊专为地方王侯织制的婚礼用锦。

“长寿明光”锦

约汉晋时期（公元1-3世纪）
长22.5、宽37cm
新疆若羌楼兰出土
新疆文物考古研究所藏

Brocade with Longevity Enlightening Pattern

Ca. Han to Jin Dynasties (1st-3rd century CE)
Length: 22.5cm, Width: 37cm
Excavated at the Loulan (Kroran) Site, Charklik, Xinjiang
Collection of the Xinjiang Institute of Archaeology

汉晋时期，丝绸之路上最能体现中国丝织传统的是经锦，它最为典型的图案就是云气动物纹。这件织有“长寿明光”汉字的云气动物纹锦，就属这类经锦。

茱萸纹锦覆面

约汉晋时期（公元1–3世纪）
长62.1、宽58cm
新疆民丰尼雅出土
新疆文物考古研究所藏

Jin Silk with a Floral Dogwood Pattern

Ca. Han to Jin Dynasties (1st–3rd century CE)
Length: 62.1cm, Width: 58cm
Excavated at the Niya Site, Minfeng, Xinjiang
Collection of the Xinjiang Institute of Archaeology

汉式织锦大多以云气动物纹为图案，其中唯一以植物为题材的就是茱萸纹锦。茱萸是一种落叶乔木，结实似椒子，实中之籽极为香烈，人们在九月九日重阳登高时佩以辟邪。覆面上织有茱萸纹，当有辟邪的用意。

锦袋与帛鱼

约汉晋时期（公元1-3世纪）
长12.5、宽10cm
新疆民丰尼雅出土
新疆文物考古研究所藏

Silk Pouch with Silk Fish

Ca. Han to Jin Dynasties (1st–3rd century CE)
Length: 12.5cm, Width: 10cm
Excavated at the Niya Site, Minfeng, Xinjiang
Collection of the Xinjiang Institute of Archaeology

锦带以黄地斑纹锦作面、毡里。出土时内盛铜镜、胭脂包、线轴、皮顶针等。帛鱼鱼身以蓝地兽纹锦为面、内衬毡，以蓝红色绢作鳍和尾。

锦梳袋

约汉晋时期（公元1-3世纪）
长18.5、宽9cm
新疆民丰尼雅出土
新疆文物考古研究所藏

Silk Comb Pouch

Ca. Han to Jin Dynasties (1st–3rd century CE)
Length: 18.5cm, Width: 9cm
Excavated at the Niya Site, Minfeng, Xinjiang
Collection of the Xinjiang Institute of Archaeology

绛红地云气动物纹经锦作面，袋内一侧装木梳，一侧装小绢包、毛发等。

传播与融合
The Exchange

魏晋南北朝时期，是养蚕技术及织造技术经由丝绸之路向西域传播的重要阶段。从甘肃和新疆地区出土的织物看，当地不仅已有养蚕活动，也有丝织生产，这是中国丝织技术西传的一个重要的过渡地域。北朝时期西方的纺织技术和题材也开始影响中国，中国的织物上也出现了大量的西方母题。

穿越艰难丝路的，有商人，有驼铃，还有东来西往的美丽。

The Wei, Jin, Southern and Northern dynasties marked an important period for the transmission of sericulture and silk weaving techniques from China to the West, through the Silk Road. Those willing to face the dangers of the Silk Road included tradesmen, camel herdsmen, and intrepid adventurers. Based on finds from archaeological sites in Gansu and Xinjiang, silkworm rearing and weaving activities took place in Xinjiang, and this region became an important center for the transmission of Chinese sericulture techniques to the West. By the Northern dynasties, Western weaving techniques and materials had begun to influence Chinese silk production. Chinese textiles subsequently began to show the influences of many Western themes and motifs.

辟邪纹绵线锦绦（部分）

约汉晋时期（公元1–3世纪）
长18、宽3.7cm；长20、宽9.5cm
新疆尉犁营盘出土
新疆文物考古研究所藏

Silk Band Decorated with Talisman Designs (Part)

Ca. Han to Jin Dynasties (1st–3rd century CE)
Length: 18cm, Width: 3.7cm; Length: 20cm, Width: 9.5cm
Excavated at the Yingpan site, Weili, Xinjiang
Collection of the Xinjiang Institute of Archaeology

两件均为经二重平纹锦绦，长方格内填辟邪纹。将红和浅棕、黄和绿、绛紫和浅棕丝线分区排列，织造时纹地色彩互换，形成整齐的长方形骨架，格内纹饰主题为奔走的动物。

红地狩猎纹锦

北朝（公元420-589年）
长16-7.6、宽6.7-4cm
新疆且末扎滚鲁克墓地出土
新疆维吾尔自治区博物馆藏

Red Brocade Decorated with Hunting Motifs

Northern Dynasties (420-589 CE)
Length: 16-7.6cm, Width: 6.7-4cm
Excavated at Zagunluke, Xinjiang
Collection of the Xinjiang Uyghur Autonomous Region Museum

新疆当地生产的丝织平纹经锦织物，使用丝质的绵经绵纬，均加有Z向强捻，设计风格模仿汉式云气动物纹锦图案。

红色大富贵人物狮子纹绮纹饰图
Diagram of Red Silk Damask Decorated with Lion Motif and Auspicious Symbols

红色大富贵人物狮子纹绮

北朝（公元420–589年）
长137、宽51cm
中国丝绸博物馆藏

Red Silk Damask Decorated with Lion Motif and Auspicious Symbols

Northern Dynasties (420–589 CE)
Length: 137cm, Width: 51cm
Collection of the China National Silk Museum

在织物中间区域有一个交脚坐于高台上的神像，可能是印度佛教中的提婆形象。提婆两侧有两人持花，其下为双凤和双狮，双狮之间还织有“大富贵”三字。龙身两侧莲花台上为对人形象，莲台之下还有“善吉”两字。虽然整件织物采用的还是中国风格的龙和吉祥文字，但神像已不再是中原的传统，可以看出其受到外来文化的明显影响。

对羊纹锦覆面

北朝（公元420–589年）
长34.5、宽26.5cm
新疆吐鲁番阿斯塔那出土
新疆维吾尔自治区博物馆藏

Silk Face Cover Covering Decorated with a Motif of Facing Goats

Northern Dynasties (420–589 CE)
Length: 34.5cm, Width: 26.5cm
Excavated at Astana, Turfan, Xinjiang
Collection of the Xinjiang Uyghur Autonomous Region Museum

覆面由绿地对羊纹锦裁剪的面心和白绢荷叶边饰构成，色彩对比强烈。白色羊纹在绿地上一字排开，形成首相对、尾相连的布局。北朝时期西方的纺织技术和题材也开始影响中国，中国的丝织品开始出现大量来自西方的动物纹样。北朝时来自西亚的山羊形象出现在中国的织锦上，这种羊头部长有两只弯曲的角，身形矫健，四腿修长作站立状，颈部系有绶带，随风向后飘成三角形。

联珠对鸡纹锦

唐（公元618–907年）
长26.8、宽17.7cm
新疆吐鲁番阿斯塔那出土
新疆维吾尔自治区博物馆藏

Silk Covering with Facing Birds Motif

Tang Dynasty (618–907 CE)
Length: 26.8cm, Width: 17.7cm
Excavated at Astana, Turfan, Xinjiang
Collection of the Xinjiang Uyghur Autonomous Region Museum

属于中亚织锦，曾用作覆面。织锦图案是联珠对鸟纹，上下两行鸟纹有明显不同，下行鸟纹较上行鸟多一颈后的飘带，这类织锦是用一种只能控制纬向循环而不能控制经向循环的织机织成。

三彩骆驼及牵驼俑

驼高84、俑高62cm
唐（公元618–907年）
河南洛阳出土
河南博物院藏

Tang Tri-colored Camel Led by a Figure

Tang Dynasty (618–907 CE)
Camel's height: 84cm, Figure's height: 62cm
Excavated at Louyang, Henan
Collection of the Henan Museum

骆驼嘶鸣前行，有一胡人俑，握着缰绳的双手好像在用力地拉着骆驼，引导驼队走过那茫茫大漠。唐代大量的丝织品通过驼队由丝绸之路运往西方，使中国有了“丝国”之称。

丝绸之路

北方草原之路是开辟最早的中西贸易通道，亚欧大陆北部的大草原是这条丝路的主通道。其西端是古希腊，东端为蒙古高原，匈奴、突厥和蒙古等马背民族曾先后是蒙古草原的主人。

公元前2世纪，以张骞凿空西域为标志，由沙漠绿洲相连而成的陆上丝绸之路出现了。这条古道以西安为起点，沿黄河流域西行，过河西走廊，经新疆至中亚内陆、西亚两河流域及地中海东岸地区，全长约7000公里，是汉唐时代最具影响力的文化通道。

随着航海技术的发达，公元10世纪以后丝绸贸易转由海路进行。中国的丝绸和瓷器由东南地区的港口出口至世界各地，更伟大的时代在哥伦布环球航海后来到，世界贸易由此进入一个新的阶段，丝绸之路开始谱写新的篇章。

The Silk Road

The earliest Silk Road wove through the great northern grasslands of the Eurasian continent. This ancient trade route was the first to connect China and the West, with Greece on the western end and the Mongolian steppes on the eastern end. The Xiongnu, Turkic, Mongolian and other nomadic peoples took turns ruling over these ancient grasslands.

By the 2nd century BCE, Han explorer Zhang Qian's expeditions to the Western Regions paved the way for a new Silk Route that made its way through the desert from oasis to oasis. This ancient route spanned 7000km and began at Xi'an. It followed the flow of the Yellow River westward, crossed the Hexi Corridor, and passed through Xinjiang and inner Central Asia, to the Mesopotamia and Mediterranean regions. This Silk Road was the greatest influence on cultural exchanges from the Han to the Tang Dynasties.

From the 10th century onwards, the development of maritime capabilities turned the silk trade to sea routes. Chinese silks and ceramics were traded through the Southeast Asian ports to various parts of the world. Global trade reached new levels by the time of Christopher Columbus and the story of the Silk Road began a new chapter.

花本式提花
Weave Patterns with Variations in Floral Motifs

隋末唐初，中国的丝织技术中吸取了西方的纬向循环技术，制成了新型的花本式提花机，这种提花机既能控制经向，也能控制纬向循环，是真正意义上的提花机。自此以后，提花机的原理就基本没变，一直到法国在此基础上研制成功贾卡织机。

In the late Sui-early Tang dynasties, the Chinese weaving process was influenced by western textile production techniques. This led to the invention of a new draw loom that could control the pattern repeats in both warp and weft directions. The principle behind the draw loom would remain fundamentally unchanged until the invention of the Jacquard loom in France.

灯树对羊纹锦

唐早期（约公元7世纪中叶）
长13.8、宽26.1cm
新疆吐鲁番阿斯塔那出土
新疆维吾尔自治区博物馆藏

Jin Silk Decorated with Lamp Tree and Goats Motifs

Early Tang Dynadty (mid 7th Century CE)
Length: 13.8cm, Width: 26.1cm
Excavated at Astana, Turfan, Xinjiang
Collection of the Xinjiang Uyghur Autonomous Region Museum

波斯艺术中经常出现生命树的纹样，生命树是一种古老的植物崇拜的遗存，图案通常是作两动物对称的中心轴形式。吐鲁番文书中有“阳树锦”之名，即是羊树锦，织锦纹样作树下对羊状。

联珠小花纹锦

唐早期（约公元7世纪中叶）
长19.7、宽20.5cm
新疆吐鲁番阿斯塔那出土
新疆维吾尔自治区博物馆藏

Jin Silk with Pearl Ring and Little Flowers

Early Tang Dynadty (ca.mid 7th Century CE)
Length: 19.7cm, Width: 20.5cm
Excavated at Astana, Turfan, Xinjiang
Collection of the Xinjiang Uyghur Autonomous Region Museum

隋到初唐时，织物上小花图案十分流行，敦煌壁画和西安等地隋至唐初墓葬所出彩塑中亦多有描绘，有联珠环小团花和类似菊花的小团花等。此件织物的纹样，是由四朵小花组成的菱形状的十样花。

对龙纹绫

唐（公元618–907年）
长21、宽25.1cm
新疆吐鲁番阿斯塔那出土
新疆维吾尔自治区博物馆藏

Damask Decorated with a Facing Dragon Motif

Tang Dynasty (618 – 907 CE)
Length: 21cm, Width: 25.1cm
Excavated at Astana Turfan, Xinjiang
Collection of the Xinjiang Uyghur Autonomous Region Museum

原为覆面，以双层联珠作团窠环，环外以十样花作宾花，环内是主题纹样对龙。这类图案的织物在丝路沿途出土非常多，是联珠纹中国化的另一集中表现。

➲ 宝花纹锦

唐（公元618–907年）
长60、宽78cm
中国丝绸博物馆藏

Silk Samite with Floral Motifs

Tang Dynasty (618–907 CE)
Length: 60cm, Width: 78cm
Collection of the China National Silk Museum

宝花图案在许多出土实物及敦煌壁画中都可看到，唐代的宝花纹样大体可分为四种，一是瓣形宝花，二是装饰性很强的蕾式宝花，三是写生味较强的侧式宝花，四是常有鸟鹊蜂蝶绕飞的景象宝花。此件宝花纹锦图案属于蕾式宝花，体现出一种盛唐气象。

宝花狮纹锦

唐（公元618–907年）
长46、宽29cm
中国丝绸博物馆藏

Silk Samite Decorated with Lions and Floral Motifs

Tang Dynasty (618–907 CE)
Length: 46cm, Width: 29cm
Collection of the China National Silk Museum

花卉环中的动物纹样创自唐代初期，称为"陵阳公样"，是将西域团窠联珠环内的动物纹样与中国花卉纹样相结合的产物。织锦采用辽式纬锦，纹样已带有自由的写实风格，是陵阳公样在唐代晚期流行的见证。

➲ 花鸟纹锦

唐（公元618–907年）
长36.5、宽24.4cm
新疆吐鲁番阿斯塔那出土
新疆维吾尔自治区博物馆藏

Silk Samite Decorated with Bird-and-Flower Motif

Tang Dynasty (618–907 CE)
Length: 36.5cm, Width: 24.4cm
Excavated at Astana, Turfan, Xinjiang
Collection of the Xinjiang Uyghur Autonomous Region Museum

这件织锦是唐代鸟鹊蜂蝶绕飞景象宝花锦的代表。图案主题为以大小花朵组成宝花纹样，绕以各种禽鸟、行云和零散小花。外侧又杂置折枝花和山石、远树。锦边还有带状花边，图案繁缛，组织严密。

束综提花机工作原理

织机利用花本来储存经线的提升规律，花本由脚子线与耳子线编成，脚子线上部受控于耳子线，下部用以控制经线。脚子线与耳子线的每个交点表示织物上经纬线的一次交织，脚子线压在耳子线上时提升经线，反之则不提。一根耳子线与所有脚子线相交即是一纬与所有经线的交织规律。每织一纬，拉花工拉动一根耳子线，将花本的提花信息转换成经线的提升，以完成一个图案的提花开口。

The Principles of Draw Loom

The pattern produced by the draw loom is controlled by a program, which consists of leashes and lashes, to control the warps moving up and down. The draw boy lifts one leash when the weaver inserts one weft. The whole pattern is formed after the whole program is finished.

从束综提花机到计算机

束综提花机通过挑花结本，以线来存储纹样织造的程序。公元18世纪法国人贾卡(Jacquard)发明提花织机，织机采用预先打孔的卡片——纹版控制提花程序，这不仅是丝织业的革命，也为人类打开了一扇信息控制的大门。1836年计算机先驱查尔斯·巴比奇(Charles Babbage)利用打孔卡片的原理，为世界上第一台机械计算机器差分机编程。公元19世纪末美国统计学家赫尔曼·霍尔瑞斯(Herman Hollerith)借鉴纹版的原理，利用凿孔把字母信息在卡片上编码，发明了制表机。20世纪40年代，计算机时代到来，仍利用打孔卡片编程，一直延续到80年代后期最终被电子媒介所取代。

From the Draw Loom to the Computer

The draw loom was able to create and repeat weaving movements to produce patterned textiles. In the 18th century, a Frenchman by the name of Jacquard invented the Jacquard loom, which used cards with pre-punched holes to control the weaving process. Jacquard's innovation completely revolutionized the silk weaving industry. In 1836, Charles Babbage used the principle of the punched-hole card to invent the world's first mechanically controlled loom. By building on these inventions, the American statistician Herman Hollerith developed a tabulating machine at the end of the 19th century by coding alphabetical letters onto the punched cards. Although the age of the computer had arrived in the 1940s, the use of the punched cards continued until replaced by electronic media in the 1980s.

木身锦衣裙女俑

唐（公元618—907年）
高29cm
新疆吐鲁番阿斯塔那张雄夫妇墓出土
新疆维吾尔自治区博物馆藏

Wood Woman Figurine in Silk Dresses

Tang Dynasty(618–907CE)
Height: 29cm
Excavated from Tomb of Zhang Xiong and his Wife in Astana, Turfan, Xinjiang
Collection of the Xinjiang Uyghur Autonomous Region Museum

女俑为木胎加彩，头挽高髻，阔眉细目，额饰花钿，颊敷红粉，在眼角外下侧各饰“斜红”，唐罗虬《比红儿诗》中“一抹浓红傍脸斜”就是指这种妆饰，女俑的两手在腹前作交叉状，上身穿螺青色柿蒂纹绮窄袖对襟短襦，外罩红地联珠对鸟纹锦制成的半臂，半臂为直领、对襟，身披草黄色绞缬罗制成的披帛。女俑下身着由红、黄两色的绢、绮织物间隔拼缝而成的“间道”裙，此条裙尚外罩一天青色薄纱裙。

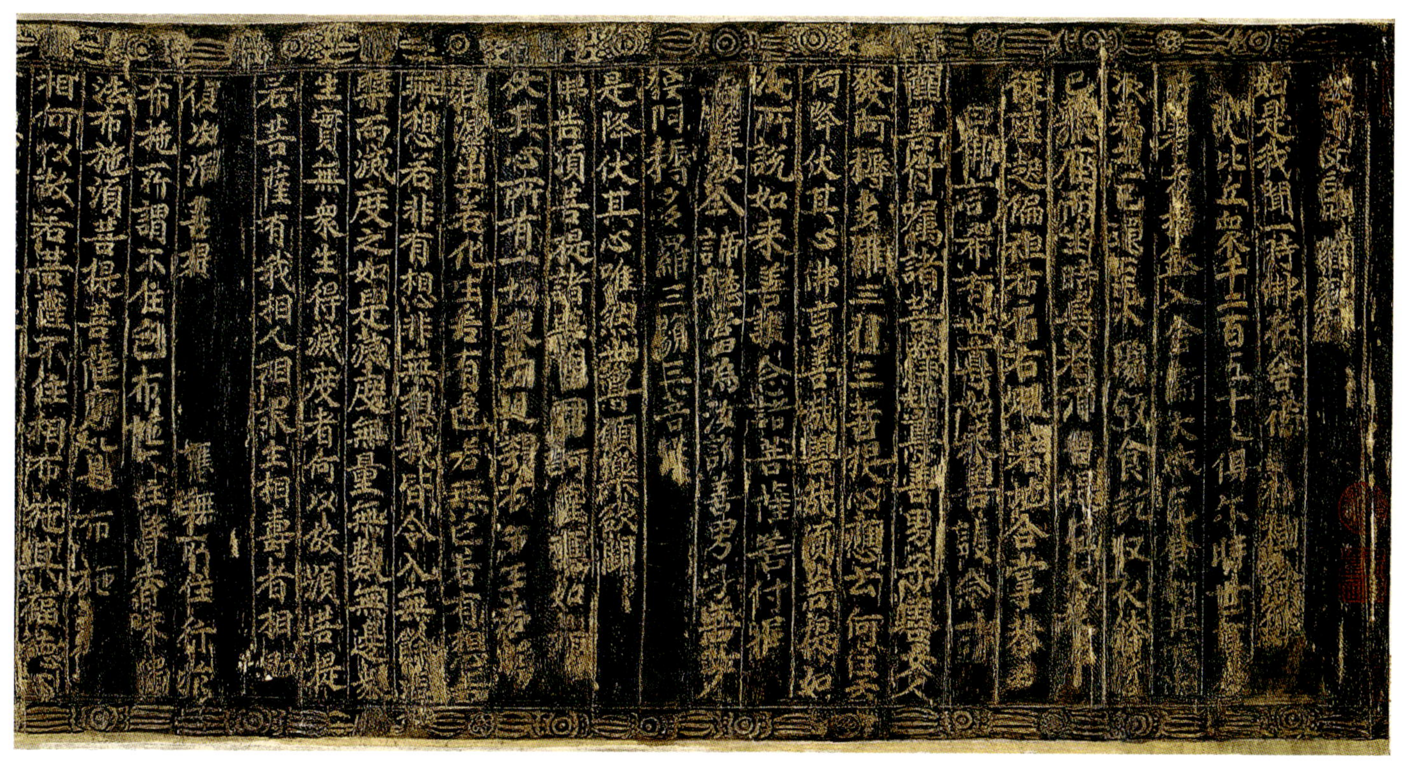

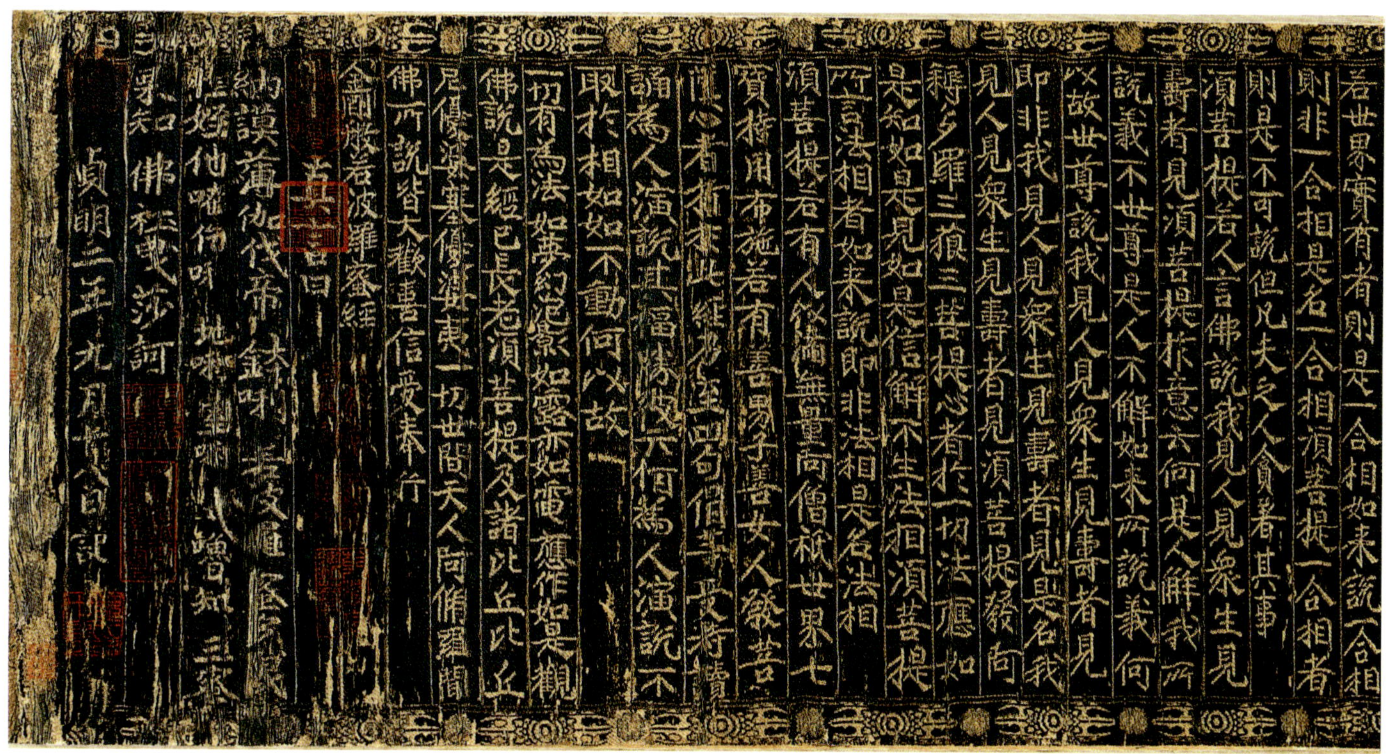

织成金刚经（部分）

后梁贞明二年（公元916年）
长713.4、宽29.6cm
辽宁省博物馆藏

Silk Woven Diamond Sutra (Part)

The 2nd year of Zhenming of Late Liang Dynasty (907–923 CE)
Length: 713.4cm, Width: 29.6cm
Collection of the Liaoning Provincial Museum

佛教经文出现在丝绸上，大多以刺绣而成，此金刚经是在织机上织成。经文为金刚般若波罗蜜多经，共计5000余字，采用蓝地黄字以模仿蓝叶泥金的写经方法，行间以界栏隔开，是历代织制佛经之冠。按纬密56根/厘米计算，需要约40000根纬线才能织出一个循环，这样的织物一定要用大花楼束综提花机才能完成。

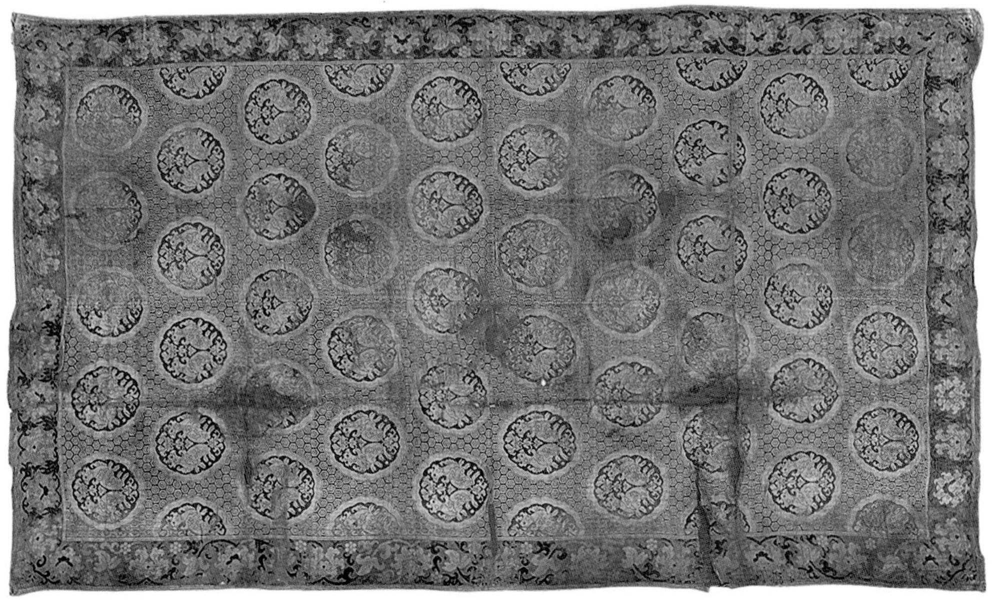

龟背纹地格力芬锦被

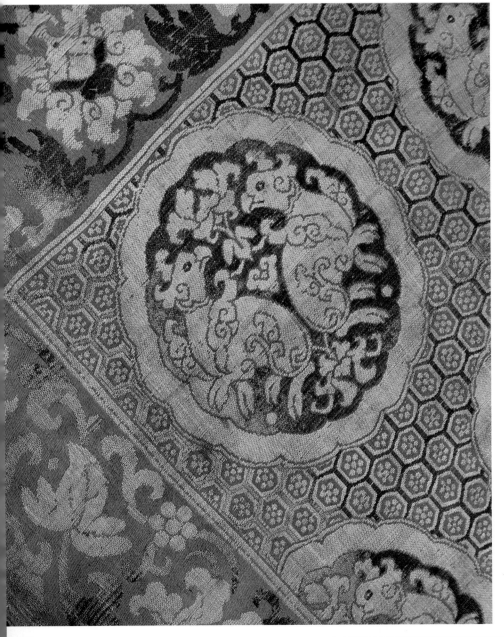

元（公元1271－1368年）
长204、宽118cm
内蒙古集宁路故城遗址出土
内蒙古博物馆藏

Silk Blanket with Griffins on a Hexagon Background

Yuan Dynasty (1271－1368 CE)
Length: 204cm, Width: 118cm
Excavated at the Ruins of Jininglu, Inner Mongolia
Collection of the Inner Mongolia Museum

格力芬是西方传说中的神兽，体形如兽，两角雕嘴，四足双翅。元代织物中常以格力芬为图案题材，而外框的缠枝牡丹花纹样则是典型的中原风格，这件织物是当时中外文化融合的产物。

➲ 西方极乐世界织锦

清（公元1644－1911年）
长448、宽196cm
故宫博物院藏

Brocade with Design of the Pure Land

Qing Dynasty (1644－1911 CE)
Length: 448cm, Width: 196cm
Collection of the Palace Museum

原藏故宫乾清宫，清乾隆初年根据宫廷画师丁观鹏的画稿由苏州织造府织成，以《阿弥陀经》的西方极乐净土为题材，全幅场面宏伟，各类人物共计278人。

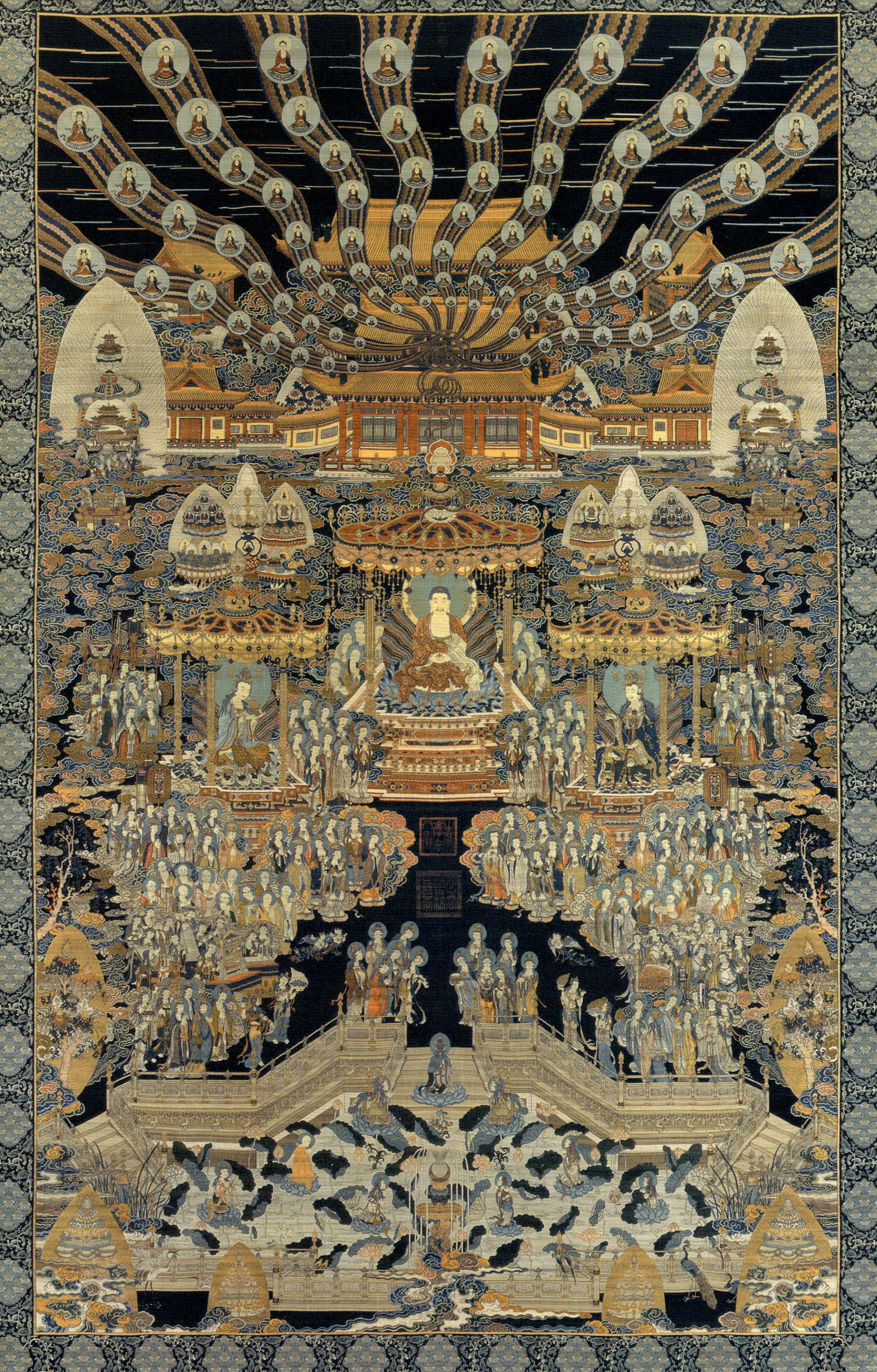

彰施五彩
Dyes and Colors

古代的丝绸印染技术在早期的涂彩、画缋基础上发展起来，手绘施彩，是中国丝绸印染的开端。真正开始印花，是采用类似于印章那样的凸版印花技术，这种用颜料直接印花的方法效率很低。汉唐时期，改以绞缬、蜡缬、夹缬、灰缬等防染印花技术为主，生产效率空前提高，印染图案绚丽多彩。中国古代对印花技术的最大贡献，是雕版防染印花“夹缬”。

The dyeing of Chinese silks began with the direct hand application of color pigments to textiles and found its early inspiration from the art of painting. Print seals, with designs in relief, came later. However, this method of applying colored patterns to create printed textiles was not very efficient. Resist dyeing techniques were developed between the Han and Tang dynasties. These included tie dyeing, wax resist dyeing, clamp resist dyeing, ash-resist dyeing, which were based on the principle of creating designs by protecting certain parts of the cloth from contact with dye.

These four dyeing techniques, along with stencil printing, made it possible to achieve designs with intricate patterns, complex motifs and many gorgeous colors. The production level of these textiles was very high and these dyeing techniques laid the foundation of China’s tradition in printed textile patterns.

手绘与印花
Hand-drawing and Printing

将染料或颜料拌以黏合剂，并用凸纹版或镂空版将其直接印在织物上显花，丝织物呈现出绚丽的色彩。早在西汉开始，中国已经发明了凸版印花技术与手绘相结合的方法，以后又有了进一步的发展。

Color pigments were mixed into dye substances before being applied onto the printing blocks, which could have designs either in relief or in intaglio. The blocks were then pressed onto fabrics to create a printed pattern. Printed silks could thus display beautiful designs with brilliant colors. At the beginning of the Western Han dynasty, China had already discovered the techniques of pattern printing by combining printing blocks and hand drawing techniques.

金银色印花纱（部分）

西汉（公元前206–公元8年）
长64、宽48、幅边宽0.3cm
湖南长沙马王堆出土
湖南省博物馆藏

Silk Gauze Printed in Gold and Silver Colors (Part)

Western Han Dynasty (206 BCE–8 CE)
Length: 64cm, Width: 48cm, Margin width: 0.3cm
Excavated at Mawangdui, Changsha, Hunan
Collection of the Hunan Provincial Museum

在印花时使用三套色凸版颜料印花：一是用龟背骨架版印出银白色，二是用火焰纹曲线版印出银灰色，三是用山形小圆点印出金色，或由手绘而成。图案由均匀细致的曲线和小圆点组成，单元外廓呈菱形。

印花敷彩纱袍

西汉（公元前206–公元8年）
衣长128–130、通袖长250、
腰围51、袖口宽25cm
湖南长沙马王堆出土
湖南省博物馆藏

Silk Gown with Printed Designs

Western Han Dynasty (206 BCE–8 CE)
Length: 128–130cm, Sleeves: 250cm, Waistline: 51cm, Cuff width: 25cm
Excavated at the Mawangdui , Changsha, Hunan
Collection of the Hunan Provincial Museum

袍服的袖口、领缘等处以素纱制成，夹绵。面料采用印花和敷彩相结合的工艺，首先用花版印出暗灰色枝蔓，然后进行花蕾、花穗和叶片等的手绘敷彩，最后用粉白加点。

绞缬与灰缬
Tie Dyeing and Ash-resist Dyeing

防染印花技术首先出现在绞缬和蜡染上，“以丝系缯染之，解之成文谓之缬”。防染印花是古代染缬的主流，唐代出现以灰代蜡的防染印花，亦称灰缬。明清时灰缬被广泛用于棉织物，现今仍能见到的蓝印花布采用的正是这个技术。

Tie-dyeing and wax-resist dyeing were the first techniques that were developed based on the principle of dye resistance, as demonstrated by a quote from an ancient text, "…silk fabrics tied with threads and put into dyes; when the fabric is untied, the pattern is done: this is called tie dyeing…" By using the silk ties as a dyeing tool, it was possible to separate the sections to be patterned. Dye-resist methods soon became the preferred technique for producing dye-patterned textiles. During the Tang dynasty, ash replaced wax and the process became known as ash-resist dyeing. This technique was later used on cotton textiles as well, during the Ming and Qing dynasties. Today, the principle behind these dyeing techniques is still found in the production of blue calico cloth.

绞缬绢

约汉晋时期（公元1−3世纪）
长23.5、宽20cm
新疆尉犁营盘出土
新疆文物考古研究所藏

Tie-dyed Silk Fragment

Ca. Han to Jin Dynasties (1st−3rd century CE)
Length: 23.5cm, Width: 20cm
Excavated at the Yingpan, Yuli, Xinjiang
Collection of the Xinjiang Institute of Archaeology

绞缬绢采用汉晋南北朝时期的典型工艺绑扎制成，即将织物按点镊起，用线环扎，而后染色，得到的花纹通常是满幅散点布列的单纯小圈纹。

绞缬绢衣

北朝（公元420–589年）
中国丝绸博物馆藏

Tie-dyed Silk Jacket

Northern Dynasties (420–589 CE)
Collection of the China National Silk Museum

上衣对襟短身，两襟微微相交，喇叭形宽袖，属于当时流行的襦，面料全部采用绞缬绢染出褐色地黄色小点纹。绞缬又称扎染，在北凉时期开始流行，保存如此完整的绞缬服装极为罕见。

绞缬工作原理

绞缬又称撮缬，现在称作扎染，它利用线或织物本身将织物缝绞、捆绑、扎结后入染，以使染液在织物处理部位不能上染或不等量渗透，纹样具有晕色效果。

Principle of the Tie-Dyeing

The dyeing process that is now referred to as "tie-dyeing" makes use of string or other pieces of fabric to tie, bind or seal off parts of the textile from the dyeing process. Dyes were thus prevented from reaching the fabric portion that was bound by a tie knot, or a gathered knot, or other uneven portions. The resulting designs often had a clouded appearance.

狩猎纹灰缬绢

唐（公元618–907年）
长18.1、宽48.9cm
新疆吐鲁番阿斯塔那出土
新疆维吾尔自治区博物馆藏

Silk with Hunting Motif

Tang Dynasty (618–907 CE)
Length: 18.1cm, Width: 48.9cm
Excavated at Astana, Turfan, Xinjiang
Collection of the Xinjiang Uyghur Autonomous Region Museum

印染工艺在唐代已经相当成熟，吐鲁番出土了大量的丝绸防染印花织物。狩猎纹灰缬绢，原为浅黄色绢，织物对折后用夹板夹持，施以防染剂，打开夹板，进行染色，染得浅红色为地，防染剂处显花。

灰缬工作原理

灰缬采用灰浆进行防染印花，工艺操作较为简单，只需将灰浆涂在织物上所需描绘的地方，被灰浆覆盖的部分仍保留织物原有的颜色，其余部分则会染上染料的颜色。

Principle of Ash-resistant Dyeing

The ash-resist dyeing process involved using ash and glue as a dye-resistant paste. The dyeing process was relatively straightforward. Ash would be applied directly to the fabric in places that were to be left untouched by the dye. These areas, which would make up the design, would retain the original color of the fabric.

宝花水鸟纹灰缬绢（部分）

唐（公元618–907年）
长110.5、宽39cm
新疆吐鲁番阿斯塔那出土
新疆维吾尔自治区博物馆藏

Silk with Motif of Flowers and Water Bird (Part)

Tang Dynasty (618–907 CE)
Length: 110.5cm, Width: 39cm
Excavated at Astana, Turfan, Xinjiang
Collection of the Xinjiang Uyghur Autonomous Region Museum

灰缬绢图案采用花蕾式的宝花形式作环，其中填入立鸟纹样，每个团窠之间以十字宾花装饰，是流行于初唐至中唐之际典型的“陵阳公样”。

夹缬
Clamp-resist Dyeing

将丝绸夹于两块镂空花版之间，利用花版紧夹防染，解开花版，花纹显现。夹缬始于盛唐，《唐语林》说发明者是玄宗(公元712–756年)柳婕妤之妹，她“性巧慧，因使工镂版为杂花象之，而为夹缬”。后来夹缬技术传出宫廷，在民间广为传播，宋元时十分盛行，明清时期依然使用。

With the clamp-resist dyeing process, silk is clamped between two engraved blocks then dyed. Upon removal of the blocks then dyed, the pattern is revealed on the silk. According to the Tang Yu Lin (Collection of Tang Sayings), clamp-resist dyeing was believed to have been invented by a sister of Liu Jieyu, an imperial concubine of the Xuanzong emperor(712-756 CE). She was thought to be extremely clever and skilful, and came up with the idea of engraving floral designs on the blocks before clamping a piece of silk between them. This technique eventually spread beyond the Tang court and was widely used during the 11-13th centuries, and remained in use till the 19th century.

花卉纹夹缬绢幡身

唐晚期（约公元9世纪）
甘肃敦煌发现
旅顺博物馆藏

Silk Flag with a Clamp-resist Dyed Floral Motif

Late Tang Dynasty (ca. 9th century CE)
Discovered at Dunhuang, Gansu
Collection of the Lushun Museum

幡，是佛教所用的旌旗，是用以供养菩萨、庄严道场的道具。此三件幡均出自敦煌地区，全部或局部使用了夹缬工艺制作。

花卉纹夹缬绢幡

唐晚期（约公元9世纪）
长56、宽43.3 cm
甘肃敦煌发现
旅顺博物馆藏

Silk Flag with Clamp-resist Dyed Floral Motif

Late Tang Dynasty (ca. 9th century CE)
Length: 56cm, Width: 43.3cm
Discovered at Dunhuang, Gansu
Collection of the Lushun Museum

花卉纹夹缬绢幡

唐晚期（约公元9世纪）
长104、宽41.5 cm
甘肃敦煌发现
旅顺博物馆藏

Fragment of a Silk Flag with Clamp-resist Dyed Floral Motifs

Late Tang Dynasty (ca. 9th century CE)
Length: 104cm, Width: 41.5cm
Discovered at Dunhuang, Gansu
Collection of the Lushun Museum

南无释迦牟尼佛夹缬绢

辽（公元907–1125年）
长65、宽56.5cm
山西应县佛宫塔出土
应县木塔文物保管所藏

Namo Sakyamuni Clamp-resist Dyed Silk

Liao Dynasty (907–1125 CE)
Length: 65cm, Width: 56.5cm
Found at Fogong Pagoda, Yingxian, Shanxi
Collection of the Preservation Institute of the Wooden Pagoda, Yingxian

画面为佛说法图。佛端坐莲台，双手扶膝，上出花盖，两侧有折技花朵，飘丽花雨，前有方案，上置摩尼宝珠，两侧各有4弟子合十侍立，又有协持与化生童子各1人。榜题“南无释迦牟尼佛”七字。采用单色印制方法套印加彩绘完成。

夹缬工作原理

夹缬是利用两块刻成对称花纹的镂空板相互夹制对折的坯布防染印花，采用浸染法工艺，使染液通过在印版侧壁和版面局部凿开的洞孔染色于织物上。

Principle of Clamp-resist Dyeing

The clamp-resist method of dyeing uses two engraved blocks, which are clamped together. The dye seeps into the textile from the hollowed patterns engraved on the blocks.

锦上添花
Embroidery

穿刺运针、以针带线的刺绣，为织物增添了新的色彩。历代刺绣艺术，无不工巧精丽，令人叹为观止。

先秦及汉以锁绣独领风骚，魏晋南北朝流行劈针。唐代绣技转以平绣为主，并有接针、戗针和套针等针法相佐。宋明时代采用画绣结合，相得益彰。

Embroidered fabrics have added much color to the gamut of available textiles. Further advancements in embroidery techniques with each successive dynasty have resulted in the breathtakingly beautiful textiles we see today. The chain stitch was the predominant embroidery technique from the pre-Qin to the Han dynasties. The split stitch became popular during the Wei, Jin, Southern and Northern dynasties period. By the Tang dynasty, plain embroidery stroke stitches had taken over. Other stitches in use included the backing stitch, long and short stitch, etc. Embroidery during Song and Ming dynasties became an art form in its own right and was often joint with painting. Many new themes thus became the subject of embroidered works.

锁绣
Chain Stitch

西周出土物上见到的刺绣印痕，有的是前针勾后针形成曲线的针迹，这种针法被称为“锁针”，是中国古代的发明。锁绣在战国秦汉时期也极为流行，湖北地区的楚墓中就有这样的绣品出土，其中以荆州马山楚墓所出最为丰富多彩。

Some textiles excavated from Western Zhou tombs feature a curved embroidered stitch, which is known as a chain stitch and appears on very early Chinese fabrics. In chain stitched designs, the outline was first stitched and then the shape was filled in. Examples of this kind of embroidery have been excavated at Chu Tombs in Hubei province, with many excellent examples from the Mashan site at Jingzhou, and indicate that this technique was also popular during the Warring States period through to the Qin and Han Dynasties.

龙凤虎纹绣

战国（公元前475−221年）
长112、宽53.5、袖口宽32cm
湖北荆州马山出土
荆州博物馆藏

Embroidery with Dragon, Phoenix and Tiger Motifs

Warring States Period (475−221 BCE)
Length: 112cm, Width: 53.5cm, Width of sleeves: 32cm
Excavated at Mashan, Jingzhou, Hubei
Collection of the Jingzhou Museum

绣片为龙凤虎纹绣罗单衣的左袖，在灰白色四经绞素罗织物地上以红棕、棕、黄绿、土黄、橘红、黑、灰等色丝线以锁绣技法刺绣。图案由龙、凤、虎缠绕穿插排列，一侧是一只凤鸟，双翅张开，有花冠，脚踏小龙；另一侧是一只浑身布满红黑色（或灰色）条纹的斑斓猛虎，正张牙舞爪地奔向大龙，大龙作抵御状。龙凤之间相互交错、缠绕，形成一种暗中的骨架，使图案的布局满而不乱，显示了一种飘逸、神奇的美，是浪漫楚风的典型代表。

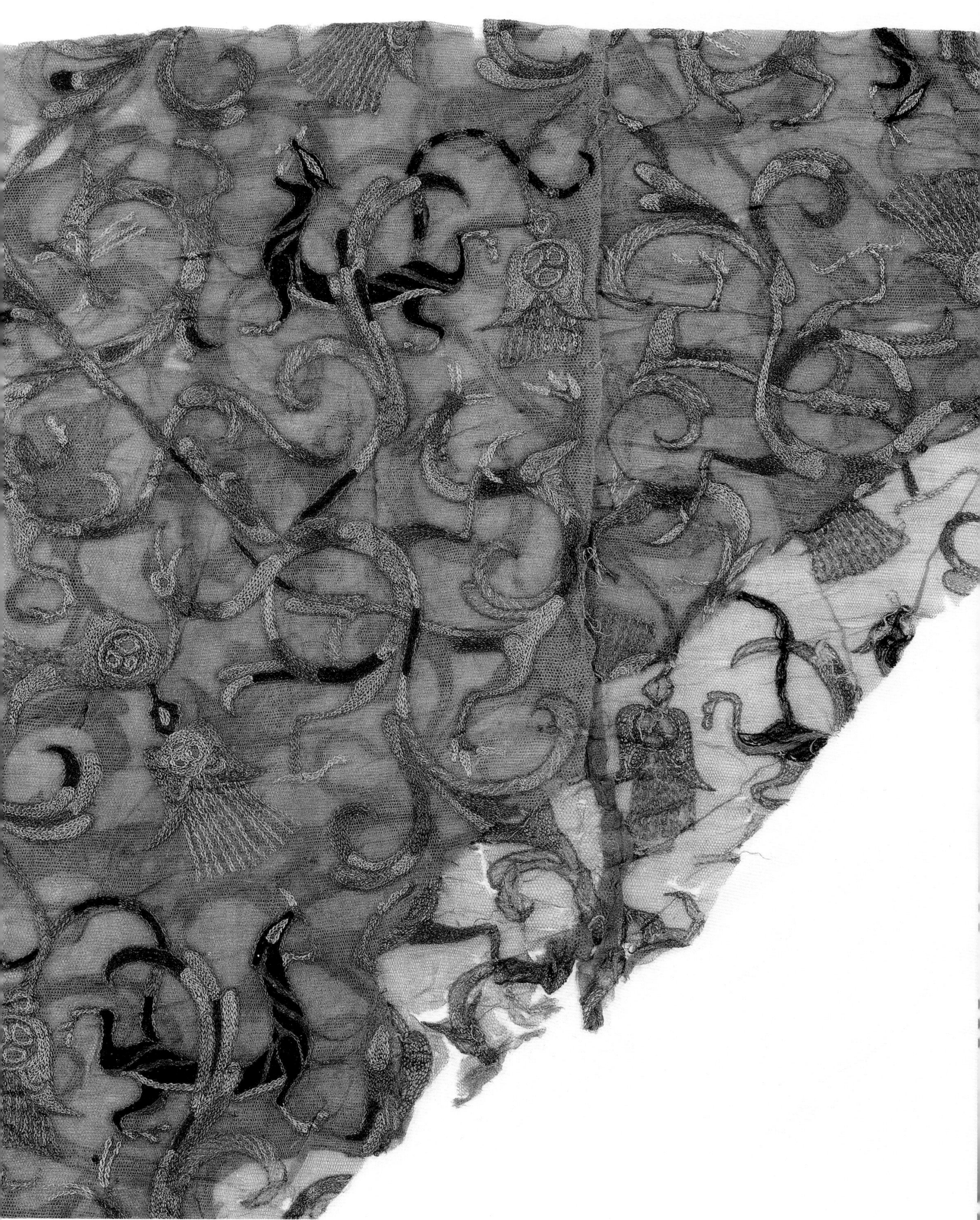

转折中的劈绣
Split Stitch

南北朝时期佛教的盛行扩宽了刺绣题材，善男信女往往不惜工本，以绣像积功德。绣像是为了布施，刺绣中的每一针代表了一句颂经，一粒佛珠，一次修行，一针即一福，通过刺绣过程祈福是一种风尚。

由于制作大面积大密度的作品费时费工，绣工开始尝试用表观效果基本一致的劈针来代替锁针，从而大大提高生产效率，这是当时刺绣技法的一大进步。劈针绣是在锁针与平针之间的一个过渡。

During the Northern and Southern Dynasties Buddhism became widespread in China, bringing in a whole new range of textile subject matter. As followers of the religion did not hesitate to perform any task that might express their devotion, some diligently produced Buddhist themed embroidered textiles. In fact, the very act of making embroidery became a popular type of worship. Each stitch represented a sentence from a sutra or one thumbing of a Buddhist prayer bead.

As fine embroidery was a labor intensive, time-consuming occupation, the split stitch technique was a major innovation that was introduced in an effort to speed up production time. This stitch gradually placed the chain stitch, as their embroidered results were quite similar.

绮地乘云绣绮 (局部)

西汉（公元前206–公元8年）
长50、宽40cm
湖南长沙马王堆出土
湖南省博物馆藏

Damask Embroidered with a "Swirling Cloud" Pattern (Part)

Western Han (206 BCE–8 CE)
Length: 40cm, Width: 50cm
Excavated at Mawangdui, Changsha, Hunan
Collection of the Hunan Provincial Museum

"乘云绣"之名得自墓中竹简文字，绣片以黄色对鸟菱纹绮为地，以朱红、绛红、浅棕、藏青等色丝线用锁绣技法刺绣，图案祥云缭绕，云间又有眼部夸张的凤头，凤身同云纹相连。马王堆汉墓出土的众多绣品采用了这种刺绣方法，其主题图案由战国时流行的龙凤纹样变为各种云气图案。

广阳王造佛像绣

北魏（公元386–534年）
正身长75、宽51cm，边长62、宽13cm
甘肃敦煌莫高窟出土
敦煌研究院藏

Embroidery of the Buddha by Prince of Guangyang

Northern Wei Dynasty (386–534 CE)
Length of the main figure: 75cm, Width 51cm;
Length of the side: 62cm, Width: 13 cm
Excavated at Mogao Caves Dunhuang, Gansu
Collection of the Dunhuang Academy

绣品为北魏广阳王元嘉（法名慧安）于太和十一年（公元487年）所施，应是在洛阳制作，通过其他高僧带至莫高窟地区。绣有佛像的幢幡，在当时被称为"绣像"，是僧人讲经说法时悬挂的，通常由施主供奉。刺绣的中心部分有坐于莲花座之上的佛像，着红色袈裟，作双脚盘坐的结跏式。

C 红色绫地宝花织锦绣袜

唐（公元618–907年）
长27.3、宽22.5cm
青海都兰热水出土
青海省文物考古研究所藏

Red Damask Stockings Embroidered with Rare Flower Motifs

Tang Dynasty (618–907 CE)
Length: 27.3cm, Width: 22.5cm
Excavated at Reshui, Dulan, Qinghai
Collection of the Qinghai Institute of Archaeology

袜子分袜筒、袜背和袜底三部分。袜筒以蓝地黄花宝花锦制成；袜背及袜底均以暗花纹绫为底，用彩色丝线分别绣出宝花和矩形格子纹样。三部分间的连接使用了罕见的绕环编绣。这样的锦袜可能是少数民族在帐篷内所用。

D 黄地大型宝花绣鞯

唐（公元618–907年）
长49.88、宽34.9cm
青海都兰热水出土
青海省文物考古研究所藏

Saddle Blanket with Large Floral Motifs Embroidered on Yellow Silk

Tang Dynasty (618–907 CE)
Length: 49.88cm, Width: 34.9cm
Excavated at Reshui, Dulan, Qinghai
Collection of the Qinghai Institute of Archaeology

绣片原为马匹鞍鞯残片，以黄绢为地，用各色以锁绣针法绣出具有唐草风格的宝花花瓣，花瓣呈桃形，瓣内有蕾，四瓣形成一朵宝花，花瓣连成一片，显得极为华丽。劈针针法在刺绣时后一针从前一针绣线的中间穿出再前行，在外观上看起来与锁针十分相似。

永远的平绣
Plain Stitch

唐代宫廷贵妃院有绣工七百人，规模很大，主要工作是制作日用装饰性刺绣，为提高刺绣效率，大量采用平绣成为一种趋势。平绣运针平直，是以平针为基础针法，只依靠针与针之间的连接方式进行变化的刺绣技法，常用多种颜色的丝线绣作，色彩丰富，又称为“彩绣”。平绣以罗为绣地，绣品背后又有平纹绢作衬，将罗和绢绣在一起史称“罗表绢衬”。以罗为绣地的风格是对战国秦汉时期刺绣传统的继承，又因为是日用刺绣，不像绣像那样致密。

明清之际，是中国刺绣艺术最为发达的一个时期，各地都形成了自己独特的风格，产生了众多的地方性绣种，刺绣的技法系统也更为完善。

During the Tang Dynasty the Inner Quarters of the Imperial Palace employed more than seven hundred needlework artists. The majority of the pieces they created were used for decorative purposes on items for daily use. In order to increase their productivity, the embroiderers frequently used the technique of plain stitching. This technique was based on the usage of a straight needle that was used to pull thread from needlepoint to needlepoint. Therefore, a large array of designs could be created quite simply. This kind of needlework was normally done using silk threads of several different colors, so was also called multicolored embroidery. Plain stitch embroidery was done on gauze with thin tabby silk used for background.

The Ming and Qing Dynasties represented the golden age of Chinese embroidering techniques. Different regions produced their own unique styles of embroidery leading to a dazzling array of textiles available during the period. In addition, as new techniques were discovered and integrated with older methods, the art of embroidery became increasingly more complex.

花鸟纹刺绣罗

唐（公元618–907年）
长102、宽48cm
中国丝绸博物馆藏

Silk Gauze with Bird and Flower Embroidery

Tang Dynasty (618–907 CE)
Length: 102cm, Width: 48cm
Collection of the China National Silk Museum

织物右边有一条刺绣带，用彩色丝线绣出花树、鸾凤和蝴蝶等纹样，背后有黄色平纹绢作衬。左边的织物亦有刺绣，为一些单独的小花，呈直线状排列。织物上还钉缝有两块多彩夹缬罗。

蓝地梅花夹竹纹绣罗

辽（公元907–1125年）
长66、宽40cm
内蒙古庆州白塔出土
巴林右旗博物馆藏

Blue Silk Gauze Embroidered with Plum Blossom Motifs

Liao Dynasty (907–1125 CE)
Length: 66cm, Width: 40cm
Excavated at the White Pagoda, Qingzhou, Inner Mongolia
Collection of the Balinyouqi Museum

绣品以梅花飞鸟为图案主题。居中有梅枝，梅两侧各饰草蔓一簇。梅上方两侧有灵芝云一片。山石之间尚有飞鸟穿插其间，左右下三边有白色联珠勾边。

红地梅花夹竹纹绣罗

辽（公元907–1125年）
长67、宽53.5cm
内蒙古庆州白塔出土
巴林右旗博物馆藏

Red Silk Gauze Embroidered with Plum Blossoms and Bamboo Motifs

Liao Dynasty (907 – 1125 CE)
Length: 67cm, Width: 53.5cm
Excavated at the White Pagoda, Qingzhou, Inner Mongolia
Collection of the Balinyouqi Museum

图案主题为梅竹荷花蜂蝶湖石。居中处为一竹一梅，左边梅竹之间，饰有荷花一簇。梅竹根边有山石若干，上缀四瓣、五瓣、六瓣小花。山石之上有蓝色小树若干，山石之旁有浅绿小草数簇。远方有云状山石，亦有树林小山。又有灵芝云、蝴蝶和蜜蜂穿插其间，一片蝶飞蜂舞景象。

红地梅花夹竹纹绣罗局部
Part of Red Silk Gauze Embroidered with Plum Blossoms and Bamboo Motifs

花鸟纹刺绣罗衫

元（公元1271－1368年）
衣长106、通袖长60cm
内蒙古集宁路遗址出土
内蒙古博物馆藏

Silk Gauze Jacket Embroidered with Flower and Bird Designs

Yuan Dynasty (1271－1368 CE)
Length: 106cm, Sleeve length: 60cm
Excavated at the Ruins of Jining Circuit, Inner Mongolia
Collection of the Inner Mongolia Museum

这是目前所知元代刺绣服饰中最为重要的佳作，属汉族服饰款式，对襟直领，直筒宽袖。在紫色四经绞素罗地上以平针为主，并结合打籽针、辫针、戗针、鱼鳞针等针法刺绣，刺绣图案多达99个。整件绣衫构图一如绘画，写实自然，在元代织绣品中实属罕见。

花鸟纹刺绣罗衫局部
Part of Silk Gauze Jacket embroidered with Flower and Bird Designs

明黄色缎绣彩云金龙夹袍

清雍正（公元1723—1735年）
身长143、通袖长193、下摆宽126cm
故宫博物院

Lined Bright Yellow Satin Robe Embroidered with Multi-colored Clouds and Golden Dragons

Yongzheng Era of the Qing Dynasty (1723–1735 CE)
Length: 143cm, Sleeves: 193cm, Width: 126cm
Collection of the Palace Museum

这件龙袍为清世宗雍正皇帝御用吉服之一，龙袍，又称彩服。主要用于元旦、万寿、冬至等重大吉庆节日、筵宴以及祭祀前后的“嘉疏”（《春秋繁露》：“祭礼先嘉疏”）活动，如：太和殿、中和殿前阅视祝版、先农坛耕耤礼等场合。其式为：圆领，大襟右衽，马蹄袖，裾四开，直身式袍。缀铜鎏金錾花扣四。

此袍采取二至三色间晕与退晕相结合的装饰方法，运用平针、套针、戗针、平金、缠针等传统刺绣针法，在明黄色素缎地上，以盘金绣的技法在前胸、后背及两肩处绣五爪正龙各一，下襟绣侧龙各二。其余部分则皆以彩色丝线绣成。构图威严庄重，绣工精巧细腻，线条舒展流畅。无论从龙袍的前身或后面看，都只见金龙五条，体现出中国古代皇权至上的“九五之尊”（《周易》：“九五，飞龙在天，利见大人”）。金碧辉煌的巨龙，在五彩云蝠的衬托下，扶摇升腾栩栩如生。不但具有很好的装饰效果，还将清雍正时期高超精湛的刺绣工艺水平充分表现出来。

丝绸曾是人类重要的物质生活资料，也是美化自身和生存空间的精神创造。
中国是丝绸的发源地，
中国丝绸不仅以它精巧的织造技术、绚丽的图案色彩、滑爽柔软的质感和浓郁的艺术特点，
在很长一段时间里领先于世界前列，而且还通过“丝绸之路”传往各地，
成为与世界各国经济、政治和文化交流的桥梁，在世界历史上产生了深远的影响。
取之于桑蚕的丝绸为人类带来了锦绣华服，也为历史增添了绚烂的色彩。
我们下面要欣赏到的是诞生于烈火的青铜器，
它铸就了历史雄浑的篇章，带来了一个威武的青铜时代。

Since ancient times, silk has been valued for its beauty and contributions to cultural history. It originated from China and is one of the most precious materials in the world. It was the product of the most advanced weaving techniques developed over time. It is not only soft and smooth to the touch, but also has a rich history as an art form as silk designs came in an array of beautiful colors and exquisite designs. As one of the most important and sought after commodities traded along the famous Silk Road, Chinese silk played an important role in world economy, as well as facilitated political and cultural exchanges between China and the West. Its profound influence on world history stands uncontested.

雄奇宝器

古代青铜铸造术

中国的青铜时代具有独特的风采，青铜铸造的文明，成就了一种永恒的记忆。

钟鸣鼎食的时代，贵族是青铜器的拥有者，铜器是子孙永宝之器，是地位尊卑的象征。国家有国之重器，所谓“九鼎”是国家政权的象征。

“国之大事，在祀与戎”。古代中国青铜器的主要功能是祭祀与征战，大量制作的是礼乐器和兵器，与其他文明用青铜主要制作工具、兵器和饰品有所不同。大量繁缛华丽青铜礼乐器的制作，在技术上形成了以陶范铸造为主，辅以失蜡铸造和多种表面装饰工艺的传统技艺，这与世界上其他青铜文明有明显的不同。

Techniques of Ancient Bronze Production

China's great Bronze Age was an epoch of such unmatched achievement both in terms of human civilization and artistic elegance that its splendor is still clearly apparent today. During this period of affluence in Chinese history, the use of bronze items fell under the domain of the aristocracy and was treasured in those families for generations. The types of bronze vessels a family owned were clear indicators of their social status. This was true even for the rulers of China as possession of the famous “Nine Ding Vessels” were potent symbols of the right to rule.

The Chinese saying “great affairs of the nation lie in sacrificial rites and warfare” demonstrates that in ancient China the two most important functions of bronze items were for use as ceremonial vessels in rituals, including musical instruments, and weapons of war. These practices are in contrast to other bronze producing civilizations in which the primary items of production were utensils and ornaments, although weapons were also produced in great numbers in other countries.

Perhaps the feature that most distinguishes Chinese bronze production from that of other civilizations was a manufacturing technique known as the clay piece-mold method. This method relied on the production of an initial clay master model for each bronze piece. It was that the clay mold casting techniques as well as the lost-wax casting and magnificent surface decoration techniques for bronzes distinguished the ancient Chinese Bronze Culture from the other ancient cultures in the world.

九鼎八簋

春秋（公元前770–前476年）
鼎：通高54.4–47.6、口径53.4–45.3cm，重19.6–13.8kg
簋：通高23.8–22.7、口径19.7–19.2cm，重3.9–3.2kg
河南新郑郑韩故城遗址祭祀坑出土
河南博物院藏

Nine *Ding* Tripods and Eight *Gui* Vessels

Spring and Autumn Period (770–476 BCE)
Ding: Height: 54.4–47.6cm, Diameter of mouth: 53.4–45.3cm, Weight: 19.6–13.8kg
Gui: Height: 23.8–22.7cm, Diameter of mouth: 19.7–19.2cm, Weight 3.9–3.2kg
Excavated from the Sacrifice Pit at the Ruins of Zhenghan, Xinzheng , Henan
Collection of the Henan Museum

古代中国青铜器是地位和权力的象征，九鼎八簋是周朝天子所用。郑韩故城遗址是春秋、战国时的著名都城，郑、韩两国先后在此建都长达530年之久，城内发现多处贵族墓地及铸铜、铸铁、制骨作坊，郑国祭祀遗址还出土了四套九鼎八簋。九件列鼎的形制相同，大小依次递减，八件列簋的形制、大小基本一致。鼎和簋均采用复合陶范法和分铸铸接工艺成形，鼎身外范由六块组成，预铸的鼎耳、足、扉棱与鼎身铸接连接，鼎耳、足内含泥芯；簋耳空心，与器体铸接连接。

定鼎与问鼎 Settling Down the *Ding* (*ding ding*) and Asking for the *Ding* (*wen ding*)

相传大禹铸九鼎，商汤灭夏后，迁九鼎于宗庙。周武王灭商后，又迁九鼎于宗庙。春秋时期，楚国扬威于王畿近郊，楚庄王询问九鼎之轻重，大有取代周天子之意。因此，鼎在中国古代是权利的象征，是统治者身份的标志，具有重要的政治意义。定鼎象征着权位的合法化，问鼎则有权利更替的意味。

According to legend, Da Yu (the third mythical emperor who created the Chinese state) cast the original nine imperial ding vessels. After King Tang of the Shang overthrew the Xia Dynasty (2100 - 1600 BCE), he moved the nine ding into his ancestral temple. After King Wu of the Zhou overthrew the Shang Dynasty, he then moved the nine ding into his own ancestral temple. During the Spring and Autumn Period (722 - 481 BCE) the State of Chu grew stronger and stronger, encroaching on the Zhou king's territory. Finally, King Zhuang of Chu formally requested to be presented with the nine ding vessels, declaring his intention to replace the Zhou Dynasty. Thereupon, ding vessels were intrinsically linked to those in power, symbolizing their right to rule. The phrase, ding ding, means to settle down the ding and is indicative of an individual's legitimate right to power. Wen ding, means to ask for a ding and symbolizes a quest for power.

铄石成金
Melting Stone into Metal

中国古代的青铜主要是铜和锡、铅的合金，它们来自于矿石。烧造陶器过程中成熟起来的高温技术，最终让人们从矿石中得到了宝贵的金属资源。中国至迟在公元前3000多年前已经有了青铜冶铸生产活动，二里头文化时期进入青铜时代。从此青铜文化成为中国早期文明的重要内容，青铜的生产和加工持续繁荣了2000多年。

In ancient China bronze was comprised of an alloy of copper, tin, and lead, which were smelted from ores. The technology of firing at high temperatures came from the already developed ceramic making industry and allowed these natural resources to be fully exploited. Based on archaeological evidence, bronze foundries were active in China by at least 3000 BCE and by the era of the Erlitou Culture (2100 – 1800 BCE) a true Bronze Age had been reached. Bronze production continued to develop and flourish for roughly 2000 years after Erlitou.

早期铜器
Early Coppers

考古发掘已发现了多例仰韶文化中晚期（约公元前6500－前5000年）的原始冶铜遗物，那个时代是用矿石冶炼金属的开端。考古发现的早期青铜铸件多为小型工具和容器，采用等壁厚及薄壁件设计，多为素面或铸造有简单纹饰。

Several items have been excavated from Yangshao Culture (ca. 6500－5000 BCE) sites that provide evidence for early coppers smelting activities as well as nascent techniques for making metal alloys. copper casting in these early periods mostly focused on the production of small utensils and vessels. Walls of individual vessels were cast with equal thickness and the surface decorations were quite simple.

铃形铜器

新石器时代陶寺文化（约公元前2085年）
高2.65、长对角线6.3、短对角线2.7 cm
山西襄汾陶寺遗址出土
中国社会科学院考古研究所藏

Bell-shaped Bronze Object

Taosi Culture, Neolithic Period(ca. 2085 BCE)
Height: 2.65cm, Length across the Bottom: 6.3cm, Width across the Bottom: 2.7cm
Excavated from the site of Taosi, Xiangfen Shanxi
Collection of the Institute of Archaeology, Chinese Academy of Social Sciences

考古发现年代最早的铜礼乐器。经化学定量分析含铜97.86%，铅1.54%，锌0.16%。器壁厚度不匀，有铸造气孔。铸造工艺虽较原始，却是采用比较复杂的两块外范与一块泥芯相组合的双合范陶范技术铸造成形的早期铜器。

爵

夏晚期（约公元前18世纪）
高26.5、流尾长31.5 、壁厚0.1 cm
河南偃师翟四角楼村南遗址出土
洛阳市博物馆藏

Jue Vessel

Latter Xia Dynasty (ca. 18th century BCE)
Height: 26.5cm, Length: 31.5cm, Thickness: 0.1cm
Excavated from an Erlitou Culture grave south of Sijiaolou Village, Zhaizhen, Yanshi, Henan
Collection of the Luoyang Municipal Museum

铜爵为贵族饮酒器具，夏代出现，商周时代沿用。这件铜爵为发现年代最早的完整容器之一，典型陶范铸造均匀薄壁铸件，表现了当时陶范铸造技术在合范、定位等工艺方面已经比较成熟。二里头遗址已出土了100多件青铜礼器，发现了铸铜遗址，表明中国在夏代已经进入青铜时代。

锻造铜器
Forging Bronzes

除了铸造成形主流技术外，青铜时代也常采用锻造方法制作青铜器。考古发现在齐家文化时期（约公元前2000年）已采用锤击红铜、青铜等来制造小件铜器，在西周时期则出现了锻造容器。

In addition to the predominant production method of casting, craftsmen in the Bronze Age would also forge bronze Vessels and tools. Archaeological evidence for this includes small copper and bronze tools forged with a hammer from the Qijia Culture (ca. 2000 BCE). Forged vessels have also been discovered from the Western Zhou period (1046 - 771 BCE).

盘

西周（公元前1046–前771年）
高3.3、口径14.6、底径11.5 cm
甘肃崇信于家湾墓葬出土
甘肃省文物考古研究所藏

Dish

Western Zhou (1046–771 BCE)
Height: 3.3cm, Diameter of mouth: 14.6cm, Diameter of base: 11.5cm
Unearthed at Yujiawan, Chongxin, Gansu
Collection of the Gansu Provincial Institute of Cultural Relics and Archaeology

墓葬群中至少出土10件铜盘，检验其中5件，有4件均为热锻及冷锻成形，1件为铸后经过加热和轻微冷锻。4件锻造铜盘的壁厚分别为0.51–1.26毫米，其中3件为铅锡青铜、1件锡青铜，含铜在80.4%–84.4%、锡12.2%–16.4%、铅0%–5.0%，是目前发现年代最早的锻造成形青铜容器。

江西瑞昌铜岭商代中期
古铜矿遗址采铜井巷
Well lane of Copper Mining Relics of Middle Shang Dynasty, Tongling, Ruichang, Jiangxi

古老的冶金术
Ancient Metallurgy

发达的矿石开采和冶炼是铸造青铜器的基础。商周古铜矿冶遗址已发现多处，当时已能有效地解决探矿、采矿、选矿等一系列复杂的技术问题。冶铜炉从早期的坩埚炉、坑炉发展到结构较完善的竖炉，加上人力鼓风的运用，使获得的铜锭纯度很高。

The technology of mining and smelting of copper and tin ores are the fundamental requirements for bronze production. Based on a number of ancient copper mines and foundry sites excavated from the Shang and Zhou it is clear the processes of prospecting for minerals, mining, and refining ores had reached a high level of development in these early periods. Furnaces for smelting copper ores were developed early in the form of crucible furnaces. In addition, excavated pit furnaces and shaft furnaces were remarkably advanced in structure. Manually forced drafts in the furnaces were also used and so the quality of copper obtained was astonishingly high.

铜锭

西周（公元前1046–前771年）
长41、宽10cm
安徽南陵古铜矿遗址出土
上海博物馆藏

Bronze Ingot

Western Zhou Dynasty (1046–771 BCE)
Length: 41cm, Width: 10cm
Excavated from the Ruins of the Nanling Copper Mine, Anhui
Collection of the Shanghai Museum

铜矿石开采后，多在开采地冶炼成铜锭后再运输到铸铜作坊。此件铜锭为炼铜制品，经X射线荧光光谱分析，含铜96.60%、铁2.50%、锌0.05%，纯度很高，表明西周时期的炼铜炉及其冶炼技术已经达到相当高的水平。

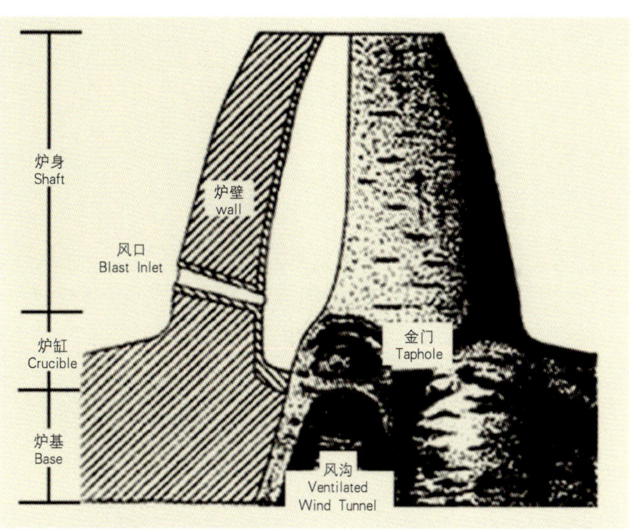

春秋时期炼铜竖炉结构复原图
Reproduced Picture of Shaft Furnace Structure of Spring and Autumn Period

木铲

春秋时期（公元前770–前476年）
通长18.2、铲宽6.4cm
湖北黄石铜绿山矿冶遗址出土
黄石市博物馆藏

Wooden Shovel

Spring and Autumn Period (770–476 BCE)
Total Length 18.2cm, Width of the shovel: 6.4cm
Excavated from the ruins of a mine at Tonglu Mountain, Huangshi, Hubei
Collection of the Huangshi Municipal Museum

铜绿山矿冶遗址出土和采集的木工具共241件，有铲、锹、锤、瓢、桶、船形斗、钩、槌、梯、辘轳、扁担等，主要为探矿、铲装、选矿、排水、提升等工具。其中各种形制的长、短柄木铲数量最多，计有89件，多用整木削制而成，主要用于铲装矿石。此件属短柄木铲。

铜斧

春秋时期（公元前770–前476年）
通长34.5、刃宽30.4cm，重11kg
湖北黄石铜绿山矿冶遗址出土
黄石市博物馆藏

Bronze Axe

Spring and Autumn Period (770 – 476 BCE)
Length: 34.5cm, Width of blade: 30.4cm, Weight 11kg
Excavated from the ruins of a mine at Tonglu Mountain, Huangshi, Hubei
Collection of the Huangshi Municipal Museum

从铜绿山矿冶遗址出土和采集了大量石、铜、铁、木、竹、骨等生产工具，其中铜工具34件，有斧、锛、凿、铲、锄、镢等，大都为挖掘和铲装工具。挖掘矿石的大小铜斧共11件，此件器身较大，刃部已有磨损，三个长方形铸孔用于固定木把手，采用两块均有型腔的陶范合范铸造成形。

湖北黄石大冶铜绿山东周矿冶遗址
Site of Mining of Eastetn Zhou Dynasty, Tonglu Mountain, Daye, Huangshi, Hubei

铸造辉煌

Casting: The Superlative Technique

青铜器制作主要采用陶范铸造法，依靠活块模与活块范、分铸铸接等技术制作形状复杂的器物，纹饰和铭文也同时铸造成形。春秋中期之后出现了毋需分范的失蜡法，技艺绝伦。复合金属技术和成套编钟的铸造，表明了人们对青铜性能的高度认知，技术达到成熟，已形成专业化分工生产。

The clay piece-mold casting technique was a remarkably flexible yet complex process. Since a model and as many mold pieces as necessary were made for each individual vessel this allowed for the creation of complex shapes and unique decorative patterns. In addition, all inscriptions and decorations are added to the vessel during the initial casting procedure, negating the need for additional manufacturing techniques. Towards the end of the Spring and Autumn period (770 - 476 BCE) Chinese bronze casters began to use the lost wax casting process. This technique allowed for the casting of exquisitely complex pieces that were devoid of seam marks associated with the piece-mold method. Bronze casters, who were clearly professional craftsmen, were not only highly proficient at forming vessels but as the use of composite metals and the production of tonally matched sets of chime bells indicate, technical achievements reached in early China were impressive.

陶范铸造技术

The Clay Mold Casting Techniques

陶范材料由多种原料配置而成，经特定工艺处理后具有良好的铸造性能。制范技术有复合模范与印模块范拼合、纹饰和铭文的刻制与翻印、内范支钉及芯撑应用、刮板制范与规范化制范等多项工艺，浑铸、分铸、铸接、铸焊等为陶范铸造技术的主要手段，又配之以精湛的青铜熔炼术，举世闻名的商周青铜器才得以出现。

The process of casting bronzes relied on several materials and evolved as a technique over time until it became a highly sophisticated procedure. There were several methods of production employed in ancient foundries including, piece-mold casting, casting in one piece, casting in several Pours, as well as welding. Ornamental designs and inscriptions were incised onto clay molds by hand or with stamp plates. The stability of a clay core was insured by pegs or chaplets placed between the clay core and mold that created an even distribution of molten bronze. Such technology and craftsmanship account for the wide variety in shape, size, and decoration of bronzes from the Shang and Zhou Dynasties.

铜罍铸造

The Casting of Bronze *Lei* (Wine Vessel with Wide Shoulder and Narrow Foot)

铜罍涡纹模

商晚期（公元前13-前11世纪）
高5.3、泡径5.5cm
河南安阳孝民屯东南地出土
中国社会科学院考古研究所安阳工作站藏

Model with Whorl Patterns of a Bronze *Li* Vessel

Late Shang Dynasty (13th-11th centuery BCE)
Height: 5.3cm, Diameter of Design: 5.5cm
Unearthed from Southeast of Xiaomin Village, Anyang, Henan
Collection of Anyang Station, Institute of Archaeology, Chinese Academy of Social Sciences

青铜器纹饰的制作方法，除了在泥质母模上雕刻、从母模上翻制外范复印纹饰之外，还有直接在外范上雕塑、压印纹饰等工艺。大涡纹常见于铜罍的肩部，此涡纹模背面附带捉手，使用方式可能是在罍肩部外范翻制成形后，直接将涡纹压印施加于外范上。纹饰压印模的使用提高了陶范纹饰制作的效率。

铜罍外范

商晚期（公元前13–前11世纪）
A高8.5、厚约5.2cm；B高15.4、厚约4.8cm
河南安阳孝民屯东南地出土
中国社会科学院考古研究所安阳工作站藏

Clay Mold of a Bronze *Lei* Vessel

Late Shang Dynasty (13th–11th century BCE)
A–Height: 8.5cm, Thickness: 5.2cm; B–Height: 15.4cm, Thickness: 4.8cm
Unearthed from Southeast of Xiaomin Village, Anyang, Henan
Collection of Anyang Station, Institute of Archaeology, Chinese Academy of Social Sciences

两块陶范残件的纹饰与同时期出土青铜罍相似，四周边缘均修治平整，型腔面上纹饰清晰精细。陶范A是罍口、颈部外范，右侧面有一合范定位榫。陶范B是罍的下腹部范，侧面带牛首半环耳型腔，顶面和右侧面设有定位卯，底边设两个榫。铸造铜罍的外范，是由这些小块的块范拼合构成。

A

B

亚址罍与外范、涡纹模对应示意图
The Mapping of the Molds of Body and Whorl Patterns and Finished Ware of Ya Zhi *Lei* Vessel

亚址罍

商晚期（公元前13–前11世纪）
通高44.8、口径17.5cm，重14.2kg
河南安阳郭家庄西160号墓出土
中国社会科学院考古研究所藏

Ya Zhi *Lei* Vessel

Late Shang Dynasty (13th–11th century BCE)
Height: 44.8cm, Diameter of mouth: 17.5cm,
Weight: 14.2kg
Excavated No. 160 tomb, west of Guojia Village, Anyang, Henan
Collection of the Institute of Archaeology, Chinese Academy of Social Sciences

罍为商周时代的大型盛酒器。肩部有一对牛首半环形耳，耳内连一圆环。下腹一侧有一牛首形耳。表面装饰三角蝉纹、夔龙纹、涡纹、大蕉叶纹等，以云雷纹衬地。颈部和腹内铸有铭文。对照安阳出土陶范和罍表面铸造痕迹，应由多块块范拼合构成两大块复合陶范，与腹泥芯和足底范组合后浑铸成形。

铜分裆鼎铸造
The Casting of Bronze Ding-tripod with Splitting Lower Belly

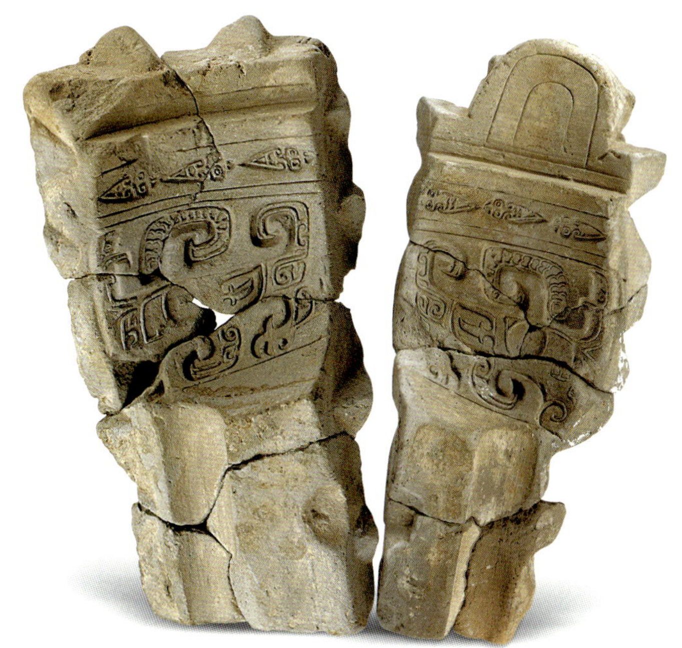

分裆铜鼎外范

商晚期（公元前13-前11世纪）
高22、厚1.4-3.3cm
河南安阳孝民屯东南地出土
中国社会科学院考古研究所安阳工作站藏

Clay Molds for a Bronze *Ding* Vessel

Late Shang Dynasty (13th-11th century BCE)
Height: 22cm, Thickness: 1.4-3.3cm
Unearthed from Southeast of Xiaomin Village, Anyang, Henan
Collection of Anyang Station, Institute of Archaeology, Chinese Academy of Social Sciences

以榫卯定位扣合的两块陶范，组成铜鼎两足间三分之一的外范，鼓腹分裆，有蝉纹、兽面纹和倒夔龙纹。侧面和顶面也设置了与相邻陶范合范的定位榫卯，两足型腔之间的圆卯，则是外范与足部泥芯的合范定位。此类鼎的铸型，应有6块垂直分型的外范、1块鼎腹泥芯和1块足部泥芯组合而成。

分裆铜鼎模

商晚期（公元前13-前11世纪）
腹高约9.4、厚5.2cm
河南安阳孝民屯东南地出土
中国社会科学院考古研究所安阳工作站藏

Clay Model for a Bronze Ding Vessel

Late Shang Dynasty (13th-11th century BCE)
Height: approximately: 9.4cm, Thickness: 5.2cm
Unearthed from Southeast of Xiaomin Village, Anyang, Henan
Collection of Anyang Station, Institute of Archaeology, Chinese Academy of Social Sciences

鼎模残件。以泥雕塑，质地细密，经过焙烧和烟薰。空心结构，表面雕刻有纹饰。以模垂直分型翻制外范，与泥芯相合组成铸型，可一次整体铸造铜鼎成品。模表面常用烟薰方法施以分型碳烟层，便于翻范脱模。

亚寠鼎

商晚期（公元前13-前11世纪）
通高21、口径17.1cm
河南安阳郭家庄西160号墓出土
中国社会科学院考古研究所藏

Ya Fu *Ding* Vessel

Late Shang Dynasty (13th – 11th century BCE)
Height:21 cm, Dianeter of mouth:17.1 cm
Excavated in No. 160 tomb, west of Guojia Village, Anyang, Henan
Collection of Institute of Archaeology, Chinese Academy of Social Sciences

鼎是青铜时代最为重要的礼器，具有煮食或盛食功能。该墓同出两件分裆鼎，形制、纹饰、铭文相同。立耳，直口，方唇，三柱形足，腹部饰三组以云雷纹为地纹的兽面纹，每个兽面纹的两侧饰倒置的夔龙纹，与安阳出土分裆鼎模相似。器口下内壁有铭文。陶范法整体铸造成形。

铜器铭文铸造

The Casting of Bronze Inscriptions

铜器铭文活块泥芯

商晚期（公元前13-前11世纪）
高6.2、宽4.4、厚3cm
河南安阳孝民屯东南地出土
中国社会科学院考古研究所安阳工作站藏

Clay Piece-core (inner mold) with Inscription

Late Shang Dynasty (13th – 11th century BCE)
Height: 6.2 cm, Width: 4.4 cm, Thickness: 3 cm
Excavated at the southeast of Xiaomin Village, Anyang, Henan
Collection of Anyang Station, Institute of Archaeology, Chinese Academy of Social Sciences

青铜器铭文通常位于器内壁，为阴文，常用制作方法是将带有反阳字铭文的活块镶嵌于主体泥芯上，组合成复合泥芯整体铸造而成。该泥芯型腔面有弧度和11个反字，原应为阳文，浇注后清出泥芯时造成字口断损。泥芯背面规整，上部有一榫，应是镶嵌在铜器主体泥芯上的铭文活块泥芯，为殷墟迄今发现文字最多、最完整的一件。

戍嗣子鼎

商晚期（公元前13-前11世纪）
通高48、口内径37.8、腹深24.6cm，重21.5kg
河南安阳后冈出土
中国社会科学院考古研究所安阳工作站藏

Shu Si Zi *Ding* Vessel

Late Shang Dynasty (13th – 11th century BCE)
Height: 48 cm, Diameter of inner mouth: 37.8, Width at the widest point: 24.6 cm, Weight: 21.5 kg
Excavated at Hougang, Anyang, Henan
Collection of Anyang Station, Institute of Archaeology, Chinese Academy of Social Sciences

商代晚期著名青铜器，器腹的内壁铸有阴字铭文共3行29个字，内容为记录商王赏赐戍嗣子贝二十朋，戍嗣子铸造这件方鼎来祭祀他的父亲的事情。铭文制作方法是先刻制阴字铭文模，然后翻制反阳字铭文活块，镶嵌于鼎主体泥芯上组成复合泥芯，最后与鼎一并铸成。

戍嗣子鼎铭文拓片
Rubbing of the Inscriptiob of
Shu Si Zi Vessel

铜卣铸造

The Casting of Bronze *You* (Wine Vessel with Swing Handle)

凤纹卣

西周早期（公元前11–前10世纪）
高27.6、腹宽17.9cm
上海博物馆藏

You Vessel with the Design of a Phoenix

Early Western Zhou Dynasty (11th–10th century BCE)
Height: 27.6cm, Width at the widest point: 17.9cm
Collection of the Shanghai Museum

卣是一种盛酒器。卣腹部、颈部、圈足和盖上装饰华美的凤鸟纹和直棱纹，肩部有4个歧出甚长的脊棱。器身和盖用陶范法复合范技术浑铸成形，歧出的脊棱分铸成形后用铸焊法与器身连接，器盖空心耳采用小泥芯浑铸成形，提梁分铸，整体铸造技术精湛娴熟。

铜卣外范

商晚期（公元前13–前11世纪）
A残高6.5、厚约3cm；B残高8.4、厚约3.5；C残长12.2、残宽10.5、厚约2.8cm
河南安阳孝民屯东南地出土
中国社会科学院考古研究所安阳工作站藏

Clay Molds of Bronze *You* Vessel

Late Shang Dynasty (13th–11th century BCE)
A–Height: 6.5cm, Thickness: 3cm; B–Height: 8.4cm, Thickness: 3.5cm; C–Length: 12.2cm, Width: 10.5cm, Thickness: 2.8cm
Unearthed Southeast of Xiaomin Village, Anyang, Henan
Collection of Anyang Station, Institute of Archaeology, Chinese Academy of Social Sciences

孝民屯铸铜作坊遗址是迄今发现的规模最大的一处商代铸铜遗址，有制范、浇铸和修整铜器遗迹，出土陶范已超过3万块，大多为各种青铜礼器的范和模。3件卣范残件的纹饰与青铜凤纹卣相似，陶范A为卣腹部齿冠鸟头纹和直棱纹处残范；陶范B为卣腹部带扉棱型腔的长尾凤鸟纹处残范；陶范C为卣肩部歧出棱脊的外残范。陶范型腔面上的纹饰是从卣模上翻制形成。

铜卣与陶范对应示意图
Bronze *You* Vessel and Mold Fragments for Similar Vessels

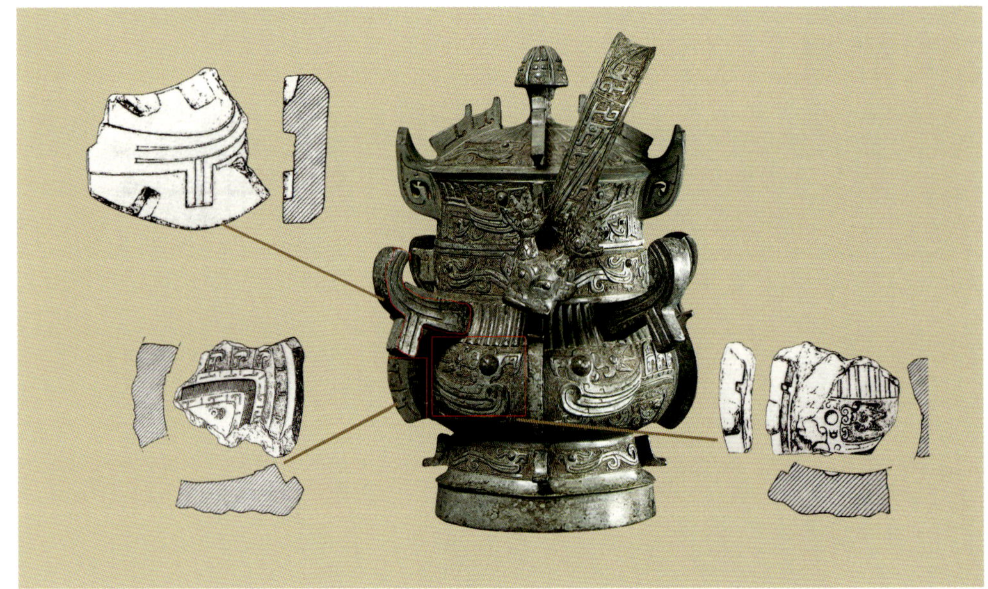

铜卣外范示意图
Caly Molds Fragments of Bronze *You* Vessel

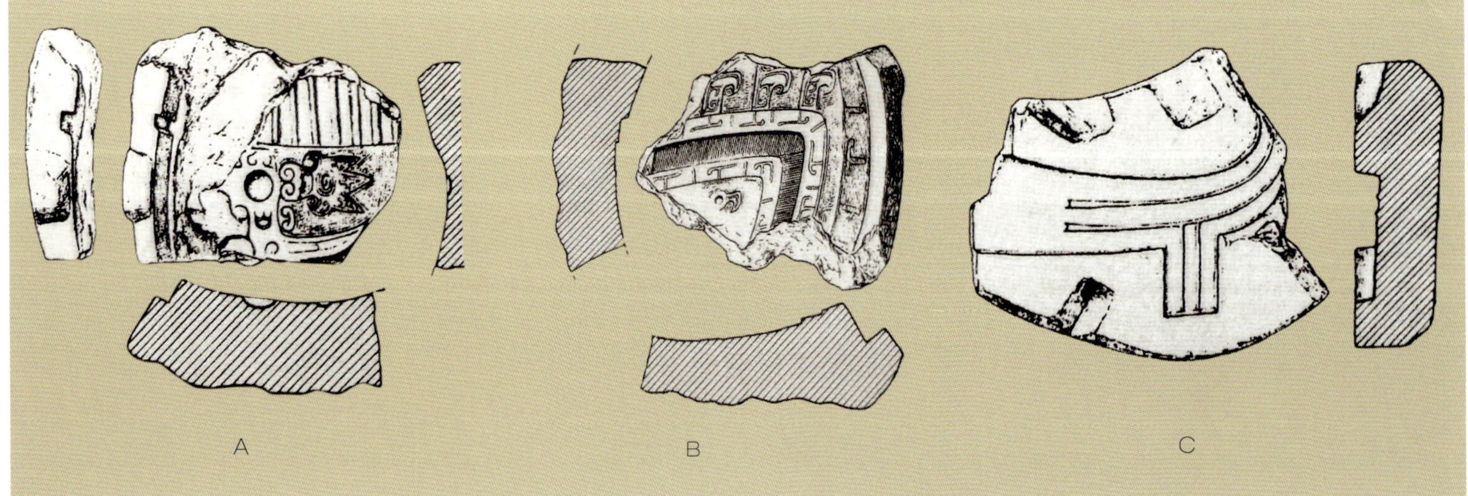

铜附件铸造
The Casting of Bronze Attachments

铜人形器足整套陶范

春秋晚期（公元前6-前5世纪）
合范高11.5、宽8cm
山西侯马晋都城铸铜遗址出土
山西博物院藏

Clay Molds of Human Figure Stand

Late spring and Autumn Period (6th–5th century BCE)
Height: 11.5cm, Width: 8cm
Excavated from the foundry Site at the Jin Capital at Houma, Shanxi
Collection of the Shanxi Museum

成套完整铸型，出土时已合好待浇铸。由六块外范与一块泥芯组成，外范与外范之间依靠分型面上的榫卯定位，外范与泥芯之间依靠泥芯上的芯撑定位和控制器物壁厚，足底的一块外范兼作浇口，充分体现了当时精湛的复合范工艺。整套陶范用于铸造空心人形器足，所铸人形属“断发纹身”的南方异族形象。

铜虎形器耳整套陶范

春秋晚期（公元前6-前5世纪）
高8、通长18.3、宽6.6cm
山西侯马晋都城铸铜遗址出土
山西博物院藏

Clay Molds for a Tiger Shaped Vessel Handle

Late Spring and Autumn Period (6th–5th century BCE)
Height: 8cm, Length: 18.3cm, Width: 6.6cm
Excavated from the foundry Site at the Jin Capital at Houma, Shanxi
Collection of the Shanxi Museum

同出两套形制相同的完整陶范，未使用。前、上、下三表面标有合范号。整套铸型由3块范组合而成，虎的左、右侧各一块范，腹底部一块范，以分型面上众多的定位榫卯正确合范，浇口设于虎尾。该套陶范用于铸造晋式铜器中常见的实心虎形器耳，虎身饰草叶状云纹。

人足虎耳双盖方鼎

春秋（公元前770-前476年）
高8.7、长10、宽6.5cm
山西闻喜上郭村出土
山西博物院藏

Square *Ding* Vessel with a Lid and Human Figure Stand

Spring and Autumn Period (770–476 BCE)
Height: 8.7cm, Length: 10cm, Width: 6.5cm
Excavated at Shangguo Village, Wenxi, Shanxi
Collection of the Shanxi Museum

长方形鼎形方盒，顶部有两扇可以对开的小盖，均铸有小虎钮。盒外壁四面附虎形耳，两宽面下部各有一对人形足。整器充分运用了陶范法分铸技术，4个虎形耳和4个人形足分别铸造成型后，镶嵌于鼎体陶范中，在浇铸鼎身时与鼎体铸接，小盖上的虎形钮亦铸接。分铸铸接技术是陶范法的特色工艺之一，大大简化了复杂造型青铜器的制作难度。

铜牺立人擎盘铸造

The Casting of Bronze Dish Held by a Sculpture of a Human Riding an Animal

牺立人擎盘与陶范对应示意图
Bronze Dish Held by a Sculpture of a Human Riding an Animal and Clay Mold Fragments for a Animal

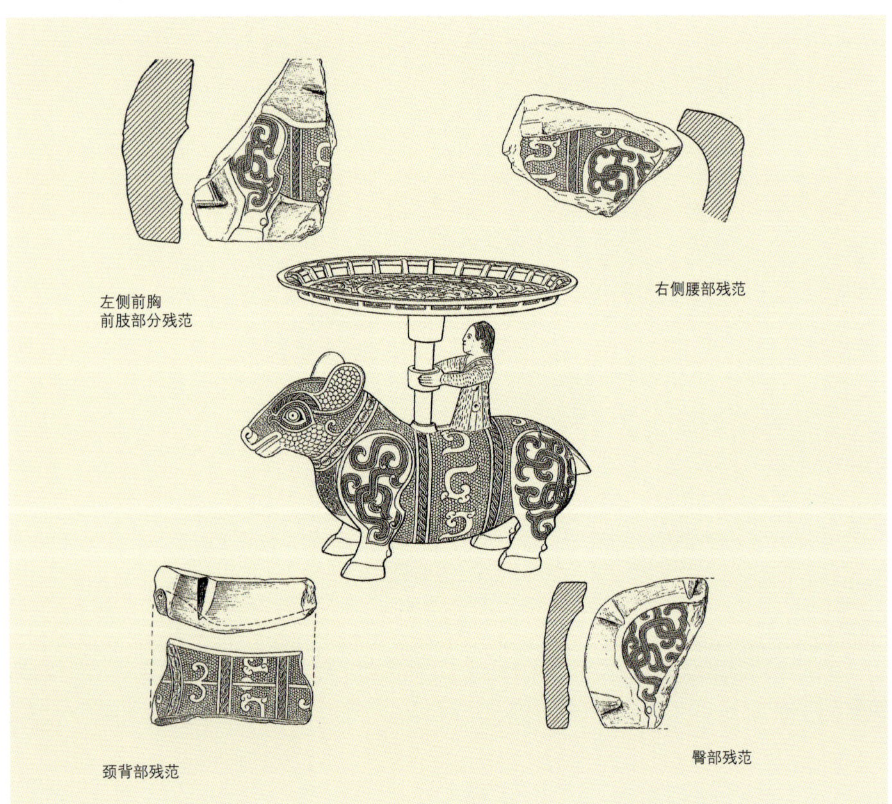

铜牺立人擎盘陶范

春秋晚期（公元前6–前5世纪）
残高11–4.5、长9.5–7cm
山西侯马晋都城铸铜遗址出土
山西博物院藏

Clay Molds Fragments of a Bronze Dish Held by a Sculpture of a Human Riding an Animal

Late Spring and Autumn Period (6th–5th century BCE)
Height: 11–4.5cm, Length: 9.5–7cm
Excavated from the foundry Site at the Jin Capital at Houma, Shanxi
Collection of the Shanxi Museum

侯马铸铜遗址中出土的一些牺牲类残范和残泥芯，包括镂空盘残范，造型和纹饰基本与山西省长治市分水岭126号墓出土的战国铜牺立人擎盘相似，分别可对应于前胸、前肢部位，颈背部，腰部，臀部，前胸、前足等部位。部分残范的分型面上设有合范定位榫卯，外侧有合范号。

陶范铸造工艺 陶范配料由原生土等多种材料组成，经特定工艺处理后具有良好性能。制范前一般需要先制作带纹饰的泥模，然后在泥模上分块翻制陶范并补刻纹饰，最后制作泥芯、铭文范及浇注系统。陶范在浇注前，必须经过600℃—900℃左右的长时间烘焙以脱除水分。

The Technique of Casting with Clay Molds The main ingredient in the production of clay molds was the earth needed to make the clay. In fact, only after the ceramic industry attained a high level of development could the manufacturing of bronzes commence. After the clay was prepared a model was created in the exact shape of the final vessel, complete with all decorative motifs and fixtures. The mold pieces were pressed against this model to absorb the shape of the final piece. Next clay cores were made. Then clay piece-molds and cores were assembled and baked at about 600℃-900℃. Finally the molten bronze was pouring into the mold's cavity. Upon cooling, the mold pieces were chipped away leaving the finished bronze vessel behind.

牺立人擎盘

战国（公元前475-前221年）
通高14.6、长17.5、盘径11cm
山西长治分水岭126号墓出土
山西博物院藏

Bronze Dish Held by a Sculpture of a Human Riding an Animal

Warring States Period (475-211 BCE)
Height: 14.6cm, Length: 17.5cm, Diameter of plate: 11cm
Excavated from the Tomb 126 at Fenshuiling, Changzhi, Shanxi
Collection of the Shanxi Museum

"牺"是古代对祭祀用牲畜的称谓。此"牺"综合多种畜禽的特征，神态温顺，体态肥壮，竖耳，蹄足，短尾。牺背站一女俑，两臂前伸，擎住套环，内置镂空盘支撑柱。器身满饰华美的鳞片纹和盘龙纹，以绞索纹、贝纹作界带。牺体浑铸而成，背上立人分铸成形后与牺牲铸接连接，旋转镂空盘单独铸造后插入套环装配。

制范材料

陶范原料：①原生土 ②细砂 ③植物纤维 ④草木灰 ⑤熟料 ⑥陶范混合料

取当地的原生土，经筛选后羼入细砂、植物纤维、草木灰和焙烧过的黏土粉熟料等（配料），充分混合后加水练制（练泥）并存放一段时间（陈腐），便能得到雕塑性、复印性和铸造性能俱佳的陶范制作材料。范料中加砂是用以提高耐火度，加植物纤维和草木灰可增强透气性，加熟料是为了控制收缩性。

Materials for Making Molds

Materials for Making Clay Molds and Models
①loess, ②sand, ③plant fiber, ④plant ash, ⑤grog, ⑥mixed materials for clay molds

Several different techniques were employed to create different types of ceramics. If sand is added to the clay mixture the fire-resistant nature of the final ceramic is increased. If chamotte (powder from ground up fired ceramics) is added this controls the shrinkage factor seen during the firing process. When plant fibers or charred plants were added this increased the porous quality of the ceramics. Finally, when a suitable amount of water is added to the mixture the plasticity and flexibility of the resulting clay allowed the creation of sculptured molds and models that were highly suitable for bronze casting.

陶范铸造示意模型

Models Showing the Process of Piece-mold Casting for Bronze *Zhi*

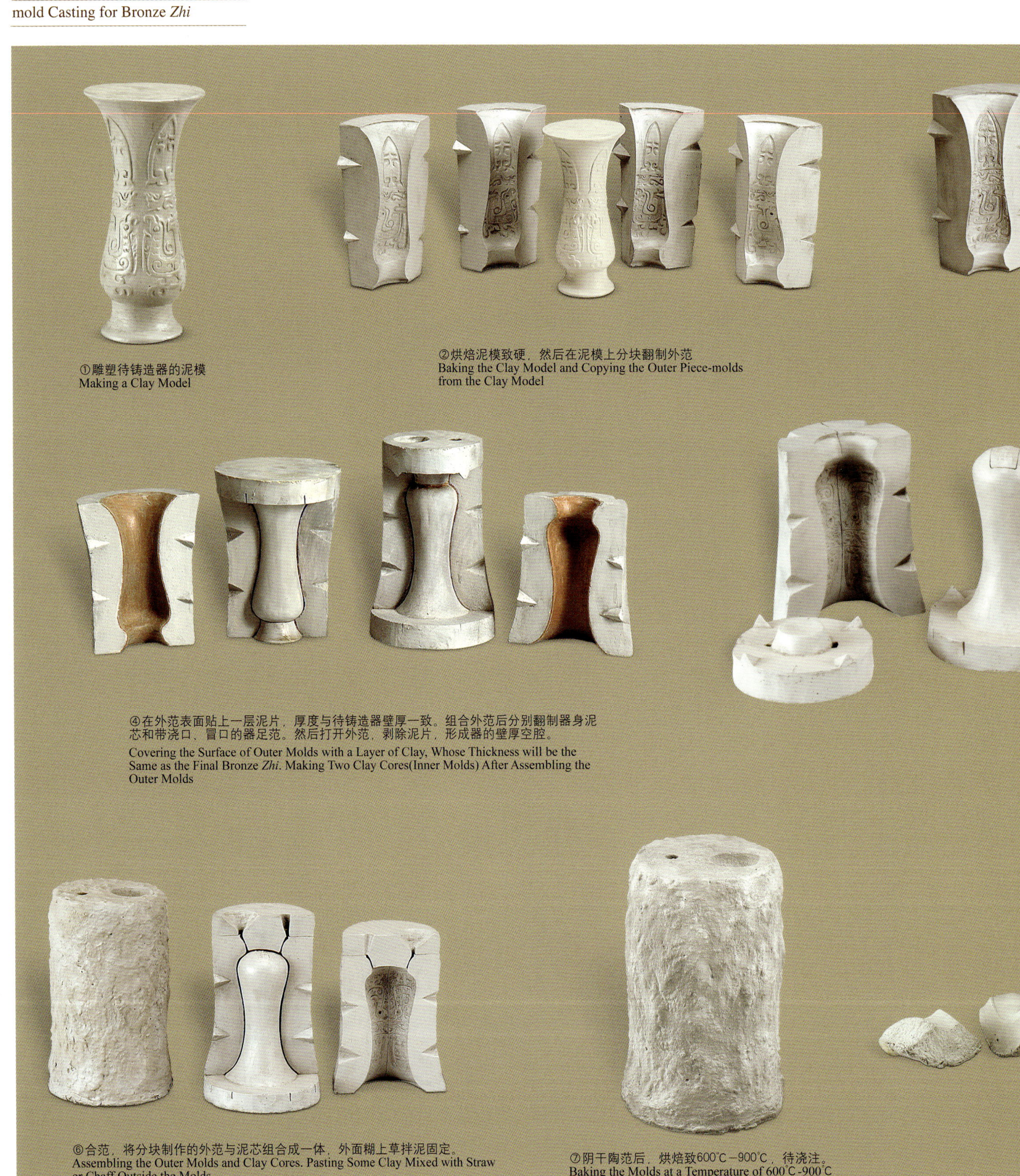

①雕塑待铸造器的泥模
Making a Clay Model

②烘焙泥模致硬，然后在泥模上分块翻制外范
Baking the Clay Model and Copying the Outer Piece-molds from the Clay Model

④在外范表面贴上一层泥片，厚度与待铸造器壁厚一致。组合外范后分别翻制器身泥芯和带浇口、冒口的器足范。然后打开外范，剥除泥片，形成器的壁厚空腔。
Covering the Surface of Outer Molds with a Layer of Clay, Whose Thickness will be the Same as the Final Bronze *Zhi*. Making Two Clay Cores(Inner Molds) After Assembling the Outer Molds

⑥合范，将分块制作的外范与泥芯组合成一体，外面糊上草拌泥固定。
Assembling the Outer Molds and Clay Cores. Pasting Some Clay Mixed with Straw or Chaff Outside the Molds

⑦阴干陶范后，烘焙致600℃-900℃，待浇注。
Baking the Molds at a Temperature of 600℃-900℃

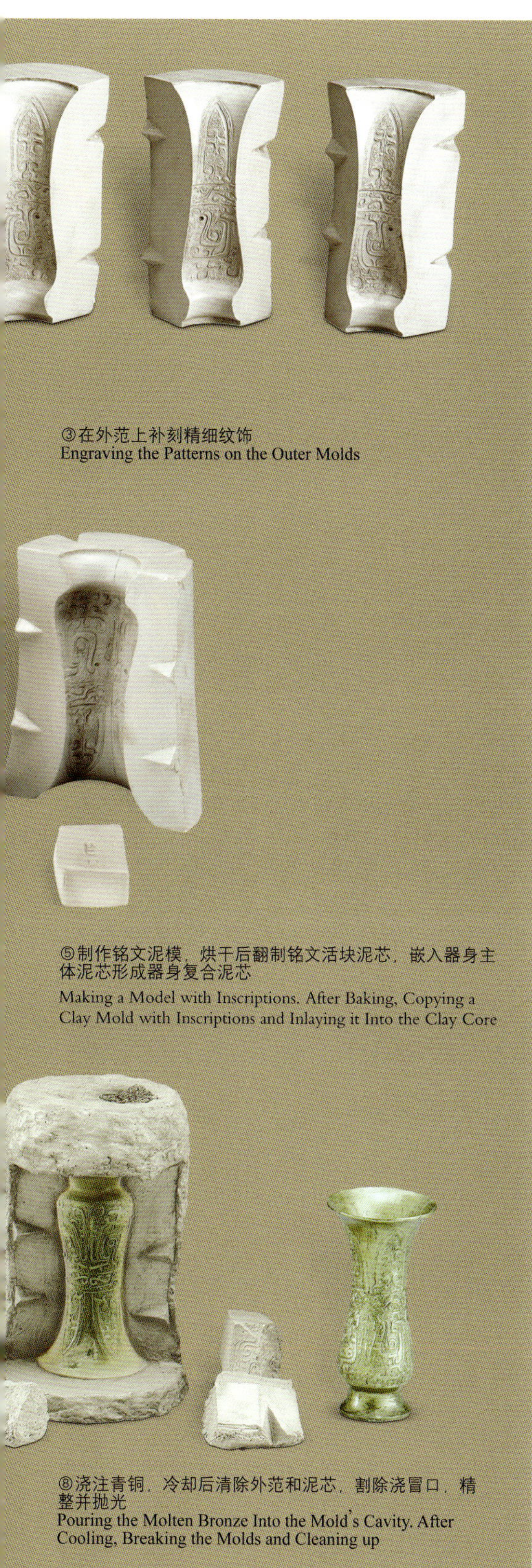

③在外范上补刻精细纹饰
Engraving the Patterns on the Outer Molds

⑤制作铭文泥模，烘干后翻制铭文活块泥芯，嵌入器身主体泥芯形成器身复合泥芯
Making a Model with Inscriptions. After Baking, Copying a Clay Mold with Inscriptions and Inlaying it Into the Clay Core

⑧浇注青铜，冷却后清除外范和泥芯，割除浇冒口，精整并抛光
Pouring the Molten Bronze Into the Mold's Cavity. After Cooling, Breaking the Molds and Cleaning up

父庚觯

西周早期（公元前11−前10世纪）
高14.9、口径7.6cm
上海博物馆藏

Fugeng *Zhi* Vessel

Early Western Zhou Dynasty (11th−10th century BCE)
Height: 14.9cm, Diameter of mouth: 7.6cm
Collection of the Shanghai Museum

觯为饮酒器，出现于商代晚期，流行于西周，春秋晚期以后不再铸用。该器呈细长体喇叭口式，长颈，垂腹，圈足，腹部饰两对垂尾凤纹，颈部饰蕉叶纹和鸟纹，器内底有铭文“作父庚”，是被祭祀者的名字。陶范法浑铸成形，纹饰及内底铭文与青铜觯一起铸成。

“模 范”

在青铜器陶范铸造工艺中，“模”是指用于制范的原型，“范”是指依照模型的形状和纹饰翻制出来用于铸造青铜器的铸型，“模”与“范”决定了青铜器的形状。因此，“模范”一词指同类中最完美的事物，后来引申为值得仿效的人或物。

“Model versus Mold”

In bronze casting technology, the role of the model is to create the shape of the vessel and the role of the mold is to transfer the decorative elements and inscriptions onto the vessel. Both are vital elements in determining a vessel's form and are the twin keys to successful casting of all bronze vessels.

纹饰的制作 制作泥模和陶范纹饰通常使用骨质、铜质等雕刻工具。除了直接在泥模和外范上刻制纹饰以外，还发明了印模法印制块状纹饰技术，或采用刮板造型方法制作环带形纹饰或造型。

Creating Decorative Patterns To create the intricate decorative patterns featured on most bronze vessels craftsmen used bone or bronze tools to carve their designs directly into the clay model or outer mold pieces. In addition to this technique, the use of pattern stamp blocks was introduced. This increased the rate of production and also insured standardization of identical motifs on bronze vessels.

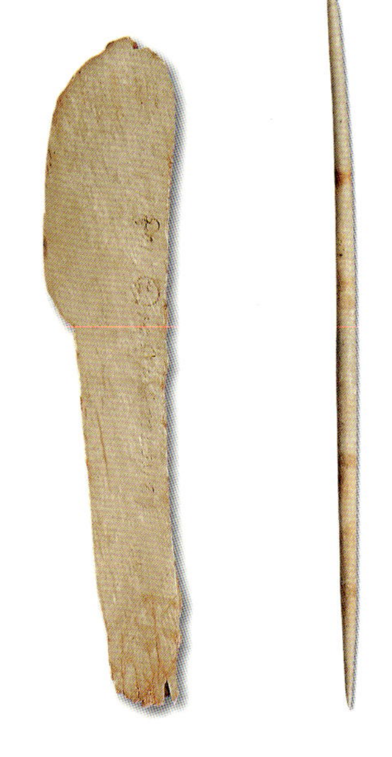

刻范、模的骨工具

春秋晚期（公元前6–前5世纪）
通长16.5–8.3cm
山西侯马晋都城铸铜遗址出土
山西博物院藏

Bone Tools for Engraving Models and Molds

Late Spring and Autumn Period (6th–5th century BCE)
Length:16.5– 8.3cm
Excavated from the foundry Site at the Jin Capital at Houma, Shanxi
Collection of the Shanxi Museum

非金属制范工具主要有骨、角、蚌等材料制成，其中以骨制工具为主。该铸铜遗址中共出土骨刻刀122件、骨锥29件，大多用兽类与鸟类肢骨磨制，或用锯开和砸劈的骨条、骨片加工而成。骨刻刀有平刃、铲形、柳叶形、尖刃、三角刃等形制；骨锥则有一端或两端尖刃、钝刃等。用于制范及刻制纹饰。

制范、模的铜工具

春秋晚期(公元前6–前5世纪)
大件长23、刃宽8cm；小件长13.4cm
山西侯马晋都城铸铜遗址出土
山西博物院藏

Bronze Tools for Engraving Models and Molds

Late Spring and Autumn Period (6th–5th century BCE)
Lenth of the larger one: 23cm, width of blade: 8cm; Length of the smaller:13.4cm
Excavated from the foundry Site at the Jin Capital at Houma, Shanxi
Collection of the Shanxi Museum

侯马铸铜遗址出土铜刻刀和铜锥共96件、铜錾和铜凿各3件，是制范和刻制纹饰主要工具。铜刻刀形色多样，最大一件即长23厘米，刃宽8厘米；铜錾形体较小，可能为嵌装到木柄上使用的錾头。

刻制法制纹饰
Carving Patterns on Clay Molds and Models

A

兽面纹模

春秋晚期（公元前6–前5世纪）
残长20、宽18.5cm
山西侯马晋都城铸铜遗址出土
山西博物院藏

Fragment of a Model Incised with a Wild Animal Design

Late Spring and Autumn Period (6th–5th century BCE)
Length: 20 cm, Width: 18.5 cm
Excavated from the foundry Site at the Jin Capital at Houma, Shanxi
Collection of the Shanxi Museum

陶模上的纹饰采用雕、刻方法制成，可用于翻制外范。

兽面纹模

春秋晚期（公元前6–前5世纪）
残长42、宽18cm
山西侯马晋都城铸铜遗址出土
山西博物院藏

Mold Fragment with an Animal Face Mask

Late Spring and Autumn Period (6th–5th century BCE)
Length: 42cm, Width: 18cm
Excavated from the foundry Site at the Jin Capital at Houma, Shanxi
Collection of the Shanxi Museum

刻制法是青铜器纹饰最常用的制作方法。青铜器纹饰按刻制对象可分三类：模纹是指刻于母模、翻制复印到外范上的纹饰；范纹是指直接施加于外范上的纹饰；模范复合纹是指在外范已翻印的模纹上再加刻范纹的组合纹饰。制模材料选用不含粗沙粒的细腻泥料，可以获得精致、繁复的浅浮雕纹饰。经焙烧的母模较坚实，可延长使用寿命。陶范A是以云雷纹为底纹的兽面纹母模残件，陶范B是一块较完整的兽面纹母模，也以云雷纹为底纹，是用于翻制器物的分块外范，经过焙烧。

B

云雷纹卣

商晚期（公元前13–前11世纪）
通高（不含提梁）29.9、底径14.8–18.2cm
河南罗山莽张后李村出土
河南博物院藏

You Vessel with a Cloud and Thunder Pattern

Late Shang Dynasty (13th–11th century BCE)
Height (with the handle down): 29.9cm, Diameter: 18.2–14.8cm
Excavated in Houli Village, Mangzhang, Luoshan, Henan
Collection of the Henan Museum

盛酒的器具。器盖和器身均装饰精细规整的雷纹和空心联珠纹。雷纹线条极为细薄、高突、密集，很难从母模上又深、又窄、又密的阴刻沟槽中复印翻制，应是在外范上直接刻制形成。空心联珠纹可以使用类似鹅毛管的空心管直接在外范上压印形成。此青铜器纹饰应属范纹。绳纹提梁分铸链接。

➲ 镶嵌蟠蛇纹扁壶

战国（公元前475–前221年）
高31.1、腹宽32.2cm
上海博物馆藏

Hu Vessel with a Coiled Snake Motif

Warring States period (475–221 BCE)
Height: 31.1cm, Width at the widest point: 32.2cm
Collection of the Shanghai Museum

青铜壶为盛酒器，兴始于商代中期，汉代仍常见。扁壶出现于战国，小圆口，短颈、器身扁圆形，长方形短圈足，双肩有铺首衔环耳。该壶口外圈、颈部和腹部均镶嵌红铜，腹部以宽线条为界栏，将腹分为五层长方格，格内满饰蟠蛇纹。纹饰是用一块长方形纹饰印模，以印模法逐一在外范上印制形成。印模法制作的纹饰统一，加工简便快速。

印模法制纹饰
Executing Decoration by Stamping

刮板法制纹饰
Making a Clay Mold for a Pommel with Thread-relief Rings

剑

战国（公元前475–前221年）
长45.3cm
上海博物馆藏

Sword

Warring States period (475–221 BCE)
Length: 45.3cm
Collection of the Shanghai Museum

剑身满饰菱形网格暗纹，剑首有同心圆纹。同心圆纹由厚仅0.2–0.8毫米、凸起达0.5–2.2毫米、间距为0.3–1.2毫米不等的多圈高同心度、高凸起、薄壁状凸棱与放射状底纹组成，有的剑首同心圆凸棱圈数多达11道之多，系采用刮板造型法在刮制外范时同步构成，最后用刻制法在同心圆陶范上刻划两周放射状线地纹。剑首与剑柄铸接而成。

剑首同心圆纹
A Pommel with Thread-relief Concentric-Circles Pattern

剑首同心圆复制件

长约3.6、直径约3.8cm　上海博物馆提供

模拟实验复原铸造的带同心圆纹饰剑首。刮板法制作陶范与同心圆纹饰技术的基础是新石器时代已经运用的轮制法制陶术。此类剑首通常采用两块刮板造型的外范与剑柄铸接连接，纹饰面陶范采用一块带齿的模板车刮外范及其同心圆凸棱，剑首背面陶范使用一块带弧度的模板车刮造型。

A Reproduction Pommel

Length: 3.6 cm, Diameter: 3.8 cm
Provided by the Shanghai Museum

Models, such as this piece, have been created in an attempt to understand how concentric circles were made in early bronze pieces. The scraping method and other techniques used to make concentric circle designs evolved from Neolithic period wheel formed ceramic technology. Sword pommels, such as this example, were usually formed with two scrapers, one used on the outer mold and one used on the sword handle. One wheel scraper with notches was used to impress convex rings onto a clay mold. The clay mold used to create the underside of the sword head was impressed with a wheel scraper with spikes.

剑首同心圆陶范刮板造型模型
Model Showing a Pottery Wheel for Making a Clay Mold for a Concentric-Circles Pommel

浑铸与分铸 陶范法铸造青铜器，或采用一次铸造成形的浑铸技术，或依靠部件分铸铸接、铸造焊接、机械连接等技术手段，将分次铸造的各个部件连接成一个整体，以获得结构复杂、具有立体感的青铜器物。铸造过程中经常运用的金属芯撑技术，保障了复杂形状铸件壁厚的均匀性。

One Piece Casting and Casting in Several Pours Bronzes cast using the clay piece mold technique were not all cast in a single pour. Sometimes casters used sequential casting and soldering to create bronzes with interlocking parts of great complexity. Casters also often used spacers in order to maintain an even thickness for the vessel walls.

浑铸技术
One Piece Casting

妇好觚

商晚期（公元前13–前11世纪）
高25.8、口径14.4、圈足径8.3cm，重1.15kg
河南安阳殷墟妇好墓出土
中国国家博物馆藏

Fuhao *Gu* Cup

Late Shang Dynasty (13th–11th century BCE)
Height: 25.8cm, Diameter of mouth: 14.4cm, Diameter of base: 8.3cm, Weight: 1.15kg
Excavated from the Tomb of Fuhao, in the Ruins of Yin, Anyang, Henan
Collection of the National Museum of China

觚为饮酒器。敞口，薄唇，束颈，鼓腹，高圈足，颈饰焦叶纹。腹部饰对称倒置龙纹，圈足饰同向卷体夔纹，夔纹边沿皆透雕。自腹至圈足有四道棱脊。圈足内铸铭文两字。四块外范与两块泥芯组合整体一次铸造获得精细纹饰和镂空结构，为典型浑铸青铜器。

芯撑技术
Securing Cores with Spacers

鬲

商早期（公元前16–前14世纪）
通高31.6、口径16cm，重3kg
湖北黄陂盘龙城李家嘴1号墓出土
湖北省文物考古研究所藏

Li

Early Shang (16th–14th century BCE)
Height: 31.6cm, Diameter: 16cm, Weight: 3kg
Excavated from Tomb 1 at Lijiazui at Panlongcheng, Hubei
Collection of the Hubei Provincial Institute of Cultural Relics and Archaeology

烹煮食物的炊器之一。侈口束颈，小立耳，分裆鼓腹，空锥足。使用三块外范与一块泥芯组成铸型浑铸成形。为控制器物壁厚，合范时在足内侧器底部位的泥芯与外范之间，共放置了6小块青铜芯撑，浇铸时与青铜液结合成一体。这是最早使用陶范法金属芯撑技术的青铜器之一。

分铸技术
Casting in Several Pours

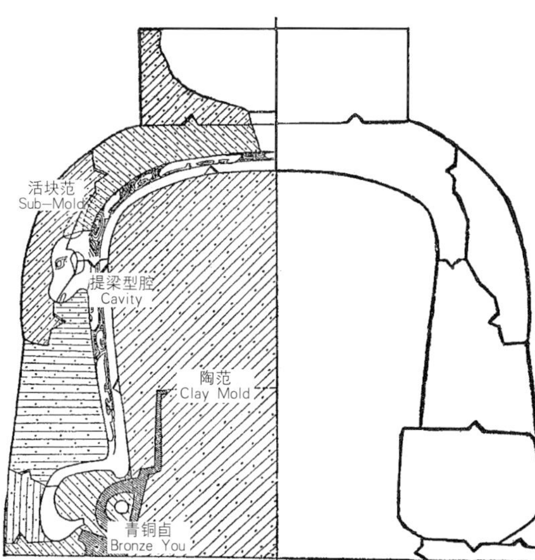

伯格卣提梁分铸和复合范示意图
Sketch of Clay Molds for a Handle Casting-on a Bronze *You*

伯格卣

西周早期（公元前11-前10世纪）
通盖高29.7、口径10.4-12.6、腹深17cm，
重4.98kg
陕西宝鸡竹园沟出土
宝鸡市青铜器博物馆藏

Boge *You* Vessel

Early Western Zhou (11th-10th century BCE)
Height: 29.7cm, Diameter of mouth: 12.6-10.4cm, Depth of body: 17cm, Weight: 4.98kg
Excavated from Zhuyuangou in Baoji, Shaanxi
Collection of the Baoji Municipal Bronze Museum

同时出土一对，直颈，高圈足，配提梁。整器装饰华丽，纹饰立体感强。主体兽面纹上设高浮雕卷曲羊角，以雷纹为地。提梁两端置立体羊首，梁中部设一对牛首。盖沿、器肩和圈足饰龙纹，四条棱脊自盖至足，器内铸铭文六字。该器卷曲羊角、羊首、牛首处均用活块范拼合构成型腔，提梁在铸成器身后再用复合陶范法浇铸链接，铸造精良，是陶范法复合范技术和分铸技术的典型青铜器。

铸接技术
Casting in Several Pours

簋

商早期（公元前16–前14世纪）
通高17.4、口径22cm，重2.8kg
湖北黄陂盘龙城李家嘴1号墓出土
湖北省文物考古研究所藏

Gui Vessel

Early Shang Dynasty (16th–14th century BCE)
Height: 17.4cm, Diameter of mouth: 22cm, weight: 2.8kg
Excavated from Tomb 1 at Lijiazui at Panlongcheng, Hubei
Collection of the Hubei Provincial Institute of Cultural Relics and Archaeology

盛放谷物类食物的器具。宽折沿，鼓腹，圈足，腹部饰粗犷兽面纹，设一对兽首半环耳，器耳对应的内壁各有三个乳钉状凸起。器身与器耳采用依次铸造方法连接成一体，先铸器身，在配耳的相应部位各预留三个孔洞；然后在器身外侧合上器耳外范，从器内预留孔浇注铸接器耳。铸接方法巧妙，为中国最早使用分铸铸接工艺的青铜器。

铜器耳分铸整套陶范

春秋晚期（公元前6–前5世纪）
合范高14.8、宽11.5、厚7–4.5cm
山西侯马晋都城铸铜遗址出土
山西博物院藏

Complete Clay Mold Sets for Assorted Handles

Late Spring and Autumn Period (6th–5th century BCE)
Height: 14.8cm, Width: 11.5cm, Thickness: 4.5–7cm
Excavated from the foundry site of the Jin State capital at Houma, Shanxi
Collection of the Shanxi Museum

单独铸造空心器耳的整套陶范，出土时已合好待浇注，由二块外范、一块活块范和一块泥芯组成。泥芯表面有多个突起的三棱锥，为合范时泥芯定位和控制器耳壁厚的泥芯支钉。

鼎耳剖面件

战国（公元前475-前221年）
约长11、宽8.7cm
上海博物馆藏

Fragment of a *Ding* Tripod Vessel's Handle

Warring States Period (475–221 BCE)
Length: 11cm, Width: 8.7cm
Collection of the Shanghai Museum

可见鼎耳与器身铸接连接结构，空心鼎耳内含有泥芯，鼎身青铜包裹咬合器耳。先铸造空心器耳，不清除鼎耳中的全部泥芯，仅挖除接口处少量泥芯，埋入器身陶范中相应部位，然后浇铸器身并与鼎耳牢固连接。

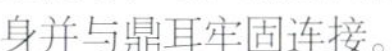

圆鼎

战国（公元前475年-前221年）
通高25、口径19cm
上海博物馆藏

Round *Ding* Tripod Vessel

Warring States Period (475–221 BCE)
Height: 25cm, Diameter of mouth: 19cm
Collection of the Shanghai Museum

鼎盖上三个环形钮，鼎身设一对附耳，圆体，鼓腹，三长兽蹄足，器盖与器身有相同的曲折雷纹，为战国流行圆鼎形制。钮、耳和足先分别铸造成形，然后埋入翻制的器体外范相应部位，在浇铸器体时两者铸接连接。应用铸接技术，可以减少或避免陶范活块结构，降低青铜器陶范制作的难度。

铸焊技术
Soldering Technique

龙耳尊

春秋早期（公元前8–前7世纪）
通高33.6、口径27.5、腹深20.8cm
安徽南陵出土
南陵县文物管理所藏

Zun Vessel with Dragon Handles

Early Spring and Autumn Period (8th–7th century BCE)
Height: 33.6cm, Diameter of mouth: 27.5cm, Depth of belly: 20.8cm
Excavated from Nanling, Anhui
Collection of the Culture Relics Administrative Institute of Nanling County

盛酒器。同出两件，大口，广肩，束颈，圈足，尊体饰横条脊纹和云雷纹，肩腹部两侧对称设置一对巨大的龙形耳为把手，具有典型吴越文化特征。龙耳与尊身分别单独浑铸成形，器耳与器身连接采用在两者结合处浇注青铜液的铸焊方法。铸焊技术在复杂青铜器铸造中有广泛的应用，战国时期的铸焊多用低熔点铅锡合金。

陶范铸就的宝器 中国古代青铜器以繁多的种类、独特的功能、奇特的造型、瑰丽的纹饰、丰富的铭文和精湛的制造技术，在世界艺术史和技术史上占有独特的地位，产生了许多技术发明和工艺创新。其中，陶范铸造技术是各种工艺技术的精髓，创造了辉煌的青铜文明。

Treasures Cast By Clay Molds Ancient Chinese bronzes are greatly varied both in their shapes, functions, decorations, inscriptions, and the casting technique used. They have a special position in the history of art and technology in the world based the innovative methods used to produce these vessels. The foundation of this great tradition is the clay mold casting technique.

兽面纹方鼎

商早期（公元前16－前14世纪）
通高100、口径62.5cm，重86.4kg
河南郑州张寨南街出土
中国国家博物馆藏

Large Square *Ding* Vessel

Early Shang Dynasty (16th–14th century BCE)
Height: 100cm, Diameter of mouth: 62.5cm, Weight: 86.4kg
Excavated on Zhangzhai Nan Street, Zhengzhou, Henan
Collection of the National Museum of China

此鼎是迄今已知商代早期最大的一件青铜器，直口，深腹，平底，立耳，柱足，腹的四壁和足装饰兽面纹和乳钉纹带。大鼎铸造采用多次铸接的技术，将整个大器化成多个小铸件逐一铸接成形。先铸造鼎底，在鼎底的四角预留圆孔，然后用于分别铸接上四足；再在鼎底上分别组合鼎腹和耳的陶范，浇铸连接上鼎腹和耳。鼎壁较薄，陶范铸造技术已经比较娴熟。

司母戊方鼎

商晚期（公元前13-前11世纪）
通高133、口长116、宽79cm，重832.84kg
河南安阳武官村出土
中国国家博物馆藏

Si Mu Wu *Ding* Vessel

Late Shang Dynasty (13th-11th century BCE)
Height: 133cm, Length at the lip: 116cm, Width at the lip: 79cm, Weight: 832.84 kg
Excavated at Wuguancun in Anyang, Henan
Collection of the National Museum of China

商后期王室青铜祭器，浑厚凝重，是中国迄今发掘出土最大、最重的青铜礼器。长方形，双立耳，四柱足中空，腹部饰兽面纹和夔纹，足饰兽面纹，耳饰双虎食人纹，鼎腹内壁铸有铭文。整器由复合陶范分铸而成，鼎身和四足先行浑铸成形，器身各面采用复合陶范拼接，其中鼎底就用四块陶范拼合，局部有二次补铸痕迹；两立耳在器口沿处合范分别后铸铸接；鼎足和鼎耳均为等壁厚空心设计，内有泥芯，器身普遍使用金属芯撑控制铸件壁厚。造型、纹饰、工艺均达到极高水平，是商代青铜文化顶峰时期的代表作品。

四羊方尊

商晚期（公元前13-前11世纪）
高58.3、口边长52.4cm
湖南宁乡月山铺出土
中国国家博物馆藏

Four Ram *Zun* Vessel

Late Shang Dynasty (13th–11th century BCE)
Height: 58.3cm, Length of one side of the lip: 52.4cm
Excavated at Yueshanpu in Ningxiang, Hunan
Collection of the National Museum of China

像形尊是青铜礼器中高贵的艺术器。羊在古代寓意吉祥,方尊肩部的四角为写实的四个卷角羊头，两羊相邻处各探出一双角龙首，通身满饰繁缛的凤鸟纹、兽面纹、蕉叶纹和云雷纹。整器采用陶范法分铸铸接技术铸造，先分别铸造羊角和羊头，然后将其分别配置于器身外范中，再进行整体浇铸。此器形体端庄典雅，造型优美雄奇，寓动于静，是陶范铸造工艺臻于极致的典范。

象尊

商晚期（公元前13–前11世纪）
高22.8、长26.5cm
湖南醴陵狮形山出土
湖南省博物馆藏

Elephant *Zun*

Late Shang Dynasty (13th–11th century BCE)
Height: 22.8cm, Length: 26.5cm
Excavated at Shixingshan in Liling, Hunan
Collection of the Hunan Provincial Museum

鸟兽尊是以动物形象为器形的一种造型奇特的青铜器。该器上扬象鼻为中空的流，象鼻前端饰鸟纹和虎纹，前额饰一对蟠蛇纹，腹部饰兽面纹和夔龙纹，前足饰虎纹，后足饰兽面纹，通体共装饰了11种动物纹饰，在高凸的主体纹饰之下为细密的云雷纹衬底，纹饰层次丰富。整器将象的形体特征与器物用途和谐地结合于一体，是商代鸟兽尊中的一件精品。该器采用复合陶范法整体一次铸造而成，工艺精良。

大禾人面纹方鼎

商晚期（公元前13–前11世纪）
高38.5、口长29.8、口宽23.7cm
湖南宁乡黄材出土
湖南省博物馆藏

Square *Ding* Tripod with Human Face Motif

Late Shang Dynasty (13th–11th century BCE)
Height: 38.5cm, Length of mouth: 29.8cm, Width of mouth: 23.7cm
Excavated at Huangcai, Ningxiang, Hunan
Collection of the Hunan Provincial Museum

商周青铜器中唯一以人面为饰的方鼎，为陶范法浑铸。器内侧中部近口处，铸铭文“大禾”。

何尊

西周早期（公元前11–前10世纪）
通高39、口径28.6cm
陕西宝鸡贾塬出土
宝鸡市青铜器博物馆藏

He *Zun* Vessel

Early Western Zhou Dynasty (11th–10th century BCE)
Height: 39cm, Diameter at the lip: 28.6cm
Excavated at Jiayuan in Baoji, Shaanxi
Collection of the Baoji Municipal Bronze Museum

西周早期青铜器上开始出现了长篇铭文。何尊器内底有一篇12行共122字的铭文，记载了周王在成周营建都城，对武王进行祭祀，是周成王的一篇重要诰文，证实了周武王灭商后筹建洛邑为东都和成王继续营建成周的史实，是研究西周初年历史的珍贵资料。尊腹部饰卷角兽面纹，卷角高高翘出器表面，通体有四道镂空棱脊，圈足饰兽面纹。全器浑铸，长篇铭文铸造沿袭了商代翻制活块泥芯、镶嵌于器物主体泥芯上的整体铸造工艺，高突卷角采用分块组合范整体铸出，是西周时期复合陶范法铸造的典型器。

何尊铭文拓片
Inscription Rubbing from He *Zun*

子龙鼎

西周早期（公元前11－前10世纪）
通高104、口径80cm
传河南辉县出土
中国国家博物馆藏

Zi Long *Ding* Vessel

Early Western Zhou Dynasty (11th–10th century BCE)
Height: 104cm, Diameter of mouth: 80cm
Said to be unearthed at Huixian, Henan
Collection of the National Museum of China

具有商代遗风。方唇，宽沿，立耳稍外倾。垂腹圜底，三粗壮蹄足。口内壁铸“子龙”铭文，口沿下饰饕餮纹，以雷纹衬地，有六道扉棱。鼎腹素面无纹饰，鼎足上部饰卷角突起的兽首，附扉棱，下衬两道弦纹。整器浑厚凝重，铸制精良，保存完好，为商末周初陶范铸造青铜器的力作。

鸟尊

春秋早期（公元前8–前7世纪）
通高25.3、长33cm
山西太原金胜村出土
山西博物院藏

Bird Shaped Zun Vessel

Early Spring and Autumn Period (8th–7th century BCE)
Height: 25.3cm, Length: 33cm
Excavated at Jinsheng Village, Taiyuan, Shanxi
Collection of the Shanxi Museum

整器作昂首挺立的鸟形，体态硕壮有力，通体饰细密的羽纹。鸟尾部有一昂首卷尾的小虎，与双蹼足形成器的三足，虎形提梁立于背上，通过链条与盖连接，鸟上喙可活动，当鸟身倾斜时，上喙可自动张开流出酒液。整器的制作采用了铸接、焊接和铆接等多种工艺。尊主体、虎形提梁和虎形足分别单独铸造后，以低熔点锡铅合金焊接成一体；器盖、链条以多次分铸铸接技术串连并与虎形提梁铸接连接；活动鸟上喙用销子与下喙铆接，壁厚均匀。

莲鹤方壶

春秋中期（公元前7-前6世纪）
通高125.6、口径长31.6、口径宽26cm
河南新郑李家楼出土
河南博物院藏

Square *Hu* with a Crane

Middle Spring and Autumn Period (7th–6th century BCE)
Height: 125.6cm, Length at the mouth: 31.6cm, Width at the mouth: 26cm
Excavated at Lijialou in Xinzheng, Henan
Collection of the Henan Museum

青铜盛酒器，同出一对。盖顶部对称分布着两重共24瓣透雕莲瓣和一展翅欲飞的立鹤。壶颈部配一对大型龙形双耳，有花冠形角。壶腹下部四角饰有攀缘飞龙，作回首向上攀附之状。圈足下有承托壶身的双兽，与壶体上的龙、兽等相互应合。壶身的纹饰为浅浮雕并有阴线刻镂的龙、凤纹饰，有的以鸟兽合体的形式表现，虬曲蟠绕，布满壶体。多种附饰和纹饰组合形成清新、生动活泼的造型，反映了春秋时期青铜器艺术审美观念的重要变化。龙形耳、兽足、立鹤等附饰采用分块复合陶范法铸造，采用铸焊技术与器体连接；莲瓣与盖铸接连接，铸造技艺高超。

王子午鼎

春秋中期（公元前7－前6世纪）
高63、口径81cm
河南淅川下寺出土
河南博物院藏

Prince Wu *Ding* Vessel

Middle Spring and Autumn Period (7th–6th century BCE)
Height: 63cm, Diameter of mouth: 81cm
Excavated from Xichuan, Xichuan, Henan
Collection of the Henan Museum

同出共7件，形制相同，大小相次，为一组列鼎，形体雄伟。立耳外撇，束颈，平底，蹄足，有盖，整器纹饰华美，多用浮雕技法。盖面饰窃曲纹，器身和耳满饰半浮雕或深浮雕夔龙纹、窃曲纹、云纹。器腹内壁与盖铸有85字长篇铭文，记叙了王子午选用精铜铸鼎，以祭祀先祖文王。器身腰上攀附六条立体构造的龙形怪兽，结构复杂，系用陶范法复合范工艺先行铸造成形，再与鼎身焊接连接，是复合范铸造技术和分铸成形工艺流行时期的代表作品。

镬鼎

春秋晚期（公元前6-前5世纪）
通高93、口径102、腹深50cm，重220kg
山西太原赵卿墓出土
山西博物院藏

Huo *Ding* Vessel

Late Spring and Autumn Period (6th–5th century BCE)
Height: 93cm, Diameter of mouth: 102cm, Depth from waist: 50cm, Weight: 220kg
Excavated from the Tomb of Zhao Qing in Taiyuan, Shanxi
Collection of the Shanxi Museum

镬鼎是贵族在祭祀、宴飨时煮牲肉的炊具，为迄今所知春秋时期最大的青铜礼器。鼎耳和鼎足单独铸造成形，嵌埋于鼎身外范中与鼎腹铸接连接成一体，鼎腹部的环耳采用分块复合范与鼎身整体铸造而成。

蛇纹尊

春秋晚期（公元前6-前5世纪）
高21、口径15.5cm
湖南衡山霞流出土
湖南省博物馆藏

Zun Vessel with a Snake Pattern

Late Spring and Autumn Period (6th–5th century BCE)
Height: 21cm, Diameter of mouth: 15.5cm
Excavated in Xialiu, Hengshan, Hunan
Collection of the Hunan Provincial Museum

此器形体为西周时期中原地区尊常见的形制，但其蛇纹纹饰，与中原地区常见的纹饰不同，属于百越文化风格。器身纹饰精细，颈饰三角云纹，腹有群蛇纠结图案，圈足饰雷纹。口沿上共有两周20组昂首相对的蛇纹，呈立体造型，系用活块复合范铸造工艺整体一次铸造，显示了高超的铸造工艺水平。

失蜡铸造技术
The Lost Wax Casting Process

春秋时期已经使用的失蜡铸造技术，是中国古代青铜器成形加工的重要工艺之一。失蜡铸造是用蜡料制模，外糊范料，烘焙时蜡料熔失而得到无分型面的整体陶范，可一次获得具有三维空间构造、立体透雕效果的复杂铸件，是中国青铜铸造工艺技术的重大进展。

During the Spring and Autumn period lost wax casting was already in use. Lost wax casting was an important technique in ancient Chinese foundries. The process involves creating a wax model, which is then encased with clay to make a mold. When the assembled elements were heated, the wax melts out leaving a hollow mold for casting. The lost wax technique allowed casters to create a single mold for complex three-dimensional shapes. It was a major innovation in the technical repertoire of ancient Chinese casters.

透雕夔龙纹禁

春秋晚期（公元前6-前5世纪）
高28.8、长131、宽67.6cm
河南淅川下寺出土
河南博物院藏

Jin Stand with a Design of Openwork Kui Dragons

Late Spring and Autumn Period(6th–5th century BCE)
Height: 28.8cm, Length: 131cm, Width: 67.6cm
Excavated at Xiasi, Xichuan, Henan
Collection of the Henan Museum

陈列酒器的案几。由禁体、附兽、足兽三部分组成。铜禁案面中部为长方形平面，四侧攀附12条透雕龙形兽，器底另有12只张口咋舌的透雕怪兽作器足。采用陶范法、失蜡法、钎焊等多种工艺精工制作而成，结构复杂，工艺精湛。禁体多层镂空云纹构件、各龙形兽附饰和怪兽器足的多层透雕结构部分均用失蜡法铸造，案面、龙形兽附饰和怪兽器足采用陶范法复合范工艺铸造，以低熔点金属钎焊方法将全部部件焊接组装成器。一般认为该铜器是目前出土的最早、最大、最复杂的失蜡法青铜铸件。

饰件

春秋晚期（公元前6−前5世纪）
长8、宽6cm
河南叶县许岗4号墓出土
叶县文化局藏

Ornament

Late Spring and Autumn Period (6th−5th century BCE)
Length: 8cm, Width: 6cm
Excavated from the Xugang Tomb 4 in Yexian , Henan
Collection of the Yexian Cultural Affairs Bureau

为铜器耳首饰件。呈龙首形，器顶有众多蟠蛇纹与卷云纹以相互交叉和穿插的铜梗支撑，构成立体镂空结构。检验分析认为纹样、铜梗和饰件本体都是整体铸造成形，为失蜡铸造件。用便携式X光荧光仪分析金属成分为铜78.4%，锡15.0%，铅6.5%,银0.1%，属铅锡青铜合金。

曾侯乙尊盘

战国早期（公元前5−前4世纪）
盘高23.5、盘口径58，尊高30.1、尊口径25cm
湖北随州曾侯乙墓出土
湖北省博物馆藏

Marquis Yi of Zeng's *Zun* Vessel and Basin

Early Warring States Period(5th−4th century BCE)
Height of Basin: 23.5cm, Diameter of Basin: 58cm, Height of zun: 30.1cm, Diameter of zun' s mouth: 25cm
Excavated from the Tomb of Marquis Yi of the Zeng State in Suizhou, Hubei
Collection of the Hubei Provincial Museum

由上尊下盘两件器物组成。尊口沿装饰一圈以铜梗纠结支撑形成的多层镂空蟠螭纹立体构件，颈部附四条镂空吐舌怪兽，腹部和圈足均附立体蟠龙装饰。盘口沿为镂空花环，口沿上有四组对称分布的长方形多层镂空附饰，附饰下有两条扁体兽和一条双体龙蟠，足上盘体附立体蟠龙装饰。采用陶范法、失蜡法、钎焊、铆接等多种工艺精工制作而成，全器造型优美，纹饰繁复。尊、盘口沿多层立体镂空构件以失蜡法铸造，尊、盘主体由陶范法铸造，其他单层透雕部件和立体盘曲部件多用复合陶范法铸造或加焊接，最后以低熔点金属钎焊方法或铆接工艺组装成尊、盘整体。

青铜合金技术
Bronze Alloying Techniques

青铜合金随含锡量不同，具有不同的性能。古代工匠从实践中逐渐认识了合金成分与各种性能间的关系，公元前5世纪的《周礼·考工记》是世界上最早记载青铜合金配比和掌握熔炼火候的文献。铸造演奏的成套编钟和双金属复合剑，是当时高度认识青铜合金性能的范例。

Bronze has different characteristics based on the tin content in the alloy. Ancient casters gradually came to realize the relationship between alloy composition and the differences in the bronzes they produced. The 5th century BCE Zhouli-Kaogongji is the earliest record in the world of a mastery of bronze alloying techniques and smelting. The casting of sets of chimes bell and bimetallic bronze swords are examples of the high level of understanding ancient bronze casters had of alloying techniques.

盏
战国（公元前475–前221年）
湖南岳阳凤形嘴山1号墓出土
湖南省博物馆藏

Zhan Vessel

Warring States Period (475 – 221 BCE)
Excavated from Tomb 1 at Fengxingzui Mountain, Yueyang, Hunan
Collection of the Hunan Provincial Museum

盏为楚文化独有的青铜器。器盖圆弧，中部有蛇盘曲而成的二层立体透空结构圈形捉手，另有四个环耳。器身束腰，圆鼓腹，有一对兽形耳，兽头部位也为蛇盘绕而成的二层立体透空结构。三器足，由两条小蛇盘曲成镂空结构。装饰有陶范法模制的蟠螭纹、蟠虺纹和变形蝉纹。采用失蜡法、陶范法和分铸铸接工艺制作，立体透空结构的盖捉手、兽形耳和镂空足用失蜡法铸造成形，盖与器身上的六个环耳用陶范法分铸，这些部件最后用陶范法浇铸成整器。盖内和器内均有二行八字铭文“愠儿自乍铸其盏盂”。

《考工记 · 六齐》记载与青铜合金

《周礼 · 考工记》将青铜合金成分配比归纳为六类，称之为"六齐"，其配比递进关系与现代冶金学理论非常吻合，在当时极为不易，是中国古代工匠对青铜冶铸生产活动经验的积累和总结。

随含锡量的增加，锡青铜合金的硬度增加，韧性降低，颜色则由红变黄，当锡大于20%时将转白，锡含量在12%－18%时的强度为最大，含锡量小于17%时的延伸率大于5%，为塑性材料。如在含锡12%－18%的锡青铜中加入小于6%的铅，总的机械性能降低不多，但可大大降低熔点，提高铸造的流动性。

Bronze Alloys and Records in the *Kaogongji-Liuji*

The *Zhouli-Kaogongji* divides bronze alloying into six formulas called "*liuji*", which coincide largely with modern metallurgy. This was a huge achievement in bronze production and was the result of centuries long accumulated experience of ancient Chinese casters.

When tin is added to bronze alloys, the resulting vessels have harder, yet more brittle walls and the bronze color turns from red to yellow. When the tin content is more than 20%, the vessel will turn white. When the tin content is between 12% and 18%, the strength of tin bronze alloy is strongest. If the tin content is less than 17%, the elongation is more than 5% and the alloy becomes a plastic-like material. If less than 6% of lead is added to a tin bronze alloy with a tin content between 12% and 18%, then the total mechanical features are barely reduced, but the alloy has a much lower melting point, which enhances the fluidity of casting.

圆鼎

战国（公元前475年–前221年）
通高24、口径22.5cm
上海博物馆藏

Ding Ve 1

Warring States Period (475 – 221 BCE)
Height: 24cm, Diameter of mouth:22.5cm
Collection of the Shanghai Museum

《考工记 · 六齐》中"钟鼎之齐"为"六分其金，而锡居一"。即铜85.71%，锡或其他成分14.29%。钟、鼎为实用礼器，需要较高的强度和韧性。实验研究表明，当青铜合金的含锡为13%–14.8%时，钟的音色最佳。某青铜鼎分析成分铜82.5%、锡14.13%、铅2.10%与记载配比相符。

斧

战国（公元前475–前221年）
通长15、宽6.6cm
上海博物馆藏

Axe

Warring States Period (475–221 BCE)
Length: 15cm, Width: 6.6cm
Collection of the Shanghai Museum

《考工记·六齐》中的“斧斤之齐”，为“五分其金，而锡居一”。即铜83.33%，锡或其他成分16.67%。斧、斤为实用工具，使用中要触及硬物、遭磨损、受冲击，因此要求材料有良好的综合机械性能。迄今不多的实际分析与此记载均有差距。

剑

战国（公元前475–前221年）
长40.7cm
上海博物馆藏

Sword

Warring States Period (475–221 BCE)
Length: 40.7cm
Collection of the Shanghai Museum

《考工记·六齐》中的“大刃之齐”，为“三分其金，而锡居一”。即铜75%，锡或其他成分25%。大刃指刀、剑兵器，需要有高的硬度和良好的综合机械性能。如一般青铜剑的铜73.85%，锡17.48%，铅6.84%的分析成分，含锡量均低于记载配比，锡和铅的总量基本符合。

镜

战国（公元前475–前221年）
直径15cm
上海博物馆藏

Mirror

Warring States Period (475–221 BCE)
Diameter: 15cm
Collection of the Shanghai Museum

《考工记·六齐》中的“鉴燧之齐”，为“金，锡半”。即铜66.66%，锡和其他成分33.33%。鉴、燧均为用于照面的铜镜，含锡量高的青铜色泽呈浅黄至银白色。分析一战国铜镜含铜68.81%，锡23.75%，铅7.68%，含锡量虽未达到记载配比，但一般都高于其他几类器物。

戈

战国（公元前475–前221年）
通长25、宽12.5cm
上海博物馆藏

Dagger

Warring States Period (475 – 221 BCE)
Length: 25cm,Width: 12.5cm
Collection of the Shanghai Museum

《考工记·六齐》中的“戈戟之齐”，为“四分其金，而锡居一”。即铜80%，锡或其他成分20%。戈、戟为安装手柄的长兵器，也要求有高的硬度和良好的综合机械性能。如铜80.74%，锡18.09%，铅0.17%的一批实际分析数据，与记载基本相符。

削

战国（公元前475–前221年）
长21.6cm
上海博物馆藏

Scraper

Warring States Period (475–221 BCE)
Length: 21.6cm
Collection of the Shanghai Museum

《考工记·六齐》中的“削杀矢之齐”，为“五分其金，而锡居二”。即铜71.43%，锡和其他成分28.57%。削为有柄小刀，杀矢即箭镞，需要注重材料的硬度。实际分析箭镞成分，含锡量虽然没有记载那样高，但一般都要达到14%–20%。

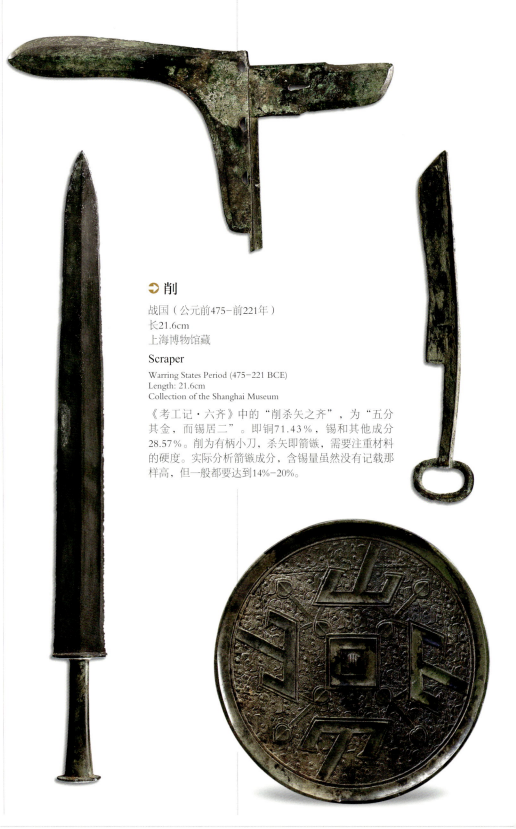

复合金属技术
Bimetallic Techniques

复合金属技术是运用两种成分金属，通过二次铸造方法铸成一器，可以充分发挥金属的综合性能。除了青铜与玉复合制造工艺外，还发明了不同成分双青铜复合及青铜与铁复合铸造技术。

Bimetallic techniques use metals of two different alloys to make into one object by casting-on. This process mode an object with high mechanical properties. Other than the invention of techniques for combining jade and bronze, bimetallic techniques led to the creation of bronzes composed of two different alloys of bronze and the combination of bronze and iron.

青铜复合兵器 随含锡量的增加，青铜合金的硬度提高但韧性变差。春秋战国时期发明的双青铜复合兵器，以高锡青铜铸造高硬度的刃部，以低锡青铜铸造韧性好的脊部，使兵器具有刚柔相济的综合性能。

Bimetallic Bronze Weapons Increasing the amount of tin raises the hardness of bronze alloys but also increases the alloy's brittleness. During the Spring and Autumn and Warring States periods casters invented bimetallic bronze swords. Using high tin content bronze in the sword's cutting-edge for hardness and low tin content bronze in the sword's spine for toughness, casters created weapons that combined both rigidity and flexibility.

复合剑X光片
X Ray Film of Bimetallic Sword

镶嵌鸟纹玉援戈

商晚期（公元前13–前11世纪）
通长27.8、玉援长15.8、穿径0.5cm
河南安阳殷墟妇好墓出土
中国国家博物馆藏

Jade Blade Dagger with Inlaid Bird Motif

Late Shang Dynasty (13th–11th century BCE)
length: 27.8cm, Length of jade portion: 15.8cm, Diameter of hole: 0.5cm
Excavated from the Tomb of Fuhao, Yinxu, Anyang, Henan
Collection of the National Museum of China

陶范铸造青铜与玉复合件。戈援部用玉石制作，戈内部以青铜铸造，镶嵌绿松石。当先以陶范法铸造青铜内，留出安装玉援的槽和固定销钉孔，然后将玉援插入预铸的安装槽内，用销钉等机械连接法将玉援与铜内固定连接成一器，最后用绿松石镶嵌出青铜内前端的兽面纹和后端的鸟纹。戈为钩击兵器，玉石质硬而脆，并不适合用于制作兵器的刃部，该器系仪仗用器。

复合剑

战国（公元前475–前221年）
长54.2、宽5cm
湖南长沙黄泥坑出土
湖南省博物馆藏

Bimetallic Sword

Warring States Period (475–221 BCE)
Length: 54.2cm, Width: 5cm
Excavated at Huangnikeng in Changsha, Hunan
Collection of the Hunan Provincial Museum

剑是古代重要的冷兵器，直身，尖锋，两刃，后接短柄。在东周时期，吴越地区首先出现了一种青铜复合剑，剑脊和剑柄用韧性好的低锡青铜铸造，剑刃以硬度和强度高的高锡青铜与剑脊复合铸接成一体，从而得到具有刚柔相济综合机械性能的青铜兵器，反映了古代工匠对青铜合金成分与性能之间关系的深刻了解。

复合剑断面

战国（公元前475–前221年）
残长4.9、宽4.1cm
上海博物馆藏

Section of a Bimetallic Sword

Warring States Period (475–221 BCE)
Length: 4.9cm, Width: 4.1cm
Collection of the Shanghai Museum

从断面观察，制作青铜复合剑，首先是铸造剑脊和剑柄，剑脊两侧为菱形榫头结构，然后再铸接上剑刃。剑刃与剑脊通过榫卯结构紧密结合。分析剑脊合金含铜87.03%、锡11.22%、铅<0.1%，含锡低，韧性好，不易折断；剑刃青铜含铜79.13%、锡19.35%、铅0.19%，含锡高，硬度大，刃口锋利。

铜铁复合器 考古发现多例商代中晚期的青铜与陨铁合铸复合兵器。西周晚期发明了人工冶铁，促使铜铁复合铸造技术进一步发展，不仅用于铸造兵器，还常用于铸造金属容器。

Bimetallic Bronze and Iron Objects There have been many archaeological discoveries of late Shang period bronze and meteoric iron composite weapons. During the Late Western Zhou Dynasty man–made iron was invented which caused a development in the techniques for casting bronze and iron composites, not only for weapons but also for vessels.

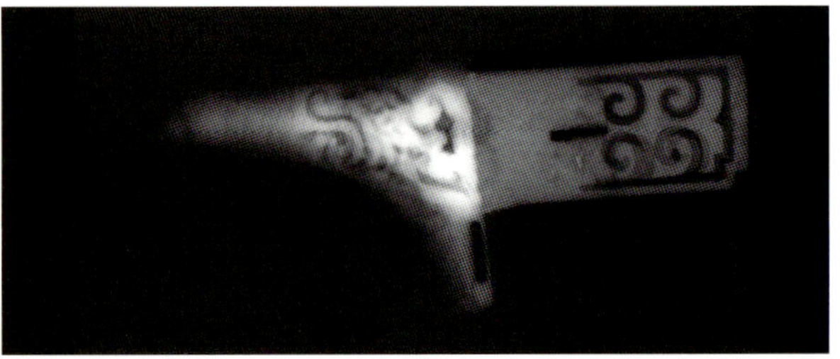

镶嵌铜内铁援戈X光片
X Ray Flim of Inlaid Dagger with Bronze Tang and Lron Blade

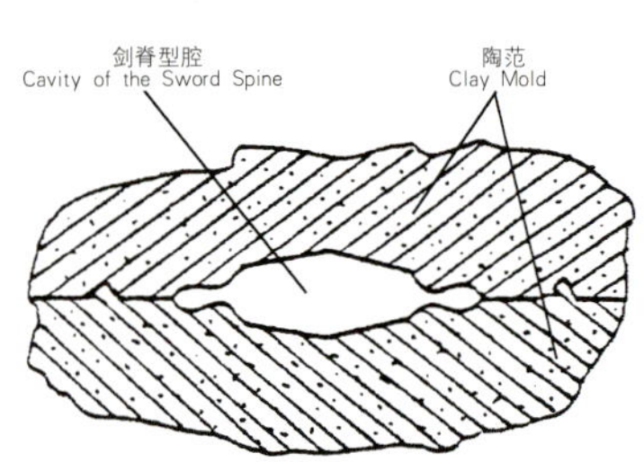

复合剑剑脊铸造示意图
Diagram of the Casting Mold for the Spine of a Bimetallic Sword

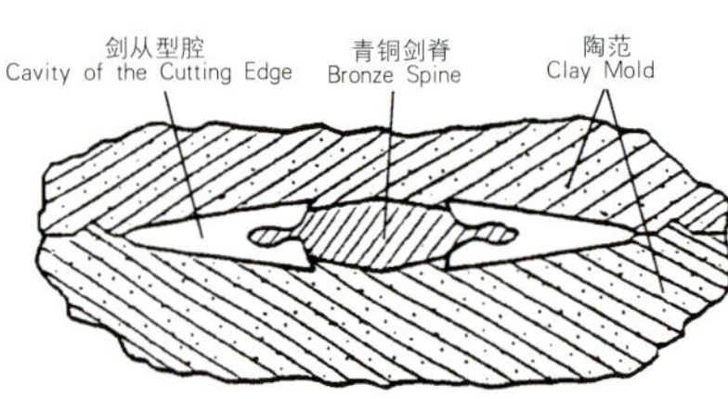

复合剑剑刃二次铸造示意图
Diagram of the Casting Mold for the Cutting Edge of a Bimetallic Sword

镶嵌铜内铁援戈

西周（公元前1046–前771年）
残长17.4、内长7.5、内厚0.5cm
河南三门峡虢国墓地2001号墓出土
河南博物院藏

Inlaid Dagger with Bronze Tang and Iron Blade

Western Zhou Dynasty (1046–771 BCE)
Length: 17.4cm, Length of Tang : 7.5cm, Thickness: 0.5cm
Excavated from Tomb 2001 at the State of Guo Graveyard in Sanmenxia, Henan
Collection of the Henan Museum

戈铁援锻打成形，嵌入铜内部分有防脱落结构。铜戈内后铸，包覆铁援铸接组合成一体。铁援表面镶嵌绿松石，出土时表面尚附有木柲残痕。分析证明铁援为块炼铁，是目前中国发现最早的人工冶铁制品之一。块炼铁是铁矿石在较低温度下用木炭在固态条件下还原得到的，是中国古代发明的早期冶铁技术之一。

铁足铜鼎

战国（公元前475–前221年）
通高51.5、口径42、最大径65.8cm，重60kg
河北平山中山王墓出土
河北省博物馆藏

Bronze *Ding* Vessel with Iron Legs

Warring States Period (475–221BCE)
Height: 51.5cm, Diameter of mouth: 42cm, Diameter at the widest point: 65.8cm, Weight: 60kg
Excavated in the King of Zhongshan's Tomb, Pingshan, Hebei
Collection of the Hebei Provincial Museum

为王墓中同时出土的九件列鼎中的首鼎，铜身铁足，圆腹圜底，双附耳，蹄形足，上有覆钵形盖，盖顶有三环钮，是我国迄今发现的最大的铁足铜鼎。整器采用分铸铸接工艺制作成形，盖环形钮先铸并与鼎盖铸接，方形附耳先铸后与鼎腹铸接。三蹄形铁足为最后铸接，其中一铁足有缺陷而用铜铸造补焊。该鼎是战国时期所发现铭文字数最多的器物，鼎盖及腹外侧刻有铭文469字，此鼎为奉祀宗庙的礼器。

铜骹铁叶矛

西周（公元前1046–前771年）
残长12.7、上端厚1.6、铁叶残宽2.9cm
河南三门峡虢国墓地2001号墓出土
三门峡市虢国博物馆藏

Bimetallic Spear with a Bronze Socket and Iron Blade

Western Zhou Dynasty (1046–771BCE)
Length: 12.7cm, Thickness of socket end: 1.6cm, Width of the iron blade: 2.9cm.
Excavated from Tomb 2001 of the Guo State in Sanmenxia , Henan
Collection of the Sanmenxia Municipal Guo State Museum

矛是一种长柄格斗兵器，由铁叶和铜复合而成。铁叶的下端呈圆形，与铜骹上部锻接在一起，铁叶是目前中国发现最早的人工冶铁制品之一。分析证明铁为块炼渗碳钢，块炼铁在加热锻打制作产品的过程中与碳接触，碳渗入铁中，成为块炼渗碳钢，对钢铁技术的传播和发展起重要的作用，是中国古代使用的早期冶铁技术之一。

编钟铸造技术
The Casting of Bell Chimes

编钟是用于演奏的成组乐器。编钟铸造是独特的铸件结构、合适的合金配比、娴熟的复合陶范工艺、巧妙的音律调制方法等技术的综合表现。完整的音律、良好的音色、精美的形制和恢宏的气势，使中国古代编钟在世界铸造史和音乐史上占有重要的地位。

Bell chimes were used as a set of musical instruments for performances. The casting of bell chimes is a high level of technology that required the creation of appropriate alloy compositions, a formidable knowledge of the piece mold casting technique, and a procedure for ensuring the proper tuning of the instrument. The comprehensiveness of their musical scales, the beauty of the sound, and fineness of their casting are features that give the bell chimes created by ancient Chinese casters an important place in the history of music and bronze casting in the world.

立象兽面纹铙

商晚期（公元前13–前11世纪）
通高71、铣间46.5、鼓间35.6cm，重70kg
湖南宁乡老粮乡出土
湖南省博物馆藏

Nao with Standing Elephant and Animal Mask

Late Shang Period (13th–11th century BCE)
Height: 71cm, Width of bell face: 46.5cm, Depth: 35.6cm, Weight: 70kg
Unearthed at LaoLiangxiang in Ningxiang, Hunan
Collection of the Hunan Provincial Museum

中国最早使用的青铜打击乐器之一，仰击发音。铙的钲部为合瓦式结构，敲击正鼓和侧鼓，可以发出不同的乐声。铜铙的侧鼓有立象纹，钲部饰粗线条的兽面纹，周边有虎、鱼和乳钉相间排列的纹饰。甬有干无旋，与腹腔相通。采用复合陶范法整体铸造成形。湘江流域出土了较多数量的商代铜铙。

兽面牛首纹钟

商晚期（公元前13–前11世纪）
通高31.6cm，重12.6kg
江西新干大洋洲商墓出土
江西省博物馆藏

Bell with Animal Mask and Ox Head Decoration

Late Shang Period (13th–11th century BCE)
Height: 31.6cm, Weight: 12.6kg
Excavated at Dayangzhou in Xingan, Jiangxi
Collection of the Jiangxi Provincial Museum

中国最早使用的青铜打击乐器之一，由铙演化而来，用于祭祀和宴享奏乐。器表面满布三层花纹，主体纹饰为兽面牛首纹，并以云雷纹衬底。采用陶范法复合范技术整体铸造成形。

人面纹錞于

春秋晚期（公元前6–前5世纪）
高43、肩长径26.5、口长径20.8cm
江苏丹徒出土
镇江博物馆藏

Chunyu with Human Face Decoration

Late Spring and Autumn Period (6th–5th century BCE)
Height: 43cm, Diameter at the shoulder: 26.5cm, Diameter at the mouth: 20.8cm
Excavated at Dantu, Jiangsus
Collection of the Zhenjiang Museum

古代军中乐器，常与鼓配合用于战争中指挥进退，也用于祭祀集会。圆筒形体，上大下小，顶部和侧面各有一兽形钮，在侧面的钮上有一人面纹，鼻梁高高凸起，器顶和器身饰涡纹和云纹。先铸造两兽形钮，筒身陶范法整体铸造，同时铸接上两兽形钮。

曾侯乙编钟合金成分

曾侯乙编钟的铸造合金与《周礼·考工记》中的"钟鼎之齐"配比一致，是符合现代金属学发声原理的最佳合金配比。

The Alloy Composition of the Bell Chimes of Marquis *Yi* of Zeng

The alloy composition of the bell chimes of Marquis *Yi* of Zeng matches the alloy composition suggested in the vessel and bell section of the *Zhouli's Kaogong ji*. This alloy composition also matches that suggested by modern metallurgical studies for the most favorable resonance.

编钟名称 Bell Chime	1号甬钟 Bell Chime #1	2号甬钟 Bell Chime #2	3号甬钟 Bell Chime #3	4号甬钟 Bell Chime #4	钮钟 Niu Bell
铜含量Copper（%）	85.08	83.66	78.25	81.85	77.54
锡含量Tin（%）	13.76	12.49	14.60	13.44	14.40
铅含量Lead（%）	1.31	1.38	1.41	1.40	2.19

1978年出土于湖北随县擂鼓墩1号墓，65件编钟按大小和音高编成8组悬挂在3层钟架上，总重量达2500多千克，音律准确，音色优美，是世界音乐史上的奇迹。

The Bell Chimes of Marquis *Yi* of Zeng

This bell chime set was discovered in 1978 in Leigudun Tomb One in Suizhou City, Hubei Province. The sixty-five bells of the set are divided by size and pitch into eight sets suspended from a three-tiered bell rack. The chime set weighs a combined 2500 kilograms. Each bell is carefully tuned and has a pure sound. Marquis Yi's chime set is a great monument in the history of musical cultures of the world.

编钟各部位名称

编钟的基本形式，是两侧尖锐的合瓦形扁体共鸣箱上设一个可悬挂的柄。《周礼·考工记》中对钟体各部位的名称有明确说明。

Illustration of the Names for Various Parts of Bell

The basic structure of a bell chime is composed of two pointed-tile shaped pieces with a protruding stem for suspension. The *Zhouli's Kaogong ji* has a description of the names of each part of a bell chime.

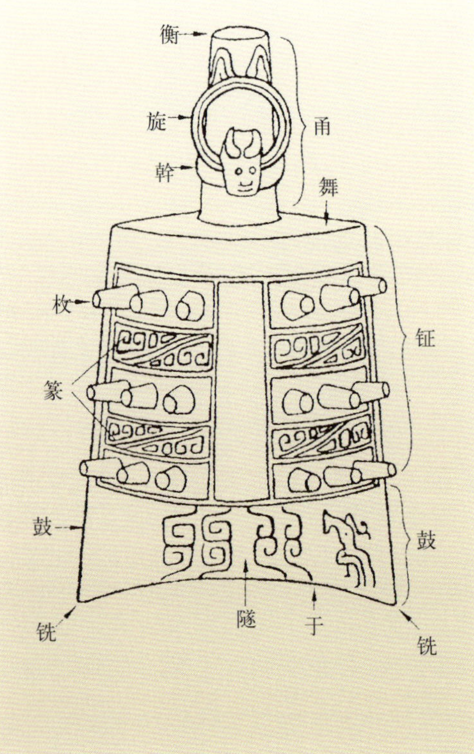

1981年湖北随州擂鼓墩2号墓出土编钟一套36件
36 Bell Chimes in a Set form Tomb 2 of Leiguduan Excavated in 1981,Suizhou,Hubei.

编钟

战国中期（公元前4-前3世纪）
通高98-30cm，重量79.5-4.3kg
湖北随州擂鼓墩2号墓出土
随州博物馆藏

Bell Chimes

Middle Warring States Period (4th-3th century BCE)
Height: 98-30 cm, Weight: 79.5-4.3 kg
Excavated in the Leigudun Tomb 2, Suizhou, Hubei
Collection of the Suizhou Museum

编钟是用于演奏的成组乐器，整套编钟由8件大甬钟和28件小甬钟组成，其独特的合瓦式结构，使每件编钟都具有两个乐音。为保证编钟的声学性能，钟体及其高突的枚必须整体铸造，因此编钟是以复合陶范法浑铸成形，每个枚以及甬、舞、篆部的兽面纹、变形蟠螭纹等浮雕纹饰都分别制作成活块范，最后将这些总数在数十至上百件的活块范嵌合于铸造编钟的钟体范与甬部范内，组合成铸型，复合范铸造工艺达到了相当娴熟的水平。

湖北随州擂鼓墩 2 号墓出土编钟
Excavated in the Leigudun Tomb 2, Suizhou, Hubei Bell Chimes

编钟铸造工艺 为保证编钟音质纯正，要求编钟的钟体及其高突的枚必须整体铸出，因此复合陶范法是编钟铸造的首选制范工艺。将众多陶范组合后不变形、不错位、不开裂，充分体现当时的复合陶范法技术已非常成熟。

The Craft of Bell Chime Casting In order to ensure the sound quality of a bell chime, The entire bell and its raised studs had to be cast in one pour. Therefore, complex composite mold assemblies were the main technique used for bell casting. The fact that the complex casting molds fit together well and did not change shape or leak attests to the high level of sophisticated techniques achieved in the piece mold casting technique.

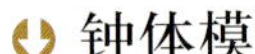

钟体模

春秋晚期（公元前6–前5世纪）
A通高9.5、上宽6.5、厚2.7、底宽7.6、厚3.2cm；B通高9、上宽6.7×5.3cm
山西侯马晋都城铸铜遗址出土
山西省考古研究所侯马工作站藏

Bell Model

Late Spring and Autumn Period (6th–5th century BCE)
A–Height: 9.5cm, Width at the top: 6.5cm, Thickness at the top: 2.7cm, Width at the bottom: 7.6cm, Thickness at the bottom: 3.2cm
B–Height: 9cm, Dimensions of the upper part: 6.7 x 5.3cm
Excavated from the foundry Site at the Jin Capital at Houma, Shanxi
Collection of the Houma Workstation of the Shanxi Provincial Archaeological Institute

用于翻制钟外范的母模。泥质，胎质含较多的沙粒，表面涂有一层细腻的泥料，使表面光滑。钟模经过高温焙烧，增加了强度，从而延长使用寿命。模A为完整钟模的半模，钟面上刻划出各部位的细线轮廓，由于钟体为对称的合瓦式，从半模上制作的钟体陶范两两对合，组成铸造钟体的铸型；模B为带有芯头的实心整体钟模残件，舞部与钟面刻有细的轮廓线或定位线，尚未制作完成。

A

B

钟体外范

春秋晚期（公元前6–前5世纪）
通高16、上宽14.1、下宽15.4、厚2.5cm
山西侯马晋都城铸铜遗址出土
山西博物院藏

Outer Mold for Bell Chime

Late Spring and Autumn Period (6th–5th century BCE)
Height: 16 cm, Width at the top: 14.1cm, Width at the bottom: 15.4cm, Thickness: 2.5cm
Excavated from the foundry Site at the Jin Capital at Houma, Shanxi
Collection of the Shanxi Museum

半扇铸钟外范，基本完整。型腔面上的鼓部、篆部、枚等部位的纹饰都已完成。外范上有三个用于合范的卯，二个长条形卯在上分型面上，与舞部范上的榫对合定位；一个长条形卯在下部，与泥芯上的榫合范定位。这样相同的两扇外范与泥芯可组成一套完整的钟体铸型。

钟枚模

春秋晚期（公元前6–前5世纪）
高3.2、底部直径7cm
山西侯马晋都城铸铜遗址出土
山西博物院藏

Model for the Studs of a Bell Chime

Late Spring and Autumn Period (6th–5th century BCE)
Height: 3.2cm, Diameter at the base: 7cm
Excavated from the foundry Site at the Jin Capital at Houma, Shanxi
Collection of the Shanxi Museum

翻制钟枚的母模。由底板和其上突起的鹰状枚组成。先选用细腻的泥料制作底板，并堆塑出锥形突起，阴干后在其上雕刻出纹饰，高温焙烧，完成钟枚模的制作。可反复多次用于翻制钟枚活块范。

钟枚活块范

春秋晚期（公元前6–前5世纪）
最大4.2×4.2、最小1.8×1.8cm
山西侯马晋都城铸铜遗址出土
山西博物院藏

Molds for Bell Studs

Last Spring and Autumn Period (6th–5th century BCE)
Largest: 4.2 x 4.2cm, smallest 1.8 x 1.8cm
Excavated from the foundry Site at the Jin Capital at Houma, Shanxi
Collection of the Shanxi Museum

系列钟枚活块范。为前大后小的方形锥体，翻制于钟枚模，有蟠蛇纹，经阴干焙烧后，可嵌入铸钟外范组成复合钟体范。钟枚活块范的大小不一，其大小依编钟的大小而定，一件编钟上钟枚的大小一致，一般翻制于同一件钟枚模。

钟鼓纹饰模

春秋晚期（公元前6–前5世纪）
高8–6、弧面宽19cm
山西侯马晋都城铸铜遗址出土
山西博物院藏

Part Model the *Gu* of a Bell

Late Spring and Autumn Period (6th–5th century BCE)
Height: 8–6cm, Width of the curved face: 19cm
Excavated from the foundry Site at the Jin Capital at Houma, Shanxi
Collection of the Shanxi Museum

用于翻制钟鼓纹饰活块范的母模。由左右两块组成，表面为蟠螭纹，蟠螭口衔虺，左右各与一凤相互缠绕，组成复杂的兽面纹。选用经过练泥、陈腐的细腻泥料，制作出呈弧形陶模并雕刻纹饰，阴干后经高温焙烧即具有了较高的强度，可反复用于翻制钟体鼓部纹饰活块范。

编钟的乐律学成就

先秦的编钟达到了很高的乐律学成就，主要体现在七声音阶的使用、“三分损益法”的创立、十二律的形成、十二音位体系的确立等，形成了一套完整的具有中华文化传统的乐律体系。

Temperament Achievements of Bell Sets

Pre-Qin bell chimes achieved a high temperament level, referring to the relationship between pitches. This is seen in the production of bell sets with a seven-note scale, the creation of “subtracting and adding of one-third”, the formation of twelve-tone scales, and the successful production of a twelve-tone set of bells. These achievements indicate that ancient casters were fully versed in creating sets of bells with precise temperament relations.

编钟与西洋圆钟的声学性能比较

中国古代编钟具有独特的合瓦式结构，在振动中形成两条音响节线走向，使一件编钟具有了两个乐音。西方的圆钟，钟体结构绕中心轴的各部分都对称，基频共振态的振型只有一种，只能产生一个基音。

Comparison of Acoustic Abilities of Chinese Bell Sets and Round Bells from the West

Bell chimes in ancient China were composed of bells that were in the shape of tapered ellipses. This unique structure produced two sounds when struck at different points, thus one set of bells could produce two musical scales. Round bells from the West were symmetrically around a central axis and so would only vibrate in one direction, thus producing a single musical tone.

奇巧装饰
Marvelous Decorations

应用多种表面装饰工艺美化青铜器，是中国古代青铜文化的重要特色。夏代晚期已出现镶嵌宝石工艺，随着青铜加工技术的进步，又逐步发明了镶红铜、错金银、鎏金银、填漆、彩绘、刻纹等表面装饰工艺，加上春秋战国时期流行的独特表面富锡技术，使中国青铜器更加绚丽多彩。

A great variety of techniques for surface decoration were used to ornament bronzes. This is a special characteristic of ancient Chinese bronze culture. In the late Xia dynasty techniques for inlaying precious stones had already appeared. With the advance of bronze metallurgical and machining technology gradually techniques were invented for enhancing surface decoration. These include inlaying copper, gold, and silver, gilding, color painting, lacquer overlay, and carving. Including the Spring and Autumn and Warring States period technique of tin surface enrichment, all of these techniques for enhancing surface decoration added to the spectacular achievements of ancient Chinese bronze metallurgy.

镶嵌工艺
Inlay Techniques

青铜器上的镶嵌工艺，可分为镶嵌金属和非金属两类，借助镶嵌物与青铜器本身的色泽反差，在铜器表面铸造或开凿的沟槽中镶嵌构成纹饰、铭文或作点缀，形成各种绚丽的图案。

Techniques for inlaying on bronzes can be divided into metal inlays and non-metal inlays. Inlays were placed in troughs on the surface of a bronze vessel and were created by casting or chiseling. Using the difference in color between the inlaid material and the bronze metal artists created intricate surface patterns.

镶嵌绿松石兽面纹牌饰

商早期（公元前16-前14世纪）
长16.5、宽11cm
河南偃师二里头出土
洛阳市博物馆藏

Plate with Inlaid Turquoise and an Animal Mask Pattern

Early Shang Dynasty (16th–14th century BCE)
Length: 16.5cm, Width: 11cm
Excavated at Erlitou, Yanshi, Henan
Collection of the Luoyang Municipal Museum

装饰品。长方形，四圆角，面微凸起，整体形似盾牌，两侧附有四个穿孔。铜牌本体用陶范法铸造，预留大面积的凹槽，然后用生漆、树胶等天然黏合材料胶镶嵌绿松石。所嵌绿松石形状各异，排列规整，切割、打磨工艺精致。

镶嵌绿松石兽面纹牌饰X光片
X Ray Film of Plate with Inlaid Turquoise and an Animal Mask Pattern

镶嵌绿松石兽面纹方缶

商晚期（公元前13–前11世纪）
高10.7、口径6.2、底径7.5cm
传河南安阳出土
中国国国家博物馆藏

Square *Fou* with Turquoise Inlay

Late Shang Dynasty (13th–11th century BCE)
Height: 10.7cm, Diameter at the mouth: 6.2cm, Diameter at the base: 7.5cm
Said to be unearthed at Anyang, Henan
Collection of the National Museum of China

嵌槽铸造而成，遍身嵌满绿松石，共形成上下8个兽面纹。腹部每面用绿松石镶嵌成一巨大兽面纹，中间用一条直棱作分界线。肩部四角凸扉棱两侧的半个兽面纹组成一个整体。肩部每面中间各有一个小牺首，亦镶嵌有绿松石。

镶嵌红铜龙纹方豆

春秋晚期（公元前6–前5世纪）
通高29.7、口径17.3cm
河南固始侯古堆出土
河南博物院藏

Square *Dou* with Dragon Decoration and Copper Inlay

Late Spring and Autumn Period (6th–5th century BCE)
Height: 29.7cm, Diameter at the mouth: 17.3cm
Excavated at Hougudui, Gushi, Henan
Collection of the Henan Museum

盛食器。覆斗形盖，四角有环钮，两侧又设环形耳，斗状腹盘两侧也有环形耳，下有八棱柱形高足，覆盆形圈足座。盖与盘用四面八个小兽首为子母扣合口。盖、盘、圈足均用红铜镶嵌龙纹图案，作跳跃奔腾状，形象生动逼真，富有生趣。嵌错红铜的方法，一般是先按照预先铸就的嵌槽图案剪裁纯铜片，然后压入铸槽中挤合牢固并错磨平整(嵌错法)，或将事先制得的纹饰铜片固定于外范型腔表面，在浇注青铜时嵌于器物表面形成纹饰(铸镶法)。

镶嵌宴乐攻战纹壶

战国早期（公元前5–前4世纪）
通高40、口径13.4、腹径28cm
四川成都百花潭出土
四川省博物馆藏

Inlaid *Hu* with Scenes of Banquets with Musical Performances and Battles

Early Warring States Period (5th–4th century BCE)
Height: 40cm, Diameter of mouth: 13.4cm, Diameter at widest point: 28cm
Excavated at Baihuatan in Chengdu, Sichuan
Collection of the Sichuan Provincial Museum

容酒器，有盖。肩部有兽面衔环双耳，盖面有三只鸭形钮，其余饰满各类纹饰。壶身以三条带纹分为四层画面，分别为习射、采桑图；宴乐、弋射和习射图；水陆攻战图；狩猎图及一周双兽组成的13个桃形图案。繁复的写实画面，更显当时铸造、镶嵌工艺达到了登峰造极的水平。X射线探伤无损检测反映，此器镶嵌物应是密度高于铸器青铜的其他金属，显示出独特的地域风格。

镶嵌宴乐攻战纹壶纹饰图
Pattern of Inlaid *Hu* with Scenes of
Banquets with Musical Performances and Battles

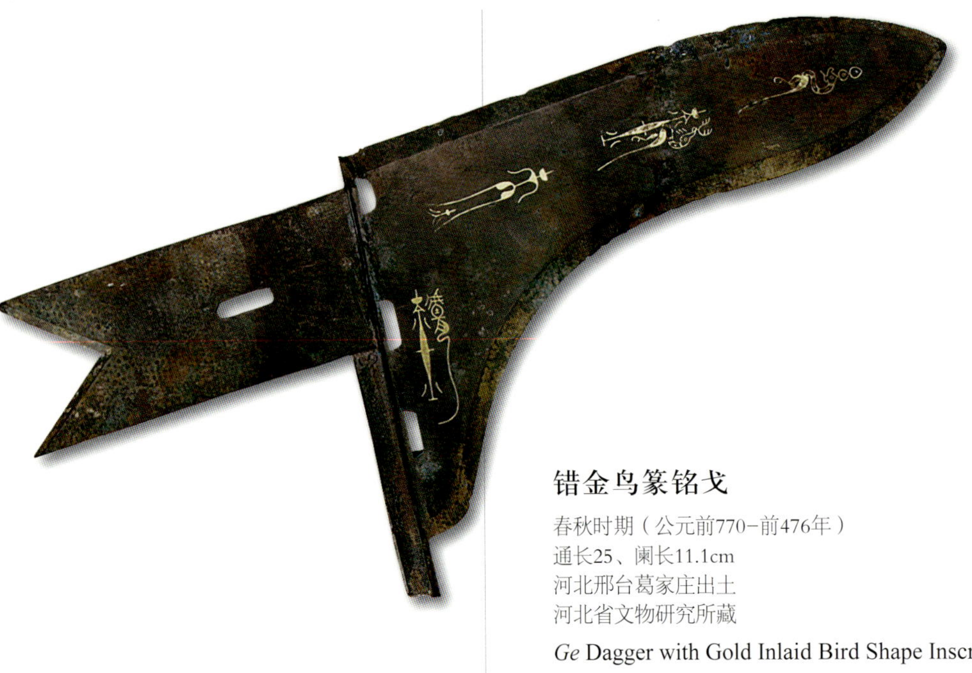

错金鸟篆铭戈

春秋时期（公元前770－前476年）
通长25、阑长11.1cm
河北邢台葛家庄出土
河北省文物研究所藏

Ge Dagger with Gold Inlaid Bird Shape Inscription

Spring and Autumn Period (770－476 BCE)
Length: 25cm, Length of lan: 11.1cm
Excavated at Gejiazhuang in Xingtai, Hebei
Collection of the Hebei Provincial Cultural Relics Institute

错金银是中国传统装饰工艺之一。此戈利用金的良好塑性和鲜明的色泽，将金锻制成丝状，嵌在戈表面预留的凹槽内，在援部正、背面形成错金鸟篆铭文8字。笔画之细腻，加工之精良，足见当时错金工艺的高超。此戈虽为晋国墓出土，但从戈上的鸟篆文看，应属于吴越地区青铜器铭文风格。

错金夔纹盖豆

战国早期（公元前5－前4世纪）
通高19.2、口径17、底径11cm
山西长治分水岭出土
山西博物院藏

Dou with *Kui* Dragon Pattern Inlaid in Gold

Early Warring States Period (5th－4th century BCE)
Height: 19.2cm, Diameter of mouth: 17cm, Diameter of base: 11cm
Excavated at Fenshuiling in Changzhi, Shanxi
Collection of the Shanxi Museum

盛食器。盖顶捉手较大，倒置似盘；深腹，附一对环形耳；短柄足，盘形圈足座，有四穿孔。通体满布错金精细纹饰，盖顶饰云纹、莲瓣纹和斜三角纹；盖面和器身装饰变形夔纹和玄纹；圈足上为垂叶纹。整器彰显富丽堂皇的高贵气质，是战国通体错金青铜器的代表作品，反映了当时高超的金属加工技艺。

错银鸟纹双翼兽

战国中期（公元前4–前3世纪）
高23.9、通长40.1cm，重10.7kg
河北平山中山王墓出土
河北省博物馆藏

Silver Inlaid Winged Beast with Bird Surface Decoration

Middle Warring States Period (4th–3th century BCE)
Height: 23.9cm, Length: 40.1cm, Weight: 10.7kg
Excavated from the tomb of the King of Zhongshan at Pingshan, Hebei
Collection of the Hebei Provincial Museum

陈设器。神兽圆目突出炯炯有神，双翼微展欲要高飞，利爪撑地稳健有力，圆颈直竖昂首咆哮，神态威严，造型矫健。全身纹饰主要用错银工艺表现，用于勾勒口、眼、耳、鼻、毛、羽和遍体的漫圈云纹，使神兽整体形象更加栩栩如生。两翼尾部和神兽后尾有铸造长羽纹或长毛纹。整器造型生动，错银纹饰刻画细腻，陶范铸造和表面装饰工艺极为精湛。

错金银龙纹方案

战国中期（公元前4-前3世纪）
通高36.2、上框边长47.5cm，重18.65kg
河北平山中山王墓出土
河北省博物馆藏

Square Tray Stand with Dragon Decoration and Gold and Silver Inlay

Middle Warring States Period (4th–3th century BCE)
Height: 36.2cm, Length of the side of the upper frame: 47.5cm, Weight: 18.65kg
Excavated from the tomb of the King of Zhongshan at Pingshan, Hebei
Collection of the Hebei Provincial Museum

战国中期错银工艺在错金工艺基础上发展起来。此方案满错金银，黄白相间，使本来精致的造型更加熠熠生辉。方案由底座、龙凤和框架三部分组成。各部分采用复合陶范法分铸成形，经铸接、铸焊、榫卯结构连接。整体造型疏密得当，动静结合，龙飞凤舞跃然眼前。

鎏金银工艺
Gold and Silver Gilding

鎏金银工艺最早出现于战国时期，盛行于汉代。鎏金是用金—汞涂敷器物表面，经烘烤去除汞后获得，鎏银用银汞齐。器物表面通常用局部鎏金或通体鎏金，还常和鎏银、镶嵌等工艺一起使用。

The technique of gilding bronzes first appears during the Warring States period before becoming widely used in the Han dynasty. Gilding is a process where by a vessel is first covered in a solution of gold and mercury and then heated until the mercury evaporates leaving a thin layer of gold on the surface. The technique is sometimes used for only parts of the surface and sometimes for the entire object. It is also used with silver as well as in conjunction with inlay techniques.

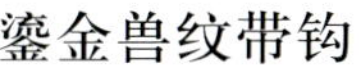

鎏金兽纹带钩

战国中期（公元前4-前3世纪）
通长19.2、宽3cm
河北平山出土
河北省文物研究所藏

Gold Gilt Belt Clasp with Animal Patterns

Middle Warring States Period (4th–3th century BCE)
Length: 19.2cm, Width: 3cm
Excavated from Beiping Mountain, Hebei
Collection of the Hebei Provincial Institute of Cultural Relics

腰带扣饰。蛇头形钩首，细颈，钩身长条形，钩尾平直，正面中部略偏向钩尾设有一圆形钩钮。带钩表面以半浮雕铸造装饰一大二小相互缠绕的螭龙纹饰，以及极细密的针刺羽纹、点纹和涡纹等。铸造纹饰精致细腻，通体作鎏金表面装饰处理，是为数不多的早期鎏金青铜器的精品。

鎏金长臂猿带钩

战国（公元前475-前221年）
通高16.7cm
山东曲阜3号战国墓出土
山东省博物馆藏

Gold Gilded Belt Clasp with the Design of a Gibbon

Warring States Period (475–221 BCE)
Length: 16.7cm
Excavated in Tomb 3 atQufu, Shandong
Collection of the Shandong Provincial Museum

腰带扣饰。猿猴形，猿身微拱，两臂长伸似抓物，回首机警观察，后肢微蹲，作欲起身跳跃状，姿态生动。猿身表面以鎏金和包金作装饰，金光灿灿；两目嵌蓝料珠，炯炯有神。鎏金是用金—汞齐涂敷器物表面，经烘烤驱除汞后留下金层作装饰的一种表面处理工艺，通常用在铜、铜合金、银等金属器物局部或通体的表面装饰。

陽信家

鎏金银蟠龙纹壶

西汉（公元前206年–公元8年）
高59.5、腹径37、圈足径22.6cm
河北满城陵山中山靖王刘胜墓出土
河北省博物馆藏

Gold and Silver Gilt *Hu* Vessel with Dragon Interlace Decoration

Western Han Dynasty (206 BCE –8 CE)
Height: 59.5cm, Diameter at widest point: 37cm, Diameter of foot: 22.6cm
Excavated in the Tomb of Liu Sheng, the Prince Jing of Zhongshan, at Lingshan in Mancheng, Hebei
Collection of the Hebei Provincial Museum

通体纹饰鎏金银，龙凤主纹以鎏金为主，部分辅助云纹则鎏银，鼓腹上饰一对鎏金铺手，盖上有鎏银的三个卷云纹状钮，整体装饰交相辉映，光彩夺目。壶底有18字铭文，记载了壶的主人及壶的容量等信息。

鎏金长信宫灯

西汉（公元前206–公元8年）
高48cm，重15.85kg
河北满城陵山中山靖王刘胜之妻窦绾墓出土
河北省博物馆藏

Changxin Palace Lantern

Western Han Dynasty (206 BCE–8 CE)
Height: 48cm, Weight: 15.85kg
Excavated in the Tomb of Dou Wan, wife of Liu Sheng, the Prince Jing of Zhongshan, at Lingshan in Mancheng, Hebei
Collection of the Hebei Provincial Museum

汉代时青铜器已走向衰落，但出现了一些新的实用器，“长信宫灯”就是其中一件构思巧妙的器物。宫灯通体鎏金，璀璨夺目。灯盘、灯座及执灯宫女的右臂处可拆卸，灯罩与灯盘可转动开合，便于调节灯光亮度和角度。右臂为烟道，烟经底层水盘过滤，可减少室内的烟臭以保持清洁。灯上有九处刻铭，计65字，有汉文帝皇后窦氏所居宫名“长信”二字。整体设计精妙，造型优美，体现了古代匠师的创造才能及当时的科技水平。

表面富锡工艺
Surface Tin-enrichment Techniques

随含锡量的增多，青铜颜色由红色、黄色逐渐增白。表面富锡技术，是运用金属锡熔点较低、高锡铜合金色泽银白和耐腐蚀性良好等性能的一种特殊的铜器表面装饰工艺，反应了中国古代对锡金属的深刻认知和高超运用。

As the tin content of bronze is increased the color of the resulting alloy will gradually turn from red and yellowish hues to white. The surface tin-enrichment technique uses the lower melting point of tin and its effect of turning bronze alloys white to produce surface decoration and increase resistance to corrosion. The technique demonstrates great understanding of the properties of tin among ancient Chinese metal workers.

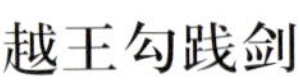

越王勾践剑

春秋晚期（公元前6–前5世纪）
长55.7、宽4.6、柄长8.4cm
湖北江陵望山出土
湖北省博物馆藏

Sword of King *Goujian* of the State of *Yue*

Later Spring and Autumn Period (6th–5th century BCE)
Length: 55.7cm, Width: 4.6cm, Length of handle: 8.4cm
Excavated at Wangshan in Jiangling, Hubei
Collection of the Hubei Provincial Museum

剑首向外翻卷作圆箍形，采用刮板法制范技术铸成了剑首内11道同心圆纹饰，达到了陶范铸造水平的极致。剑格正面以蓝色琉璃、背面以绿松石镶嵌入预铸凹槽，以点缀纹饰。剑身满饰黑色的菱形暗纹，是以含锡材料热扩散处理成银白色高锡纹饰，在2000多年腐蚀作用下，形成了现今的灰黑色纹饰。近格处有“越王勾践自作用剑”两行八字鸟篆铭文。铭文错金，精致华美。

吴王夫差矛

春秋晚期（公元前6–前5世纪）
长29.5、宽3cm
湖北江陵马山出土
湖北省博物馆藏

King *Fuchai* of Wu's Spearhead

Late Spring and Autumn Period (6th–5th century BCE)
Length: 29.5cm, Width: 3cm
Excavated at Mashan, Jiangling, Hubei
Collection of the Hubei Provincial Museum

矛身与剑身相似而稍短，锋部呈弧线三角形。中脊凸起，脊上有血槽，其后端各铸一兽头。骹中空，骹首两侧有对称凹口，用以插柲。通体满饰菱形几何暗纹，与越王勾践剑工艺相同。基部有错金铭文两行八字，记为“吴王夫差自作用矛”。此矛冶铸精良，花纹典雅，保存完好。

菱形纹矛

战国（公元前475–前221年）
通长24cm
湖南益阳新桥山出土
益阳市博物馆藏

Spearhead with Lozenge Pattern Decoration

Warring States Period (475–221 BCE)
Length: 24cm
Excavated at Xinqiao Mountain, Yiyang, Hunan
Collection of the Yiyang Municipal Museum

宽体狭刃，骹尾呈弧形，中脊自锋起至骹部，脊尾饰浮雕兽面纹。全身装饰有菱形暗格纹，其装饰和工艺同“越王勾践”剑相仿。

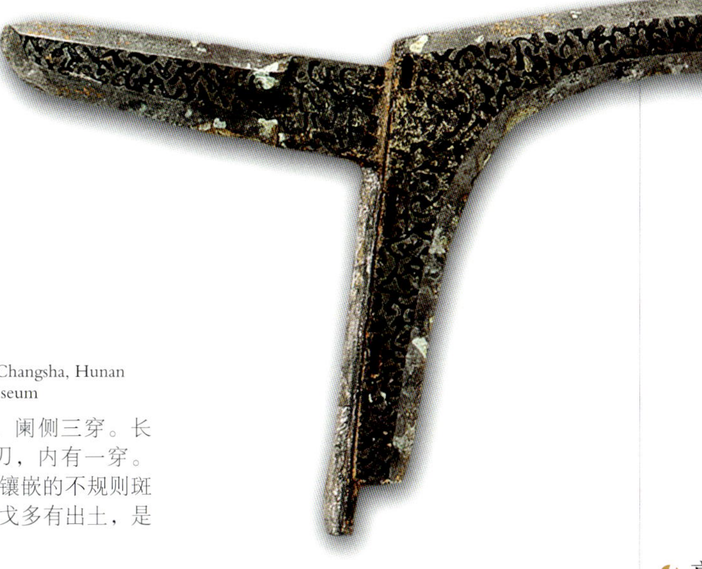

亮斑戈

战国（公元前475–前221年）
全长25.6、援长15.5cm
湖南长沙魏家堆10号墓出土
湖南省博物馆藏

Dagger with Bright Spots

Warring States Period (475–221 BCE)
Length: 25.6cm, Blade length: 15.5cm
Excavated from Tomb 10, Weijiadui, Changsha, Hunan
Collection of the Hunan Provincial Museum

长援上昂，锋部略宽。长胡，阑侧三穿。长内，后半段上、下尾部均有刃，内有一穿。全身装饰表面富锡处理非机械镶嵌的不规则斑纹。楚戈中饰亮斑暗纹的青铜戈多有出土，是楚戈的特征之一。

亮斑矛

战国（公元前475年–前221年）
残长24.7、刃宽3.6cm，重0.128kg
湖南长沙烈士公园出土
湖南省博物馆藏

Spearhead with Etched sparkling Patterns

Warring States Period (475–221 BCE)
Length 24.7cm, Blade width: 3.6cm, Weight 0.128kg
Excavated at Martyrs Park, Changsha, Hunan
Collection of the Hunan Provincial Museum

矛身与剑身相似而稍短，锋部呈弧线三角形。中脊凸起。骹中空，用以插柲，口部略残。除刃口和中脊外，通体装饰非机械镶嵌怪异图形的暗纹，略有规律。此类黑色暗斑纹饰，当时应采用表面富锡处理技术加工成银白色亮斑，因长期埋葬而腐蚀成现今的黑灰色。亮斑青铜矛较少见。

虎斑纹亮斑戈

战国（公元前475年–前221年）
长28cm
四川成都新都区晒坝出土
四川省博物馆藏

Dagger with Bright Spot Decoration

Warring States Period (475–221 BCE)
Length: 28cm
Excavated from Shaiba, Xindu District, Chengdu, Sichuan
Collection of the Sichuan Provincial Museum

此器具有巴蜀文化特征。援呈狭三角形，中间有凸脊，近阑处有一圆孔，内上也有一水滴形穿，用于绑制木柲。援及内饰陶范铸造兽面纹、云纹、叶纹和巴蜀文字。援上还装饰有亮斑暗纹，似虎皮斑，手感略有凸起，根据检测分析结果，此类亮斑高富锡，其加工工艺与楚式兵器表面的亮斑处理工艺不同。

背面
Back

表面富锡处理工艺

将特制的锡基材料按设计图案施于青铜器表面，经扩散处理使锡元素渗入而形成富锡铜合金的白色纹饰，未涂布锡基材料的表面则仍呈青铜合金的黄颜色，构成黄、白相间的华丽图案。经过千百年的腐蚀作用，有些青铜器的黄、白纹饰区因其耐蚀性的差异，演变成了多种色泽相间的纹饰。

The Art of the Surface Tin Enrichment Techniques

First a special tin alloy paste was spread on the object surface according to the desired decorative pattern. After a process that led the surface to tin enriched, the tin alloy paste was cleaned off and the result was a surface with a decorative pattern created by the white areas in contact with the high-tin alloy paste and the ordinary reddish surface of the original bronze alloy. After several thousand years of corrosion the difference between the corrosion resistance of the white areas and the plain yellow bronze alloy has created a pattern of multiple colors.

➲ 刻纹盘

战国（公元前475–前221年）
口径51、深6cm
江苏淮阴高庄墓葬出土
淮阴市博物馆藏

Dish with Carved Decoration

Warring States Period (475–221 BCE)
Diameter of mouth: 51cm, Depth: 6cm
Excavated from a Tomb at Gaozhuang of Huaiyin, Jiangsu
Collection of the Huaiyin Municipal Museum

刻纹工艺
Carved Decoration

刻纹是在铜器表面用錾、凿等金属工具刻划出点、线或刻出浅凹面，组成一幅幅描写娱乐、狩猎、水陆攻战等线条流畅的生活画面。春秋时期冶铁术的发明，为在青铜器上镂刻纹饰和铭文提供了性能优良的钢铁工具。

Carved decoration is created by chiseling and incising marks into the surface of bronze using metal tools. These sunken carved decorations reveal vivid scenes of entertaining, hunting, and battles. The development of iron metallurgy during the Spring and Autumn period allowed for the creation of excellent tools for creating carved decoration and inscriptions.

刻纹盘纹饰图
Pattern of Dish with Carved Decoration

春秋晚期，铁器的使用，为青铜器刻纹技术的发展奠定了物质基础。刻纹器物一般以热加工捶打成形，器壁都很薄。铜盘以娴熟的线刻法刻纹，在内底及腹内壁刻有图案。内底从中心到外侧以陶纹分隔成三区：轮环纹；五条首尾相随的夔龙纹；十条首尾相缠的蛇纹；腹内壁刻山林及神人怪兽等。刻纹以写实的动物植物、社会生活和自然景色为图案，展现了当时线刻技术已进入艺术创作的成熟阶段。

火与铜的熔炼，
铸就了青铜文明的辉煌。
古老而精美的雄奇宝器，
向今人述说着先人们的智慧。
中国古代的青铜文明，
记载着三代雄浑的历史，
让世界分享着它的魅力，
这是人类文明永恒的记忆。

青铜上铸刻的文字，
将那个时代的记忆留存下来。
下面要展示的是在冶铜术之后出现的造纸术，
还有后来出现的印刷术，
它们是历史上人类最伟大的发明之一，
它改变了历史记忆的方式。
轻柔的纸张承载着厚重的文明，
承载着反思的历史、变幻的当世与希冀的未来。

The combination of high-firing techniques and metal ores came together to produce China's magnificent Bronze Age. These vessels are splendid reminders of the technical achievements and cultural practices of the ancient Chinese.

These ritual vessels, weapons and ornaments, all made of bronze, not only are fine works of art, but they are also very important historical artifacts that help unravel the complexities of the periods in which they were produced. It is through these bronze pieces that the glories of the Xia, Shang, and Zhou Dynasties come alive again before our eyes.

典藏文明

古代造纸印刷术

书籍，是人类文明的重要载体。书籍质量的提升，有赖于造纸与印刷术的发明与提高。西汉时期（公元前206－公元8年），中国发明了造纸术。东晋时期（公元317－420年），纸张逐渐取代简帛，成为主要的书写材料，并开始向世界各地广为传播。至迟在唐代初年，中国发明了雕版印刷术，同时逐渐传播到世界其他地方。一代一代传承的图籍，守望历史、典藏文明，是人类智慧的标记。

The Traditional Techniques of Papermaking and Printing

Books are vital conduits for human civilization. The increasing of book quality relied on the technical mastery of papermaking and printing. During the Western Han Dynasty (206 BCE-8 CE) the art of papermaking was invented in China; by the Eastern Jin Dynasty (317-420 CE) paper had gradually replaced bamboo slips and silk as the most important material for writing. Produced cheaply, the appeal of paper was obvious and it quickly spread to other parts of the world. Later, in the early Tang, the technique of woodblock printing was invented and it too spread to other countries.

Maps, documents, and letters printed in ink on paper are priceless records of human history and achievement. They remain as testaments to civilizations and historic events that no longer exist and so should be appreciated accordingly.

造纸术：化腐朽为神奇

Papermaking Techniques: Preserving the Written Word

中国曾使用甲骨、陶器、铜器、玉石器、简牍和帛等作为文字的载体。简牍与帛是早期应用最普遍的书写材料，但简牍体积大而笨重，不便携带，而帛又比较昂贵，难以普及。随着社会经济与文化的发展，对书写材料的需求与日俱增，创造轻巧、廉价的新型书写材料成为社会发展的迫切需要。造纸术在迫切的社会需求、丰富的原料供应和必要的技术准备中应运而生，给人类书写材料带来了巨大变革。

Before the invention of papermaking ancient Chinese used tortoise shells and bones, pottery and bronze wares, jade, bamboo reeds, and silk as writing materials. Initially bamboo slips and silks were the predominant materials for recording documents, but bamboo slips were bulky and unwieldy and silk was so expensive that it was not widely used. As Chinese society, economy, and culture developed the pressure increased to find a new and more efficient writing material. Under these conditions papermaking was invented. The dexterity of the technique along with cheap production costs, due to a steady supply of raw materials needed to produce paper, meant that the process of writing and recording underwent a radical development.

无纸时代

Before Paper

在纸发明以前，简牍和帛是普遍使用的书写材料。当造纸术发明后，它们依然作为过渡性书写材料使用过相当长的一段时间。

Before the invention of paper the main materials used to record documents were, bamboo slips and silk, All these materials had been used for centuries prior to the introduction of paper. Even after the invention of paper, bamboo slips and silk still continued to be used for a period of time.

文书竹简

战国楚国（公元前475－前223年）
长约64－72.4cm
湖北荆门包山出土
湖北省博物馆藏

Bamboo Slips

Warring States Period, Kingdom of Chu (475 – 223 BCE)
Length: 64–72.4cm
Excavated in Baoshan in Jinmen, Hubei
Collection of the Hubei Provincial Museum

这是个人给官府的文书竹简。简有竹和木两种质地。竹木材料易得且容易制作加工，经剖分、刮磨等加工程序即可制成用于书写的简。多支简按顺序用书绳编联起来称为简册（或简策）。我国早期的著作大多是写在简册上。

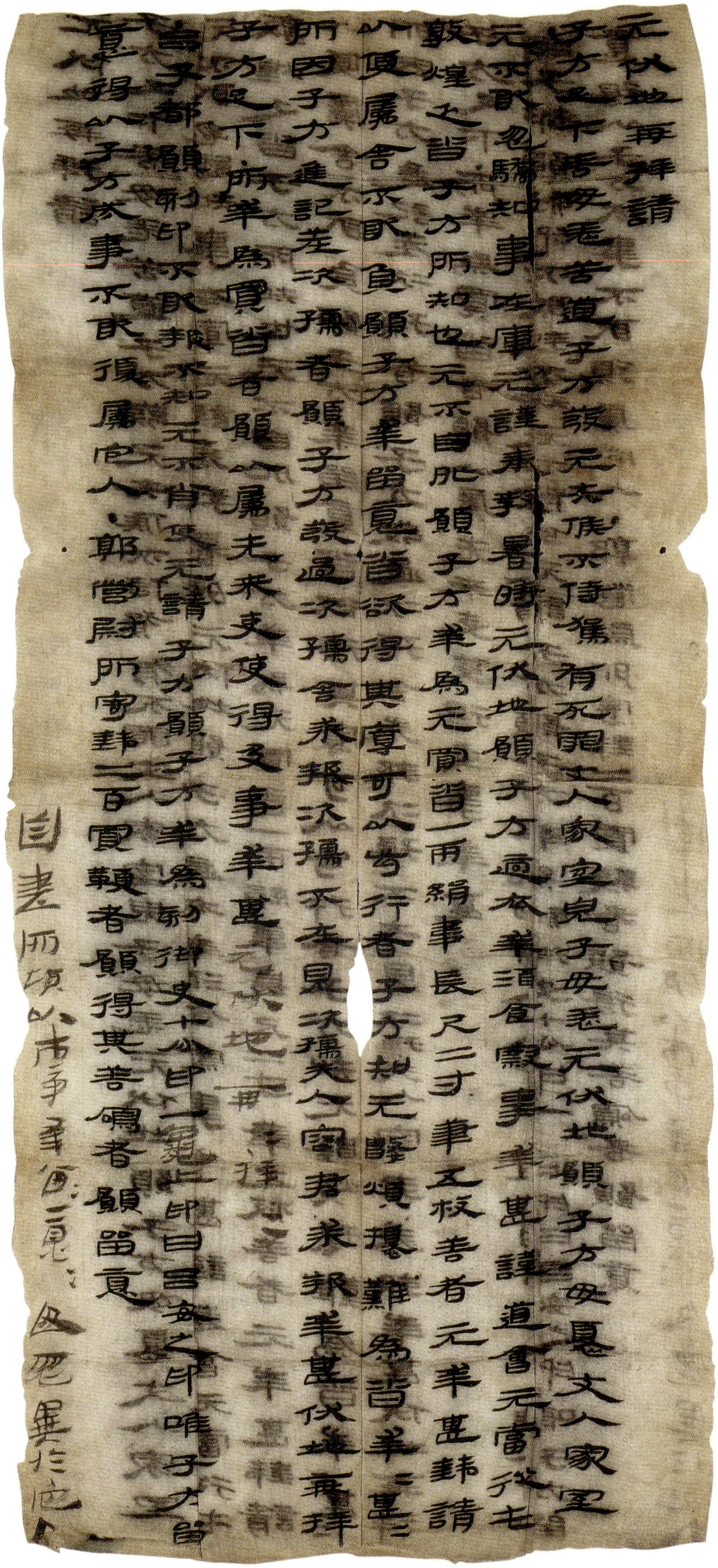

背面
Back

《元致子方书》帛书信札

西汉成帝时期（公元前32－前7年）
长23.2、宽10.7cm
甘肃敦煌甜水井悬泉置出土
甘肃省文物考古研究所藏

Letter of Yuan to Zifang, a Letter Written on Silk

Western Han Dynasty, Reign of Emperor Cheng (32–7 BCE)
Length: 23.2cm, Width: 10.7cm
Excavated from a wellat Xuanquanzhi Dunhuang, Gansu
Collection of the Gansu Prorince Institute of Cultural Relic and Archaeology

这是一封请朋友帮忙购买物品的信件，是迄今发现字数最多、保存完整的汉代私人信件。
帛书是指在丝织品上书写的文字。帛轻柔软薄，可以任意剪裁、随意舒卷，易于携带，很适合书写、绘画和制图，但价格昂贵，难以普及。文献记载古人多是先用竹简书写草稿，定本时再抄誊于帛上。

《医药》木牍

东汉（公元25–220年）
长23、宽2–4cm
甘肃武威旱滩坡出土
甘肃省博物馆藏

Wooden Tablet

Eastern Han Dynasty (25–220 CE)
Length: 23cm, Width: 2–4cm
Excavated outside of Wuwei, Gansu
Collection of the Gansu Provincial Museum

木牍记录了汉代临床医学、药物学、针灸学等方面的资料，书写工整秀丽，是汉代墨写隶书的精品。牍是指写字的木版，比简宽，一般是单片使用，通常用于记事、画图、写书信，还可以当名谒（古代的名片）使用。

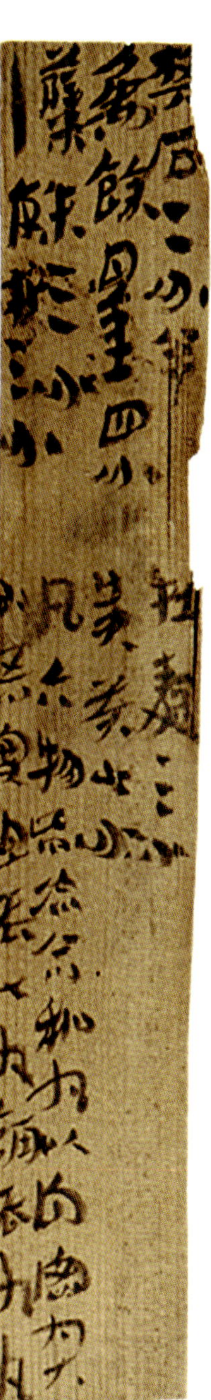

佉卢文木牍

东汉至晋（公元25–420年）
高15.9、宽5.7cm
新疆民丰尼雅遗址出土
新疆维吾尔自治区博物馆藏

Wooden Tablet Inscribed with Kharosthi Characters

Eastern Han Dynasty to Jin Dynasty (25–420 CE)
Length: 15.9cm, Width: 5.7cm
Excavated at the site of the Niya Ruins in the Xinjiang
Collection of the Xinjiang uyghur Autonomous Region Museum

这是一套完整的通信实物，包括木牍、检、封泥和绳，用于书写传递信件或机密文书。

通信使用的木牍多为一尺见方，因此信件也被称作“尺牍”。用木牍通信时，上面必须加盖一块版以使书信内容保密，版称做“检”，相当于信的封套。在检上面写收信人和发信人姓名，称为“署”。检面印齿内的黏土称为“封泥”。检与牍捆在一起，捆扎的绳子要通过检面的印齿和绳槽，并在封泥上盖印，这样可以检验信是否曾被开启。

青瓷对书俑

西晋（公元265–316年）
高17.2cm
湖南长沙金盆岭9号墓出土
湖南省博物馆藏

Celadon Figurine of Two Clerks Doing Transcription Facing Each Other

Western Jin Dynasty (265–316 CE)
Height: 17.2cm
Excavated from the 9th grave in Jinpen, Changsha, Hunan
Collection of the Hunan Provincial Museum

两俑相对而坐，中间置书案，案上有笔、砚、简册及手提箱，一人手执版，另一人执笔在版上书写，是当时以简作书的真实写照。

晋以前文献皆抄于简牍和帛之上。为避免在抄写过程中出现错误，古人非常重视校对工作。当时校书既有一人校，也有二人对校。“一人读书，校其上下，得谬误，为校；一人持本，一人读书，若冤家相对，为雠。”因此这件对书俑也被称为校雠俑。校对时一旦发现错误，使用刮刀将简牍上的字刮掉，重新填写，案上笔、砚就是为重新填写而备置的。

蔡侯纸
Marquis Cai's Paper

西汉初期，人们已能以废旧麻料为原料造纸。造纸术的发明，开启了一个书写的新纪元。公元2世纪初，东汉蔡伦总结了造麻纸的经验，改进造纸技术，扩大原料的来源，制造出高质量的植物纤维纸。

The practice of making paper from disused fibrous cloth was already known by the early Western Han Dynasty (206 BCE - 8 CE). Early in the 2nd century CE, during the Eastern Han Dynasty, Cai Lun invented the process of making paper from hemp fiber. Using materials such as tree bark, old cloth, used fishing nets, Cai Lun revolutionized the industry of papermaking. As a result paper during the Han Dynasty was often known as the "Marquis Cai's Paper". Furthermore, the resulting popularity of paper ushered in a new, prolific era of the written character.

纸地图

西汉文帝时期（公元前179–前157年）
残长5.6、宽2.6cm
甘肃天水放马滩5号汉墓出土
甘肃省博物馆藏

Map on Paper

Western Han Dynasty, Reign of Emperor Wen(179–157 BCE)
Length (remaining): 5.6cm, Width (remaining): 2.6cm
Excavated from Tomb 5 at Fangmatan, Tianshui, Gansu
Collection of the Gansu Provincial Museum

纸面平整、光滑，上面有用细黑线条绘制的山、川、崖、路等图形。这是现存最早的纸绘地图。该纸原料为麻，纸面有细纤维渣，表明造纸技术比较原始。纸地图的发现证明西汉初期不仅有纸，而且纸已被当作书写材料使用。

悬泉置带字纸

西汉成帝时期（公元前32–前7年）
残长7、宽3.5cm
甘肃敦煌甜水井悬泉置出土
甘肃省文物考古研究所藏

Fragment of Paper from Xuanquanzhi

Western Han Dynasty, Reign of Emperor Cheng (32 – 7 BCE),
Length: 7 cm, Width: 3.5 cm
Excavated from a well at Xuanquanzhi, Dunhuang, Gansu
Collection of the Gansu Province Institute of Cultural Relics and Archaeology

这是迄今所见最早的有字纸。此纸原料为麻，纸面有明显的帘纹。甘肃悬泉置出土汉代纸400多件，其中有三片残纸上用隶书书写"付子"、"细心""薰力"等药名。根据纸的形状和折叠痕迹分析，这三张纸当为包药用纸。

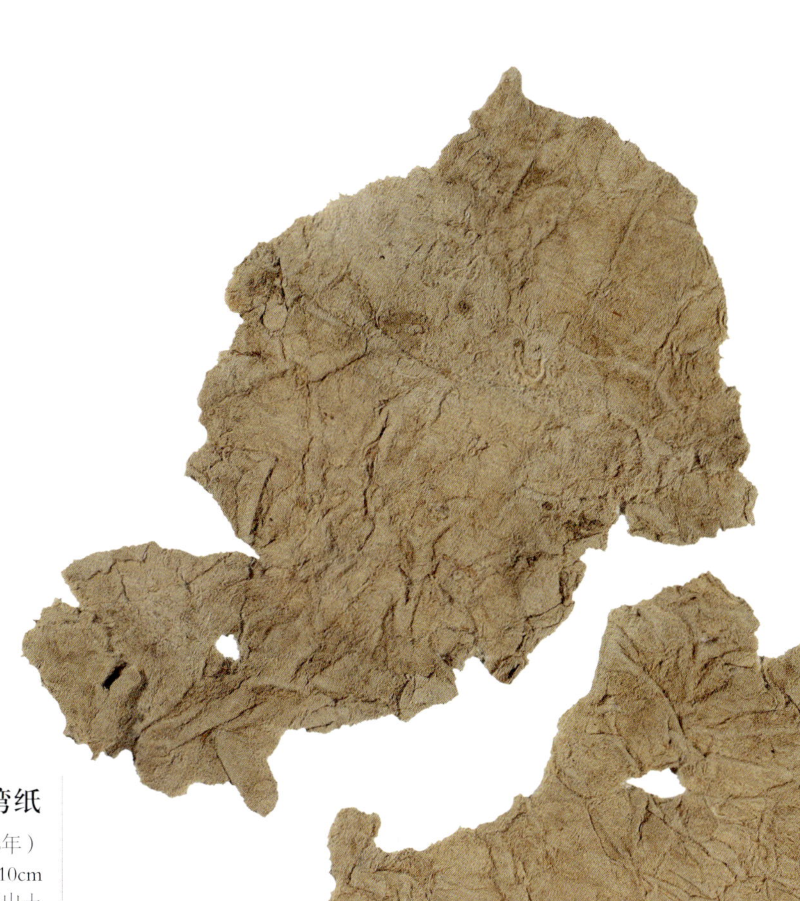

马圈湾纸

西汉（公元前206-公元8年）
长14.5、宽10cm
甘肃敦煌马圈湾烽燧出土
甘肃省博物馆藏

Paper from Majuan Wan

Western Han Dynasty (206 BCE–8 CE)
Length: 14.5cm, Width: 10cm
Excavated from Majuan Wan, Dunhuang, Gansu
Collection of the Gansu Provincial Museum

纸呈白色，纤维分布均匀，是迄今出土的西汉时期最大最完整的纸。

蔡伦像

蔡伦（？—公元121年），东汉时期桂阳（今湖南彬州）人，曾任主管御用器物的尚方令。安帝元初元年（公元114年）被封为龙亭（今陕西洋县）侯。蔡伦总结西汉以来造麻纸的经验，改进造纸技术，将经过处理的树皮和渔网增加到新的造纸原料中，进一步提高了麻纸的质量，后人将蔡伦改进制造的纸称为"蔡侯纸"。这种纸成本低，产量大，书写方便，是造纸技术的一次飞跃。

Portrait of Cai Lun

Cai Lun (? - 121 CE) was born during the Eastern Han Dynasty in Guiyang (today Chenzhou in Hunan) and became a government official. In the first year of the reign of Emperor An (114 CE) Cai Lun was given the title of Marquis of Longting (today Yangxian County, Shaanxi). Cai Lun drew on the primitive paper making techniques of the Western Han Dynasty (206 BCE - 8 CE) and invented new techniques to create better paper. As the advantages of using paper over wooden slips and silk became more evident, paper soon became the prevailing writing medium. Later generations credit Cai Lun with the invention of paper and paper is sometimes known as the "Marquis Cai's paper".

旱滩坡带字纸

东汉（公元25-220年）
残长5cm
甘肃武威旱滩坡出土
中国国家博物馆藏

Paper Fragment from Hantanpo with Characters

Eastern Han Dynasty (25-220 CE)
Length: 5cm
Excavated at Hantanpo, Wuwei, Gansu
Collection of National Museum of China

纸面均匀光滑，上面残存隶书墨迹，可辨出"青"、"贝"等字。此纸以麻为原料制成，纸面纤维交结细密，已非西汉时那种粗糙的麻纸，而是一种单面涂布加工纸，说明东汉造纸设备和技术上已达到相当高的水平。

麻纸制造工艺流程示意图

此图展示了麻纸制造的基本过程。经现代的模拟实验证实，汉代生产麻纸至少要经过浸湿、切碎、洗涤、浸灰水、蒸煮、舂捣、二次洗涤、打浆、抄纸、晒干、揭压等工序才能完成。

Diagram of the Process of Hemp Paper Making

Based on records it seems that papermaking during the Han Dynasty was composed of the following steps; soaking, sorting, and washing the raw material, followed by steaming, kneading and further washing, finally burnishing, pressing and then writing on the paper.

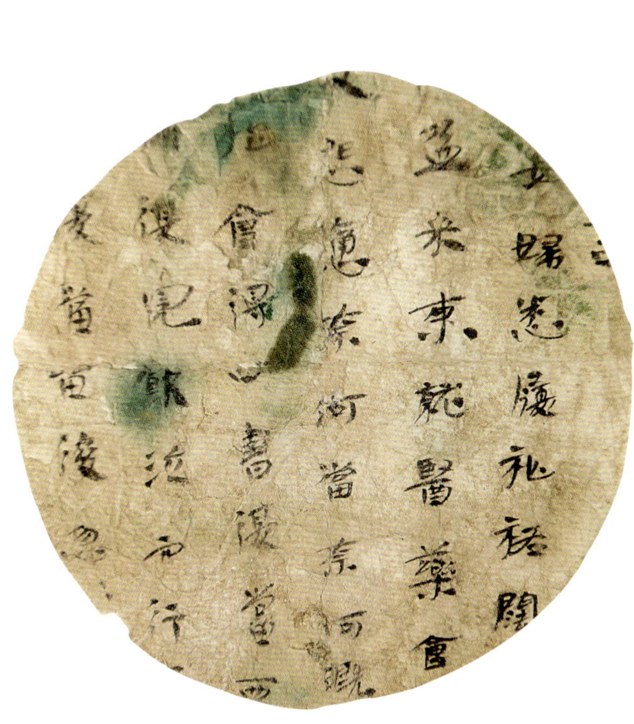

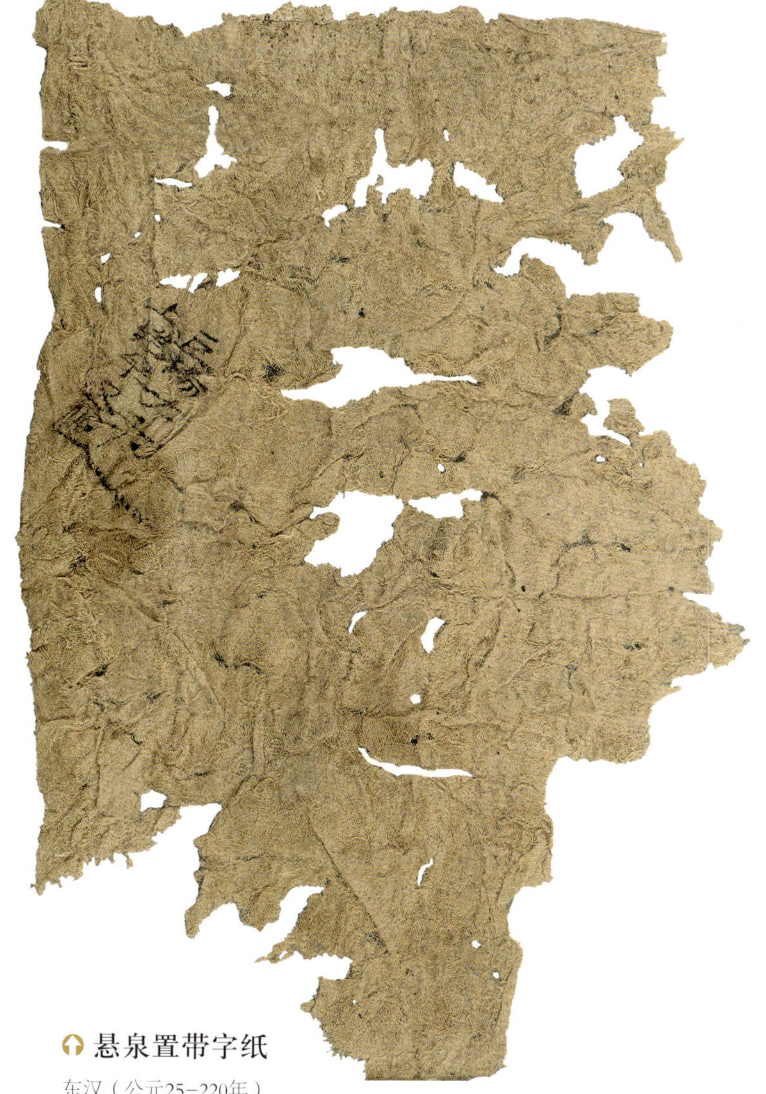

伏龙坪书信纸

东汉（公元25－220年）
直径17cm
甘肃兰州伏龙坪出土
兰州市博物馆藏

Paper Letter Fragment from FuLongPing

Eastern Han Dynasty (25–220 CE)
Diameter: 17cm
Excavated in FuLongPing, Lanzhou, Gansu
Collection of the Lanzhou Municipal Museum, Gansu

纸呈白色，纸面薄厚均匀，上书工整清晰的隶书，推测为家书残片，原衬垫于铜镜之下。此纸以麻为原料，通过使用施胶和加填料的加工技术，改善纸面平滑度和白度，说明以"蔡侯纸"为代表的东汉纸已达到可以代替简帛作为书写材料的水平。

悬泉置带字纸

东汉（公元25－220年）
长29、宽20cm
甘肃敦煌甜水井悬泉置出土
甘肃省文物考古研究所藏

Fragment of Paper from Xuanquanzhi

Eastern Han Dynasty (25–220CE)
Length: 29cm, Width: 20cm
Excavated at Xuanquanzhi, Dunhuang, Gansu Collection of the Gansu Province Institute of Cultural Relics and Archaeology

汉至唐的千余年间，主要使用麻纸，因为大麻和苎麻这类造纸原料丰富。蔡伦造纸所用原材料均含有麻纤维成分，他用废旧麻料造纸，不仅原料充足而廉价，而且还省去了沤麻工序，使打浆工序更为简便。公元2世纪，通过蔡伦的改进，纸的质量和产量均有大幅度提高，价廉物美、携带方便的纸张逐渐成为主要的书写材料。

晓雪春冰

Morning Snow, Spring Ice

“晓雪”、“春冰”是古人对洁白轻飏纸张的赞美，是造纸术不断进步的写照。魏晋至唐五代时期，造纸术进入了快速发展和兴盛的时期。随着社会需求的迅速扩大，造纸原料和技术不断创新，皮纸逐渐代替麻纸成为主要纸品；施胶、染色等纸加工技术和床架式抄纸帘等造纸设备的普遍应用，进一步提高了纸的质量和产量。纸张的大量生产，有力地促进了文化的发展和书籍的流通。写本书籍大量出现，书法艺术也由此进入新的境界，并引发了汉字字体的变迁。公元404年，东晋豪族桓玄颁布“以纸代简”令，终止了简牍书写的历史，纸终于成为主流的书写材料。

“Morning snow” and “Spring ice” are terms of praise used by those in these early periods to refer to spotlessly white, very light paper. These poetic phrases clearly demonstrate how paper had risen in esteem as an item produced within the boarders of China. During the period from the Wei, Jin Dynasties(220 - 420 CE) up to the Tang and Five Dynasties periods (618 - 960 CE), China's population grew and society developed rapidly. This situation meant that new sites to gather raw materials and new production techniques for papermaking were continually being explored. In 404 CE, the powerful official Huan Xuan from the Eastern Jin Dynasty promulgated the order of “replacing bamboo slips with paper” so paper finally became the foremost written material. With the use of equipment such as large-scale troughs, advance sizing techniques and dyes the amount of paper produced in addition to the quality of the paper increased. Different regions produced hemp paper, mulberry bark paper, mulberry fiber paper, and rattan paper, among others. In addition, specialty papers such as Shan River vine paper and Temple of the Transparent Heart paper were also made. This flurry of paper production encouraged advances in the fields of science and culture, especially in the book-reading and book-collecting arenas. During the Jin to Five Dynasties period (265 - 960 CE) a large number of books and manuscripts appeared, the art of calligraphy reached new heights, and Chinese characters underwent their own structural evolution.

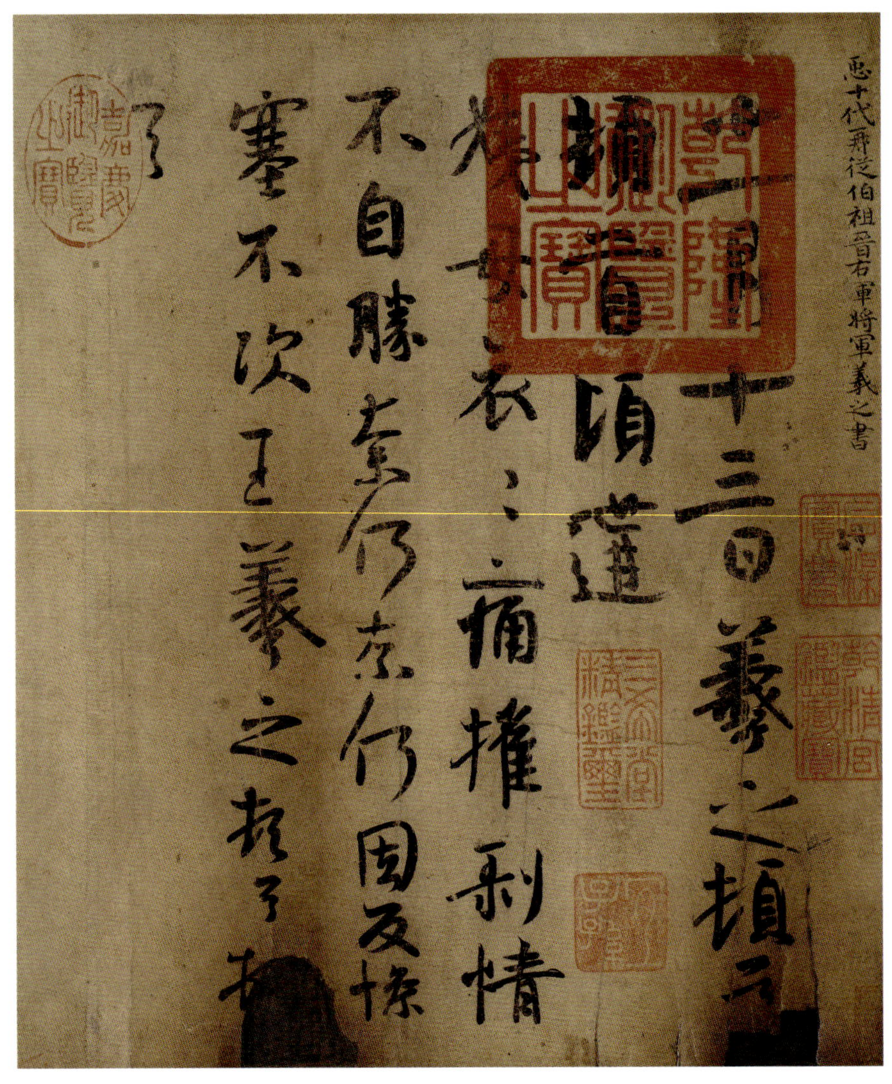

《姨母帖》

东晋 王羲之（公元303-361年）
长26.3、宽21.5cm
辽宁省博物馆藏

Memorial for an Aunt

By Wang Xizhi of the Eastern Jin Dynasty (303-361 CE)
Length: 26.3cm, Width: 21.5cm
Collection of the Liaoning Provincial Museum

此帖是王羲之在突然得到姨母故去的噩耗后，心情十分悲痛，以至于不能处理正常事务的心情记录。其书字体端美凝重，笔锋圆浑遒劲。用毛笔在狭窄的简上写字，空间上受到很大局限，即使在较宽的木牍上书写，也难以充分施展。而在洁白、平滑、柔韧的纸上可以纵情书写、绘画，笔墨的艺术魅力得以充分展示。晋代出现王羲之、王献之这样杰出的书法家，在一定程度上应归功于纸的普及。

《墓主人生活图》

东晋（公元317—420年）
长105、宽46.2cm
新疆吐鲁番阿斯塔那出土
新疆维吾尔自治区博物馆藏

Painting on Paper of a Tomb Inhabitant

Eastern Jin Dynasty (317−420 CE)
Length: 105cm, Width: 46.2cm
Excavated at Astana, Turfan, Xinjiang
Collection of the Xinjiang uyghur Autonomous Region Museum

这是现存最早的纸本绘画作品，绘画用纸由六张小纸拼接而成，描绘了墓主人生前的生活。魏晋南北朝时期，随着造纸技术的进步和纸张质量的提高，人们逐渐用纸来书写绘画。但这一时期抄纸设备多由一人操作，所抄纸幅较小，大幅纸是将多张纸粘接起来的。

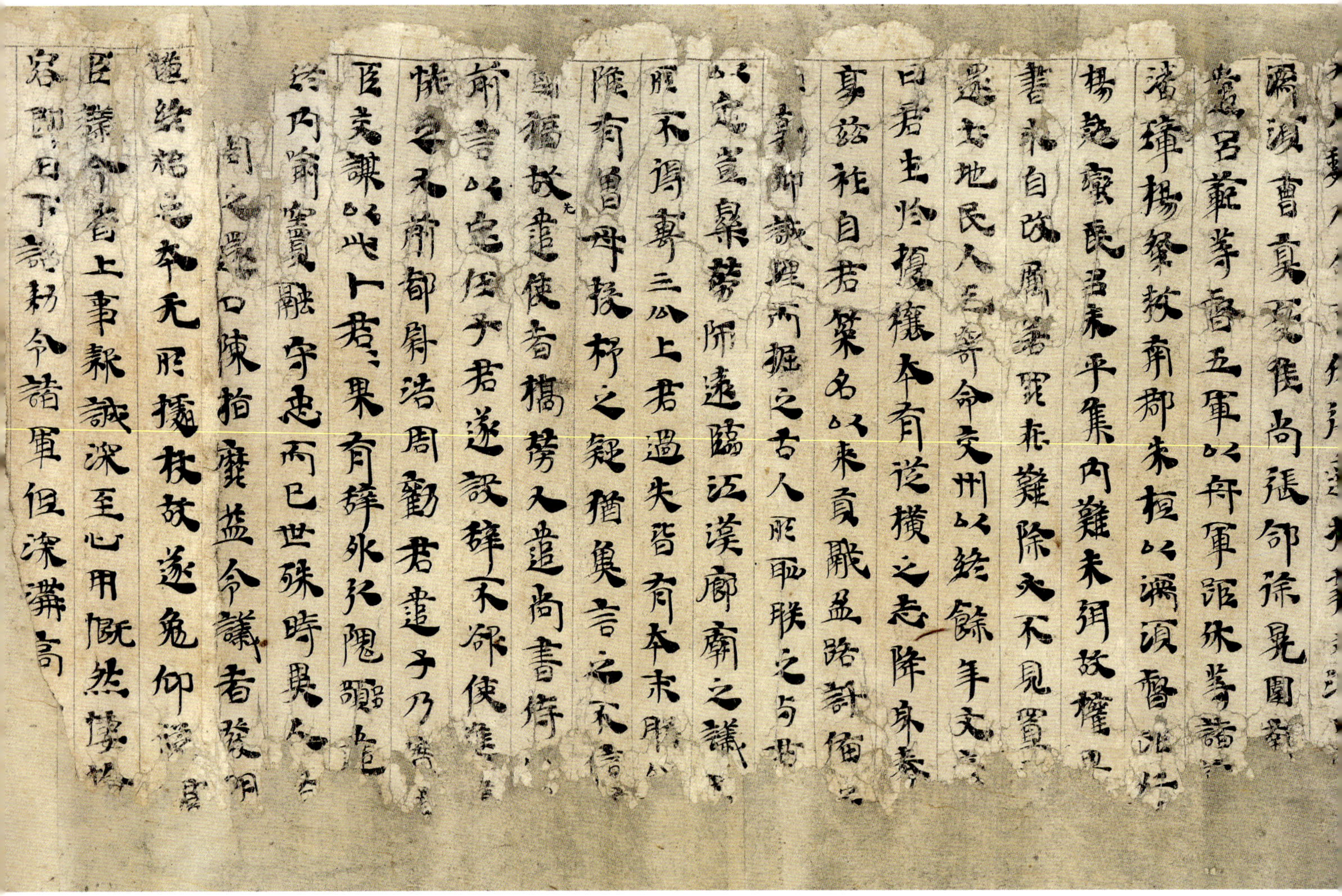

《三国志》残卷（部分）

东晋（公元317−420年）
长72.8、宽22.6cm
新疆吐鲁番出土
新疆维吾尔自治区博物馆藏

Fragment of a Legend of the Three Kingdoms Scroll (Part)

Eastern Jin Dynasty (317−420 CE)
Length: 72.8cm, Width: 22.6cm
Excavated in Turfan, Xinjiang
Collection of the Xinjiang uyghur Autonomous Region Museum

此残卷为《三国志·吴主孙权传》的部分内容，以隶书抄写而成。所用纸张已使用涂布和研光等技术。

研光技术在造纸术发明不久之后就已出现，它是用光滑的砑石将凹凸不平的纸面磨平，以消除纸面的刷痕，使纸张平滑而有光泽。涂布技术是将矿物粉颗粒（如石膏、石灰等）用黏性物质平刷在纸面上，用来提高纸张的平滑度、白度、不透明度和均匀度，改善了纸张的吸墨性。南北朝时期出土的纸张均已使用了涂布和研光技术，表明这一时期造纸技术在制浆、抄纸和加工方面较汉代有了明显进步。

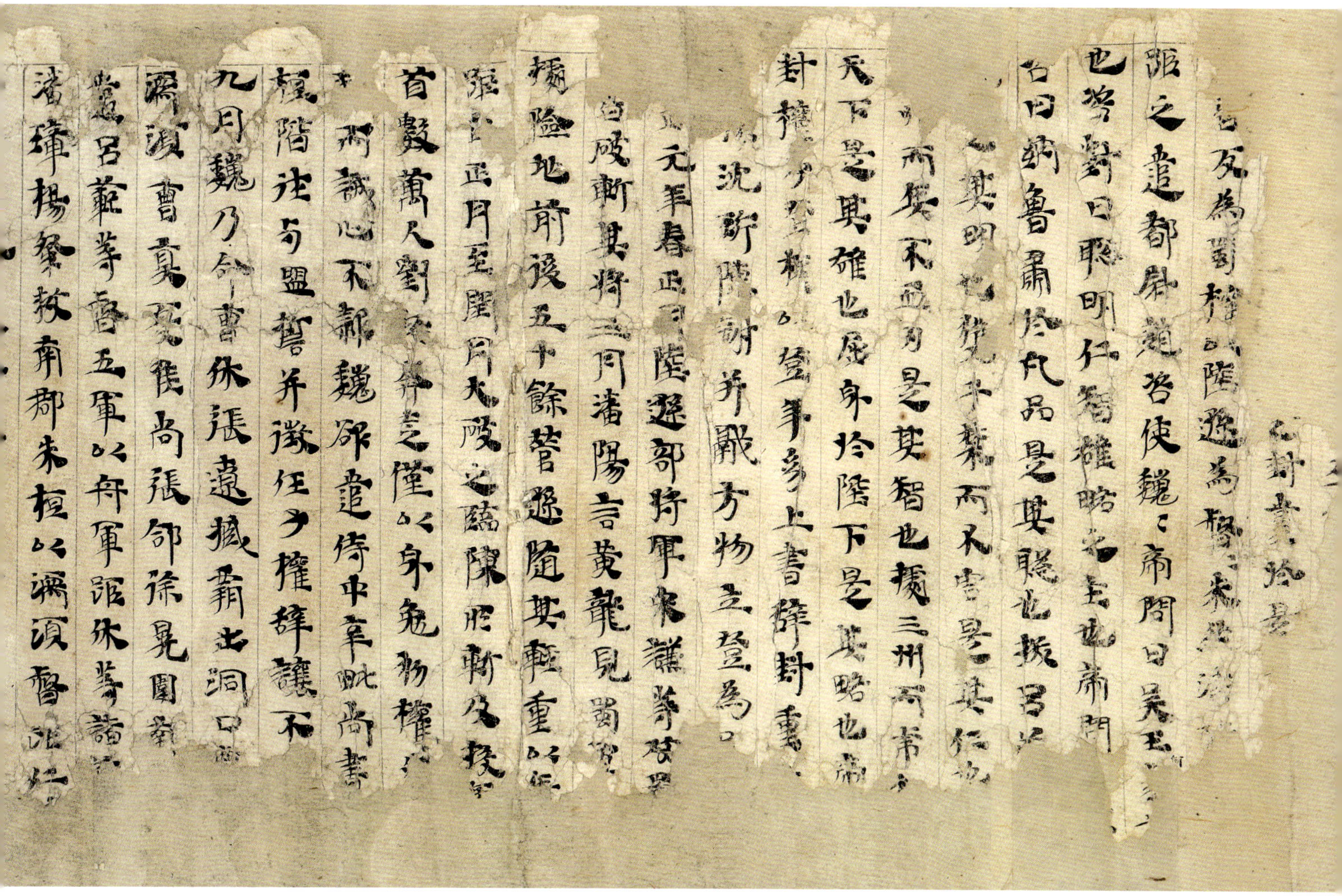

□封□□於是

乞文為蜀將以陸遜為督〻朱然潘璋

拒之遣都尉趙咨使魏〻帝問曰吳王何

也咨對曰聰明仁智雄略之主也帝問

咨曰納魯肅於凡品是其聰也拔呂蒙

□其明也獲于禁而不害是其仁也

□而兵不血刃是其智也據三州虎視

天下是其雄也屈身於陛下是其略也帝

封權子登權以登年幼上書辭封重

掾沈珩陳謝并獻方物立登為□

元年春正月陸遜部將軍宋謙等攻蜀

皆破斬其將三月鄱陽言黃龍見蜀軍

據險地前後五十餘營遜隨其輕重以兵

拒自正月至閏月大破之臨陳所斬及投降

首數萬人劉備奔走僅以身免初權外

事魏而誠心不款魏乃遣侍中辛毗尚書

桓階往與盟誓并徵任子權辭讓不

九月魏乃命曹休張遼臧霸出洞口

濡須曹真夏侯尚張郃徐晃圍南郡

遣呂範等督五軍以舟軍拒休等諸

潘璋楊粲救南郡朱桓以濡須督拒仁

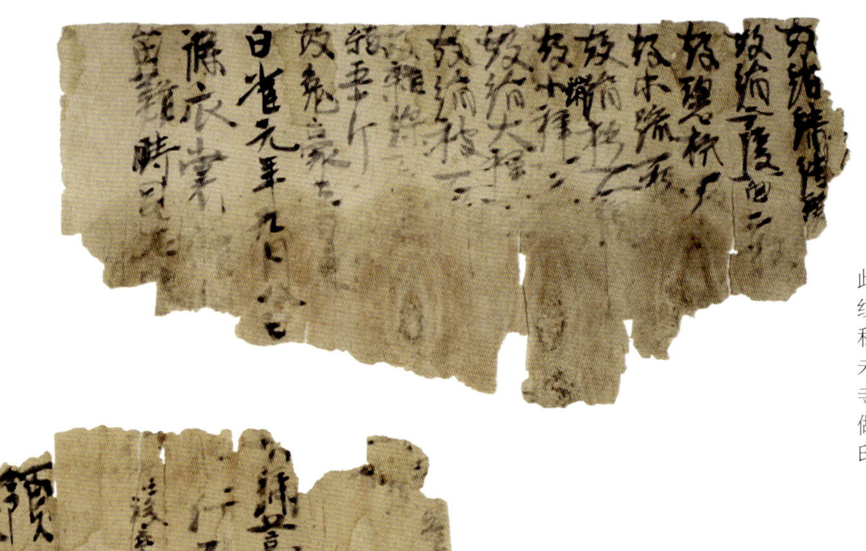

《华严经》（部分）

北魏（公元386–534年）
长769.9、宽26.2cm
中国国家博物馆藏

Avatamsaka Sutra (Part)

Northern Wei Dynasty (386–534 CE)
Length: 769.9cm, Width: 26.2cm
Colection of the Natioal Museum of China

此卷为手抄经文。纸质较细薄，表面平滑，有帘纹。魏晋南北朝时期的纸张除用于抄写书籍和公私文件外，还大量用于抄写佛经。在雕版印刷术未发明前，佛教僧侣鼓励信徒大量抄写佛经或从寺院购买抄写好的佛经，以得到佛的保佑。这种做法一方面加大了纸的消费，另一方面也加速了印刷术的发明。

白雀元年施胶纸

后秦白雀元年（公元384年）
残长12、宽10cm
新疆吐鲁番出土
中国国家博物馆藏

Sized Paper from the First Year of the Baique Era

First Year of the Baique Era, Later Qin Dynasty, (384 CE)
Length:12cm, Width:10 cm
Excavated in Turfan, Xinjiang
Collection of the National Museum of China

这是迄今发现最早的表面施胶纸。施胶技术是在造纸过程中将动物、植物、淀粉等胶剂掺入纸浆中或刷在纸面上，使纸的结构变得紧密，纸面更加平滑，纸的可塑性、抗湿性和不透水性都得以提高。这种施胶技术的使用比欧洲早1400多年。

《首行品法句经第卌八》（部分）

北朝（公元386–581年）
残长143.7、宽25cm
甘肃敦煌莫高窟藏经洞出土
甘肃省博物馆藏

Chapter XXXVIII of Dhammapada (Part)

Northern Dynasty (386–581 CE)
Length: 143.7cm, Width: 25cm
Excavated from Library Cave of Dunhuang Grottos, Gansu
Collection of Gansu Provincial Museum

此为佛教早期经典，以隶书抄写于白麻纸之上。白麻纸虽已泛黄，但表面光滑，纸质坚韧，表现出较高水平的麻纸制造技术。

《法华大智论》经卷（部分）

隋（公元581–618年）
长911、宽26cm
安徽省博物馆藏

Mahaprajnaparamita Sastra Scroll (Part)

Sui Dynasty (581–618 CE)
Length: 911cm, Width: 26cm
Collection of the Anhui Provincial Museum

经卷为《法华大智论》经卷五十三的抄写本，所用纸张为麻纸，纸质精匀，纹理细美。纸面因染有黄蘖汁而呈药黄色。

染色为较早使用的纸加工技术，是使用天然颜料将素色纸染成有色纸，用以增加纸的美观度，改善纸的性能。南北朝时期流行使用以黄蘖汁染色的染黄纸，黄蘖汁既是黄色染料，又能杀虫防蛀，对保护纸张和书籍具有良好的功效。此外，我国古代还运用染色技术制造红、黄、紫等各色纸张。

写经纸

唐（公元618–907年）
长100.7、宽25.9cm
新疆吐鲁番哈拉和卓旧城出土
中国国家博物馆藏

Sutra Writing Paper

Tang Dynasty (618–907 CE)
Length: 100.7cm, Width: 25.9cm
Excavated from the Ruins of Kara-Khoja City in Turfan, Xinjiang
Collection of the National Museum of China

这件写经纸纤维交结紧密、均匀，说明唐代造纸舂捣精细，打浆度高，已能制造出质量较高的植物纤维纸。

为了适应书写绘画的需要，唐代的纸被明确分为生纸与熟纸两类。生纸是指抄制后未经加工的纸，而经不同方法加工的纸称为熟纸。唐代的纸加工技术全面发展，当时人们已能熟练使用施蜡、研光、染色等各种纸加工技术，硬黄纸、薛涛笺、金花纸在此时最为著名。

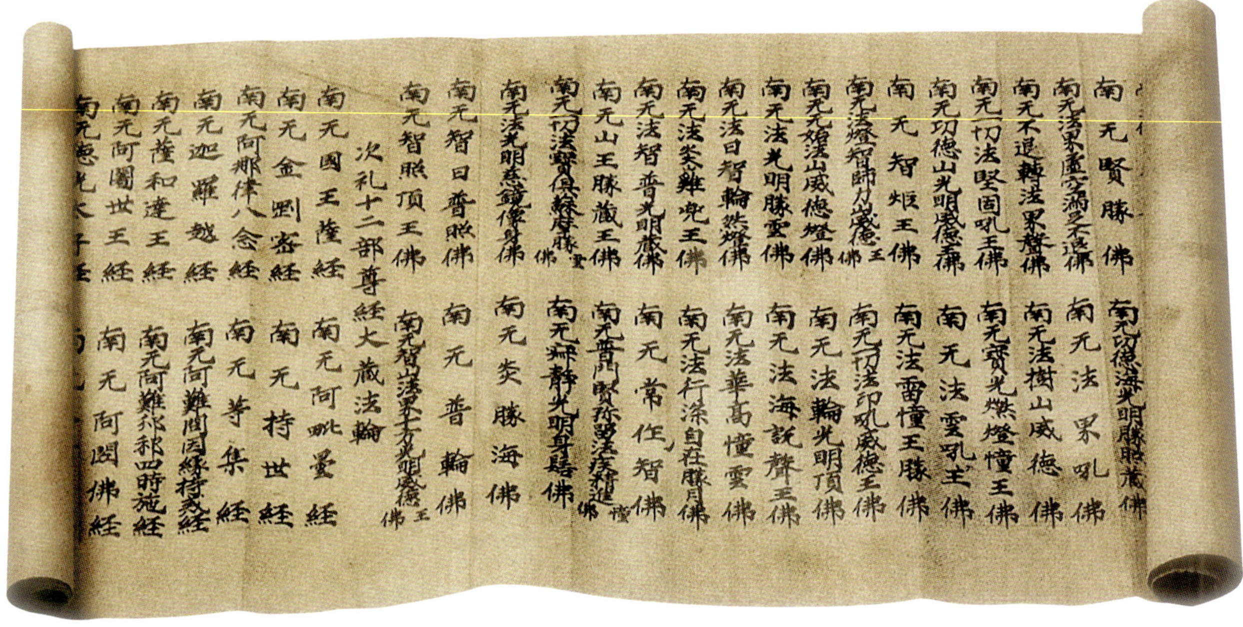

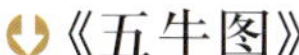

抄纸工具（模型）

扬州博物馆藏

Papermaking Tools (Moldel)

Collection of the Yangzhou Museum

中国古代最原始的抄纸方法可能是用草帘、麻布帘的浇纸法。两晋南北朝时使用床架式抄纸帘，由帘床、竹帘和捏尺三部分组成，这三部分可以自由组合和分离，操作起来极为方便，所以床架式抄纸帘又可称为“活动抄纸帘”。床架式抄纸帘可连续抄造出千万张纸，所抄纸张紧薄而匀细，这种设备生产效率高，一直沿用至今。

《五牛图》

唐 韩滉（公元723-787年）
长139.8、宽20.8cm
故宫博物院藏

Painting of Five Cows

By Han Huang of the Tang Dynasty (723-787 CE)
Length: 139.8cm, Width: 20.8cm
Collection of the Palace Museum

《五牛图》所用纸张为桑皮纸。

桑皮纸属于皮纸的一种。皮纸是以木本植物韧皮纤维为原料加工而成的纸，其原材料以楮树皮、桑树皮、藤皮、檀树皮为主。隋唐以前，人们主要使用麻纸。隋唐以后，随着雕版印刷术的发明，纸张的需求量日益增多，麻的原料供应已不能满足需求，人们不断开发新的造纸原料，树皮和竹原料丰富、成本低，以树皮为原料的皮纸逐渐代替麻纸成为占主导地位的纸品，到明清时期竹纸则成为主流。

印刷术：从转印到雕版
Printing Techniques: From Transferring to Engraving

印刷术是中国古代的四大发明之一，为人类文明的发展做出了重要贡献，它经历了雕版印刷和活字印刷两个重要的发展阶段。唐代初年，在多种转印技术的基础上，中国发明了雕版印刷术，用墨将模版上的图文转印到纸上成为主要的印刷形式。五代后唐时期，政府使用雕版印刷儒家经典。两宋时期，官刻、私刻、民间刻书兴盛，雕版印刷术进入黄金时代。

Printing was one of the great inventions that ancient China contributed to world civilization. This was a two-step invention process, the first technique that emerged was that of carved woodblock printing then movable type printing was developed. In the early Tang, innovations in printing lead to the invention of carved woodblock printing. This technique consisted of carving blocks of wood, applying ink to the surface of the block and the impressing a sheet of paper on top of the block to transfer the image or text. During the later Tang Dynasty in the Five Dynasties period the imperial government commissioned the publication of Confucian classics using this printing method. Then in the Northern and Southern Song periods, official, private, and popular printers flourished marking the high point of the era of woodblock printing.

转印——印刷术的先导
Transferring Impressions:An Ancient Technique

印刷术发明以前，人们已熟练使用多种转印技术。将印章印在泥土或纸上的钤印技术，从石碑上拓取碑文的墨拓技术，用镂花版在纺织物上印制花纹的刷印技术，在印章、碑石上刻写文字的雕刻技术，都是印刷术发明的技术先导。

Before the invention of printing there were already a variety of technologies that using some sort of movable component. These precursors included sealing with clay stamps on paper and employing openwork slats to print repeated characters or patterns on textiles or paper. Yet another method was to make rubbings of verses carved on stone steles.

秦公铜簋

春秋（公元前770–前476年）
高19.8、口径18.5、足径19.5cm
甘肃天水出土
中国国家博物馆藏

Duke of Qin's *Gui* Vessel

Spring and Autumn Period (770–476 BCE)
Height: 19.8cm, Diameter of mouth: 18.5cm, Diameter of base: 19.5cm
Excavated in Tianshui City, Gansu
Collection of the National Museum of China

器内共有铭文百余字，记载了秦国12代祖先的战功威名和秦景公守土安民的功绩，是研究秦国历史发展的重要资料。

器物上的铭文是用一个个单字模打印在泥范上后铸出来的。这种将长篇铭文拆解成单个字模的工艺与后来的活字印刷技术原理相同，它为活字印刷术的发明奠定了技术基础。

秦公铜簋铭文拓片
Rubbing of the Inscription of Duke of Qin's *Gui* Vessel

秦公铜簋铭文拓片
Rubbing of the Inscription of Duke of Qin's *Gui* Vessel

“齐铁官印”封泥

西汉（公元前206–公元8年）
残长2.5cm
中国国家博物馆藏

Sealing Clay with the Stamp “Seal of the Qi State Department of Iron”

Western Han Dynasty (206 BCE–8 CE)
Length: 2.5cm
Collection of the National Museum of China

“齐铁官印”四字为篆书，是西汉初年齐国经营铁业、自设铁官的印信。在简牍与帛作为书写材料的时代，印章不能直接钤印在书写材料上，而是将印章钤印在封泥上。封泥是古代用于封存信件、公文的工具，其上有印章钤印的印文，这对雕版印刷术的发明具有一定的启迪作用。

“牢阳司寇”铜印

战国（公元前475－前221年）
通高1.5、长1.5、宽1.5cm
中国国家博物馆藏

Bronze Printing Block with the Phrase “Laoyang Minister of Justice”

Warring States Period (475–221 BCE)
Height: 1.5cm, Length: 1.5cm, Width 1.5cm
Collection of the National Museum of China

春秋时已使用有文字的印章，其用途十分广泛，不仅钤印在封泥上，还印在陶器上、烙在修建墓葬用的黄肠木上、马身上以及铜器上。印章是一种小型雕版，上面的文字是反刻文字。印章的广泛使用说明古代的反刻技术已十分娴熟，凸雕阳文的应用更是印刷术发明的必要技术条件。

始皇诏陶量

秦（公元前221－前207年）
高9.4、口径20.4cm
山东邹县出土
中国国家博物馆藏

Imperial Ceramic Measuring Device from the First Emperor of the Qin Dynasty

Qin Dynasty (221–207 BCE)
Height: 9.4cm, Diameter of mouth: 20.4cm
Excavated from Zouxian, Shandong
Collection of the National Museum of China

这是秦代官方颁行的量器，陶量外壁有秦始皇二十六年统一度量衡的40字诏书，是以多枚印章连续押印而成。

印花敷彩纱（部分）

西汉（公元前206-公元8年）
长45 、宽55cm
湖南长沙马王堆西汉墓出土
中国国家博物馆藏

Colored Gauze with a Printed Floral Pattern (Part)

Western Han Dynasty (206 BCE–8 CE)
Length: 45cm, Width: 55cm
Excavated from the Mawangdui Western Han tomb in Changsha, Hunan
Collection of the National Museum of China

此花纹与广州象岗南越王墓所出铜质印花凸版的花纹相似。西汉纺织业发达，丝织物的花色品种丰富。此纱使用凸版印花技术将花纹捺印在织物上，这种凸版印花技术对印刷术的发明具有促进作用。

铜印花凸版

西汉（公元前206–公元8年）
长5.7、宽4.1cm；长3.4、宽1.8cm
广东广州象岗南越王墓出土
西汉南越王博物馆藏

Bronze Printing Block with a Floral Design in Relief

Western Han Dynasty (206 BCE–8 CE)
Length: 5.7cm, Width: 4.1cm;
Length: 3.4cm, Width: 1.8cm
Excavated from the Nanyue King Tomb, south of Xianggang, Guangzhou, Guangdong
Collection in the Museam of the King Nanyue of Western Han Dynasty

这是目前世界上发现年代最早的一套彩色套印织物的工具，由大小两件组成，大的是主纹版，小的是定位版，两者背面皆有穿孔小钮，可穿绳执握，如盖章般依次逐个列印，套印出彩色图形。此印花版纹样与湖南长沙马王堆1号汉墓出土的印花敷彩纱图案非常相似。

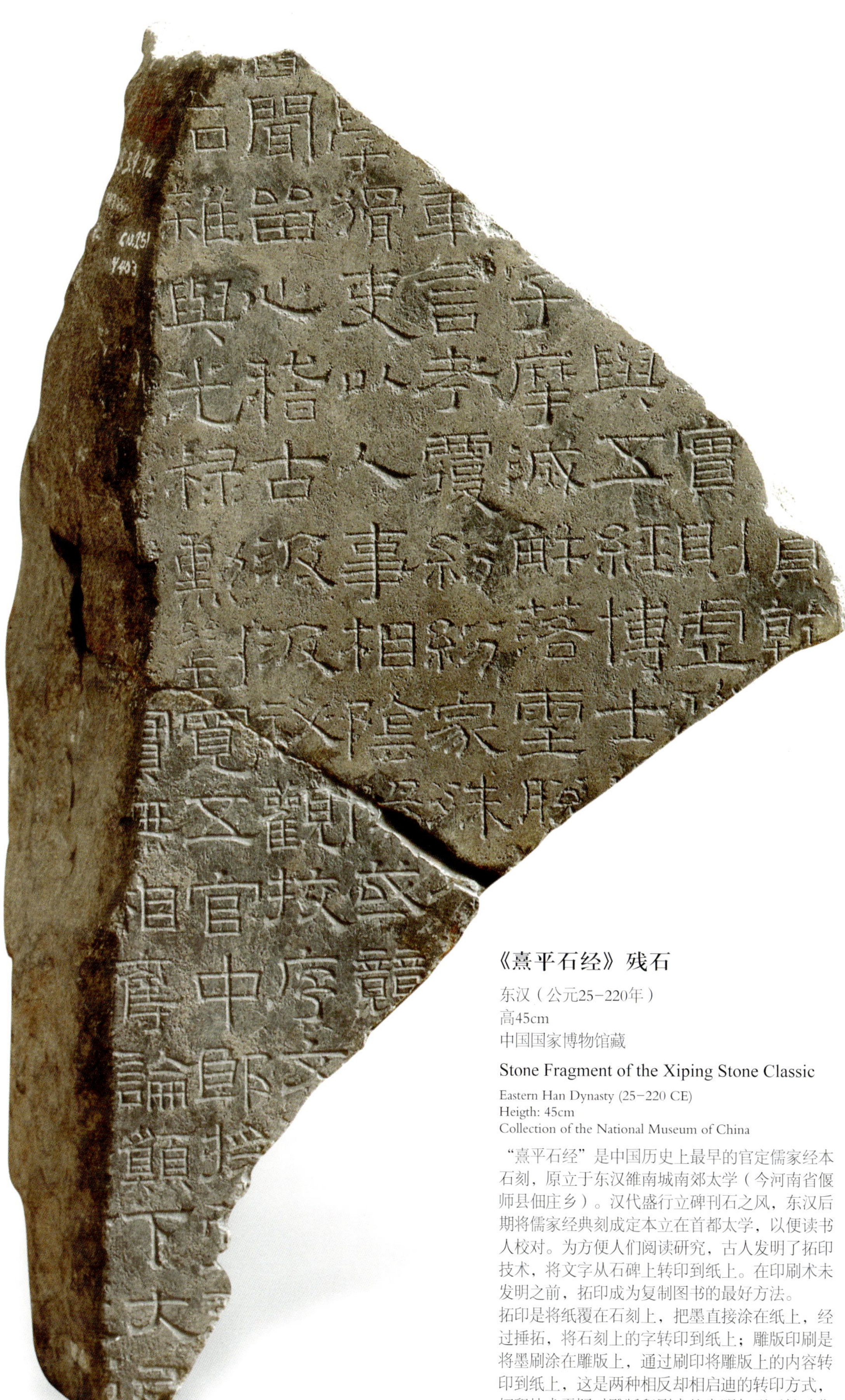

《熹平石经》残石

东汉（公元25–220年）
高45cm
中国国家博物馆藏

Stone Fragment of the Xiping Stone Classic

Eastern Han Dynasty (25–220 CE)
Heigth: 45cm
Collection of the National Museum of China

“熹平石经”是中国历史上最早的官定儒家经本石刻，原立于东汉雒南城南郊太学（今河南省偃师县佃庄乡）。汉代盛行立碑刊石之风，东汉后期将儒家经典刻成定本立在首都太学，以便读书人校对。为方便人们阅读研究，古人发明了拓印技术，将文字从石碑上转印到纸上。在印刷术未发明之前，拓印成为复制图书的最好方法。

拓印是将纸覆在石刻上，把墨直接涂在纸上，经过捶拓，将石刻上的字转印到纸上；雕版印刷是将墨刷涂在雕版上，通过刷印将雕版上的内容转印到纸上，这是两种相反却相启迪的转印方式，拓印技术无疑对雕版印刷术的发明起到了推动作用。

联珠对禽纹绢幡

隋至唐早期（公元6-7世纪）
长13、底边宽8cm
敦煌研究院藏

Silk Fabric with an Interlocking Pearl and Bird Pattern

Sui to early Tang Dynasty (6th-7th Century CE)
Length: 13cm, Width: 8cm
Collection of the Dunhuang Academy

绢幡上的花纹是先在木雕的阳纹印花版上涂色，将丝织物铺于其上，再用毛刷在背面刷印而成。这种刷印方法与雕版印刷术已十分接近。

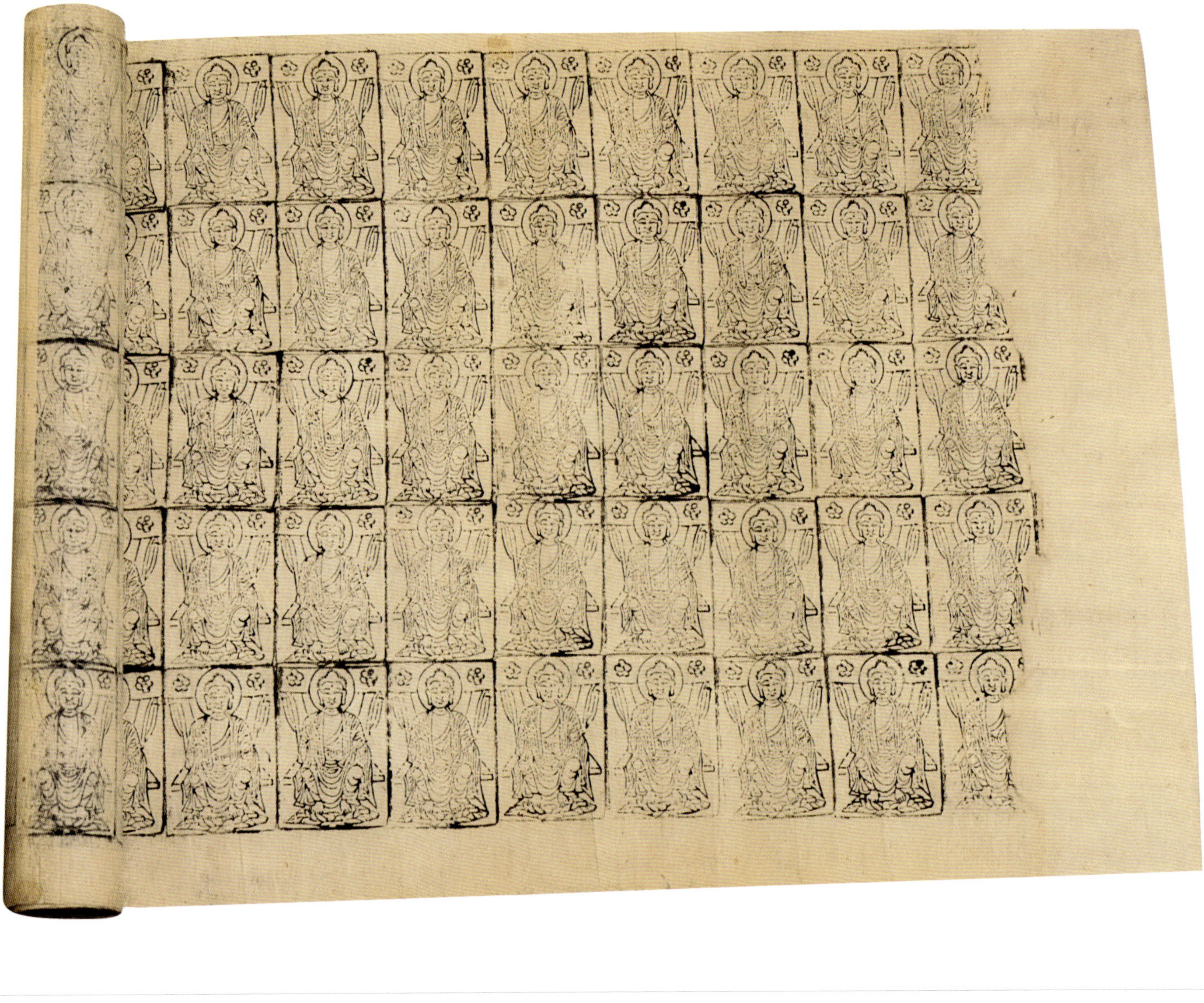

《佛像》

唐（公元618–907年）
长27、宽23cm
敦煌研究院藏

Picture of the Buddhas

Tang Dynasty (618–907 CE)
Length: 27cm, Width: 23cm
Collection of the Dunhuang Academy

图中佛像，是用事先刻好的佛像小印在纸上多次捺印而成。捺印是在印版上涂墨，将印版版面向下印在纸上，而雕版印刷则是将印版版面向上覆纸刷印，两者在技术上虽有不同，但却有着密切的联系。

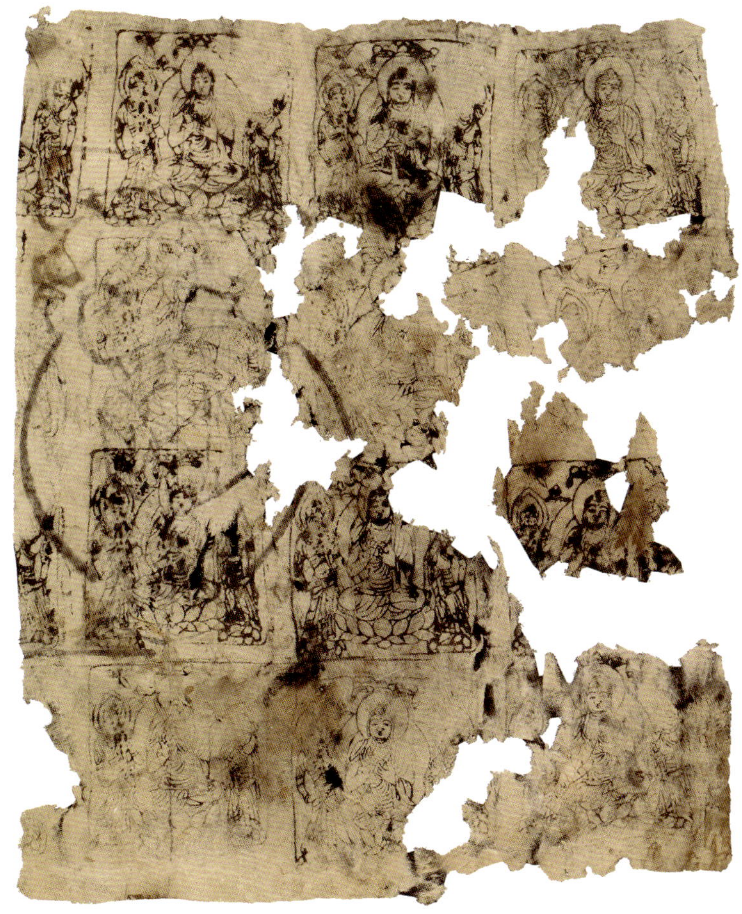

《佛像》

唐（公元618–907年）
中国国家图书馆藏

Picture of the Buddhas

Tang Dynasty (618–907 CE)
Collection of the National Library of China

此佛像为雕版捺印而成。早在南北朝时期，雕版印刷技术的雏形已经形成，图文一体的木质佛像雕版的刻制难度并不低于以文字为主的书籍雕版的刻制。

刻书雕版
Carved Print Blocks for Printing Books

隋唐科举制度的建立推动了教育的发展，促进了社会对书籍的需求，同时佛教传播也需要大量佛经复本，手工抄写已无法满足这些需求，而造纸术的普及为雕版印刷术的发明提供了先决条件。唐代中国发明了雕版印刷技术，并且很快得以传播。雕版印刷逐渐代替了手抄、刻石等书籍制作方法，加速了文化的传播，促进了文化的繁荣。

As the use of paper became widespread the cost of books dropped dramatically. Paper as a medium certainly played in role in this development but it was the invention of printing that was the main factor in this decrease in price. As for the burgeoning book market, the development of the Tang and Song Dynasty civil service examination system as well as increasing religious proselytizing activities both lead to a huge escalation in demand for printed books. At the same time, hand-copied books were in no way capable of meeting market demands and so fell out of favor.

The technique of woodblock printing was invented in the 7th century and quickly spread beyond the boarders of China to other countries. The introduction of woodblock print solved the ancient problem of relying on handwritten copies of texts that may have included mistakes in transcription. Finally a technique has been invented that could produce vast quantities of accurately written documents that in turn helped to spread information far and wide.

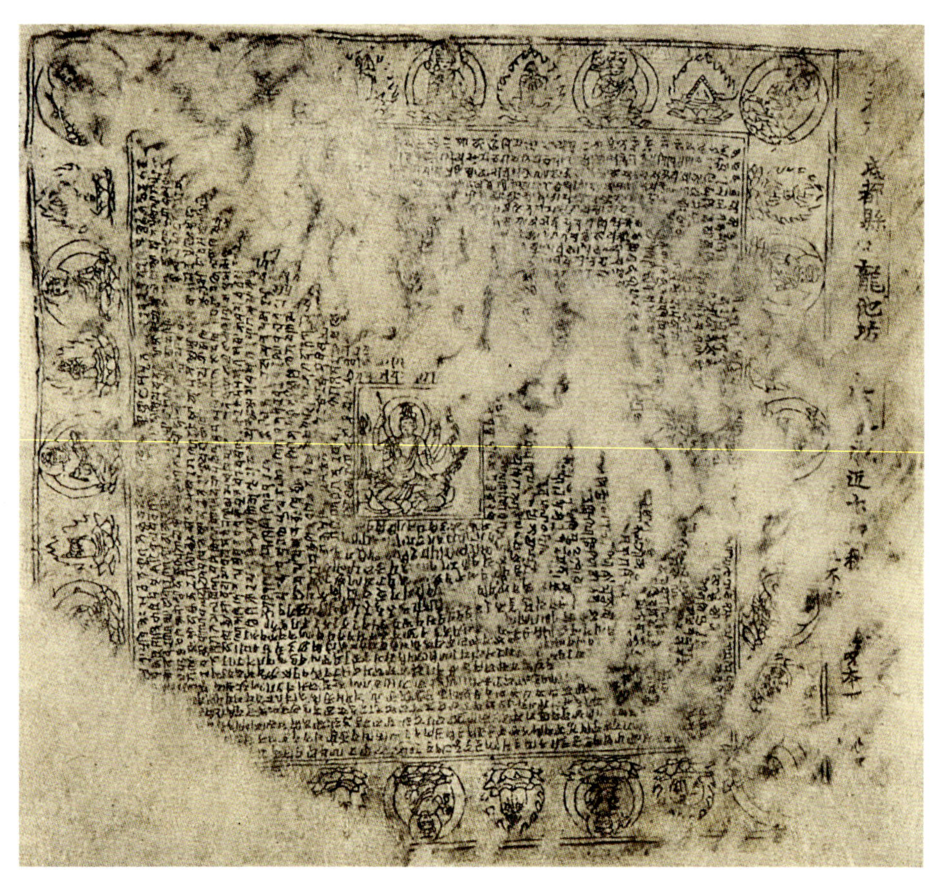

《无垢净光大陀罗尼经》

此印本1966年发现于韩国东南部的佛国寺，是目前已知最早的印刷品，印制于公元751年前。

Photograph of the Printed Book "Dharani of the Pure Immaculate Light"

This book was discovered in 1966 in the Bulguksa Temple in southeastern South Korea. It is the earliest known datable printed work and was produced before 751 CE, during the early Tang Dynasty.

《陀罗尼经咒》

唐晚期（公元9世纪）
长31、宽34cm
四川成都望江楼唐墓出土
中国国家博物馆藏

Printed Copy of the Dharani Sutra and Incantation

Late Tang Dynasty (9th century CE)
Length: 31cm, Width: 34cm
Excavated in the Wangjianglou Grave in Chengdu, Sichuan
Collection of the National Museum of China

印本由墓主手臂所带银镯内取出，纸薄呈透明状，文字刻工刀法遒劲。印本四边和中央是佛教人物图像，周围是17行梵文经文，组成圆环形。经卷的右边有一行汉字（残缺若干）“唐成都府成都县龙池坊卞家印卖咒本”，表明此经咒为印卖之物，是送葬亲属买来放在死者身上以消灾祈福的。这说明在8世纪末，中国已出现了私家经营的印书铺。

《陀罗尼经》

唐中期（公元8–9世纪）
长35、宽35cm
陕西西安冶金机械厂工地出土
西安博物院藏

A Printed Edition of the “Dharani Sutra” in Chinese Characters

Middle Tang Dynasty (8th–9th century CE)
Length: 35cm, Width: 35cm
Excavated at the site of a Metallurgy Machine Factory in Xi'an, Shaanxi
Collection of the Xi'an Museum

印本中间为佛像，四周为汉文咒语。这是国内现存较早的唐代汉文印本，其刊刻技术与印刷质量表现出唐代的雕版印刷术已相当成熟。

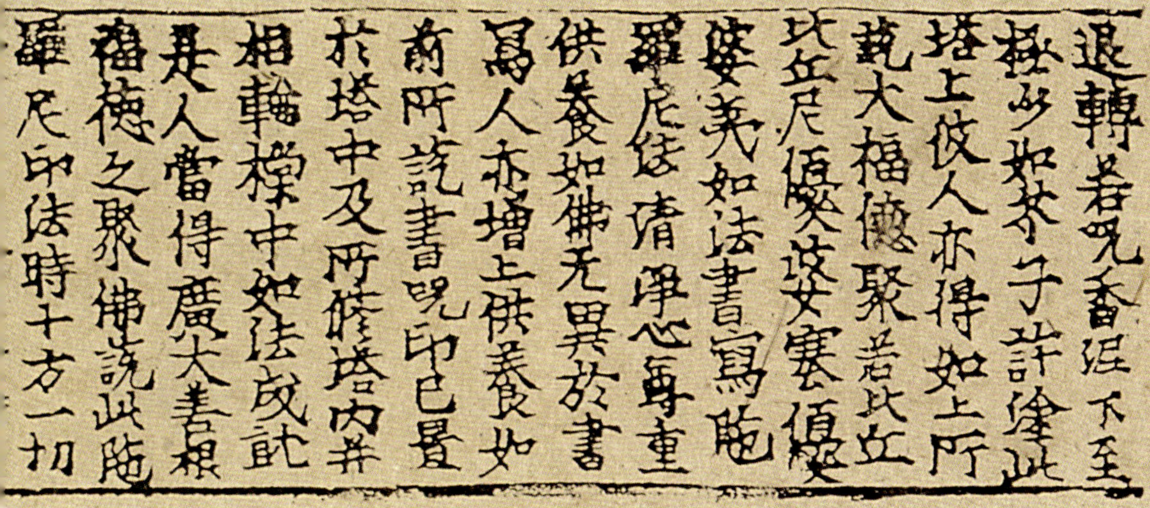
退轉若呪香泥下至
極少如芥子許塗此
塔上彼人亦得如上所
說大福德聚若比丘
比丘尼優婆塞優
婆夷如法書寫隨
羅尼法清淨心尊重
供養如佛无異於書
寫人亦增上供養如
前所說書呪印已置
於塔中及所旌塔內并
相輪橖中如法成就
是人當得廣大善根
福德之聚佛說此陁
羅尼印法時十方一切

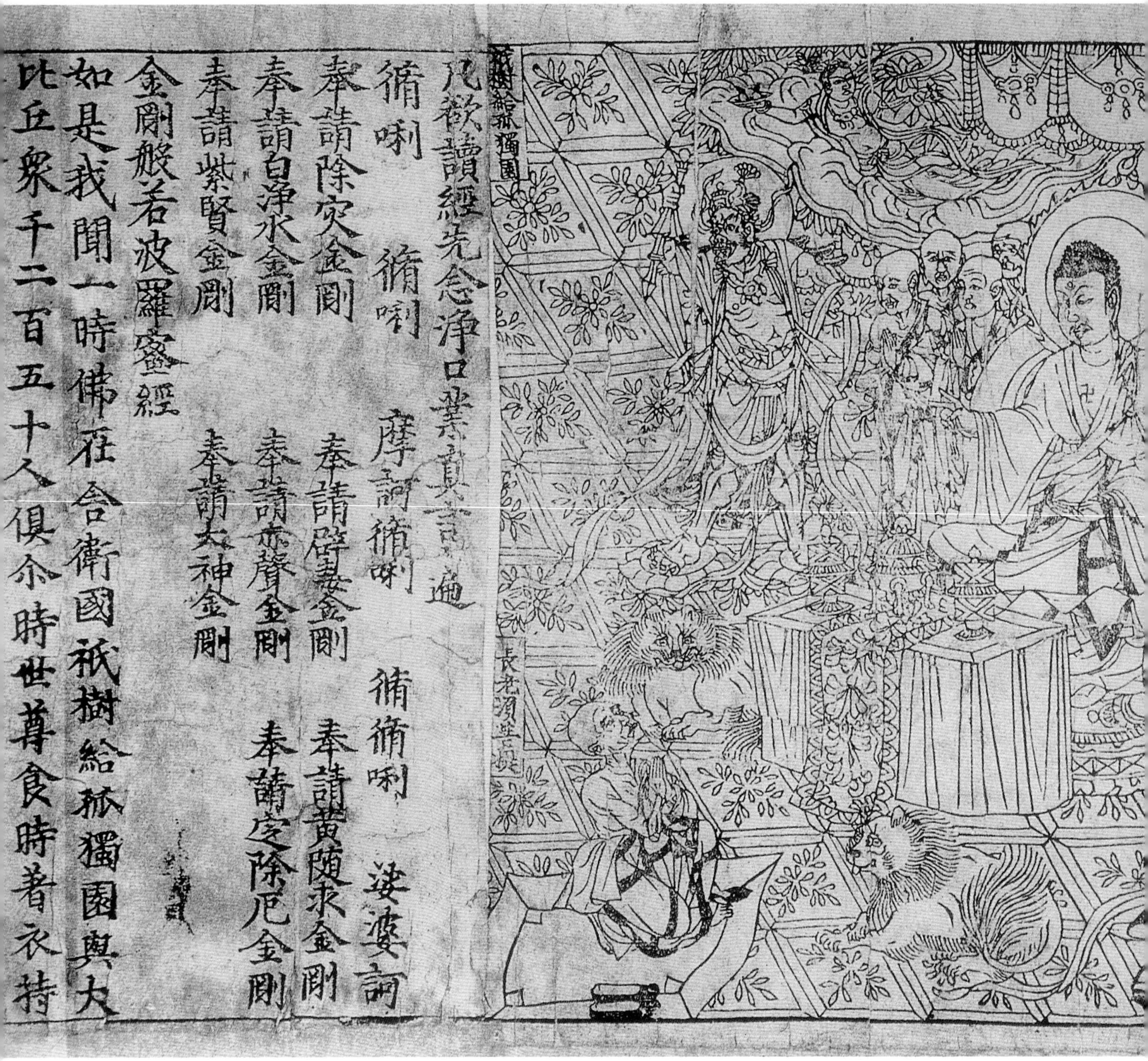

祇樹給孤獨園

長老須菩提

凡欲讀經先念淨口業真言一遍

脩唎 脩唎 摩訶脩唎 脩脩唎 娑婆訶

奉請除災金剛 奉請辟毒金剛 奉請黃隨求金剛

奉請白淨水金剛 奉請赤聲金剛 奉請定除厄金剛

奉請紫賢金剛 奉請大神金剛

金剛般若波羅蜜經

如是我聞一時佛在舍衛國祇樹給孤獨園與大

比丘衆千二百五十人俱尒時世尊食時著衣持

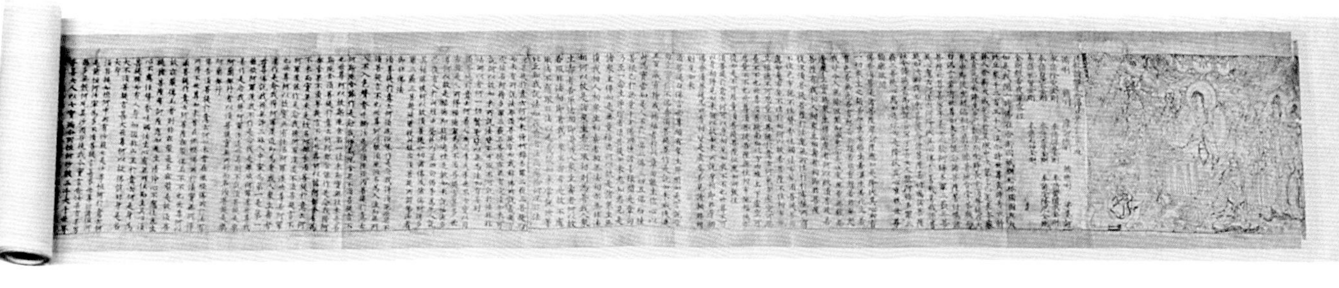

《金刚经》

唐咸通九年（公元868年）
甘肃敦煌藏经洞发现
英国伦敦博物馆藏

Printed Book the "Diamond Sutra"

9rd Year of Xiantong Reign, Tang Dynasty (868CE)
Discovered in Dunhuang, Gansu
Collection of the British Museum

此印本是现存卷轴形式印刷品中具有明确年代标志的最早印本，从扉页图画和经文字体看，唐代中后期我国的雕版印刷技术已很精湛。

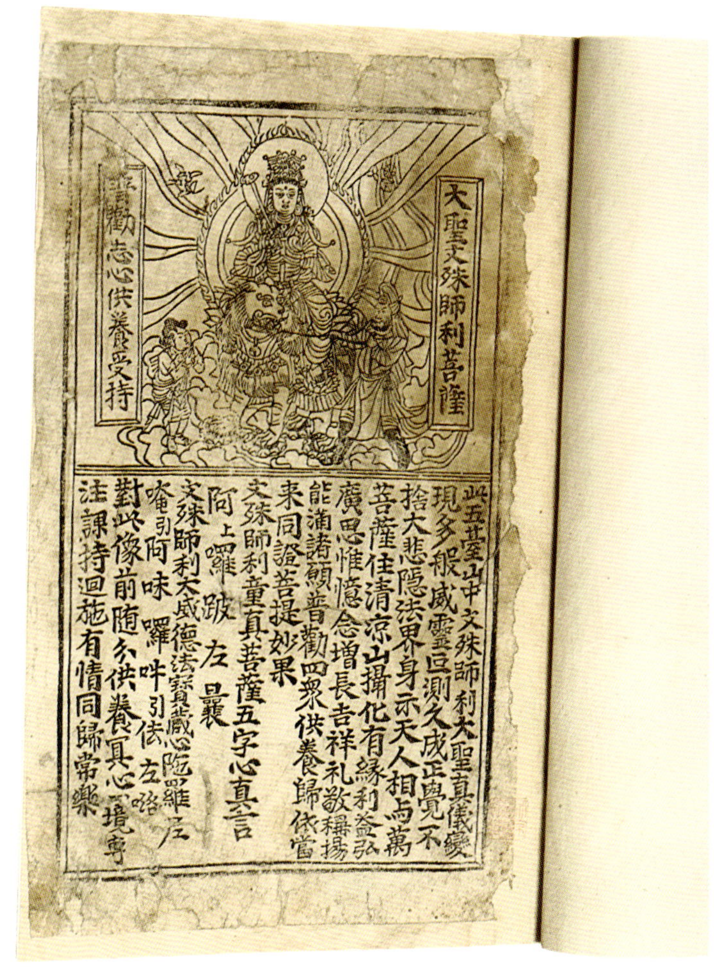

《文殊师利菩萨像》

五代（公元907–960年）
中国国家图书馆藏

Printed Copy of an Image of the Bodhisattva Manjushri

Five Dynasties (907–960 CE)
Collection of the National Library of China

此图刻画了文殊菩萨坐狮而行、普度众生的故事，图像构图严谨，刻工精湛。五代十国时期雕印了大量的佛教印刷品，许多是在一块印版上连续印制上万至十多万次，表明这一时期雕版的耐印程度很高，雕版的刻印技术已达较高水平。

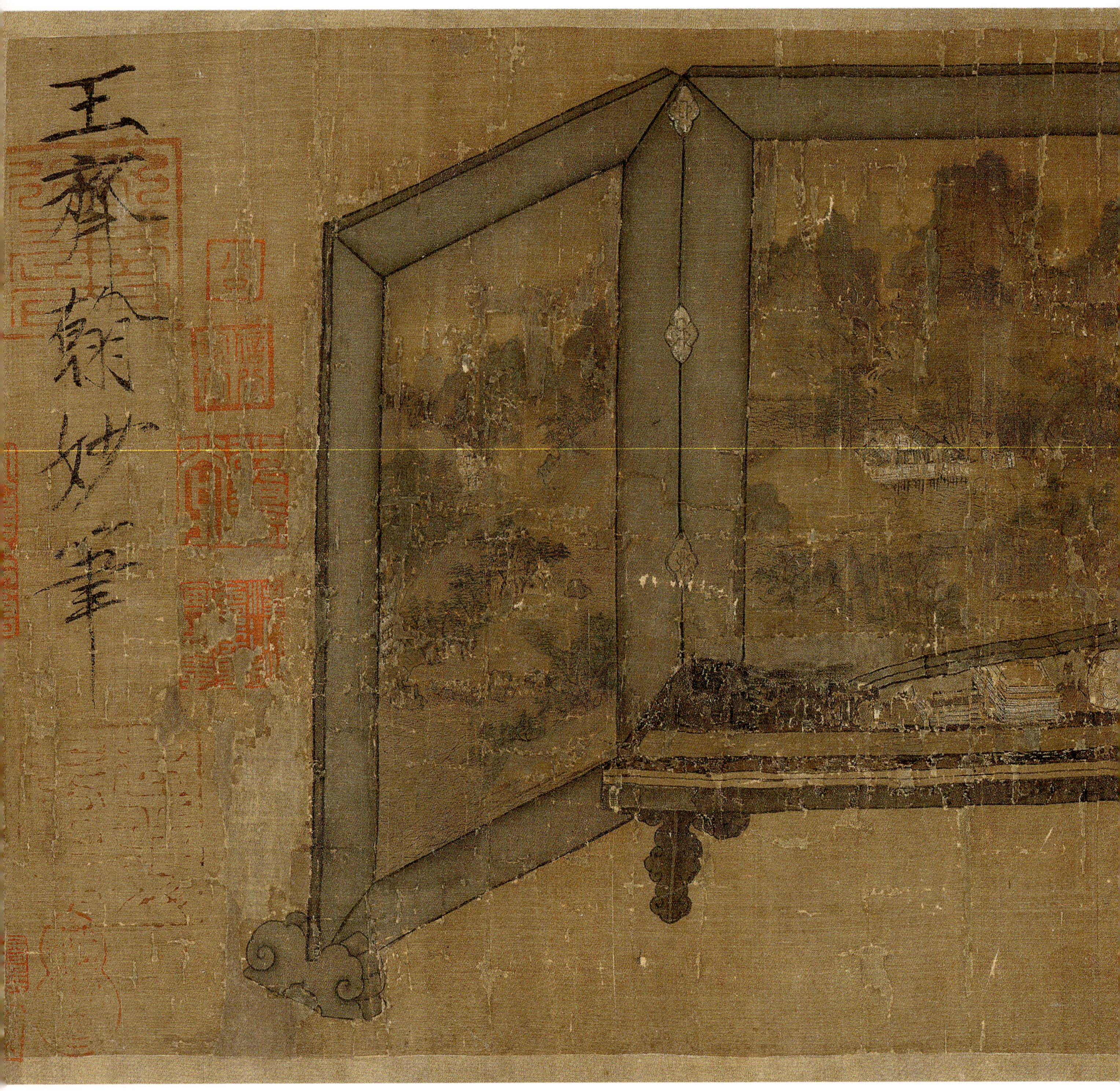

《勘书图》

南唐（公元937–975年）王齐翰
长284、宽65.7cm
南京大学藏

Scene of Collating Books

By Wang Qihan of Southern Tang Dynasty (937–975 CE)
Length: 284cm, Width: 65.7cm
Collection of Nanjing University

图中央为三叠屏风，屏风上绘着色山水，前置一长案。案上摆放小箱、书册等。右角有一书几，几上置卷册、笔砚。几后坐一长髯老者，似在校勘书籍间小憩。右上方有宋徽宗赵佶瘦金体书“勘书图”，左上方书“王齐翰妙笔”五字。

据史料记载，五代后唐长兴三年（公元932年）由政府出面雕印儒家经典，标志着唐代出现的雕版印刷术已为政府所采纳，书籍制作的主要方式开始由手写转为雕版印刷。

版印的记忆
Memories of Block Printing

两宋时期是中国雕版印刷技术的成熟期，所印书籍数量多且内容广泛，涉及到人类知识的各个领域。宋代雕版印刷已成为一门艺术，宋椠善本字体妍劲，纸墨优良，成为后世印工的楷模。

During the Northern and Southern Song Dynasties the woodblock print industry reached its peak. Books were printed that covered numerous topics and seemed to embrace all subjects readers would be interested in. Furthermore, printing techniques as well as paper and ink quality of the period were highly refined. Printed books and texts from the Song Dynasty are still looked on today as models of the technique.

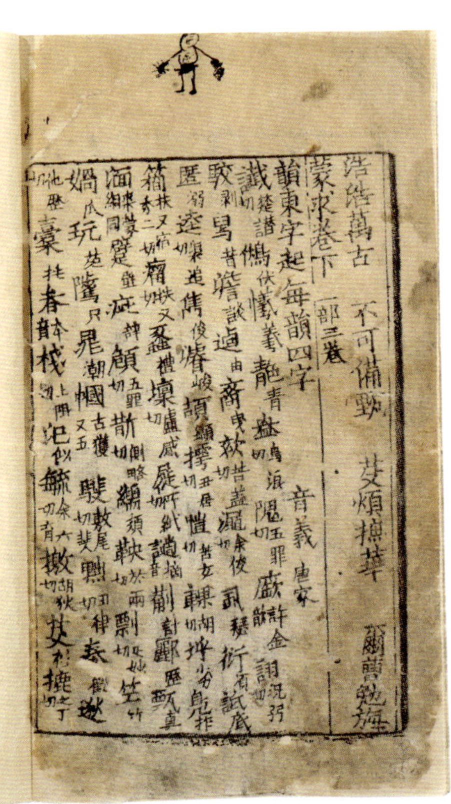

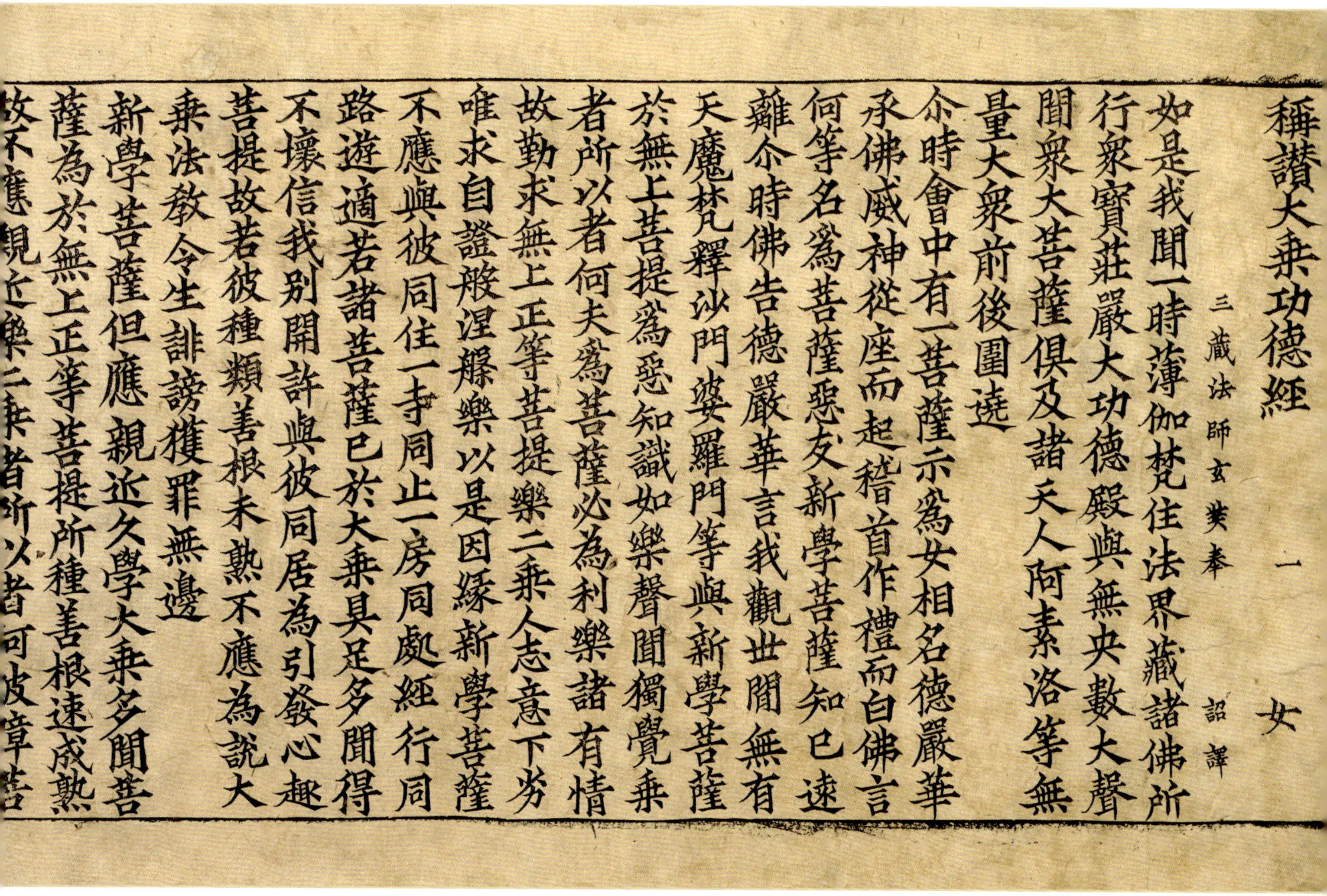

稱讚大乘功德經 一 女

三藏法師玄奘奉 詔譯

如是我聞一時薄伽梵住法界藏諸佛所
行衆寶莊嚴大功德殿與無央數大聲
聞衆大菩薩俱及諸天人阿素洛等無
量大衆前後圍遶
尒時會中有一菩薩示爲女相名德嚴華
承佛威神從座而起稽首作禮而白佛言
何等名爲菩薩惡友新學菩薩知已速
離尒時佛告德嚴華言我觀世間無有
天魔梵釋沙門婆羅門等與新學菩薩
於無上菩提爲惡知識如樂聲聞獨覺乘
者所以者何夫爲菩薩必爲利樂諸有情
故勤求無上正等菩提樂二乘人志意下劣
唯求自證般涅槃以是因緣新學菩薩
不應與彼同住一寺同止一房同處經行同
路遊適若諸菩薩已於大乘具足多聞得
不壞信我别開許與彼同居爲引發心趣
菩提故若彼種類善根未熟不應爲說大
乘法教令生誹謗獲罪無邊
新學菩薩但應親近久學大乘多聞菩
薩爲於無上正等菩提所種善根速成熟
故不應親近樂二乘者所以者何彼章菩

《蒙求》

辽（公元916–1125年）
长26、宽14.6cm
山西应县木塔发现
应县木塔文管所藏

Elementary Primer

Liao Dynasty (916–1125 CE)
Length: 26cm, Width: 14.6cm
Discovered in a Wooden Pagoda in Yingxian, Shanxi
Collection of the Wooden Pagoda Cultural Relic Bureau, Yingxian

此书辽代雕印儿童启蒙读物。《蒙求》是唐代李翰编撰的一本儿童教育的启蒙读物，它采用对偶押韵的句子来叙述历史典故。每句四字，上下两句成为对偶。这样的蒙书既可以帮助儿童识字，又可以学习典故知识。《蒙求》对以后的启蒙书籍具有极大的影响，《三字经》、《幼学琼林》中的许多内容都取材于李翰的《蒙求》。

《称赞大乘功德经》（部分）

辽（公元916–1125年）
长277、宽27.6cm
山西应县佛宫寺出土
山西博物院藏

Block Print Edition of "In Praise of Merits Mahayana Sutra"(Part)

Liao Dynasty (916–1125 CE)
Length: 277cm, Width: 27.6cm
Excavated from the Palace of Buddha Temple, Yingxian, Shanxi
Collection of the Shanxi Museum

辽刻《契丹藏》印本之一，以硬黄纸印制。版面为大字楷书，工整有力。《契丹藏》是据《开宝藏》翻刻的契丹版《大藏经》，刻印精美，表现了辽代发达的雕版印刷技术。

西夏文木雕版

西夏（公元1038－1227年）
长13.7－8.9、宽23.3－11、
厚2.3－2cm
宁夏回族自治区博物馆藏

Woodblock Printing Board with Tangut Script

Western Xia Dynasty (1038－1227CE)
Length: 13.7－8.9cm, Width: 23.3－11cm, Thickness:2.3－2cm
Collection of the Ningxia Hui Autonvmous Region Museum

西夏重视发展文化教育，专门设置了负责雕版印刷的官府机构“刻字司”。西夏的木雕版种类很多，版式不同，字体大小也有不同。

雕版印刷一般选用纹质细密坚实的木材作为原料（以梨木、枣木为佳），锯成一定大小的木板，然后刨平，把写好的文字或图像反贴在木板上，用刀刻出反写阳文（字画凸出板面），刷上墨，铺上纸，再用棕刷在纸上均匀刷印，揭下纸张，便成为正式的印刷品。

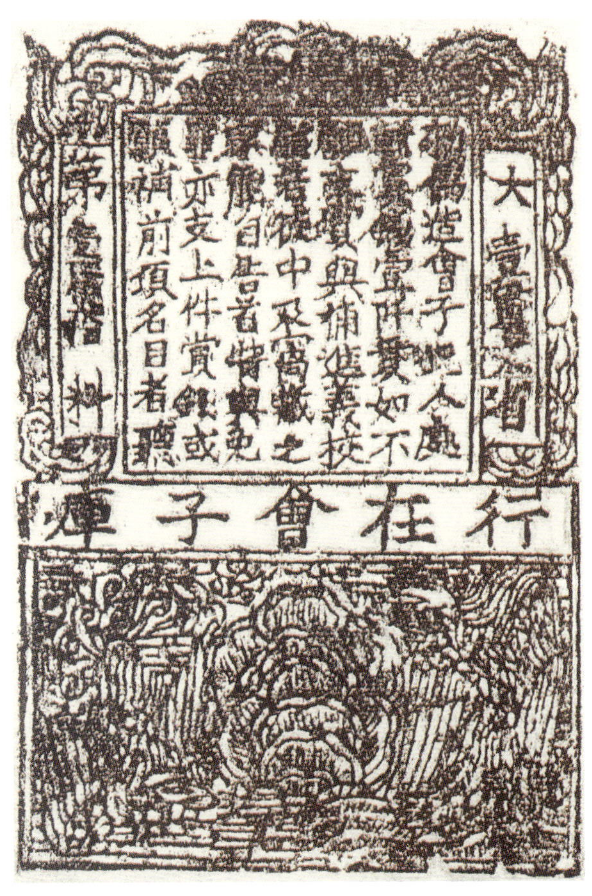

会子及铜版

南宋（公元1127－1279年）
长18.4、宽12.4cm
中国国家博物馆藏

Bronze Print Slat of Huizi Money

Southern Song Dynasty (1127－1279 CE)
Length: 18.4cm, Width: 12.4cm
Collection of the National Museum of China

这块铜版是印刷会子的印版。会子是南宋发行的主要货币之一，铜版上的文字包括发行机关的名称、面额等内容。“行在”指临安（今浙江省杭州市），“会子库”是政府主管会子的机构。南宋的纸币都用铜版印刷，说明铜版印刷在当时已经普遍流行。铜版印刷比木版印刷的技术要求更高，表明南宋的印刷技术已有很大改进。

“济南刘家功夫针铺”广告及铜版

南宋（公元1127－1279年）
长12.4、宽13.2cm
中国国家博物馆藏

Bronze Print Slat for an Advertisement for the Fine Needle Store of Jinan's Liu Family

Southern Song Dynasty(1127－1279 CE)
Lenght: 12.4cm, Width: 13.2cm
Collection of the National Museum of China

铜版为印刷广告之用。印版上方标明店铺字号“济南刘家功夫针铺”；正中有店铺标记——白兔捣药图，并注明“认门前白兔为记”，下方广告文辞称“收买上等钢条，造功夫细针。不误宅院使用，转卖兴贩，别有加饶，谓记白。”这是已知世界上最早的商标广告实物。随着宋代工商业的发展，竞争日趋激烈，不少店铺为了推销自家产品，除了装潢店面之外，还印制带有店铺标记的广告。

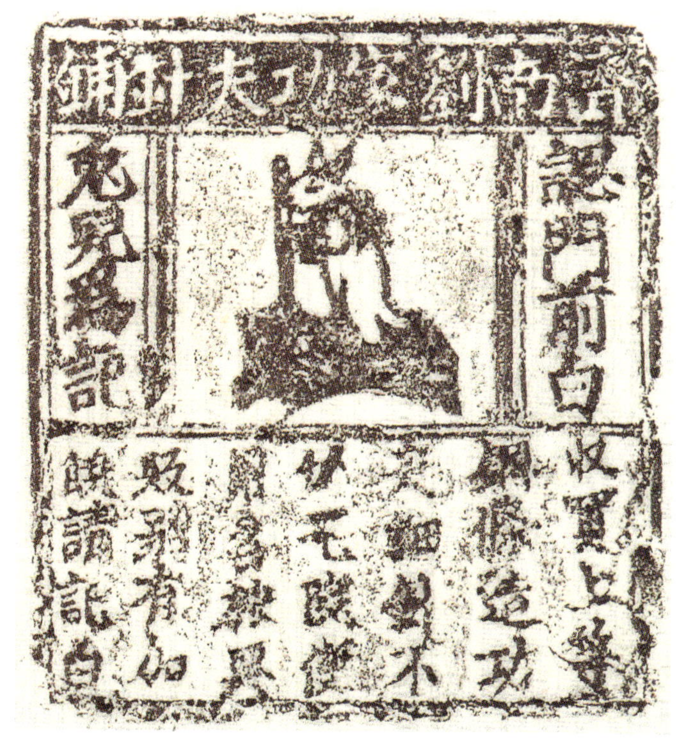

號武臣爲武信君下趙十餘城餘皆城守乃引兵
東北擊范陽范陽蒯徹說武信君曰足下必將戰
勝而后略地攻得然後下城臣竊以爲過矣誠聽
臣之計可不攻而降城不戰而略地傳檄而千里
定可乎武信君曰何謂也徹曰范陽令徐公畏死
而貪欲先天下降君若以爲秦所置吏誅殺如前
十城則邊地之城皆爲金城湯池不可攻也君若
齎臣侯印以授范陽令使乘朱輪華轂驅馳燕趙
之郊即燕趙城可毋戰而降矣武信君曰善以車
百乘騎二百侯印迎徐公燕趙聞之不戰以城下
者三十餘城陳王既遣周章以秦政之亂有輕秦

四六　通鑑紀事本末卷一　十四　李升

之意不復設備博士孔鮒諫曰臣聞兵灋不恃敵
之不我攻恃吾不可攻今王恃敵而不自恃若跌
而不振悔之無及也陳王曰寡人之軍先生無累
焉周文行收兵至關車千乘卒數十萬至戲軍焉
二世乃大驚與羣臣謀曰柰何少府章邯曰盜已
至衆彊今發近縣不及矣驪山徒多請赦之授兵
以擊之二世乃大赦天下使章邯免驪山徒人奴
産子悉發以擊楚軍大敗之周文走張耳陳餘至
邯鄲聞周章卻又聞諸將爲陳王徇地還者多以
讒毁得罪誅乃說武信君令自王八月武信君自
立爲趙王以陳餘爲大將軍張耳爲右丞相邵騷

《通鉴纪事本末》

南宋　袁枢（公元1131－1205年）
长41、宽27cm
中国国家博物馆藏

Tongjian Jishi Benmo (the Comprehensive Mirror for Aid in Government, Topically Arranged)

By Yuan Shu of the Southern Song Dynasty (1131－1205 CE)
Length: 41cm; Width: 27cm
Collection of National Museum of China

此书共42卷，是以《资治通鉴》为基本材料编纂的记事本末体史书。它不仅方便了读者阅读，还创立了以事件的因果为撰史脉络的新的史学编纂方法。

宋代是我国雕版印刷史上的黄金时代。这一时期的刻书机构设置包括官刻、私刻和民间刻印三大类型，内容涉及儒家经典、佛经、天文、历法等诸多方面。

《诗集传》

宋（公元960–1279年）
长44.6、宽31.8cm
中国国家博物馆藏

Collection of Commentaries of Poetry

Song Dynasty (960–1279 CE)
Lenght: 44.6cm, Width: 31.8cm
Collection of the National Museum of China

《诗集传》是宋代理学家朱熹研究《诗经》的一部重要著作。此刊本字体整齐，纸墨如新。宋版书刊刻艺术精湛，其字体亦是后世印刷字体的起源。

曰大哉天命善不可不傳于後嗣是以
富貴無常蓋傷微子之事周而痛殷之
亡也○無念爾祖聿于筆反脩厥德永言配
命自求多福叶筆力反殷之未喪息浪反師克
配上帝宜鑒于殷駿音峻命不易以鼓反○賦也
聿發語辭永長配合也命天理也師衆也上帝天之主宰也駿大也不易言其難也○言欲念爾祖在於自脩其德而又常自省察使其所行無不合於天理則盛大之福自我致之有不外求而得矣又言殷未失天下之時其德足以配

大文十六 三八十九 詩集傳卷十六 四 游熙

乎上帝矣今其子孫乃如此宜以爲鑒而自省焉則知天命之難保矣大學傳曰得衆則得國失衆則失國此之謂也○命之不易無遏
爾躬叶姑弘反宣昭義問有虞殷自天叶鐵因反
上天之載無聲無臭叶初尤反儀刑文王萬
邦作孚叶房尤反○賦也遏絕宣布昭明義善也問聞通有又通虞度載事儀象刑法孚信也○言天命之不易保故告之使無若紂之自絕于天而布明其善譽於天下又度殷之所以廢興者而折之於天然上天之事無聲無

印刷术：活字与彩印

Printing Techniques: Movable Type and Color Printing

印刷术的发明促进了造纸术的进一步发展，宋元时期是造纸技术发展的成熟期，造纸的原料较以前有了更广的扩充，生产设备有所改进，加工技法也不断创新，制造出为后世所称道的各种名纸。明清两代是造纸技术的总结阶段，不仅出现了许多论述纸张制造与加工技术的著作，还生产出许多加工精美的书画专用纸。

为了适应各种需求，印版材料、印刷技术和印刷工艺不断创新发展。在雕版印刷术出现以后，公元11世纪北宋毕昇发明了泥活字印刷术，宋元时期出现的套色印刷技术日渐成熟，明清时期的套色印刷与版画艺术完美结合，印刷术发展到了辉煌的阶段。

During the Song to Yuan Dynasties, traditional papermaking techniques had fully matured. Many more materials were used in the production process than in earlier periods, manufacturing equipment had seen improvements in all aspects, new innovations were introduced to the assembly process, and paper produced in this period was universally marveled at by later generations.

During the Ming and Qing periods (1368 - 1911CE) the process of papermaking entered into the final stages of its traditional development. The amount and quality of paper produced during these two dynasties surpassed all previous periods. In addition, the topic of the techniques and production processes of papermaking became a subject discussed by many commentators. The two most important factors in the success of the papermaking and printing industries in this period were the widespread use of paper in the realm of painting and the development of printing techniques by China's many minority groups.

After the Song Dynasty (960 - 1279CE), official, private, and popular carving enterprises flourished. To a great extent these techniques of woodblock printing were directed towards the goal of spreading civilization across the country. As the general range of printing activities increased, the variety of texts and images printed spread to reach every subject matter of human inquiry. Furthermore, with the invention of multi-color printing processes, printed texts took on a new brilliance.

云衣素魄

Simple Souls Wear Clothes of Clouds

宋代竹纸与稻麦秆纸的发展标志着造纸技术新纪元的到来，从使用木本植物的韧皮纤维造纸发展到使用整个植物茎杆造纸，造纸原料更加廉价易得。纸的加工技术亦不断发展进步，澄心堂纸、金粟山藏经纸、宣德纸、梅花玉版笺等，均是外观精美、性能优良且具艺术价值的名纸。

"草木轻身心自远，云衣素魄志偏长"，以草木为源的轻柔纸张，成为传播文明的重要载体。

After the flourishing middle period of the Tang Dynasty, bamboo was introduced as a papermaking material. The Song Dynasty saw the development of this material in the production process and at the same time the stalks of wheat and rice crops were used as raw materials. Manufacturers also acknowledged that fibers used in spinning and weaving could be applied to the making of paper. The expansion of papermaking with bamboo, rice and wheat plants attested to the unceasingly pace of innovation seen within the trade. Chengxin Tang paper and Buddhist sutra paper of the Song Dynasty, along with Ming Dynasty Xuande paper and Qing Dynasty Xuan paper, all became popular due to the continual advancement seen within the field of papermaking. During this long period from the 10th - 19th century, the craft of producing decorative paper in brilliant hues was developed and added to the general advancements with the field.

There is a Chinese phrase "grass makes burdens evaporate and brings the heart back from afar, in clothes of clouds simple souls have ambitions that are inclined to last" - paper made from grass was thought to not only have a certain gentle quality but also to bear the weighty burden of transmitting Chinese culture to future generations.

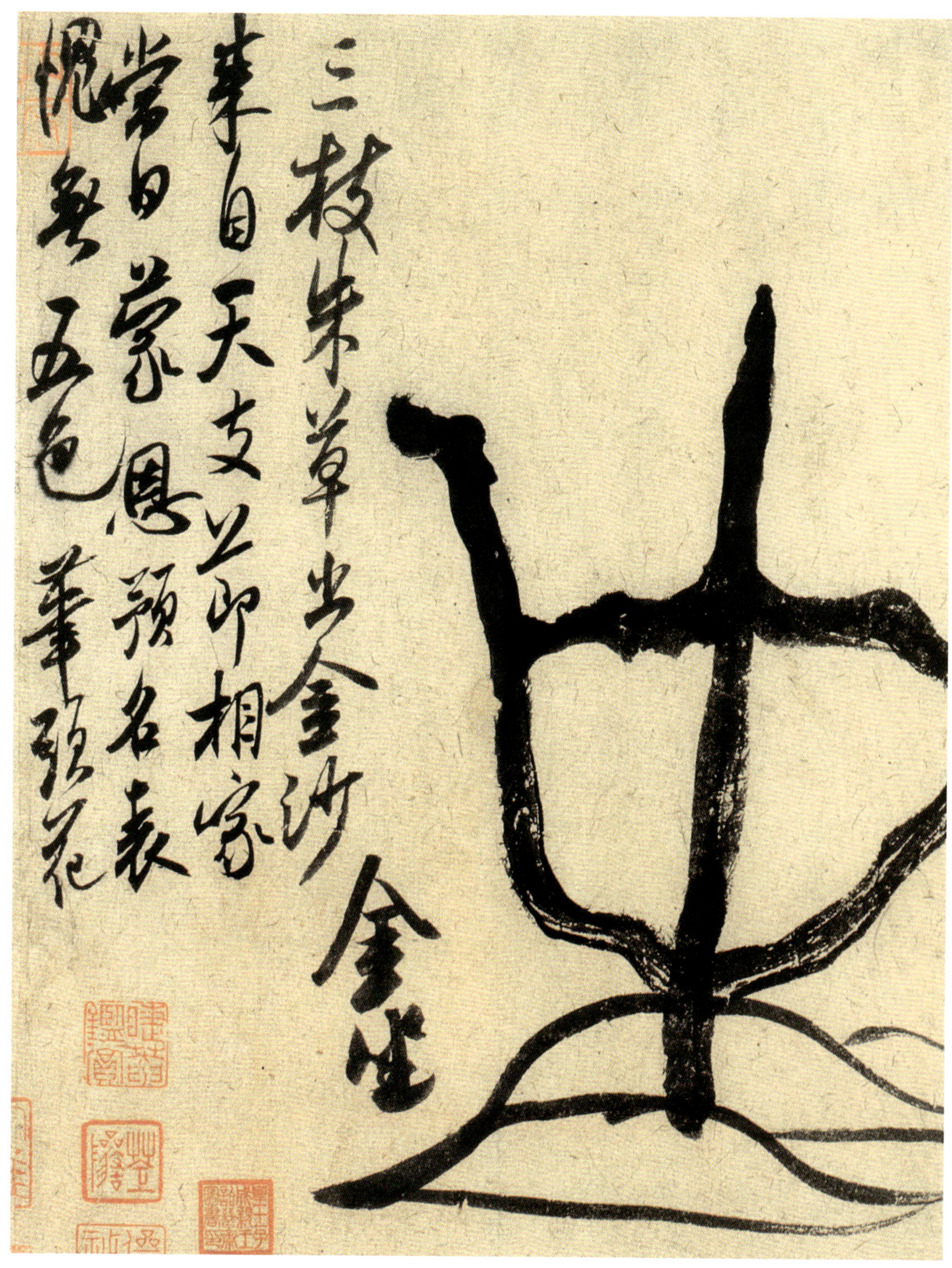

《珊瑚帖》

北宋 米芾（公元1051–1107年）
故宫博物院藏

Notes on Coral

By Mi Fu of the Northern Song Dynasty (1051–1107 CE)
Collection of the Palace Museum

此帖写于竹纸之上，纸面平滑，呈浅黄色。

竹纸是将竹子的整个茎杆加工后制成的纸，是造纸术的又一发明。竹纸在唐代已有，至宋代时广泛使用。宋代竹纸用本色原料，尚无漂白工序，因此呈浅黄色，人称“金版纸”。宋代初期所造竹纸纸质脆弱，不堪折叠，而将竹料与树皮、麻料等其他浆料按一定比例掺入，生产出的竹纸兼顾了各种纸的成本和性能，是造纸技术的又一大进步。

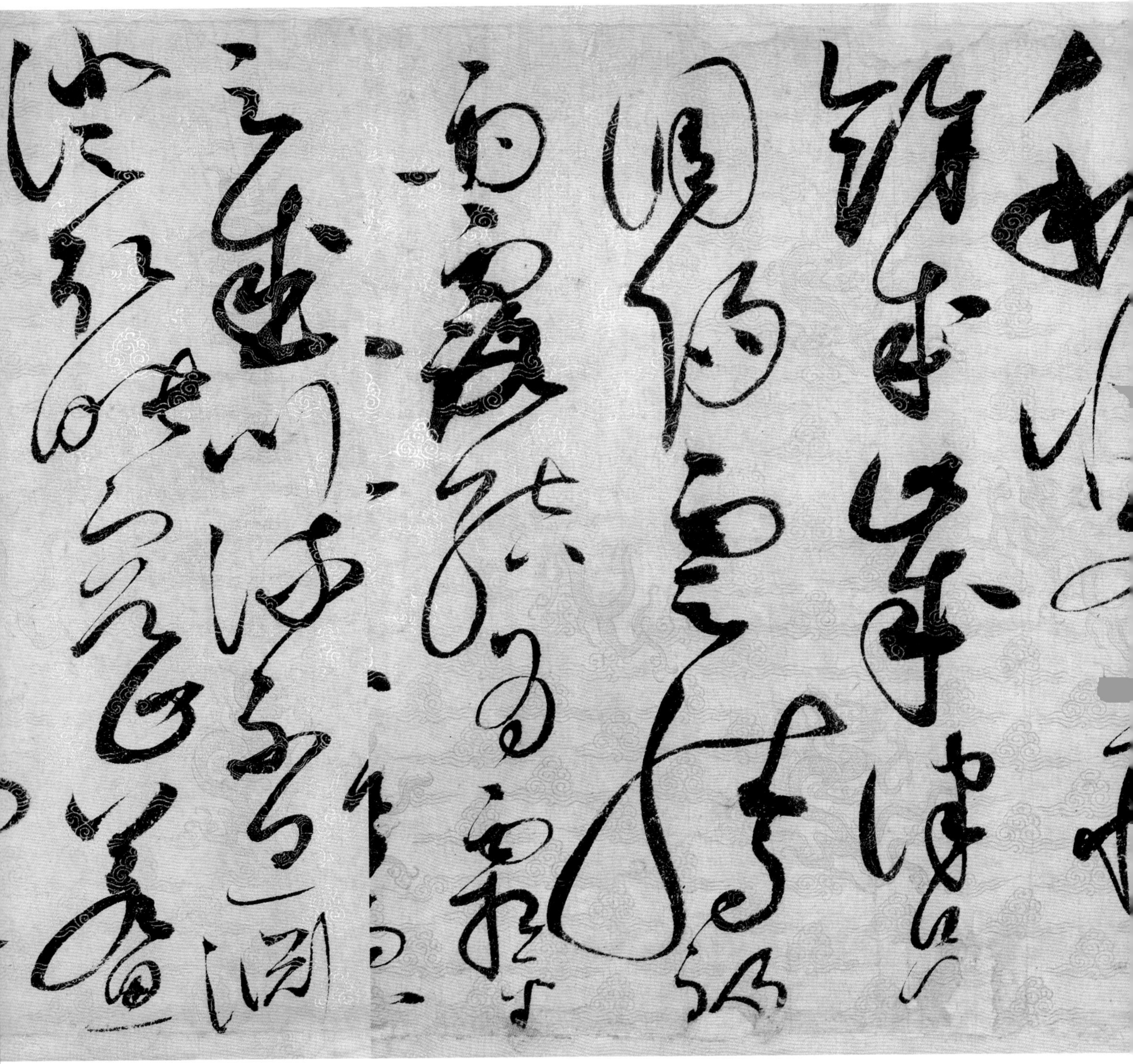

《千字文》（部分）

北宋 赵佶（公元1082–1135年）
长1172、宽31.5cm
辽宁省博物馆藏

"Essay of a Thousand Characters" in Grass Style Script (Part)

By Huizong Emperor of the Northern Song Dynasty (1082–1135 CE)
Lenght: 1172cm, Width: 31.5cm
Collection of the Liaoning Provincial Museum

纸面为泥金云龙纹图案，上有北宋徽宗赵佶草书《千字文》。这是现存抄幅最长的纸，表明宋代已能抄造大幅纸。制造巨幅纸不仅要求有特殊的造纸设备如较长的竹帘、大型纸槽和许多熏笼等，而且要求有精湛的操作技巧。西方各国在公元19世纪机制纸出现以前，未曾掌握大尺寸纸张的制作技术。

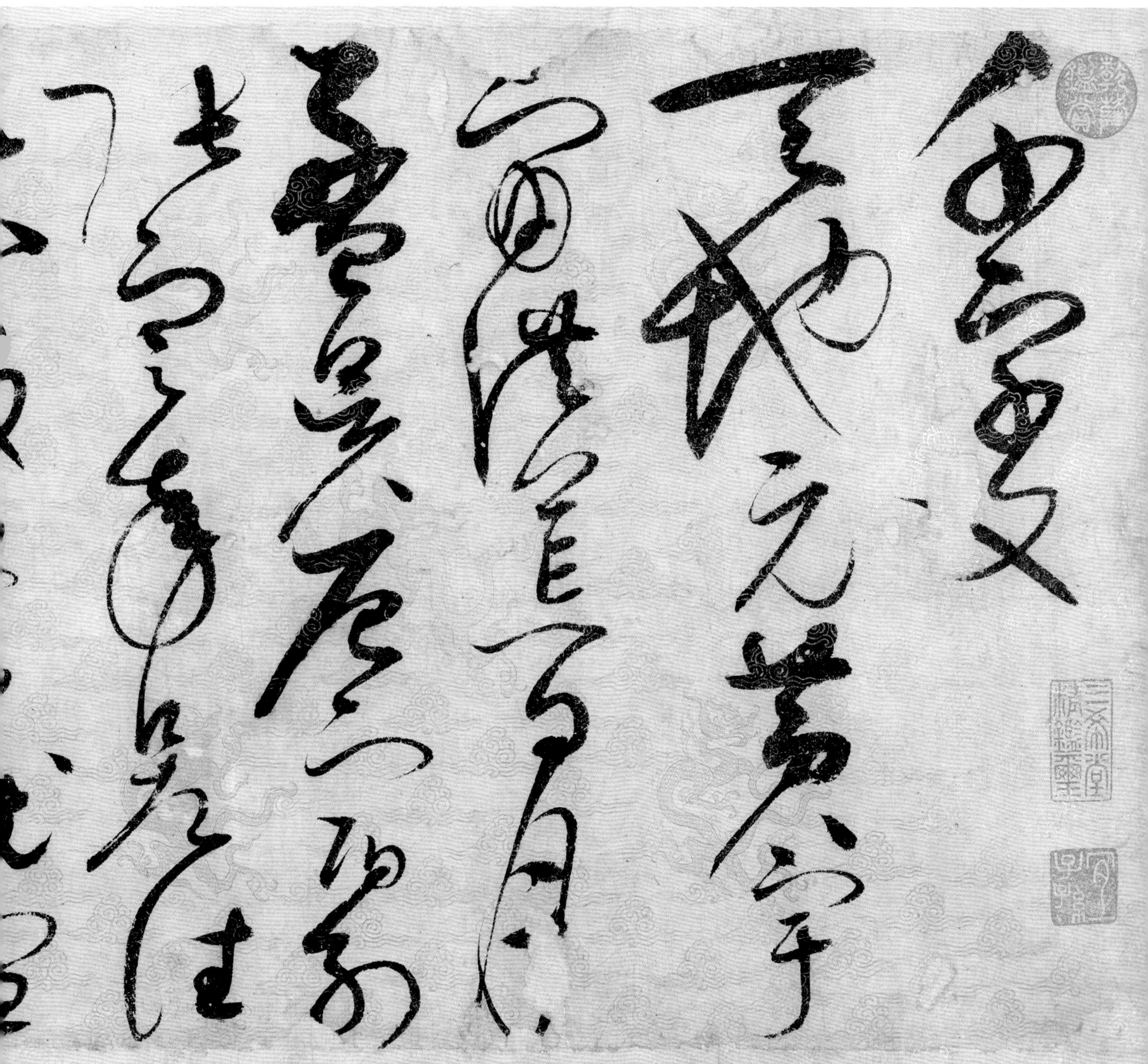

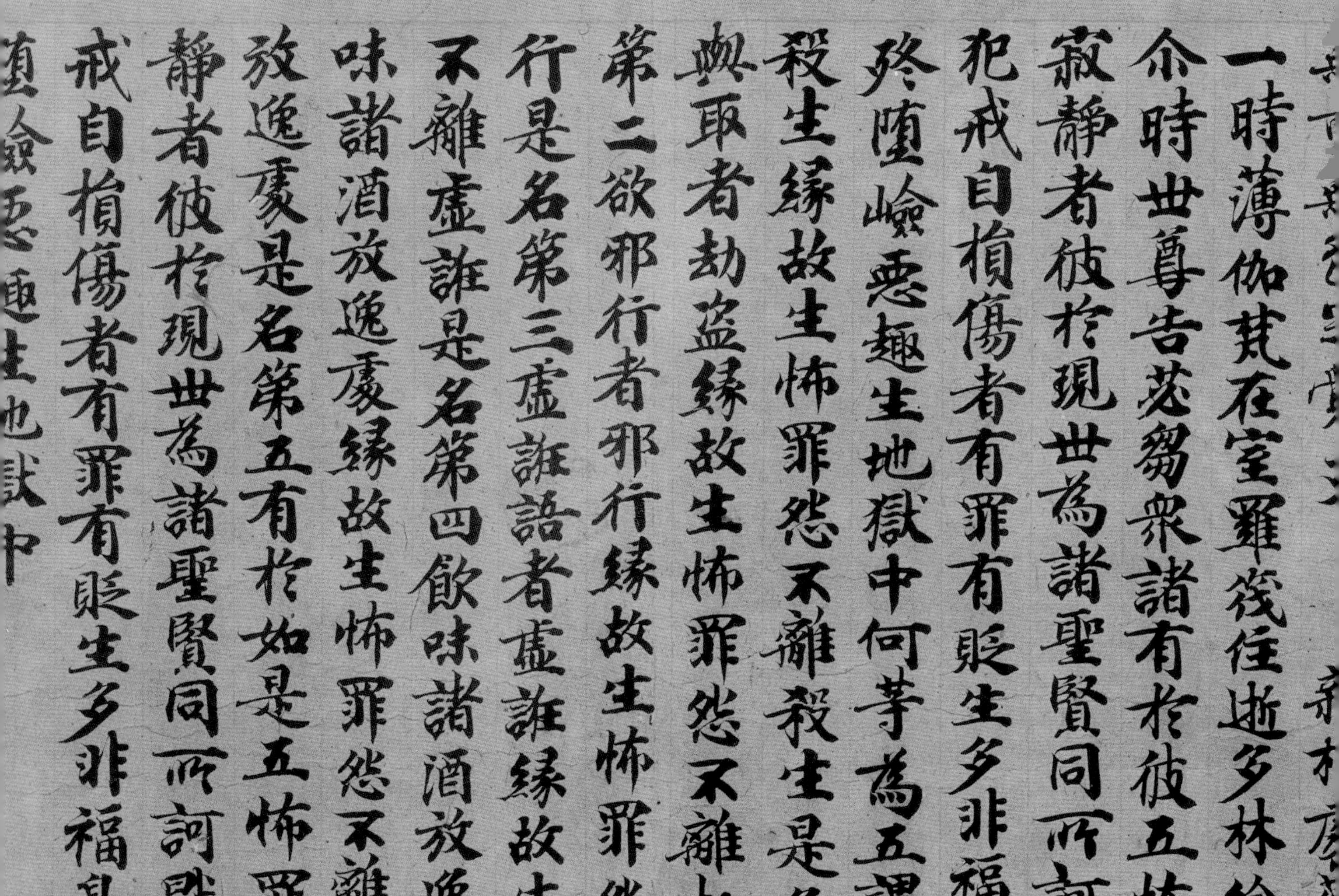

一時薄伽梵在室羅筏住逝多林給孤獨園
尒時世尊告苾芻衆諸有於彼五怖罪怨不
寂靜者彼於現世爲諸聖賢同所訶猒名爲
犯戒自損傷者有罪有愆生多非福身壞命
終墮嶮惡趣生地獄中何等爲五謂殺生者
殺生緣故生怖罪怨不離殺生是名第一不
與取者劫盜緣故生怖罪怨不離劫盜是名
第二欲邪行者邪行緣故生怖罪怨不離邪
行是名第三虛誑語者虛誑緣故生怖罪怨
不離虛誑是名第四飲諸酒放逸處者飲
味諸酒放逸處緣故生怖罪怨不離飲酒諸
放逸處是名第五有於如是五怖罪怨不寂
靜者彼於現世爲諸聖賢同所訶猒名爲犯
戒自損傷者有罪有愆生多非福身壞命終
墮嶮惡趣生地獄中

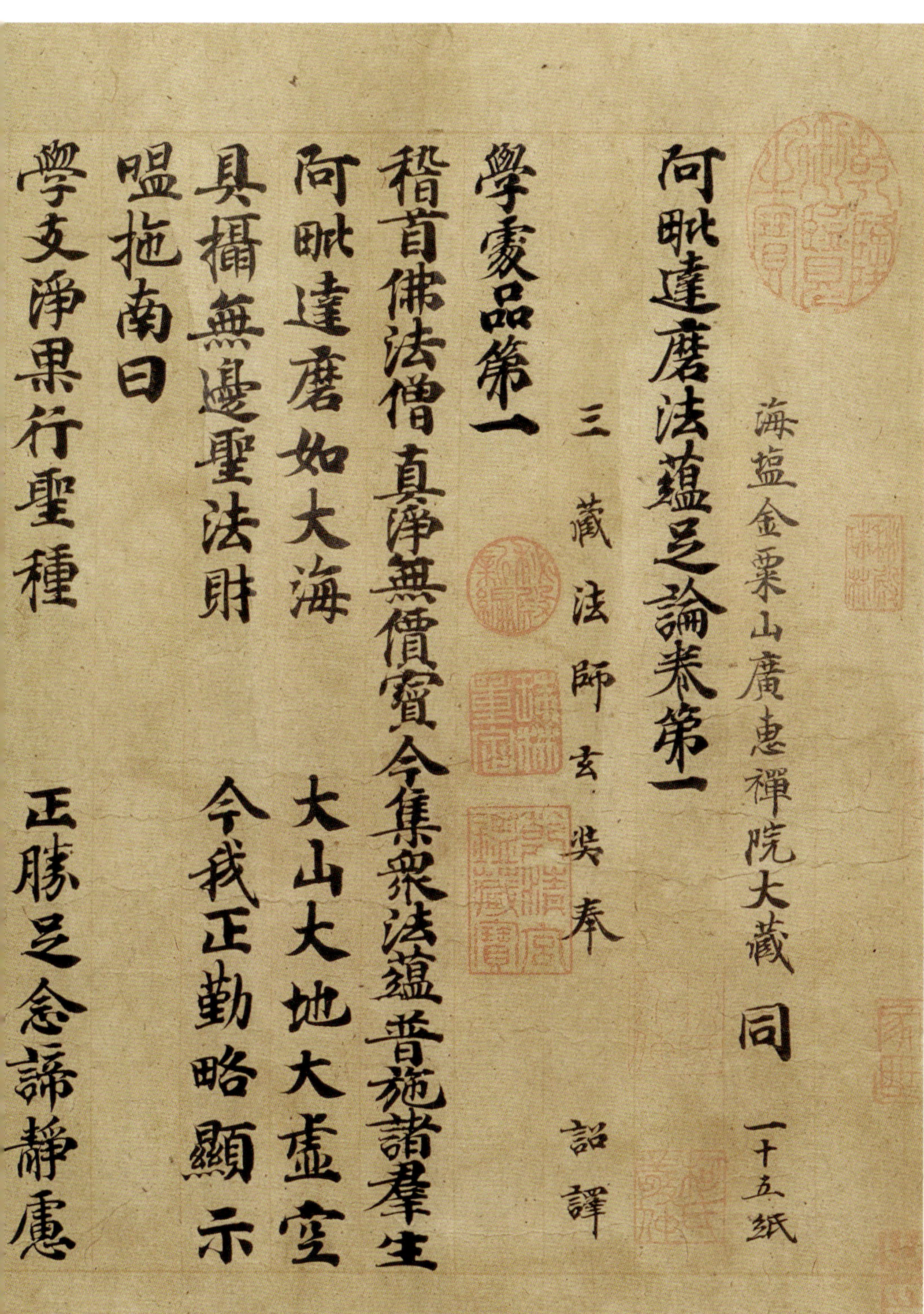

海塩金粟山廣惠禪院大藏　同　一十五紙

阿毗達磨法蘊足論卷第一

三藏法師玄奘奉　詔譯

學處品第一

稽首佛法僧真淨無價寶今集衆法蘊普施諸羣生

阿毗達磨如大海　大山大地大虛空

具攝無邊聖法財　今我正勤略顯示

嗢拖南曰

學支淨果行聖種　正勝足念諦靜慮

《阿毗达摩法蕴足论卷第一》(部分)

宋（公元960–1279年）

长857.7、宽27.8cm（每纸长60cm）

安徽省博物馆藏

The Scroll of Abhidharma-dharmaskandha pāda śāstra in Jinsu Mountain Tri-pitaka Collection (Part)

Song Dynasty (960–1297 CE)

Length: 857.7cm, Width: 27.8 cm (each sheet: 60cm in width)

Collection of the Anhui Provincial Museum

经卷用纸为皮纸，呈黄色，表面平滑具有光泽，无水线痕迹，每张纸上都印有“金粟山藏经纸”的红印。

金粟山藏经纸为宋代名纸。金粟山位于今浙江省海盐县，山下的金粟寺始建于吴赤乌年间（公元238–251年），北宋时期该寺抄写的经文被称为《金粟山藏经》，所用纸称为“金粟山藏经纸”。金粟山藏经纸大多为桑皮纸，也有麻纸，呈黄色或淡黄色。它继承了唐代硬黄纸加工技术，采用了染黄、施蜡和研光等加工工艺。金粟山藏经纸制作精细，书写效果上乘，虽历经千年沧桑，纸面仍黄艳硬韧，墨色黝泽如初。

至元通行宝钞

元（公元1271－1368年）
长31、宽21.8cm
西藏萨迦寺内发现
中国国家博物馆藏

Zhiyuan Paper Money

Yuan Dynasty (1271−1368 CE)
Length: 31cm, Width: 21.8cm
Discovered inside the Sakya Temple, Tibet
Collection of the National Museum of China

“至元通行宝钞”是元代通行的一种纸币，用北方桑皮纸印制而成。造币用纸对纸的质量要求很高，桑皮纸纸币的流通，反映了当时造纸的水平。

自宋代开始，书籍大量印刷，对纸张的需求量逐渐增多，而用麻造纸已难于满足社会的需求，所以人们都就地取材，桑树皮、楮树皮和竹逐渐成为主要的造纸原料。宋以后的书籍多使用皮纸和竹纸印刷。

《制纸图》（采自《天工开物》）

明（公元1368－1644年）
中国国家博物馆藏

Images from Tian Gong Kai Wu (Exploitation of the Works of Nature)

Ming Dynasty (1368−1644 CE)
Collection of the National Museum of China

《天工开物》是明代著名科学家宋应星编写的一部科学著作。该书第十三卷“杀青”篇中专门论述了造纸工序，这是历史上关于造纸工艺最重要的文献记录。近年江西高安华林发掘的明代造纸作坊遗迹再现了“造竹纸”的“新竹漂塘”瘸“煮楻足火”的情景。

康熙写字像

清(公元1644−1911年)
长50.7、宽32cm
故宫博物院藏

Painting of the Kangxi Emperor Writing

Qing Dynasty (1644 − 1911 CE)
Length: 50.7 cm, Width: 32 cm
Collection of the Palace Museum

康熙帝正伏案提笔，凝神静思。

虎皮宣纸

清（公元1644-1911年）
长208、宽103.6cm
故宫博物院藏

Xuan Paper with a Tiger Skin Pattern

Qing Dynasty (1644-1911)
Length: 208cm, Width: 103.6cm
Collection of the Palace Museum

虎皮宣纸是清代所特有的一种加工宣纸，因纸面有浅灰、浅绿、粉红、鹅黄、天蓝等状如虎皮的各色斑点而得名。该纸选取优质生宣，经过上矾、施胶后，再染以深浅不一、浓淡各异的颜色。

宣纸因最早产于宣州（今属安徽省）而得名。它以檀树皮和禾杆混合而成，纸质洁白、柔软，不易虫蛀，易于书写和保存。宣纸生产继承了以五代澄心堂纸为代表的皮纸制造技术，又融汇了明代宣德纸的先进工艺，其技术至明代中晚期日臻完善，成为中国皮纸的杰出代表。

宫黄地印花古钱纹蜡笺

清（公元1644-1911年）
长300、宽73cm
中国国家博物馆藏

Imperially Printed Paper with the Design of Ancient Coins

Qing Dynasty (1644-1911 CE)
Length: 300cm, Width: 73cm
Collection of the National Museum of China

纸面采用了染色、施蜡、印花等加工方法制作而成。其图案是应用印刷的方法将古钱纹印在素纸上，使其成为纸的底纹。印花是将印刷技术应用到纸的加工领域，以印花装饰纸可以达到普通染色无法达到的效果。施蜡法的应用始于唐代，在纸面上涂蜡不仅提高了纸的透明度，而且还可使纸面光滑并具有防水性。

粉白地双龙戏珠暗花纹宣纸

清（公元1644–1911年）
长133.5、宽64cm
中国国家博物馆藏

Xuan Paper Decorated with Pink and White Double Dragons Playing with Pearls

Qing Dynasty (1644–1911 CE)
Length: 133.5cm, Width: 64cm
Collection of the National Museum of China

这种带暗花的宣纸使用了“透光笺”的制作方法。先在宣纸上刻出图案，再将这张雕出图案的纸的两面各裱一层单宣纸。制成的纸迎光看去可显现出明显的图案，使纸张具有内在的美感。

斗方纸

清（公元1644–1911年）
纸长宽56.5×56.5cm，漆盒高9.8、长宽59.5×59.5cm
中国国家博物馆藏

Dou Fang Paper

Qing Dynasty (1644–1911 CE)
Each sheet is 56.5 square cm, The lacquer box is 9.8cm high, 59.5 square cm
Collection of the National Museum of China

纸呈红色，上面用泥金银粉绘制云龙纹，盛于漆盒内。

我国古代加工纸吸取了漆器和丝织品的装饰技术，发明了将金、银洒于纸上进行装饰的技术。

云母发笺

清（公元1644–1911年）
长88.5、宽62.5cm
中国国家博物馆藏

"Hair Paper" Made with Mica Fibers Mixed

Qing Dynasty (1644–1911 CE)
Length: 88.5cm, Width: 62.5cm
Collection of the National Museum of China

发笺是公元4世纪出现的一种具有独特风格的艺术加工纸。其方法是在抄造前先在纸浆中放入少量有色的纤维状物质，如绿色的水苔或黑色的发菜，打槽抄纸后，这些有色纤维纵横交织在纸面上，增加了美感。这张发笺上有闪亮斑点，是在纸浆中添加了云母，故名“云母发笺”。

绿色描金折枝花纹纸

清(公元1644—1911年)
长96、宽93.7cm
故宫博物院藏

Green Paper Sheet with Gilt Plucked Flower Pattern

Qing Dynasty (1644–1911 CE)
Length: 96cm, Width: 93.7cm
Collection of the Palace Museum

此纸两面均有装饰，一面有描金银花卉纹，另一面洒金。两面均可书写、绘画。

珊瑚色洒金粉蜡笺

清(公元1644—1911年)
长175.5、宽95.3cm
故宫博物院藏

Waxed Coral-red Paper Sheet Decorated with Golden Dots

Qing Dynasty (1644 – 1911 CE)
Length: 175.5cm; Width: 95.3cm
Collection of the Palace Museum

此笺色彩明艳华丽，两面皆洒金箔。粉蜡笺在清代康熙、乾隆年间大量制作，不仅使用单面或双面施蜡研光加工技术，还有应用了描金银、洒金、泥金等装饰方法。

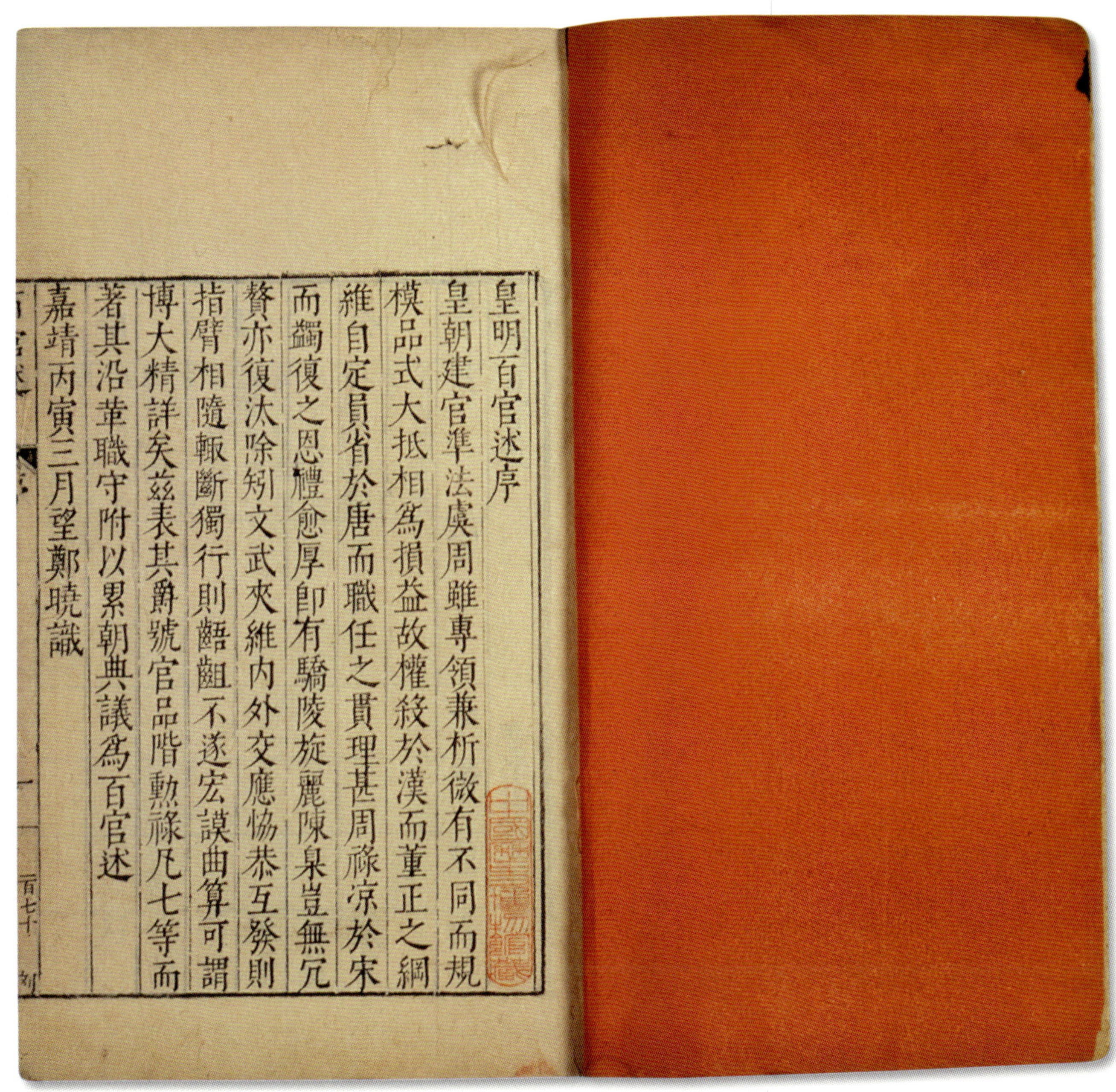

皇明百官述序

皇朝建官準法虞周雖專領兼析微有不同而規模品式大抵相爲損益故權敍於漢而董正之綱維自定員省於唐而職任之貫理甚周祿凉於宋而蠲復之恩禮愈厚卽有驕陵旋麗陳臬豈無冗贅亦復汰除矧文武夾維內外交應恊恭互發則指臂相隨輙斷獨行則齬齟不遂宏謨曲算可謂博大精詳矣茲表其爵號官品階勳祿凡七等而著其沿革職守附以累朝典議爲百官述

嘉靖丙寅三月望鄭曉識

防蛀纸扉页

清（公元1644−1911年）
长24.5、宽16cm
中国国家博物馆藏

A Title Page on a Piece of Paper Treated Against Insect Damage

Qing Dynasty (1644−1911 CE)
Length: 24.5cm, Width: 16cm
Collection of the National Museum of China

此书前后的橘红色插页表面涂有一层铅丹，有杀虫驱虫作用，这种纸亦称万年红。汉魏时期已使用黄蘗汁染纸，黄蘗汁能将纸染成黄色，既改善纸的性能，增加纸的美观度，还能起到防虫蛀的作用。宋代的印刷用纸中多添加椒汁以防虫。明清时广州一带的竹纸刊本书，首尾各附有一张万年红纸防虫蛀。

毕昇像

毕昇是泥活字印刷术的发明者，他在宋仁宗庆历（公元1041–1048年）年间，发明了用胶泥制字模，用火煅烧后排版印书的印刷方法。泥活字印刷术发明后，迅速传播到中东和近东，欧洲人因之发明了拉丁文字的活字印刷术。

Sculpture of Bi Sheng

Collection of the National Museum of China

Bi Sheng invented the technique of movable type printing. According to Sheng Kuo's Dream Pool Essays, Bi Sheng's movable type printing method consisted of three basic processes: typecasting, typesetting, and printing. After the invention of this technique, it quickly spread to Central Asia, the Middle East, and Europe where Latin letters were used on type pieces.

活字印刷术

Printing Techniques of Movable Type

为进一步改进雕版印刷术，公元11世纪北宋毕昇发明了泥活字印刷术，公元13世纪出现了木活字印刷术，元代人王祯对活字排版固定技术做了重大改进，创制了转轮排字盘。此后，木活字印刷成为中国活字印刷的主要形式之一，至清代达到了顶峰。公元15世纪晚期至16世纪还出现了铜、锡、铅等金属活字印刷，数百年间以木、铜、锡、铅和瓷、泥所造的活字，一直被交替应用。

Further improvements to the printing industry were developed by Bi Sheng in the 11th century, the Northern Song Dynasty, when he invented clay movable typesets. In the 13th century, wooden movable typesets were introduced and, during the Yuan Dynasty, Wang Zhen invented the revolving character type shelf. After the introduction of wood as a printing block material it became the predominant material for making printing tools, especially in the Qing Dynasty. In the late 15th to 16th centuries, metal typesets were also made from bronze, tin, and lead.

活字版模型

泥活字印刷是先制成单个活字，然后按照需要逐字挑选活字进行排版。活字版可根据不同的需要排成不同的版式，拆版后的活字还可以继续排印其他书籍。活字印刷可以节省印版材料、缩短印刷周期，降低印刷成本，大大提高了印刷效率。自毕昇首创泥活字印刷术以后，宋元以至清代一直都在使用。

Model of Movable Typeset

Movable typesets consist of sets with characters printed on individual small blocks. A printer could then select exactly the characters necessary to make up the body of text. The flexibility of this system is evident and it also required less printing materials then other techniques, was a faster method, and was more cost effective. After the invention of this technique by Bi Sheng in the Song Dynasty, movable type print was the predominant printing method for books until the late Qing Dynasty

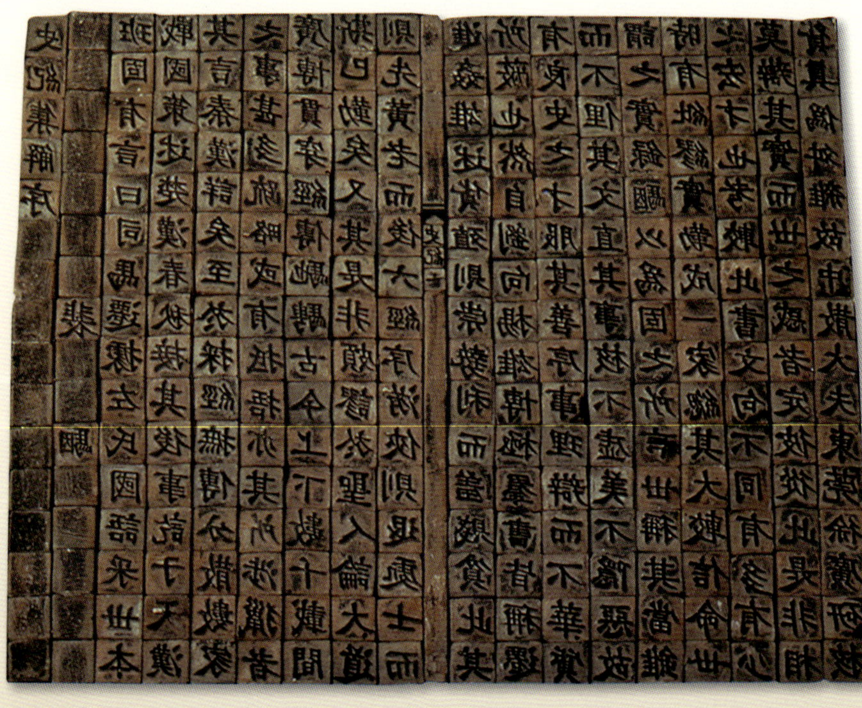

转轮排字盘模型

元朝初年，农学家王祯发明了转轮排字盘，使用简单的机械方法与设备提高了排字速度。其使用的字盘为圆盘状，分为若干格，活字字模依韵排列在格内。排版时两人合作，一人读稿，一人则转动字盘，方便地取出所需要的字模排入版内。印刷完毕后，将字模逐个还原到格内。

Model of A Revolving Character Type shelf

After Bi Sheng invented movable type printing in the Northern Song Dynasty (960 -1127), there were further attempts to create printing methods using some type of movable print pieces, but these were all abandoned due to their inefficiency. In later periods more attempts were made to invent new printing techniques and some of these met with success. In the first year of the Yuan Dynasty (1279), the agronomist, Wang Zhen, discovered a new method of typesetting that was based on revolving typeset carrousels. The typeset carrousels were circular and were divided into a grid upon which were arranged the movable type pieces, arranged according to their rhyming pattern. An axle set into a base supported the dish. This typeset carrousel required two people to operate the mechanism, one of whom read the text while the other turned the carrousel to set the necessary character pieces in order. After printing the pieces were then put back in their original positions.

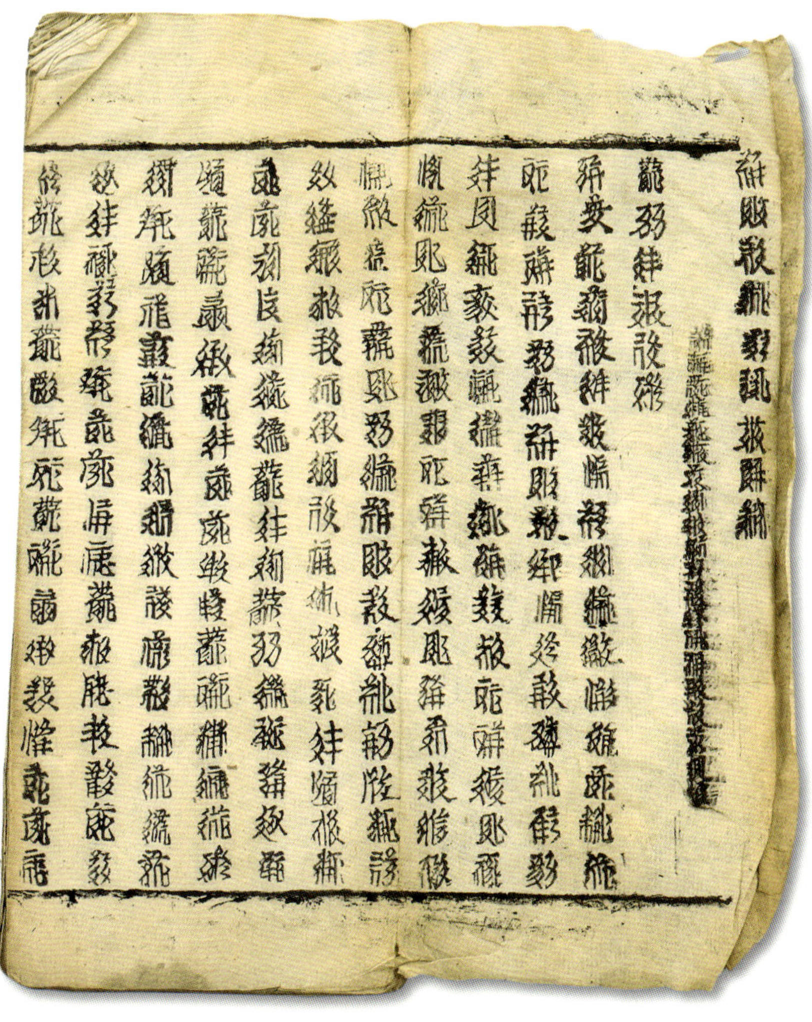

《维摩诘所说经》泥活字印本

西夏（公元1038－1227年）
长28.5、宽11.6cm
甘肃武威出土
武威市博物馆藏

Vimalakirti-nirdesa Sutra

Western Xia Dynasty (1038－1227 CE)
Length: 28.5cm, Width: 11.6cm
Excavated from Wuwei, Gansu
Collection of the Wuwen Municipal Museum

这是用西夏文印刷的佛经，是现存最早的泥活字印本。此印本具有泥活字印本的显著特征：因泥活字不坚固造成部分字的笔画不流畅，边缘不齐整；拼版时不紧凑，导致部分字行列弯曲不直；印刷墨色轻重不一，透墨深浅不同。

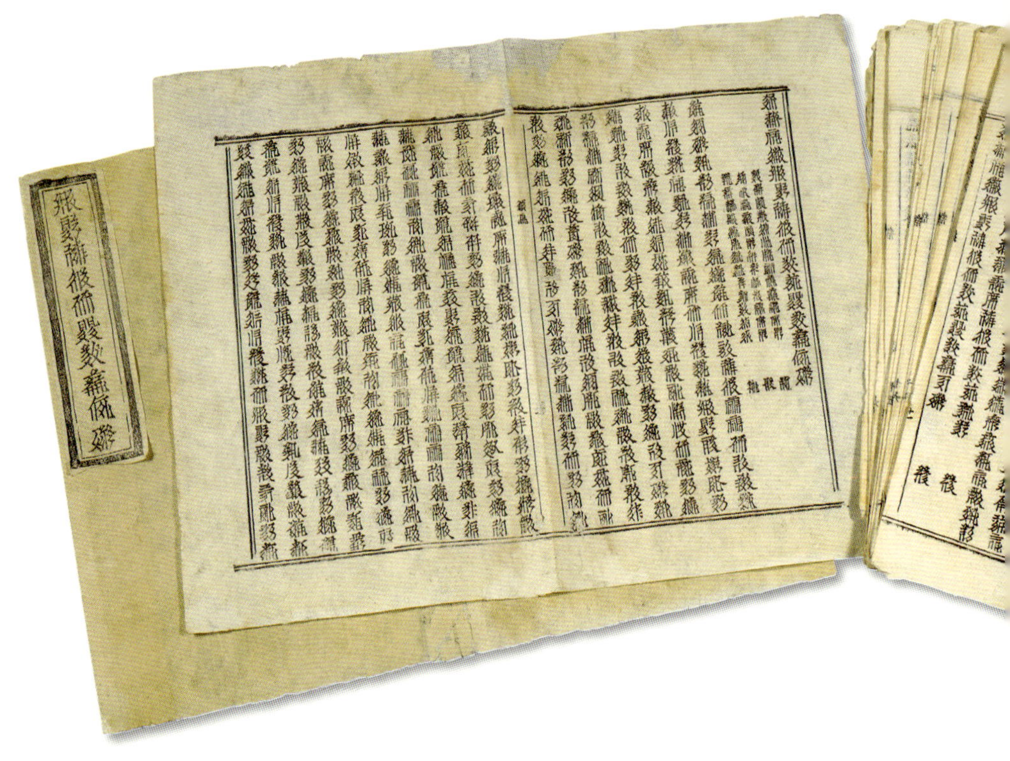

《吉祥遍至口和本续》本活字印本

西夏（公元1038–1227年）
长30.5、宽38.8cm
宁夏贺兰拜寺沟方塔出土
宁夏回族自治区博物馆藏

Ji Xiang Bian or Explanatory Notes to Buddhist Scriptures

Western Xia Dynasty (1038–1227CE)
Length:30.5cm, Width:38.8cm
Founded at the Square Pagoda of Baisigou Temple, Helan, Ningxia
Collection of the Ningxia Hui Autonomous Region Museum

这是用西夏字印刷的佛经，是最早的木活字印本之一。木活字印刷与雕版印刷的不同之处，表现在字形大小不等、字画粗细不一、版框栏线不衔接、墨色浓淡不一等方面。

回鹘文木活字（复制品）

元(公元1271–1368年)
长2.3、宽1、厚0.5–1.4cm
甘肃敦煌莫高窟内发现
中国国家博物馆藏

Wooden Movable Type Pieces with Ancient Uyghur Script (Mold)

Yuan Dynasty (1271–1368 CE)
Length: 2.3cm, Width: 1cm, Thickness: 0.5 –1.4cm
Discovered in the Dunhuang Mogao Caves, Gansu
Collection of the National Museum of China

元代木活字印刷术应用广泛，回鹘文木活字即于此时刻成。

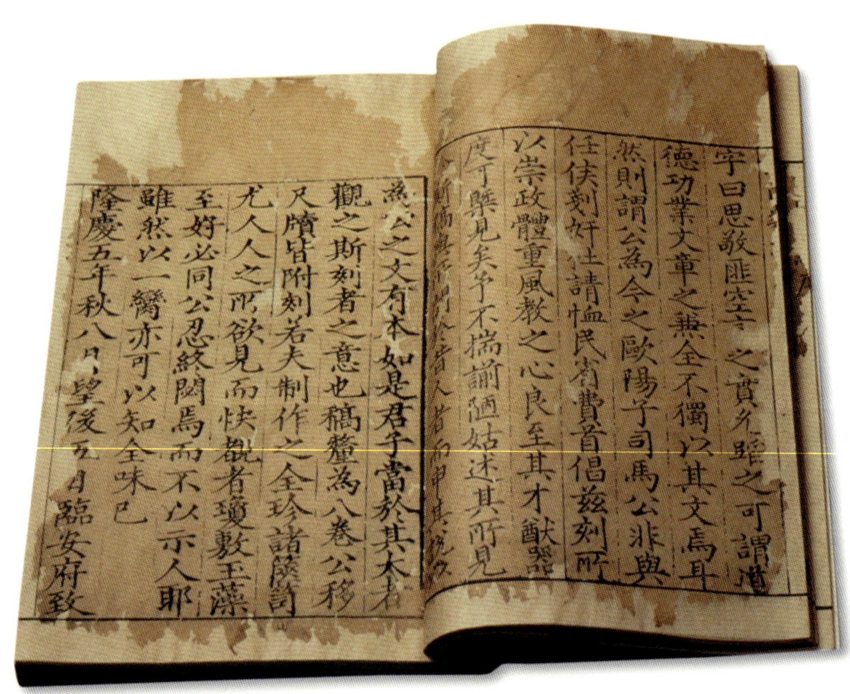
字曰思敬匪空言之實允蹈之可謂
德功業文章之兼全不獨以其文爲耳
然則謂公爲今之歐陽子司馬公非與
以崇政體重風敎之心良至其才猷器
度可槩見矣予不揣謭陋姑述其所見
然公之文有本如是君子當於其本者
觀之斯刻者之意也稿釐爲八卷公移
又牘皆附刻若夫制作之全珍諸篋笥
至妬必同公忌終闕焉而不以示人耶
雖然以一臠亦可以知全味已
隆慶五年秋八月望後五日臨安府致

《黔南类编》木活字印本

明（公元1368–1644年）
长27.2、宽20.3cm
中国国家博物馆藏

Printed Edition of Compilations from Southern Guizhou Province Using Wooden Movable Type Pieces

Ming Dynasty (1368–1644 CE)
Length: 27.2cm, Width: 20.3cm
Collection of the National Museum of China

这是在云南地区用木活字排印的一部方志，载有许多云南地方史料。明代木活字印刷的应用与普及超过前代，用木活字排印书籍的题材涉及小说、美术、科技、家谱和方志等各方面内容。

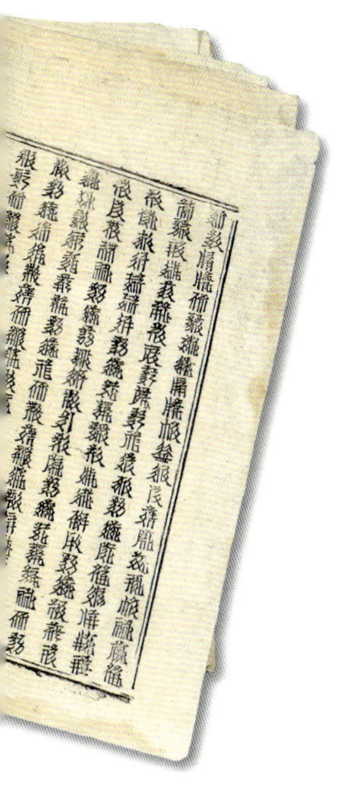

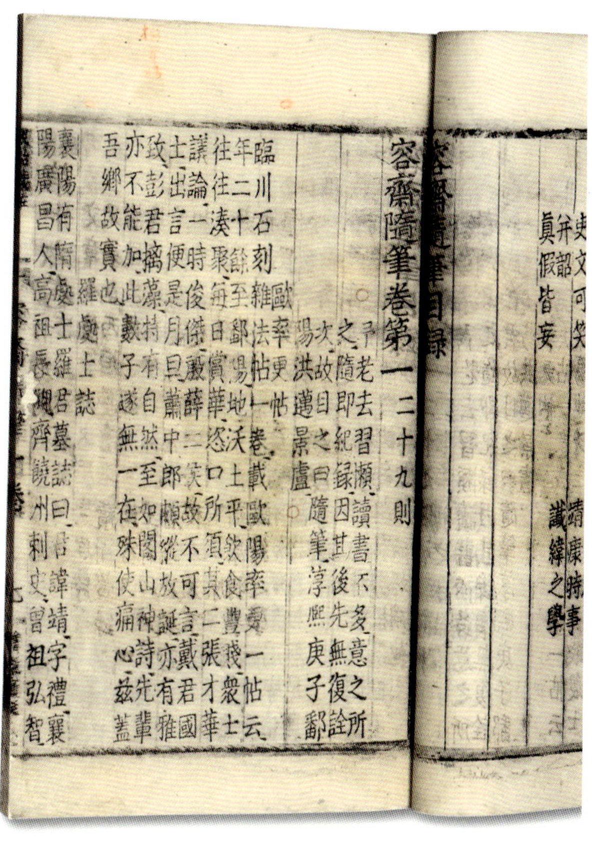

《容斋随笔》铜活字印本

明弘治三年（公元1490年）
中国国家图书馆藏

Bronze Type Printed Edition of the Notes from the Rong Studio

3rd Year of the Hongzhi Reign, Ming Dynasty, (1490 CE)
Collection of the National Library of China

明代的笔记体著作，是我国早期的铜活字印本之一。

公元15世纪末无锡人华氏开始使用铜活字印刷书籍。虽然铜活字制造工艺复杂、费时费工、投资较大，但它坚固不易变形，可反复用于印刷大量的书籍。

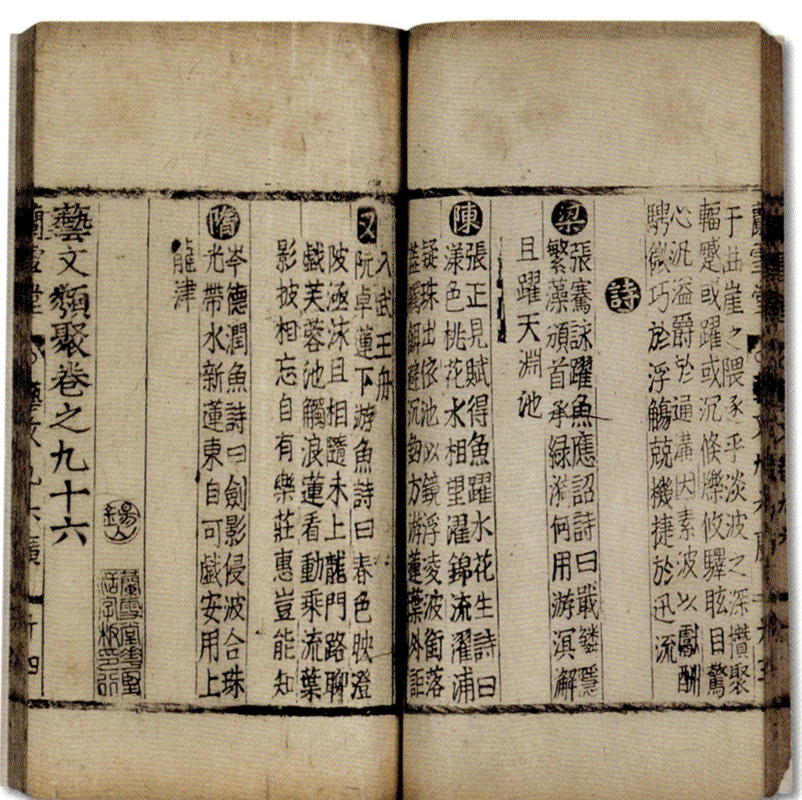

《艺文类聚》铜活字印本

明（公元1368–1644年）
长24.5、宽15cm
中国国家博物馆藏

Printed Edition of Compiled Notes on the Arts and Literature Using Bronze Movable Type Pieces

Ming Dynasty (1368–1644 CE)
Length: 24.5cm, Width: 15cm
Collection of the National Museum of China

此书是唐高祖李渊下令编纂的一部类书，全书收录各类古书1431部，分为岁时、治政、产业等46部分，共100卷，宋、明两代均有刻本传世。这是中国早期的铜活字印本之一。

1988年文物出版社用此经版所印《大藏经》
Qianlong Collection of Budhist Writings Printed by Cultural Relics Press in 1988 with Priting Slats Carved Qianlong Era

翟金生泥活字模及《翟氏宗谱》

清（公元1644–1911年）
活字模高1.2、长1、宽0.9cm；宗谱长33.5、宽17.8cm
中国国家博物馆藏

Zhai Jinsheng's Movable Type Set and the Zhai Family Geneaology

Qing Dynasty (1644–1911 CE)
Height of Type: 1.2cm, Length: 1cm, Width: 0.9cm; Length of Page: 33.5cm, Width: 17.8cm
Collection of the National Museum of China

清道光年间（公元1821–1850年）安徽泾县人翟金生仿效北宋毕昇造泥活字的方法，分五种规格造出十万泥活字。他用泥活字先后印刷自己的诗文集和翟氏宗谱等，皆得成功。《翟氏宗谱》是翟金生用自制的泥活字印刷的最后一部书。

《大藏经》经版

清乾隆（公元1736–1795年）
每块约长73.4、宽28.6cm
首都博物馆藏

Printing Slats of Qianlong Collection of Buddhist Writings

Qianlong period, Qing Dynasty, (1736–1795 CE)
Length of each Slat: ca. 73.4cm; Width: ca. 28.6cm
Collection of the Capital Museum

乾隆版《大藏经》是历代汉文《大藏经》中卷册数量最多的一部，其装潢讲究、纸质精美、字迹大而清晰。它是清代唯一官刻、也是中国最后一次官刻的汉文《大藏经》。清乾隆版《大藏经》刻版历时五年之久，经版有78230块，经书7240卷。该经奉清雍正皇帝御旨而雕刻，因此每卷首页均有雕龙“万岁”牌，故又称《龙藏经》、《清藏》。全部经版选用上好的梨木雕造，刻工精细，正反两面均雕有文字，刀法洗练，字体浑厚端秀。

昨日的美丽风景——彩印

Color Printing: Beautiful Scenes from a Bygone Era

宋元时期开始出现两色套印，明代则发展为多色套印。套印与版画艺术相结合的饾版拱花技术，更能表达出中国水墨绘画之浓淡晕染、阴阳向背的神韵，将彩印技术推向高峰。清代用雕版印制的年画，色彩鲜艳，构图饱满，成为民间点缀年景的喜庆佳品。

The government bureaucracy of the Later Tang of the Five Dynasties period (907-960 CE) published woodblock print editions of the Confucian classics. Later, in the Song Dynasty (960-1279 CE), official, private, and popular carvers saw their business thrive, ushering in a golden age of the woodblock printing industry. By the Yuan Dynasty (1279-1368 CE) printed editions appeared that made use of both red and black ink on the same page and later in the Ming (1368-1644 CE) complex pictorial prints were produced with multiple colors. In the Qing Dynasty auspicious New Year's woodblock prints in multiple colors were extremely popular. With their brilliant colors and lively compositions, such prints quickly become favored among the common people as essential ornaments for New Year's celebrations.

《炽盛光九曜图》

辽（公元916–1125年）
长94.6、宽50cm
山西省应县佛光寺塔发现
山西博物院藏

Printed Edition of the Flaming Light Buddha and Nine Luminous Whorls Picture

Liao Dynasty (916–1125 CE)
Length: 94.6cm, Width: 50cm
Discovered in the Wooden Pagoda of yingxian, Shanxi
Collection of the Shanxi Museum

此画正中是手托法轮的炽盛光佛。佛画印于皮纸之上，其方法是先以木刻墨印，印成后着色。印本刻工精细，线条遒劲，是我国迄今发现最大的木印着色佛教画。

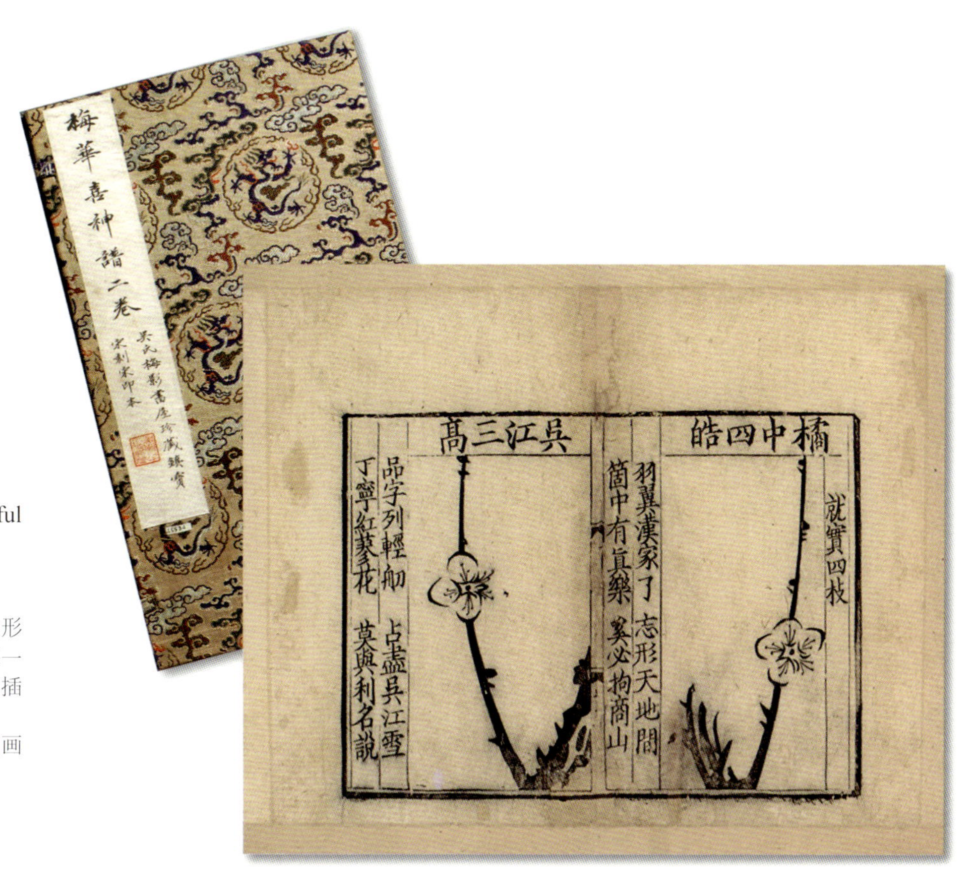

《梅花喜神谱》

宋（公元960–1279年）
上海博物馆藏

Block Print Edition of the Album of the Joyful Spirit of Plum Blossoms

Song Dynasty (960–1279 CE)
Collection of the Shanghai Museum

此书是以双刀平刻的梅花画谱，用连续插图的形式描绘了梅花从蓓蕾到结实的不同花态，且每一种花态配以雅题和诗文。这是我国现存最早的插图版画印刷品。
宋代的插图版画形式为中间插或连续插，其刻画以阳刻为主，线条稳健流利。

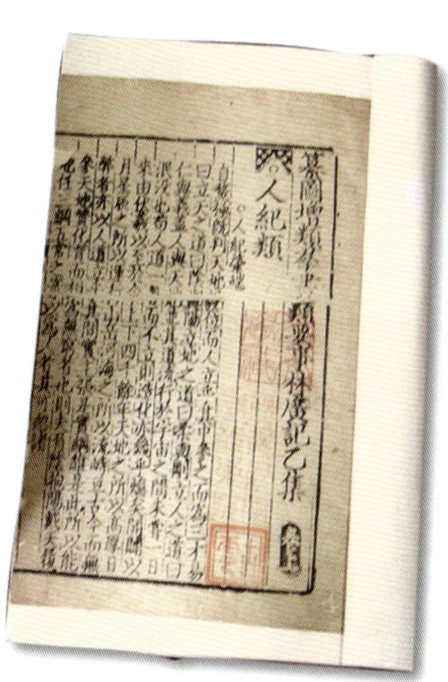

《事林广记》

元至元六年（公元1340年）
北京大学图书馆藏

Comprehensive Records on World Affairs

6th Year of the Zhiyuan Period, Yuan Dynasty,（1340 CE）
Collection of the Peking University Library

此书是元代的一部百科全书，分农桑、果实、器用、音乐、文艺、饮馔等53门，其人物、衣着、房舍等反映了元代的社会风貌。书内整版插图，构图合理，刀刻浑厚古朴，黑白对照分明。元代的插图版画取材广泛，构图的生活气息浓厚，刀刻技法更加精熟。元代书籍插图方式逐渐固定为卷首扉插、上图下文连续插及整版连插等形式，对明代的书籍插图影响颇深。

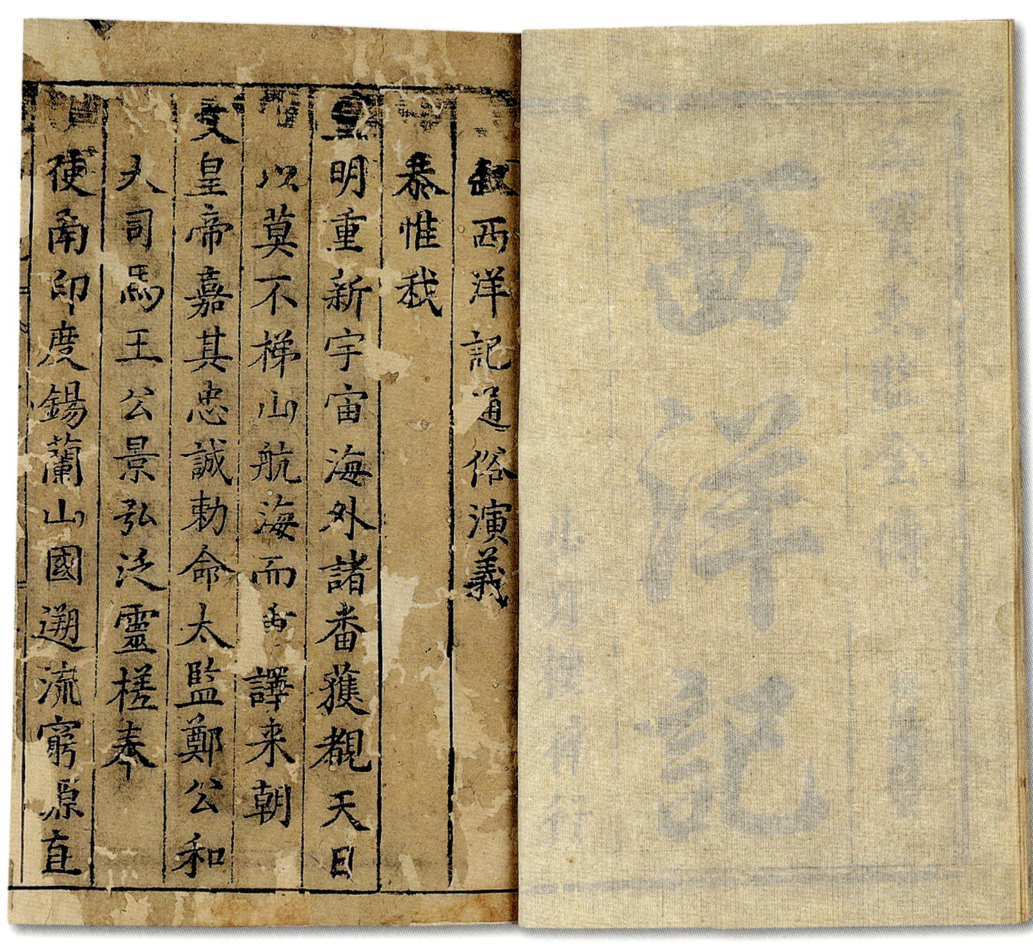

叙西洋記通俗演義

恭惟我

皇明重新宇宙海外諸番獲覲天日

以莫不梯山航海而重譯来朝

文皇帝嘉其忠誠勅命太監鄭公和

大司馬王公景弘泛靈槎奉

使南印度錫蘭山國遡流窮原直

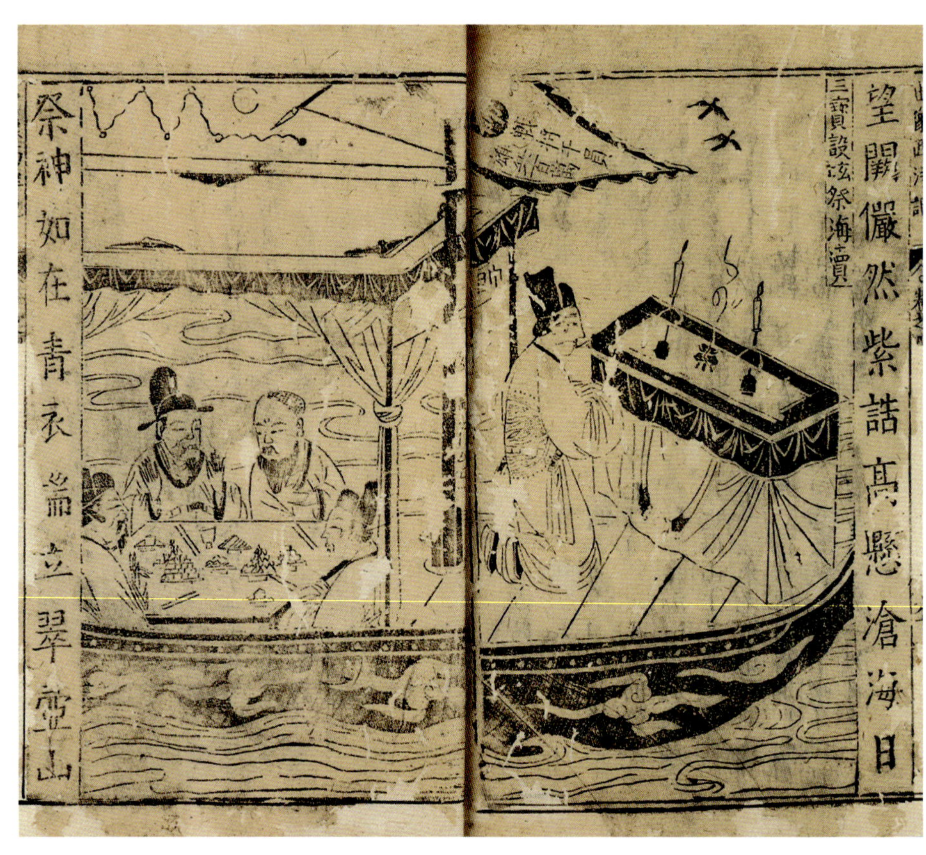

《三宝太监西洋记通俗演义》

明万历（公元1573–1620年）罗懋登
长24.5、宽16cm
中国国家博物馆藏

Tales of Eunuch Sanbao's Journey to the Western Seas

By Luomaodeng of the Wanli Period, Ming Dynasty,（1573 – 1620 CE）
Length: 24.5cm, Width: 16cm
Collection of the National Museum of China

本书描述了明代著名航海家郑和下西洋的故事，记录了西洋各国风貌及航海技术、造船技术等内容。

明代书籍中的插图版画已成为全书的一个有机部分，更形象地表现许多用语言难以叙述的内容，插图样式也由过去的上图下文改变成整版半幅、整版对幅或团扇式。 明代的插图图案设计繁密精美，线条细腻，雕刻刀法高妙，是我国插图版画发展的黄金时代。

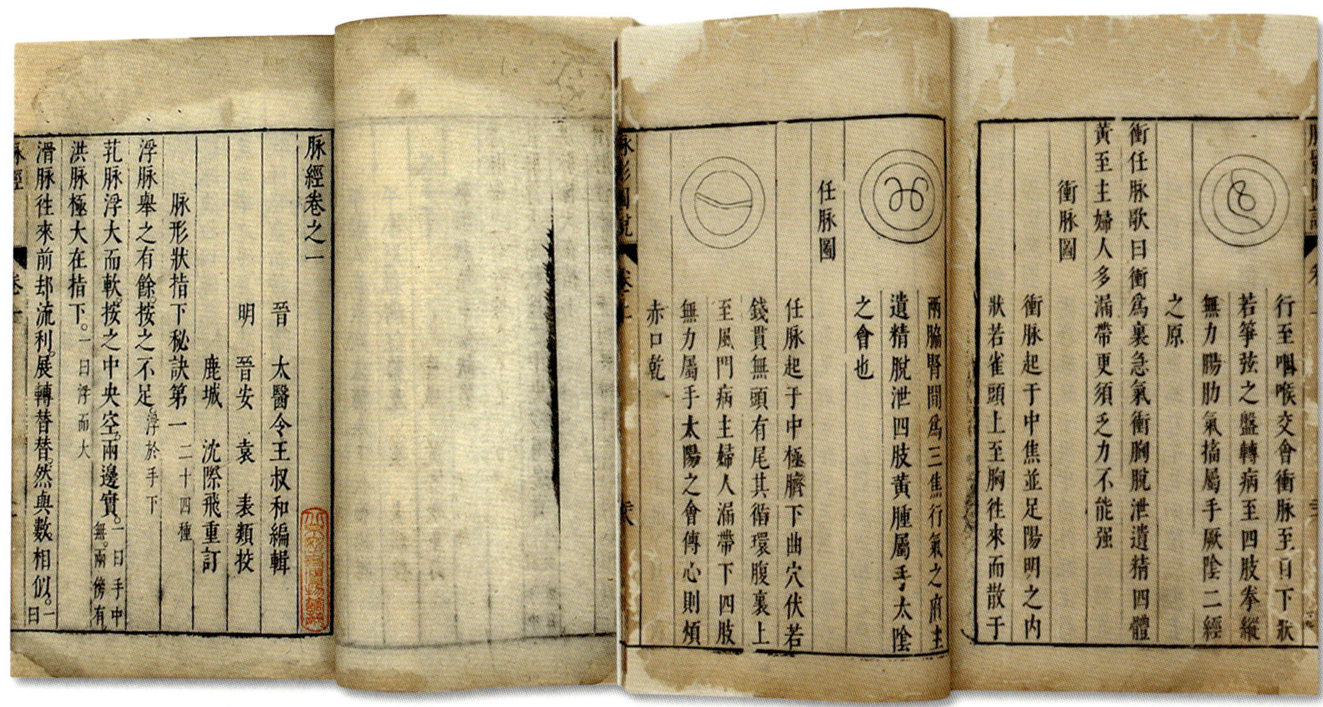

《脉经》

明（公元1368–1644年）
长27、宽17.5cm
中国国家博物馆藏

The Pulse Classic

Ming Dynasty (1368–1644 CE)
Length: 27cm, Width: 17.5cm
Collection of the National Museum of China

此书由晋代王叔和编辑，宋代时已有刊印。书中将人体脉搏跳动的各种细微差别加以区分，概括总结为24种脉象并论述了各种脉象与所反映病症之间的关系。这是我国现存最早的脉学专著，奠定了中医诊学的理论基础。

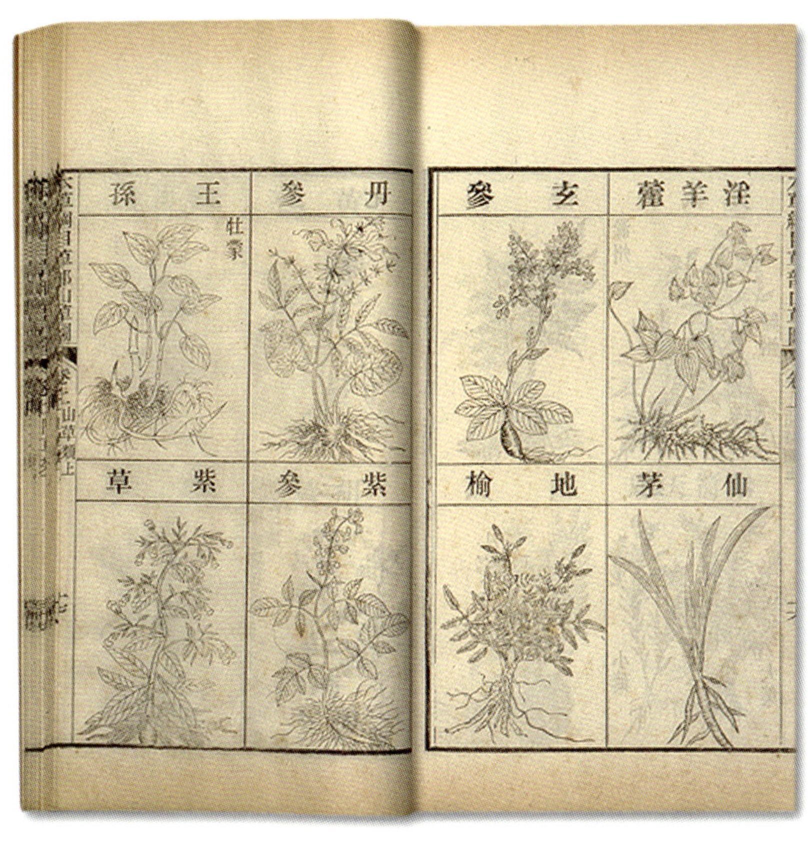

《本草纲目》

明 李时珍（公元1518–1593年）
长27、宽17cm
中国国家博物馆藏

Bencao Gangmu (Compendium of Materia Medica)

By Li Shizhen of the Ming Dynasty (1518–1593 CE)
Length: 27cm, Width: 17cm
Collection of the National Museum of China

这是中国的一部药物学巨著，全书收入中草药物1892种，药方11096个，绘制插图1110幅，形象地表现了各种药物的复杂形态和功效。

《程氏墨苑》

明万历（公元1573－1620年）
中国国家图书馆藏

Garden of Ink in the Cheng

Wanli Period, Ming Dynasty, (1573 – 1620 CE)
Collection of theNational Library of China

本书初次使用了分色分版的饾版套印法，是套色印刷技术水平高度发展的代表。从此书可以看出明代的彩色套印技术已能印制精细的版画，传统的雕版印刷术已发展到一个新的阶段。

饾版印刷是把每种颜色各刻一块小木版，犹如饾饤，所以称为饾版。其技术程序很复杂，要先勾画全画，然后再依画的本身，分成几部分，称为"摘套"。一幅画往往要刻三四十块小版，印刷时依色分次印刷，这就避免了色泽的互相印染，所印图画层次过渡自然。

《萝轩变古笺谱》

明(公元1368－1644年)
长31.5、宽21cm
中国国家图书馆藏

Ancient Painting Manual of the Studio of Vines

Ming Dynasty (1368－1644 CE)
Length: 31.5cm, Width: 21cm
Collection of the National Library of China

这是现存使用拱花和饾版印刷的最早印本之一，由江宁人吴发祥印制。笺谱的画面精美，所印画面的阴阳向背和轻重浓淡过渡自然流畅。

拱花是将纸张放置在雕有相同图案的凹凸相反的两版之间，将两版嵌合压印出花纹，是一种无色印刷技法，但它印出的画面是凸出的，能使作品具有较强的立体感，更具逼真和传神的韵味。拱花与饾版印刷技术相结合，创造了雕版印刷技术的奇迹。

《十竹斋笺谱》

明（公元1368－1644年）
长30、宽18cm
中国国家图书馆藏

Letter Sheet Manual of the Ten Bamboo Studio

Ming Dynasty (1368–1644 CE)
Length: 30cm, Width: 18cm
Collection of the National Library of China

这是现存使用拱花和饾版印刷的最早印本之一，由安徽休宁人胡正言印制。其版印精致，色调流畅，山水花木和鸟兽鱼虫都被刻画得惟妙惟肖，是中国雕版印刷技术登封造极之作。

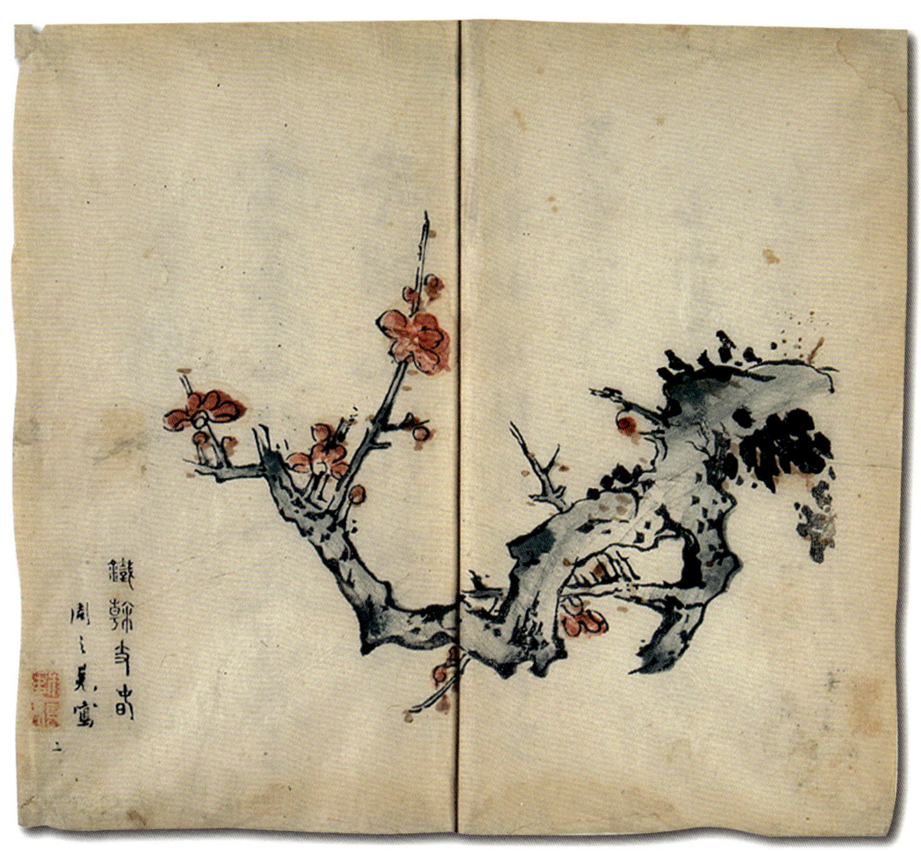

《十竹斋画谱》

明（公元1368－1644年）
长30、宽18cm
中国国家博物馆藏

Painting Manual of the Ten Bamboo Studio

Ming Dynasty (1368–1644 CE)
Length: 30cm, Width: 18cm
Collection of the National Museum of China

明朝末年安徽休宁人胡正言运用饾版印刷技术印制了《十竹斋画谱》，画、刻、印三方面都很精致。

《芥子园画传》

清康熙十八年（公元1679年）
长31.5、宽19cm
中国国家博物馆藏

The Mustard Seed Garden Painting Manual

18th Year of the Kangxi Period, Qing Dynasty, (1679CE)
Length: 31.5cm, Width: 19cm
Collection of the National Museum of China

此书是浙江钱塘人李渔编的一部画谱，以山水为主，是初学中国绘画的重要参考资料。它是清代饾版印刷的代表作，也是彩色套版印刷的精品。

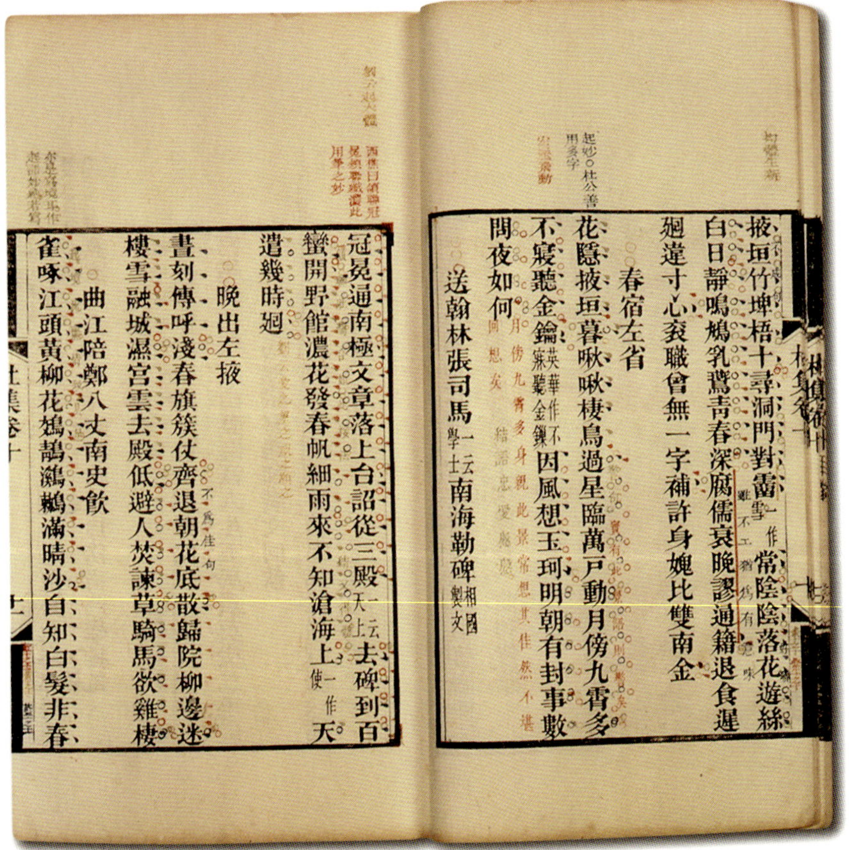

掖垣竹埤梧十尋洞門對霤常陰陰落花遊絲
白日靜鳴鳩乳燕青春深腐儒衰晚謬通籍退食遲
迴違寸心袞職曾無一字補許身愧比雙南金
春宿左省
花隱掖垣暮啾啾棲鳥過星臨萬戶動月傍九霄多
不寢聽金鑰因風想玉珂明朝有封事數
問夜如何
送翰林張司馬南海勒碑
冠冕通南極文章落上台詔從三殿去碑到百
蠻開野館濃花發春帆細雨來不知滄海上天
遣幾時迴
晚出左掖
晝刻傳呼淺春旗簇仗齊退朝花底散歸院柳邊迷
樓雪融城濕宮雲去殿低避人焚諫草騎馬欲雞棲
曲江陪鄭八丈南史飲
雀啄江頭黃柳花鵁鶄鸂鶒滿晴沙自知白髮非春

《杜工部集》

清道光十四年（公元1749年）
长31、宽18cm
中国国家博物馆藏

Compilation of Du Fu's Poems

14th Year of the Daoguang Period, Qing Dynasty, （1749 CE）
Length: 31cm, Width: 18cm
Collection of the National Museum of China

《杜工部集》是唐代著名诗人杜甫的作品集。此书为六色套印本。正文用墨笔，眉批、注、标点等分别用紫、绿、黄、蓝、红等色，色彩斑斓，阅之娱目怡情。全书印刷、装帧精工，是中国古代使用色彩最多的彩色套印刻本书籍。

在写本时代，有人用朱墨两色分别书写经文和标题，用几种颜色绘画插图，既醒目又有助于阅读。印刷术发明以后，人们开始尝试用朱墨两色套印的方法来弥补单色印刷的不足，后来发展至多色套印。明代万历年间以后，套色印刷术得到广泛应用。

《皇都积胜图》（局部）

明（公元1368–1644年）
中国国家博物馆藏

The Prosperous Imperial City (Part)

Ming Dynasty (1368–1644 CE)
Collection of the National Museum of China

《皇都积盛图》描绘了明代中后期北京城的繁荣景象。此画面展示的是明代市区街道上贩卖书籍的情景。明清两代我国的书籍印刷业走向鼎盛时期，印刷业与售书业已成为当时社会经济中的重要组成部分。

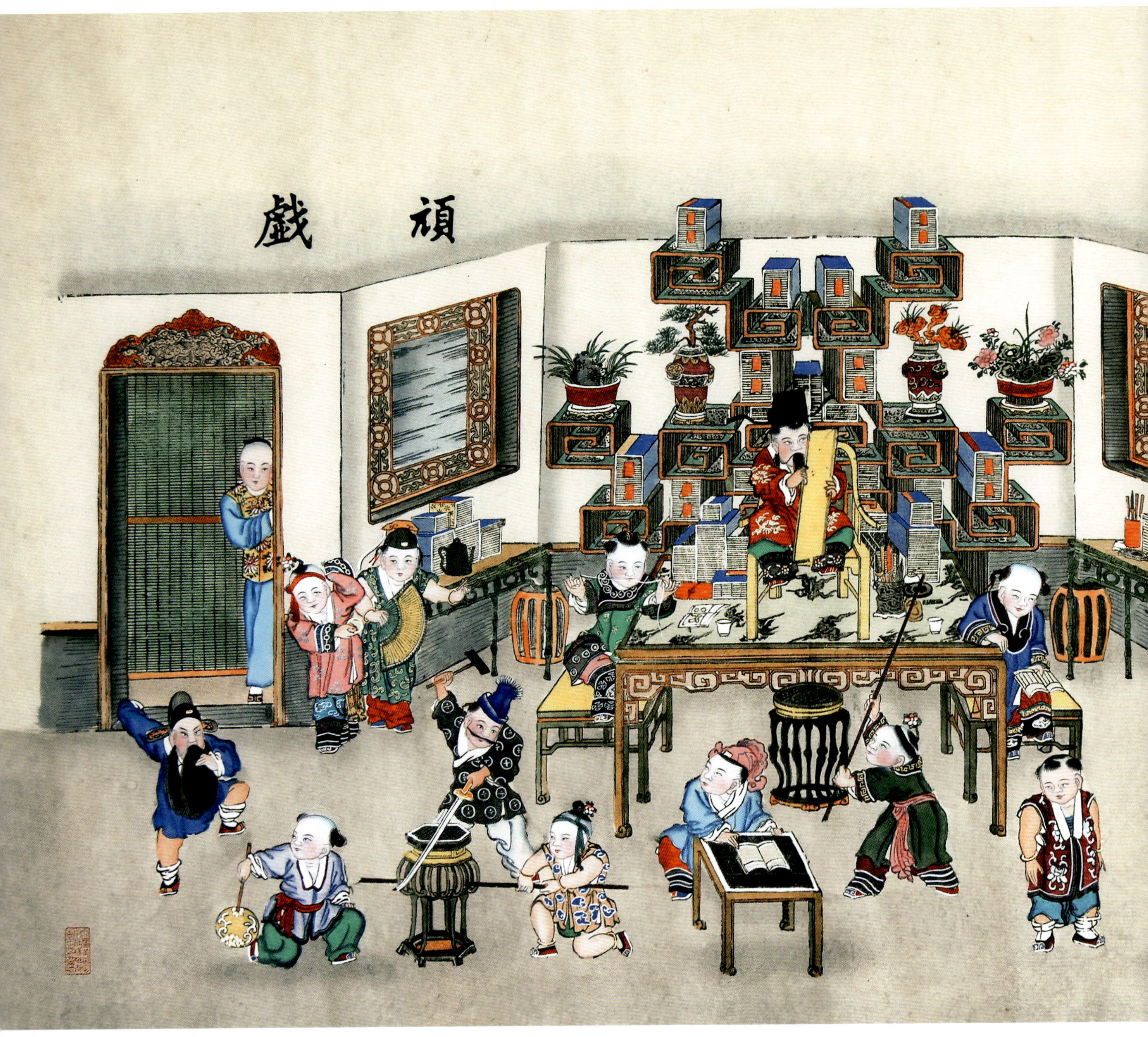

《闹学顽戏》年画

清(公元1644–1911年)
长113.5、宽68cm
中国国家博物馆藏

New Year's Print with the Phrase "Naughty Children Study Noisily"

Qing Dynasty (1644–1911 CE)
Length: 113.5cm, Width: 68cm
Collection of the National Museum of China

这是一幅反映儿童教育的年画，为天津杨柳青印制。杨柳青年画产生于元末明初，继承了宋、元绘画传统，吸收了明代木刻版画的形式，采用木版套印和手工彩绘相结合的方法印制，以寓意、写实等多种手法表现人民的美好情感和愿望，尤以反映各个时期的时事风俗及历史故事等题材为多。

《一团和气》年画

清(公元1644－1911年)
长79、宽54cm
中国国家博物馆藏

New Year's Print with the Phrase "A Prevailing Mood of Harmony"

Qing Dynasty (1644－1911 CE)
Length: 79cm, Width: 54cm
Collection of the National Museum of China

《一团和气》年画象征着吉利、祥和、圆满，是江苏桃花坞木刻年画中的经典作品。相传此画的底稿源于明宪宗朱见深所做的《一团和气图》，后为民间所采用。桃花坞年画始于明代，鼎盛于清代雍正、乾隆年间，其构图丰富，色调艳丽，具有浓郁的生活气息。

年画是中国民间于年节之际用来迎新春、祈丰年的民俗艺术品。其内容丰富，有驱凶辟邪、祈福迎祥、戏曲传说、喜庆装饰和生活风俗五类题材。这些年画线条单纯，色彩鲜明，画面具有喜庆的特色。年画的形式风格及艺术特色因民俗及地域的不同而有较大差异，以天津杨柳青、山东潍坊、江苏桃花坞和四川绵竹四大派最为著名。

大觀帖
漢韓勑碑

中国造纸术发明后，迅速传播到世界各地。
2-3世纪传到朝鲜、日本、越南，
7世纪前传到印度和巴基斯坦，
8-11世纪传往西亚和北非地区，
12世纪以后经阿拉伯传入欧洲，
17世纪从欧洲传入美洲。
而雕版印刷术于7世纪发明后，
很快东传至朝鲜和日本，
14世纪欧洲出现的雕版印刷和15世纪中叶出现的活字印刷，
都受到中国印刷术的影响。
“浩如烟海”，“汗牛充栋”，
我们常常这样形容人类拥有的图籍。
绵薄的纸片典藏着文明，传播着文明。
造纸术和印刷术作为中国古代四大发明的重要内容，
为人类的文明发展做出了不可磨灭的贡献。
当纸张从水中诞生之初，
瓷器也正在窑火中历炼。
下面展示的瓷器制作术完全改变了餐桌上的光景，
提升了全人类的生活质量，
并为历史保存了一线明亮的光彩。

After paper was invented in China the discovery was quickly transported around the world. In the 2nd - 3rd centuries the craft of papermaking appeared in Korea, Japan, and Vietnam. Before the 7th century the technique had spread to India and Pakistan. From the 8th - 11th centuries papermaking was seen in west Asia and in areas in northern Africa. After the 12th century the knowledge of papermaking jumped from Arabic Empire to Europe and in the 17th century paper was being made in the Americas.
When printing was invented in the 7th century it soon spread eastwards to Korea and Japan. In the 14th century printing appeared in Europe followed a century later by movable type printing, both techniques borrowed from China.
Two four-character phrases are frequently used in Chinese to describe humankind's attitude towards books. One translates simply as “boundless as foggy sea - voluminous” and the other means “making oxen sweat and buildings be filled - immense number of books”. It is on these thin sheets of paper that information and knowledge from long since passed eras still resonate today. Thus the twin inventions of papermaking and printing are one of the four great inventions of China that benefits humankind by preserving its past and recording its future.

泱泱瓷国

古代瓷器制作术

水、火、土的完美结合孕育了一种新的物质，创造出温润、洁净、雅致的瓷器。中国瓷器凝结了历代工匠的智慧与心血，积聚了时代与民族的精华，成为中国乃至世界科技、工艺、文化史上的奇葩，成为外国语汇里中国的代名词。

中国瓷器在造型、釉色、烧制和装饰上不断有创新，借鉴并融合了其他工艺的精华，将“形”、“意”之美发挥得淋漓尽致。淳朴洒脱的民俗意趣与恢弘典雅的皇家风貌，千余年来精彩纷呈，一路辉煌璀璨，展现了中华民族博大精深的人文精神和审美情怀。

The Techniques of Ancient Porcelain Production

The perfect collaboration of water, fire, and earth created a new material that produced an elegant substance called porcelain. After centuries of refining the technique of producing porcelain, Chinese craftsmen succeed in creating spectacularly beautiful vessels that rank highly in the annals of technical, craft, and cultural history, not only in China, but also across the globe. So prized was this substance that the word for porcelain became “china” in some languages.

Chinese porcelain, in its molding, glazing, firing and decorative motifs has evolved and assimilated the finest elements of other crafts. From the charm of folk art to the refined style found in the imperial court, Chinese porcelain encompasses the extensive and profound inner worlds and aesthetic moods of the Chinese people.

神奇出泥尘
Miracles from Mud

陶成雅器，有素肌玉骨之象。

——［明］宋应星

瓷器的诞生是个漫长过程，新石器时代制陶技术的高度发达为瓷器的产生奠定了物质和技术基础。陶器到瓷器的飞跃需要实现三大突破：瓷土的应用、釉的发明和窑炉的改进。原始青瓷在商代前期出现，经过春秋战国时期进一步发展，东汉中晚期浙江地区烧造的青瓷，达到了现代瓷器的各项标准，标志着瓷器创制过程的完成。

瓷是最能体现人类技术能力和人文情致的人工创造物。它是巧妙利用和驾驭自然力的技术成就，也是满足社会生活需要的物质财富，还是寄托和比附高尚品格的文化载体。

古代用“圆似月魂，轻如云魄”这句话，概括出瓷器清雅、飘逸、晶莹、圆润的品格。与陶器相比，瓷器胎质细腻，釉色莹润，低吸水率，不沾污物，不怕腐蚀，便于洗涤，久不褪色，美观大方，经久耐用，为工艺史上难得一见的不漏、不污、不朽之佳器。

Pottery is Refined to Porcelain, Appearing like Strong Jade Bones.

——Song Yingxing. Ming Dynasty

Centuries of pottery making finally lead to the highest achievement in the craft, the creation of porcelain. This technical feat can trace its foundation back to the Neolithic period when basic production methods and a set group of raw materials were established. The leap from pottery to porcelain was brought about by three breakthroughs: the use of porcelain clay, the invention of glaze, and the improvement of kiln furnaces. Before the Shang dynasty a prototype of celadon appeared and by the Spring and Autumn and Warring States periods such pieces became quite refined. Celadon burned in the Zhejiang area in the mid to late Eastern Han period reached a standard equal to modern porcelain, marking the completion of the porcelain creation process.

Porcelain is the manmade product that most expresses the capabilities and literary temperament of human technology. Furthermore, it is a technological success that skillfully demonstrates the ability to use and control natural forces. Porcelain also satisfies the material needs of society and is a cultural vehicle infused with elegance and style.

The Qualities of Porcelain: “the round ones are like the spirit of the moon, and the light ones are like the soul of the clouds”, this sentence reflects the refinement, elegance, crystalline nature, and mellowness traditionally associated with porcelain. Compared with pottery, the quality of a porcelain body is much finer and thinner, the glaze color is lustrous, the base does not absorb pollutants nor does it corrode. Such pieces are easy to clean, have a dignified beauty, are durable, and are rare in craftwork history as items that do not leak, corrode, or decay.

Porcelain was created upon the foundation of a long period of development of pottery technology.

火中取宝
Fetching Treasures from Fire

陶与瓷都是火的艺术。3000年前的商代，出现了比陶器明显进步的原始瓷；2000年以前的东汉，瓷器在中国浙江东部的宁绍平原诞生。与陶器相比，瓷器更经得起高温的煅炼，质地更致密，更坚固。火造就了瓷器，窑炉的温度直接决定了瓷器的成败。瓷器、印纹陶和白陶的对比很好地说明了问题。

原始瓷是瓷器发展的初级阶段。商代是原始瓷的肇始期，胎釉表现出较多原始性。西周以后原始瓷器迅速发展，到了春秋战国时期，江南地区的原始瓷器形制规整，胎体坚实，釉层均匀，距真正的瓷器只有一步之遥。苏南、浙北出土的原始瓷是这一时期的代表。

Porcelain and pottery are both included in the realm of fire arts. Proto-porcelian oringinally appeared 3000 years ago during the Shang Dynasty proto-porcelain appeared and clearly evolved from pottery production. 2000 years ago in the Eastern Han dynasty, porcelain was created in the Ningbo-Shaoxing plains of eastern Zhejiang province. If compared, porcelain, as a result of high temperature firing, is at once the more delicate and yet more solid of the two. White pottery and incised pottery vessels attest to this fragile yet durable quality.

During the Shang Dynasty proto-porcelain was burned with trace amounts of glaze. Later, after the Western Zhou period, continual technical progress was made in the field and during the Spring and Autumn, Warring States periods kilns in the Jiangnan region were producing standardized proto-porcelain. These wares had smooth bodies, even layers of glaze, and were steadily getting closer to true porcelain.

原始瓷尊

商早期（公元前16–前14世纪）
高11.5、口径18.3、底径3.5cm
河南郑州二里岗商城遗址出土
中国国家博物馆藏

Proto-porcelain Wine Cup

Early Shang Dynasty (16–14th century BCE)
Height: 11.5cm, Diameter of mouth: 18.3cm, Diameter of base: 3.5cm
Excavated from the Ruins of the Shang Dynasty Erligang City, Zhengzhou, Henan
Collection of the National Museum of China

商代晚期出现的原始瓷用瓷土做胎，烧成火候在1200℃以上，胎体坚致，表面施釉，已经具备瓷器的基本特征，是瓷器出现的先声。此器青黄釉，折肩，小圜底，整器浑厚朴实。

兽面纹白陶双系壶

商晚期（公元前13－前11世纪）
高22cm
河南安阳出土
故宫博物院藏

White Pottery *Hu* with Animal Mask Designs and Double Handles

Late Shang Dynasty (13th－11th century BCE)
Height: 22cm
Excavated from Anyang, Henan
Collection of the Palace Museum

白陶的原料与瓷土相差无几，尽管其外表洁白无暇，但是尚未达到胎体烧结的温度，它依然是陶器。新石器时代已经有白陶，商代后期白陶烧制技术高度发展，出现很多仿青铜礼器的造型和纹饰。尊为礼器中的盛酒器，此尊以瓷土做胎，敛口，鼓腹，圈足，口部两侧各有一系，端庄凝重。器身以云雷纹为地，口沿和腹部遍刻兽面纹，密而有序，繁而不乱。

瓷器和陶器的三个主要区别

一是原料。制瓷用的原料是瓷土，它是花岗岩等一类岩石长期受热液作用和风化作用而生成，助熔剂含量比制陶黏土低，在高温下不易烧塌。

二是釉料。瓷器表面往往有一层透明的玻璃态物质，称为釉。植物焚烧的灰烬中包含CaO、K_2O，Na_2O等成分，有助熔作用，能在胎体表面形成透明光亮的物质。原始瓷釉最早出现于商代，是一种高温石灰釉。

三是火候。瓷器的烧制至少需要1200℃的高温。春秋战国时期浙江地区龙窑的出现，大大提高了窑温，为瓷器的烧成奠定了物质基础。龙窑依坡而造，火膛设在低端，排烟口设在高端，窑身两侧间隔设投柴孔。龙窑的坡度能形成自然抽力，通过控制抽力从而控制窑内的温度与气氛。

The differences between porcelain and pottery are:

Selection of raw material. Porcelain clay and clay used in pottery production are different. The clay used to make porcelain is called 'china clay (or Kaolin Clay)'. Its flux content is lower than pottery clay, a facet that is evident in the higher firing temperature of china clay. Of course, china clay can also be fired at a lower temperature to make pottery. China stone, or feldspathic stone, is one type of raw material used to make porcelain, and after it has been broken up it is also known as china clay. Like granite, it is a kind of stone created from long term melting and efflorescence from heat. However, there are a variety of so-called china stones, as the chemical compositions found in such stones can be different based on the location of the mine.

The invention of glaze. Under specific temperature conditions, ash made from burned plants can melt into the outer surface of clay to create a layer with transparent glassy qualities, similar to the characteristics of porcelain glaze. This is because the ash contains a component that assists the clay in melting, such as potassium oxide or sodium oxide. Calcium oxide, the primary component of limestone, is also a flux in pottery. Based on the number of Shang dynasty prototype glazed porcelain pieces discovered it is thought that the effects of plant ash were well recognized at this early date. Thus, the process of glaze development began from a simple process of using plant ash added to the surface of clay, calcium carbonate clay or limestone clay vessels.

Raising the Heat. In early periods kiln temperatures in dragon kilns reached up to 1200 degrees centigrade. Dragon kilns were situated on hillsides with heating chambers towards the bottom and the smoke stack at the top. The firewood hole was situated at the back of the kiln or along the kiln's body. The slope angle of dragon kilns allowed the flame to naturally gravitate up the whole of the kiln. Controlling the fire's movement allowed control of the interior kiln temperature and atmosphere. Dragon kilns first appeared in Zhejiang during the Eastern Zhou period (770 - 256 BCE). The use of such kilns was the driving force behind the success of the Zhejiang kilns during the period.

原始青瓷双系罍

西周（公元前1046–前771年）
高27、口径15.2、肩宽28.8cm
河南洛阳出土
河南洛阳市文物工作队藏

Prototype Celadon *Lei* Wine Jar

Western Zhou Dynasty (1046–771 BCE)
Height: 27cm, Diameter of mouth: 15.2cm, Width at shoulder: 28.8cm
Excavated at Luoyang, Henan
Collection of the Luoyang Municipal Relics Work Team

西周原始瓷器的胎体更坚致，器形更规整，釉色更透亮均匀，与商代相比有了很大的进步。这件原始瓷罍胎色灰白，通体施青釉，流釉处颜色偏深。侈口，宽肩，圈足，肩部刻八道弦纹，绞索状耳。器形端庄浑厚，装饰朴素典雅。

印纹陶罐

春秋（公元前770–前476年）
高12、口径17.6、底径15cm
浙江绍兴窑址出土
浙江省博物馆藏

Burnt Impressed Design Pottery

Spring and Autumn Period (770–476 BCE)
Height: 12cm, Diameter of mouth: 17.6cm, Diameter of base: 15cm
Excavated from Shaoxing Kiln, Zhejiang
Collection of the Zhejiang Provincial Museum

4000年前的印纹陶已经开始用瓷土类黏土做胎，能在1000℃以上的温度中烧成，但是仍经不住1200℃以上的高温，到了春秋时期仍能见到瓷器经不住高温而烧塌的现象。

原始青瓷龙首鼎

战国（公元前475–前221年）
高14.9、口径13.6、腹径13.8cm
上海博物馆藏

Prototype Celadon Dragon Head *Ding* Vessel

Warring States period (475–221 BCE)
Height: 14.9cm, Diameter of mouth: 13.6cm Diameter at widest point: 13.8cm
Collection of the Shanghai Museum

战国时期，中国南方原始瓷制作水平已有很大的提高，无论胎釉、造型等都离瓷器仅一步之遥。龙首鼎是战国时期原始瓷器的典型代表，鼎口一侧凸起一长颈龙首，与龙首相对一侧有一小尾，两侧各有一附耳，下承三兽足。器身刻划纹饰简朴，造型生动。

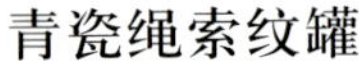

青瓷绳索纹罐

东汉熹平四年（公元175年）
高17.5、口径11.4–11.1、底径11.5–11.2cm
浙江奉化东汉墓出土
奉化县文物管理委员会藏

Celadon Rope Pattern Jar

4th year of the Xiping Ere, Eastern Han Dynasty, (175 CE)
Height: 17.5cm, Diameter of mouth: 11.4–11.1cm, Diameter of base: 11.5–11.2cm
Excavated from an Eastern Han Dynasty Tomb, Fenghua, Zhejiang
Collection of the Fenghua Relics Management Committee

这件青瓷罐是浙江早期越窑的代表。胎质细腻，釉色青绿，施釉不及底。肩部堆饰横斜交叉的绳索纹，交叉点作结索状，生动写实。

青瓷标本

东汉晚期（公元2-3世纪）
浙江上虞小仙坛窑址、大圆坪窑址出土
上虞县文物管理所、浙江省文物考古研究所藏

Celadon Sample

Late Eastern Han Dynasty (2nd-3rd century CE)
Excavated from Xiao Xiantan (Da Yuanping), Shangyu, Zhejiang
Collection of the Zhejiang Provincial Archaeological Research Department

东汉中晚期，随着原料制备技术的提高，胎和釉更为纯净了，龙窑结构的改进提高了烧成温度。在技术进步的基础上，浙江宁绍平原地区出现了完全成熟的青瓷。

成瓷技术
Porcelain Technology

原料的选择与淘洗是制瓷的关键。选取比较纯净的瓷土，经过粉碎、过筛和几次淘洗、沉淀，尽可能去除较粗的颗粒和杂质，再经过反复的踩踏、揉搓，制成纯净、具有延展可塑性的制胎坯料。

石灰釉则是将纯净的胎料稀释后加入一定量的助熔剂钙（通常是特定植物的灰烬）做成。施釉通常根据不同的器形、釉料及施釉效果采用不同的方法，有蘸釉、荡釉、浇釉、吹釉、刷釉等多种。

足够温度和保持适当气氛的窑炉是瓷器生产最关键的一步。窑炉的结构影响烧成的温度，决定了瓷器烧造的成败与质量的优劣。南方早期青瓷的创烧归功于龙窑的发明。龙窑依山而建，利用山体坡度形成自然抽力，提高炉温、装烧量和热效率。浙江地区商代晚期出现原始龙窑，以后被广泛使用，是南方主要的窑炉体系。北方采用半倒焰式馒头窑，又称圆窑，扩大了燃烧室和烟囱，有利于控制温度。清初景德镇出现“形如覆瓮”的蛋壳窑，独特的结构便于控制气氛，使受热更为充分和均匀，为官窑瓷器的发展提供了技术支撑。窑炉结构的改进，装烧技术的突破，配合各类窑具，造就了精美绝伦的中国瓷器。

Selecting and processing raw materials are crucial first steps in porcelain production. Potters first took relatively pure china clay, grinded it to powder, then sifted and washed it several times. They then let it settle in order to eliminate rough pellets and impurities. The clay was then further crushed and kneaded. All of these processes produce a pure and malleable base material for manufacturing the body of a porcelain vessel. Ingredients to create lime ash glaze was added after the refinement of the pure body material in the form of a fixed amount of calcium flux (usually the ashes of a specific plant).

After processing china clay and lime glaze materials, the most crucial step in porcelain production is the ability to reach a sufficiently high temperature and to maintain a suitable atmosphere in the kiln furnace. The kiln furnace structure influences the temperature of the firing process and decides the success or failure of the porcelain vessels produced. The production of the earliest celadon wares from the south of China was attributed to the success of the invention of the dragon kiln. The dragon kiln was built into a mountain and took advantage of the natural shape of the mountain slope to stoke the fire upwards and raise the furnace temperature. Dragon kilns were able to maintain firing temperatures and create thermal efficiency.

The original dragon kiln appeared in the late Shang Dynasty in the Zhejiang Province area. By the Eastern Han dynasty it was in wide use and was the chief kiln system seen in the south. Due to the natural geographic conditions of the north a semi-spherical kiln and inverted firing style were used, called a round kiln. This expanded the firing chamber and chimney was even more beneficial for controlling the temperature. In the Qing Dynasty an eggshell kiln 'shaped like a capsized water jug' appeared in the Jingdezhen kilns, a unique structure that provided even steadier temperature controls that advanced the technology of the production of imperial porcelain.

支钉

春秋（公元前770–前476年）
浙江越窑窑址出土
浙江省文物考古研究所藏

Spur

Spring and Autumn Period (770–476 BCE)
Excavated from the Ruins of the Yue Kiln, Zhejiang
Collection of the Zhejiang Province Institute of Cultural Relics and Archaeology

支钉是一种叠烧窑具，使用时足部向下，托面向上，再在上面放置碗碟。这种窑具自重小，可多层叠放。支钉与釉面的接触面小且在烧成后较易敲掉，在釉面只留下支痕。

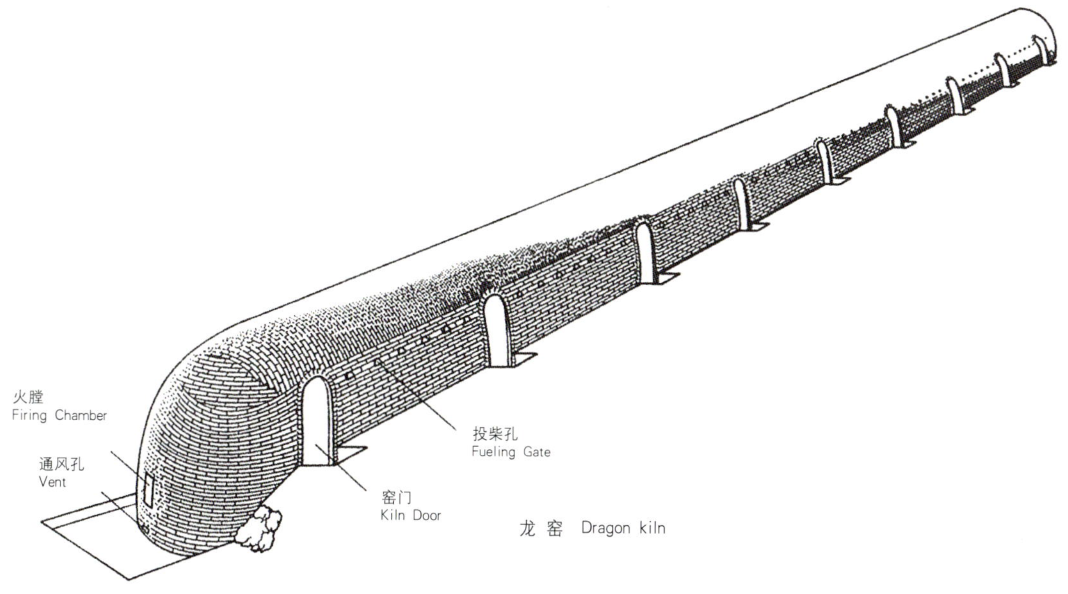

龙 窑 Dragon kiln

龙 窑

龙窑多见于中国南方，因形似龙而得名。始于商代，至宋代基本达到完善。倾斜角约8°－20°，窑长30－80米，形成自然抽力，有利于升温。以木柴为燃料，烧还原焰为主。这是宋代（公元960－1279年）浙江地区龙窑示意图。

Dragon kiln

This type of kiln was mostly seen in the south and because it was thought they resembled a resting dragon, they were called dragon kilns. They were introduced in the Shang Dynasty and reached maturity by the Song Dynasty. Most of these kilns feature a slop that was approximately 8°- 20°, kilns were 30 - 80 meters long. This allowed the formation of a natural suction that then raises the internal temperature. The kilns were mainly fueled by wood and burned carbonizing flames. This is a Song Dynasty (960 - 1279 CE) dragon kiln diagram from the Zhejiang region.

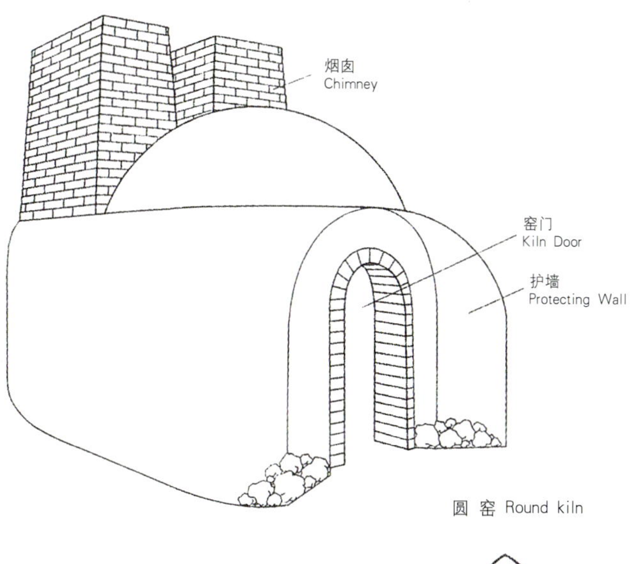

圆 窑 Round kiln

圆 窑

圆窑是中国北方传统的窑炉，因形似馒头而得名，亦名馒头窑。商代早期已经出现，唐代发展为半倒焰窑，宋代已臻成熟。燃料以煤为主，可烧还原焰或氧化焰，烧成温度达1300℃。这是北宋（公元960－1127年）陕西地区圆窑示意图。

Round kiln

Round kiln is the traditional kiln of Northern China, it's shaped like a bun, therefore is also know as bun kiln. It had already appeared in Shang Dynasty, developed to half down-draft kiln in Tang Dynasty, and matured by Song Dynasty. It is mainly fueled by coal, and is able to burn carbonizing flame or oxidizing flame, the firing temperature has reached 1300 . This is Northern Song Dynasty (960-1127 CE) round kiln diagram in Shanxi region.

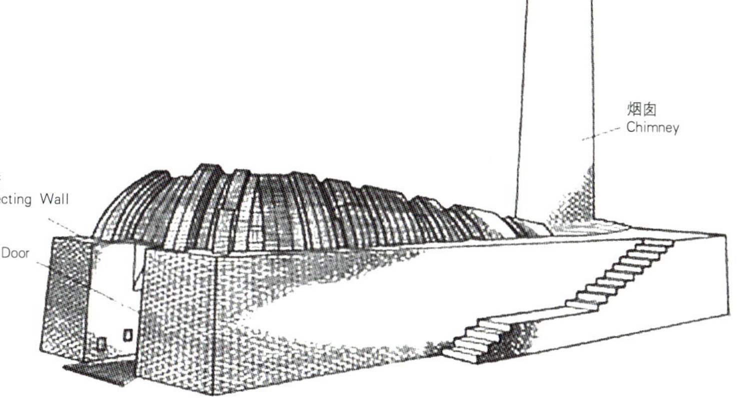

蛋形窑 Eggshell kiln

蛋形窑

蛋形窑是景德镇传统的窑炉形式，因似半个鸡蛋而得名，亦名柴窑。由元末明初的葫芦形窑发展而来。结构前部高而宽，后部低而窄，窑长7－18米。以木柴为燃料，烧还原焰。这是清代（公元1644－1911年）景德镇蛋形窑示意图。

Eggshell kiln

The eggshell kiln was the traditional kiln at Jingdezhen and was given its name because of the kiln's half egg shape, they were also known as firewood kilns. This kiln was developed from the cucurbit shaped kiln popular in the late Yuan Dynasty and early Ming Dynasty. The front of the kiln's structure is tall and wide, the back is low and narrow, and the kilns were 7 - 18 meters long. They were fueled by firewood and burned carbonizing flame. This is a Qing Dynasty (1644 - 1911 CE) eggshell kiln diagram from Jingdezhen.

匣钵

南朝（公元420－589年）
高20、 底径28cm
江西丰城洪州窑窑址出土
丰城市博物馆藏

Saggar

Southern Dynasties (420–589 CE)
Height: 20cm, Diameter of base: 28cm
Excavated from the Ruins of the Hongzhou Kiln, Fengcheng, Jiangxi
Collection of the Fengcheng Municipal Museum

匣钵是放置瓷坯的窑具，它使瓷器在烧制过程中受热均匀，避免釉面受到烟尘污染，充分利用竖向空间，扩大和升高窑室，改进了烧成质量，扩大了产量，减少了成本。匣钵最早见于南朝，以洪州窑、岳州窑使用最早。

瓷质匣钵

唐（公元618－907年）
浙江慈溪上林湖越窑窑址出土
慈溪市博物馆藏

Porcelain Saggar

Tang Dynasty (618–907 CE)
Excavated from the Ruin of Shanglin Lake Yue Kiln, Cixi , Zhejiang
Collection of the Cixi Municipal Museum

晚唐五代越窑秘色瓷以纯正、莹润的釉色被誉为“千峰翠色”，这与秘色瓷采用瓷质匣钵和匣钵釉封等独特的装烧工艺密切相关。瓷质匣钵和匣钵釉封技术显然提高了匣钵的密封性，避免了烧成后期的二次氧化，使釉色更加青绿。

景德镇窑洒蓝釉标本

明宣德（公元1426—1435年）
景德镇陶瓷考古研究所藏

Spread Blue Glaze Sample from the Jingdezhen Kiln

Xuande period, Ming Dynasty, (1426–1435 CE)
Collection of the Jingdezhen Ceramic Archaeology Research Institute

洒蓝釉是创于明宣德而盛于清康熙的一种特殊的蓝釉。它采用吹釉工艺，釉面表现为浅蓝色地上星星点点分布着水迹般的深蓝色点子，具有独特的视觉和审美效果。

制瓷技艺
Techniques of Porcelain Production

制瓷技艺包括成型技术和装饰技术。成型工艺中回旋体器物通常采用拉坯技术，较高大的器物则结合拉坯和节装技术成型。模制成型技术随着制瓷技术的成熟而得到提高，它可以制作复杂造型，使器形更加多样、美观。

公元3－6世纪，中国南北方先后采用模制技术生产瓷器，瓷胎表面装饰主要利用工具在瓷胎上作物理上的加减，包括刻划花、印花、镶嵌、镂空、堆塑等。刻划花出现最早，也最为普遍，或纤细或粗犷，随性洒脱。定窑印花借鉴缂丝技术，精致淡雅；绞胎与珍珠地划花实现了多种色彩的拼接镶嵌，营造出奇妙的视觉效果。

The techniques for making porcelain were two-fold, those for forming the shape of a ceramic body and those that created glazes. The former methods included throwing pieces on a wheel then pulling them into shape and for larger pieces sections were often formed individually then joined together. Another method of making ceramics in molds advanced over time and could be used to make items with complicated designs.

During the 3rd - 6th century CE kilns in the south followed by those in the north adopted the method of making ceramics in molds. The decoration on the surface of these items was either additive or subtractive and included surface carving, impressing, mounting, and piling. Carving appeared first and was also consistently the most popular method as it can be fine or spontaneous. Ding Kiln carved decorations referenced Silk Tapestry textile designs, both were simple and elegant.

➲ 青釉莲花尊

北朝（公元420－589年）
高66.1、口径19.2、底径20.6cm
河北衡水封氏墓地出土
故宫博物院藏

Celadon Lotus *Zun* Urn

Northern Dynasties (420–589 CE)
Height: 66.1cm, Diameter of mouth: 19.2cm, Diameter of base: 20.6cm
Excavated from the Feng Family Tombs, Hebei
Collection of the Palace Museum

模制技术的发展使得瓷器制作更为精细。南北朝时期受佛教的影响，建筑、日用品上常见佛教题材的装饰。莲花尊是北朝的典型器物，封氏墓出土的这件莲花尊造型宏伟，装饰丰富，运用模制堆贴、镶嵌、刻划等各种技法表现佛像、莲花等，精致美观。

越窑青釉羊

三国（公元220－265年）
高25、长30.5cm
南京清凉山三国吴墓出土
中国国家博物馆藏

Celadon Sheep, Yue Kiln

Three Kingdoms Period (220–265 CE)
Height: 25cm, Length: 30.5cm
Excavated from Qingjing Mountain Wu Tombs, Nanjing, Three Kingdoms Period
Collection of the National Museum of China

三国两晋时期的越窑出现许多用模制成形的动物瓷塑，青瓷羊是典型代表。羊四肢蜷曲作卧状，昂首，睁目，张嘴，额前有一小圆孔。羊身有许多刻划线条，勾勒出身体各个细节，生动细腻。

洪州窑青釉戳印花纹碗及印模

隋（公元581–618年）
碗高6.4、口径19.5、底径8cm
江西丰城出土
江西省博物馆、丰城市博物馆藏

Hongzhou Kiln Celadon Bowl with Impressed Seals and Molded Designs

Sui Dynasty (581–618 CE)
Height: 6.4cm, Diameter of mouth: 19.5cm, Diameter of base 8cm
Excavated from Fengchen Kiln, Jiangxi
Collection of Jiangxi Provincial Museum and the Fengcheng Municipal Museum

洪州窑始于东晋，终于晚唐，是唐代著名青瓷窑厂之一。隋代洪州窑就已使用模印技术，在胎体上用印模戳印出花朵草叶等纹饰，是最早的瓷器印花装饰。

越窑青釉刻花单柄壶

南朝（公元420–589年）
高21.3、口径11、足径12cm
故宫博物院藏

Yue Kiln Single Handle Carved Pot with a Green Glaze

Southern Dynasties (420–589 CE)
Height 21.3cm, Diameter of mouth: 11cm, Diameter of foot: 12cm
Collection of the Palace Museum

越窑自南朝起就有成熟的刻划花技术。此壶的肩及腹下刻划仰覆莲花纹，莲瓣肥厚硕大，中间刻划缠枝纹。刻花装饰运用剔地、划纹等不同工艺，线条流畅，纹饰自然。壶里外满釉，釉色青绿，积釉处透明呈玻璃状。壶短流，单柄，柄端翘起，造型新颖别致。

“裴家花枕”款绞胎枕

唐晚期（公元10世纪）
高9、长21.5、宽14.1cm
苏州博物馆藏

Intertwined Clay Pillow with ‘Pei Family Floral Pillow’ Inscription

Late Tang Dynasty (10th century CE)
Height: 9cm, Length: 21.5cm, Width: 14.1cm
Collection of the Suzhou Museum

绞胎是将白、褐两种颜色的胎土相互糅合相绞自然的纹饰。其装饰方式一是用绞胎坯泥直接拉坯成型，胎体白褐相间，纹理清晰，变化无穷；另一种以绞胎泥片贴面，拼成有规律的图案。唐代绞胎瓷非常出名，巩县窑、当阳峪窑都是绞胎器的著名产地。这件瓷枕枕面呈如意形，中心以绞胎拼出莲瓣纹团花，两侧也各有一组对称的绞胎团花。底部印有“裴家花枕”款，是商标的最早形式。

耀州窑狮子模具

唐（公元618−907年）
高21.6、长20.4、宽16.4cm
陕西铜川耀州窑出土
耀州窑博物馆藏

Mold in the Shape of a Lion, Yaozhou Kiln

Tang Dynasty (618−907CE)
Height: 21.6cm, Length: 20.4cm, Width: 16.4cm
Excavated from the Yaozhou Kiln Site in Tongchuan, Shaanxi
Collection of the Yaozhou Kiln Museum

耀州窑的模印技术非常出名，不仅有碗类等器物的纹样模，还有人物模和动物模，唐代黄堡窑的窑址中就出土有马模、狮子模、虎模等，都是素烧胎，或者左右合范，或者前后合范，刻划细致，生动逼真。

登封窑白釉珍珠地划花双虎纹瓶

北宋（公元960–1127年）
高31.9、口径7.1、足径9.5cm
故宫博物院藏

Double Tiger Vase with Pearl Background from the Dengfeng Kiln

Northern Song Dynasty (960–1127 CE)
Height: 31.9cm, Diameter of mouth: 7.1cm, Diameter of foot: 9.5cm
Collection of the Palace Museum

珍珠地划花是在成型的胎上施白色化妆土，再用工具在其上刻划纹饰，在空白处戳印珍珠状细密的小圆圈，在刻纹、戳纹凹下处再以赭色泥料抹平，最后上透明釉入窑烧成。这种装饰源自唐代金银器上的錾花工艺，晚唐时期始创于河南密县，北宋时传到河北、山西两省，以登封窑最为典型。瓶形似橄榄。瓶身刻二虎，一站立，一行走，在草丛中搏斗，气势凶猛。画法生动，线条流畅。

定窑白釉孩儿枕

北宋（公元960–1127年）
高18.8、长30cm
故宫博物院藏

Child's Pillow from the Ding Kiln

Northern Song Dynasty (960–1127 CE)
Height: 18.8cm, Length: 30cm
Collection of the Palace Museum

宋元时期瓷枕非常流行。李清照《醉花阴》词中写到："玉枕纱橱，半夜凉初透"，指的就是瓷枕。定窑为宋代五代名窑之一，以生产细腻光洁的白瓷著称，瓷质精细，釉色纯一，典雅大方。这件定窑孩儿枕充分体现了当时的成就。它是模制成形的典范，其外形为一伏于榻上的婴儿，双手交叠垫在头下，右手执一绣球。婴儿背部下凹为枕面。双足上翘，憨态可掬。此枕运用了印、划等技法，刻划出栩栩如生的婴儿形象，生趣盎然，是定瓷中难得一见的珍品。

定窑白釉印花撇口碗

宋（公元960–1279年）
高4.6、口径17、足径3.4cm
故宫博物院藏

Flared-Mouth Bowl with Impressed Floral Design form the Ding Kiln

Song Dynasty (960–1279 CE)
Height:4.6cm, Diameter of mouth:17cm, Diameter of foot: 3.4cm
Collection of the Palace Museum

宋代定窑白瓷印花借鉴当地盛行的缂丝，形成了独特的风格。花纹以缠枝、折枝、转枝等花卉最多，也有孔雀、凤凰、鸳鸯等禽鸟纹。整体布局繁密严整，精致细腻，含蓄典雅，具有缂丝图案意味。此碗作斗笠状，内壁印缠枝菊花三朵，碗心为六瓣朵花。胎质细腻，釉色洁白纯净，芒口镶铜圈，是定窑白瓷的精美之作。

耀州窑印花印模

宋（公元960–1279年）
高7.9、口径16.8cm
上海博物馆藏

Impressing Mold form the Yaozhou Kiln

Song Dynasty (960–1279 CE)
Height: 7.9cm, Diameter of mouth: 16.8cm
Collection of the Shanghai Museum

北宋中期以后，定窑、耀州窑相继出现印花装饰，纹饰清晰，布局严整，讲求对称，在宋代各地生产的印花瓷器中出类拔萃。瓷器上的印花花纹是在碗坯完成以后用印模印制而成的。印模通常以瓷土制作，上面刻有花纹。定窑、耀州窑印花均以清晰、满密见长。

千峰翠色·青瓷
Myriad Emerald Peaks: Celadon

巧剜明月染春水，轻旋薄冰盛绿云。古镜破苔当席上，嫩荷涵露别江渍。

——［唐］徐夤

作为最早的瓷器品类，青瓷的诞生是中国瓷器烧造历史上的重要里程碑。胎釉中含有适量的氧化铁，经还原焰烧成，呈现淡青、翠青、粉青等各种优雅悦目的青色，通称为青瓷。青瓷的雏形出现在商周（公元前16－前4世纪），至东汉（公元2世纪）发展成熟，有越窑、耀州窑、官窑、汝窑、龙泉窑等主要窑口，不同时期和不同地区的青瓷各有特色。

六朝（公元3－6世纪）青瓷的雅致迎合了士大夫的意趣，颇有时代气息。晚唐五代（公元9－10世纪）秘色瓷代表了青瓷的巅峰，“九秋风露越窑开，赢得千峰翠色来”成为咏叹青瓷的绝唱。宋代（公元11－13世纪）厚釉技术的发明为青瓷开辟了一片新天地，汝窑的“雨过天晴”、官窑的“粉青”、龙泉窑的“梅子青”、“如玉似冰”，青瓷之美让人陶醉。碧玉般沉静素雅、清丽莹润的青瓷在中国陶瓷史上享有崇高的地位，一度独揽瓷坛风光。

The exquisitely curved bright moon colors the spring waters, lightly spinning ice catches the green clouds

——Xu Yin, Tang Dynasty

As the earliest type of porcelain, the emergence of celadon is an important milestone in the history of Chinese porcelain. Celadon belongs to the class of colored glaze porcelain. The glazes used to create celadon wares contained oxidized iron and through a reductive firing process various elegant shades of green, such as light green, blue-green, and light bluish green were produced. The word, celadon, is a literal translation of the Chinese term for ‘green porcelain’. Early stages of celadon production began in the Shang and Zhou dynasties, but mature development was only achieved during the Eastern Han period. Important celadon production kilns include the Yue Kilns, Yaozhou Kilns, Ru Kilns, and Longquan Kilns. Located in different regions, each kiln's fame came in a different era and each produced a distinctive form of celadon.

In the Six Dynasties Period (229-589 CE) celadon tastes catered to the interests of the scholarly elite, and therefore embodied aesthetic characteristics of that period. Late Tang Dynasty and Five Dynasties period olive green porcelain (known as Mise wares) represented the zenith of celadon wares. This peak of celadon perfection was commemorated with such poetic phrases as: ‘the nine autumn's wind and dew began at Yue Kiln, winning the myriad peaks of green along the way’. The invention of a thick glazing technique in the Song Dynasty opened up new frontiers in celadon, such as the enchanting celadon wares of the Ru Kilns, that seemed like a ‘sky cleared after the rain’, the imperial kiln's ‘light bluish green’, and the Longquan Kiln's ‘plum green’ and ‘ice jade’. Celadon, with its emerald luster and simple elegance, its purity and mellowness, enjoys a lofty place in the history of Chinese ceramics and for a time held the spotlight entirely.

越窑
Yue Kiln

越窑是中国古代南方首屈一指的青瓷窑系，分布于浙江东北部杭州湾南岸的绍兴、上虞、余姚、慈溪至宁波、鄞县一带。早在商周时期就已烧造成功原始青瓷，经过千年的发展与积累，终于在东汉时期首先烧造成青瓷，使中国成为发明瓷器的国家。越窑始于东汉，盛于唐、五代，衰于宋，烧制时间长，生产规模大，影响深远。

越窑瓷器胎质细腻，釉汁纯净，以青和青黄色调为主，成形、装饰技法繁多，品种丰富。晚唐五代的秘色瓷更是越窑青瓷的巅峰之作，"捩翠融青"的釉色引人神往。越窑上林湖秘色瓷与同时代越窑青釉瓷在胎、釉原料化学组成上基本相同，但从外观上可见制作工艺的区别。秘色瓷胎质比越窑青釉瓷均匀细致，气孔与分层明显减少；釉层厚薄均匀，釉面光泽滋润，少见剥釉开片；成形也更加规整细致。秘色瓷还采用用釉浆密封的瓷质匣钵等独特的装烧工艺，瓷质匣钵和釉封技术提高了匣钵的密封性，避免了烧成后期的二次氧化，使秘色瓷的釉色更加青绿、纯正。

The Yue Kiln was the main celadon kiln of a series of kilns in southern China in classical times. All were in northeast Zhejiang and were in towns spread over a large area of Yinxian County and on southern banks of Hangzhou, such as Shaoxing, Shangyu, Yuyao, Cixi and Ningbo. Prototype celadon was first produced early in the Shang and Zhou Dynasties. Through a thousand years of development and continued production the first true celadon was fired during the Eastern Han Dynasty, marking China as the first nation to produce porcelain. The Yue Kiln was established in the Eastern Han Dynasty and flourished in the Tang Dynasty and Five Dynasties, finally declining during the Song dynasty. The kiln's period of activity was long, its scale of production was large, and its influence over the Chinese porcelain industry was deep. It was at the vanguard and was the driving force of Chinese porcelain production.

Yue Kiln porcelain bodies were extremely fine and its glaze pure, with a prevalence of light green, yellow and yellow-green tones. Molding and decorative technologies were varied and the assortment of vessels created was diverse. Designs were simple and tasteful, for which the wares have been praised throughout history. In the early Tang Dynasty many odes to the Yue Kilns appeared in refined and elegant verse. The olive green porcelain, known as Mise wares (Lit. "Imperial Color"), of the late Tang Dynasty and Five Dynasties period was the crowning achievement of Yue Kiln porcelain, it had an 'emerald and melted green' color scale that attracted countless admirers.

Yue Kiln Shanglin Lake olive green porcelain, known as Mise ware, and other Yue celadon wares of the same era are largely identical in terms of basic chemical composition of the glaze and body material, but in their appearance it is evident that there is something different in the burning technology. The bodies of Mise ware vessels are even finer than Yue Kiln celadon wares, with significantly decreased numbers of pores and layers. The thickness of the glaze is even and the surfaces are lustrous and sleek, with only rare instances of crackling. The forms of Mise ware vessels are also more orderly and refined. This demonstrates that the selection and processing of raw materials for such vessels were evidently highly refined techniques. The color of Mise wares is also a stronger green than Yue Kiln celadon wares. These qualities are all closely related to the use of special firing technologies including porcelain saggers bank the glaze. Use of porcelain saggers guarantees continuity in the shrinking of the product during firing and helps a vessel avoid warping. The technique of using saggers to bank the glaze increased the sealing nature of saggers and prevented oxidization during the period after burning, making the glaze tone greener.

越窑青釉熊形灯

三国·吴甘露元年（公元265年）
高11.5、口径9.5cm
江苏南京三国吴墓出土
中国国家博物馆藏

Green Glazed Lamp in the Shape of a Bear from the Yue Kiln

First year of Ganlu Era during Wu of Three Kingdoms (265 CE)
Height: 11.5cm, Diameter of mouth: 9.5cm
Excavated from the Wu Tombs, Nanjing, Jiangsu
Collection of the National Museum

灯为古代照明器具。三国两晋南北朝的瓷器中有很多动物形状的灯，如狮灯、羊灯、熊灯等。这件熊灯为越窑产品，分为灯、柱、盘三部分，灯为钵形，柱为一只蹲坐举灯的熊。盘底刻有"甘露元年五月造"铭文。

越窑青釉兽形尊

西晋永宁二年（公元302年）
高27.9、口径13.2cm
江苏宜兴西晋墓出土
南京博物院藏

Green Glazed Wine Cup in the Shape of a Mythical Beast from the Yue Kiln

2nd year of Yongning Era during the Western Jin Dynasty (302 CE)
Height 27.9cm, Diameter of mouth: 13.2cm
Excavated from a Western Jin Tomb in Yixing, Jiangsu
Collection of the Nanjing Museum

尊为盘口，颈部下方堆塑一狮形神兽，作蹲坐状，仰头朝天，双目圆瞪，口内衔珠。兽首两侧有绳索形四肢，全身用简单的线条刻划出皮毛、双翼等细节，轮廓鲜明，神形兼备。

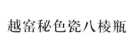

越窑青釉执壶

唐元和五年（公元810年）
高13.4、口径5.9、足径7.3cm
浙江绍兴王叔文夫人墓出土
故宫博物院藏

Green Glazed Pitcher from the Yue Kiln

5th year of Yuanhe Era during the Tang Dynasty (810 CE)
Height 13.4cm, Diameter of mouth: 5.9cm, Diameter of foot: 7.3cm
Excavated from Wang Shuwen Wife's Tomb in Shaoxing, Zhejiang
Collection of the Palace Museum

执壶又称注子。此壶器形简练，颈部一侧有八方形短流，相对另一侧有曲形双复柄，为唐代越窑最典型的器形。青釉莹澈，青中泛黄，有细小开片。

越窑秘色瓷八棱瓶

唐咸通十五年（公元874年）
高21.5、口径2.2cm
陕西扶风法门寺地宫出土
法门寺博物馆藏

Octagonal Yue Kiln Olive Green Porcelain (Mise Ware) Vase

15th year of Xiantong Era during the Tang Dynasty (874 CE)
Height: 21.5cm, Diameter of mouth: 2.2cm
Excavated from the shrine beneath the Famen Temple, Fufeng, Shaanxi
Collection of the Famen Temple Museum

八棱瓶造型简洁挺拔，釉色青绿莹润。“九秋风露越窑开，夺得千峰翠色来”，“千峰翠色”正是晚唐、五代时期越窑秘色瓷釉色的特点。秘色瓷的烧造由于使用了用釉密封的瓷质匣钵，更好地控制烧成气氛，使得釉面青翠透亮，如薄冰上的青云，秋水上的碧波，美不胜收。

耀州窑
Yaozhou Kiln

耀州窑窑址在今陕西省铜川市黄堡镇一带，是北方最著名的名窑之一，创烧于唐代，鼎盛于宋代中晚期（公元11－12世纪），以生产独特的刻花和印花青瓷著称。耀州窑瓷器釉色以橄榄青和黄绿色为主，莹透朴拙。宋代采用煤为燃料后，大大提高烧成温度，使得釉色更为晶莹润泽。

耀州窑刻花刀法犀利洒脱，线条活泼流畅，题材广泛，清新鲜活，透露出率性、生动的民间意趣。北宋晚期的印花器技法独特，纹饰丰富，刻划细腻，布局严整，有着很高的艺术审美价值。产品种类繁多，构造精妙，体现了工匠的高度智慧和创造力。

The Yaozhou Kiln was located near Huangbao Town, Tongchuan city in Shaanxi Province. It is one of the most famous kilns in the north with a production period that dates from the Tang dynasty and prospered in the mid to late Song dynasty. The kiln was well known for its unique incised design and impressed design celadon wares. Yaozhou Kiln porcelain colors were principally olive green and yellow, and were highly lustrous in quality. During the Song dynasty, after the introduction of coal for fuel, the firing temperature was significantly increased in Yaozhou furnaces, creating glazes that were even glossier than before. Yaozhou Kiln incised design methods employed lines that were lively and smooth, with subject matters that were wide-ranging and included charming folk craft details. In the late Northern Song the tools for impressed design techniques were quite distinctive and created rich designs with fine carving, as well as precise compositions with a particular emphasis on symmetry and a high aesthetic value. Yaozhou Kiln products were varied in type and skillfully constructed, reflecting the high degree of knowledge and creative ability of the kiln's artisans.

耀州窑青釉剔刻花牡丹纹壶

五代（公元907－960年）
高21.2、口径4.1cm
甘肃成县红川镇出土
成县文化馆藏

Incised Design Peony Teapot from the Yaozhou Kiln

Five Dynasties (907－960CE)
Height: 21.2cm, Diameter of mouth: 4.1cm
Excavated from Hongchuan Village, Chengxian, Gansu
Collection of the Chengxian Cultural Museum

耀州窑五代时期的剔刻花装饰以刀法精湛、纹路清晰、层次丰富著称，具有浮雕效果。此壶是耀州窑的精美之作，塔形盖，高颈，圆腹，颈、腹间连一曲形长柄。流口做成一只蹲踞怒吼的狮子，腹部主体纹饰为缠枝牡丹，花姿柔媚，枝叶婉转，美观大方。

耀州窑青釉刻花三足瓶

北宋(公元960－1127年)
通高21.4、口径8cm
上海博物馆藏

Three-Legged Carved Vase with Green Glaze from the Yaozhou Kiln

Northern Song Dynasty (960–1127 CE)
Height: 21.4cm, Diameter of mouth: 8cm
Collection of the Shanghai Museum

瓶的主体纹饰装饰于下腹部，为连续刻花纹样，刀法犀利，线条流畅，构图丰满。下承三兽足。

耀州窑青釉飞鱼形水盂

辽（公元916－1125年）
高9.3、长14cm
辽宁北票辽墓出土
辽宁省博物馆藏

Celadon Flying Fish Ink Pot from the Yaozhou Kiln

Liao Dynasty (916–1125 CE)
Height: 9.3cm, Lenght: 14cm
Excavated from the Liao Tombs at Beipiao, Liaoning
Collection of the Liaoning Provincial Museum

水盂为古代文房用具，用于往砚台上滴水溶墨。鱼形或鱼龙形器皿在辽代比较普遍，这件水盂雕成飞跃的鲤鱼，又似出水的游龙，甩尾高翘，两旁为上举的翅膀，全身鳞片历历可数，灵动之气呼之欲出。

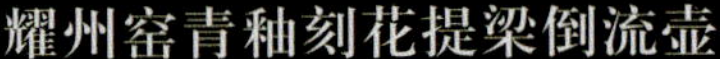

耀州窑青釉刻花提梁倒流壶

北宋（公元960-1127年）
通高18.3、腹径14.3、腹深12cm
陕西彬县出土
陕西历史博物馆藏

Green Glazed Bottom-filled Teapot with a Handle from the Yaozhou Kiln

Northern Song Dynasty (960-1127 CE)
Height: 18.3cm, Diameter at widest point: 14.3cm, Depth of bowl: 12cm
Excavated in Binxian, Shaanxi
Collection of the Shaanxi History Museum

提梁壶构造巧妙，壶盖不能开启。灌水时要将壶倒置，从底部灌入。壶内有漏柱和水相隔，使得壶放正后滴水不漏。盖壶作荷叶状，提梁为一伏卧的凤凰，流口雕刻成正在哺乳的子母狮，腹部为缠枝牡丹花，下腹近底处饰一周仰莲瓣纹。纹饰刻工精细，生动活泼。

汝窑
Ru Kiln

汝窑为宋瓷之首，烧造时间短，传世稀少，在南宋时已是“近尤难得”，历来被奉为无上珍品。《清波杂志》记载汝窑以玛瑙入釉，使其更添神秘色彩。传世汝窑器以盘碟为多，还有碗、洗、瓶、尊等器形，小巧精致。

汝窑的胎色为香灰色，迎光照看略带粉色。釉汁莹润，釉色淡雅、呈色稳定，如“雨过天青”，釉面有“蟹爪”纹。器物通体施釉，裹足支烧，底部一般有3-5个支钉痕细小如芝麻状，这是汝窑最突出的工艺特征。汝官窑青瓷釉色较之当时北方青釉瓷更为淡雅、滋润，一是由于釉中少量铁离子在还原烧成中使釉呈现出青绿色，二是由于釉层乳浊呈现半透明状。釉层乳浊是因为釉层中包含了由极小晶体、气泡、未熔物以及晶间分相等组成的细小微粒，它们对入射光线造成散射而产生的，这是汝窑青釉形成玉质感的重要因素之一。

The Ru Kiln was the most important kiln site during the Song Dynasty. The kiln's period of activity was short and little information about the kiln is available today. During the Southern Song Dynasty Ru wares were already described as the 'rarest and most outstanding', and over the dynasties these vessels have been esteemed as highly prized treasures. In the Miscellany Records of Qingbo by Zhou Hui of the Southern Song, it was recorded that the Ru Kiln used agate for glaze, which created unique colors. Most extant Ru Kiln porcelain is in the form of small dishes or plates, but there are also delicate bowls, brush-washing basins, vases, and urns that were produced by the kiln.

Ru Kiln body color is the shade of incense ash that appears slightly pink where it peeks through the glaze. The glaze is lustrous and the color is delicate and refined, like 'the sky clearing after rain'. These qualities relate to the loss of transparency in the glaze. The glaze surface also has a 'crab claw' pattern. The bases generally have three to five tiny traces of spurs left from foot firing techniques, which is the most prominent characteristic of Ru Kiln techniques.

Looking at the color, Ru Kiln celadons are even more delicate and refined than the northern style celadons of the era. One reason is due to the small amount of iron ions in the glaze. In a reductive firing process iron ions bring out the green tones of the glaze. Another reason stems from the phenomenon of translucency in the milkiness of the layers in the glaze. This translucency is due to the production of a scattered light as it enters the glaze. These fine particles are in the composition of the micro-level crystalline structure, in the air bubbles, crystalline divisions and non-fused particles of the glaze. The divisions produced in the micro-levels of the glaze structure are due to a specific chemical composition, which happens in response to the firing temperature and atmospheric conditions, creating different compositions of two non-mixing liquids. This separation is a particular physical characteristic in the glaze firing process, a chemical phenomenon that forms the jade-like quality that is one of the important elements of Ru Kiln celadons.

汝窑青釉三足洗

北宋晚期（公元11世纪末-12世纪初）
高4、口径18.5cm
故宫博物院藏

Green Glazed Tripod Writing-brush Washing Basin from the Ru Kiln

Late Northern Song Dynasty (end of 11th century - beginning of 12th century CE)
Height: 4cm, Diameter of mouth: 18.5cm
Collection of the Palace Museum

汝窑三足洗仿汉代铜洗造型。釉色为典型的天青色，釉面有细小开片。里外满釉，底部用五支钉支烧，有后刻的乾隆御制诗。

汝窑青釉圆洗

北宋（公元960-1127年）
高3.9、口径7.5、足径5.7cm
故宫博物院藏

Green Glazed Round Water Vessel from the Ru Kiln

Northern Song Dynasty (960-1127CE)
Height: 3.9cm, Diameter of the mouth: 7.5cm, Diameter of the foot: 5.7cm
Collection of the Palace Museum

洗是汝窑较多见的器形，釉色天青，釉面有开片。

汝窑以玛瑙入釉

汝窑以玛瑙入釉，玛瑙的成分是二氧化硅，完全有可能用于釉料的配比。将汝窑标本和玛瑙标本对比，对于两者的外观有直接认识，对于微观的构成也有清晰了解。

Agate, composed of silicone dioxide, was a key ingredient in Ru Kiln glazes, as the surface similarities of these two samples make clear.

汝窑青釉三足洗底部

Base of Green Glazed Tripod Writing-brush Washing Basin from the Ru Kiln

官窑
Guan Kiln

官窑有北宋官窑和南宋官窑之分。北宋官窑又称汴京官窑，文献记载少，窑址不明。南宋时，在浙江临安设立官窑，前有修内司，后有郊坛下，已被考古发掘所证实。南宋官窑吸收了北方汴京官窑、汝窑和南方龙泉窑的特点，器形既有古朴肃穆的仿古陈设瓷，又有轻巧灵便的日用器。胎色赭黑，釉色以粉青、灰青为主，“厚釉薄胎”，“紫口铁足”，创造出“璞玉”的效果。以官窑为代表的厚釉青瓷的出现，开拓了瓷器发展的新局面。

粉青如玉是南宋官窑的典型特征，这来自于南宋官窑创烧的厚釉技术。当时在釉料中增加了钾、钠的含量，创烧出在高温中黏度比钙釉大的石灰碱釉，减少了烧成中流釉现象。同时采用多次施釉工艺，使釉层明显增厚，晶莹剔透，形成特有的玉质感。另外由于胎、釉膨胀系数差异，釉面呈现出各种裂纹，疏密深浅不一，在青玉般的釉面上形成独特的自然纹饰。

The Imperial Kiln is divided into the Northern Song Imperial Kiln and the Southern Song Imperial Kiln. The Northern Song Imperial Kiln was also called the Bianjing Imperial Kiln. There is very little documentation available today about this kiln, and its location is unknown. Remaining pieces from this kiln are rare, only amounting to a few bowls, vases, and brush washers. The bodies of these vessels are thick and heavy and tend towards black in color. The glaze coloring is an elegant light green, with large crackling patterns along the surface of the vessels. Northern Song Imperial wares are known by the phrase, ‘purple mouth and iron foot’. In the Southern Song period the Imperial Kiln was established in Lin’an, Zhejiang Province. Wares produced at this kiln absorbed the characteristics of the Bianjing Imperial Kiln, the Ru Kiln and the Longquan Kiln. Important glaze colors included bluish green and sage green, with thick glazes and thick bodies, ‘purple mouth and iron foot’. The resulting vessels often were thought to resemble raw jade and had various glaze surface cracks that were at times densely packed with deep lines. A variety of vessels were produced at this kiln including as ornamental porcelains, which imitated ancient relics in a simple and solemn style. There were also elegant porcelains for daily use. With the appearance of thick glaze celadons in the Imperial Kiln a new dimension of porcelain development was created.

A bluish jade-like green was the defining characteristic of the Southern Song Imperial Kiln and came from a thick glaze burning technique. This was due to the invention of a calcium-alkaline glaze that had a higher firing degree than regular calcium glaze. It reduced the phenomenon of running in the glazing process and added stickiness and a crystalline layer to the glaze. The translucency in the glaze, which gave the vessels their jade-like appearance, was produced from the dividing structure and became even more pronounced as the technique developed. At the same time the technique of using multiple layers of glaze was used to the point that a vessel's glaze surpassed its body in thickness. Also, due to this, the glaze and body expansion coefficients differed, and a variety of crackling appeared on the glaze surface, forming a characteristic design on the surface of this celadon glaze type.

官窑青釉圆洗

南宋（公元1127–1279年）
高6.2、口径21.5、足径18.3cm
故宫博物院藏

Green Glazed Round Water Vessel from the Ru Kiln

Southern Song Dynasty (1127–1279 CE)
Height: 6.2cm, Diameter of mouth: 21.5cm, Diameter of foot: 18.3cm
Collection of the Palace Museum

直壁，口微敞，浅宽圈足，底部露胎呈褐色。粉青色釉，清亮润泽，釉面有冰裂开片。造型古朴典雅，端庄凝重。器底有后刻的乾隆御题诗。

官窑青釉弦纹瓶

南宋（公元1127–1279年）
高33.6、口径9.9、足径14cm
故宫博物院藏

Green Glazed Vase from the Imperial Kiln

Southern Song Dynasty (1127–1279 CE)
Height: 33.6cm, Diameter of mouth: 9.9cm, Diameter of foot: 14cm
Collection of the Palace Museum

长颈，鼓腹，高圈足。颈部及腰部各饰三道凸弦纹。釉色偏青，光亮润泽。有典型的“紫口铁足”。釉面开片自然，造型端庄稳重。

哥窑
Ge Kiln

哥窑是宋代五大名窑之一，其时代为南宋至元代，窑址尚未发现，产品传世罕见。从国内外各大博物馆所藏传世品看，主要造型有瓶、炉、洗、盘、碗等，釉层较厚，釉面莹润剔透，以开片装饰著称。哥窑最为典型的是“金丝铁线”，它是因为釉和胎的膨胀系数不一致在釉面形成深浅不一、疏密有致的裂纹，经人工染色而成。哥窑胎土含铁量较高，“紫口铁足”的特点与南宋官窑颇为相似。

The Ge Kiln was one of the five major kilns of the Song Dynasty. It existed from the Southern Song Dynasty through the Yuan Dynasty. The location of the kiln is not yet known and extant works are scarce. Important works in large national and international museums include vases, censers, brush washers, plates, bowls and jars. Glazes are relatively thick, the surfaces lustrous, and the ware is well known for its crackling pattern. The classic model of the Ge Kiln is 'golden threads and iron lines', called such because of the dense, deep and varied crackling pattern caused on the glaze surface by differing coefficients of expansion between the body and glaze, cracks that were also dyed by workers. The iron content of Ge Kiln clay is relatively high, earning in the name 'purple mouth and iron foot', much like the Southern Song Dynasty Imperial Kiln wares.

哥窑戟耳炉

南宋（公元1127-1279年）
高5.3、口径7.5、足径5.7cm
故宫博物院藏

Incense Burner with Halberd-Shaped Handles from the Ge Kiln

Southern Song Dynasty (1127-1279 CE)
Height: 5.3cm, Diameter of mouth: 7.5cm, Diameter of foot: 5.7cm
Collection of the Palace Museum

直口外撇，鼓腹，圈足，两侧各有一戟形耳。釉色光泽，釉面布满大小不一的“金丝铁线”。

哥窑葵口碗

南宋（公元1127-1279年）
高7.4、口径20.3cm
上海博物馆藏

Mallow-petal Rim Bowl from the Ge Kiln

Southern Song Dynasty (1127-1279 CE)
Height: 7.4cm, Diameter of mouth: 20.3cm
Collection of the Shanghai Museum

敞口，敛腹，小圈足，器身有四道凹棱，为四莲瓣状。里外布满大小不一的“金丝铁线”纹片。

钧窑
Jun Kiln

钧窑是北方著名的青瓷系统，窑址位于河南禹县，古属钧州，故名。钧窑的主要特色是它的乳浊釉，釉中含有一定量的氧化铜，烧出的釉色青中带红，艳如晚霞，主要有海棠红、玫瑰紫、钧红、天蓝、月白等釉色。

钧窑的釉是一种典型的分相釉，这是因为釉中硅、钙、镁、磷偏高，铝偏低，这种特点能促使釉在高温中产生分相。此外，各种颜色的窑变釉和釉面隐现的蚯蚓走泥纹，也是钧窑区别于其他青瓷的重要特点。

The Jun Kiln was one of the famous celadon kilns of the north and was located in Yuxian county, Henan Province, which is located in what used to be Junzhou, hence the name. The defining characteristic of Jun Kiln is its milky glaze, which contains a specific quantity of oxidized copper. When fired the green glaze color also contains a red that is the color of a late sunset. Color varieties include sky blue, lavender, flowering crabapple red, rose purple and Jun red. Jun kiln glaze is a typical divided glaze. This is due to the relatively high amounts of silicon, calcium, magnesium and phosphorus and the low amount of aluminum, which, when combined and burned at high temperature, compels the glaze to separate. Aside from this, Jun ware can also be differentiated from other types of celadon by its characteristic transmutation, or flambé, of color in the kiln and the earthworm-trail patterns in the glaze.

钧窑鼓钉三足洗

公元14世纪
高8、口径21cm
故宫博物院藏

Tripod Writing-brush Washing Basin with Drum-nail Pattern from the Jun Kiln

14th century CE
Height:8cm, Diameter of mouth: 21cm
Collection of the Palace Museum

钧窑为宋代五大名窑之一，釉色千变万化。该洗釉质肥厚，釉色富于变化。

钧窑月白釉出戟尊

公元14世纪
高32.6、口径26、足径21cm
故宫博物院藏

Pale Blue Glazed *Zun* Vessel from the Jun Kiln

14th century CE
Height: 32.6cm, Diameter of mouth: 26cm, Diameter of foot: 21cm
Collection of the Palace Museum

钧窑以独特的乳浊釉著称。钧器一般刻有一至十的数字，是器物大小的标志。数字越小，器形越大。钧窑出戟尊模仿青铜器尊的造型，腹部和足部都有扉棱出戟，底部刻“三”字。内外施月白釉。造型古朴典雅，气势雄伟浑厚，是钧窑中难得一见的珍品。

➲ 钧窑“己酉年”款天蓝釉贴花龙纹炉

元己酉年（公元1309年）
高42.7、口径25.5cm
内蒙古博物馆藏

Jun Kiln Applique Dragon Censer dated the ‘Year of Jiyou’

Yuan Dynasty, (1309 CE)
Height: 42.7cm, Diameter of mouth: 25.5cm
Collection of the Inner Mongolia Museum

元代钧窑窑系主要分布在河南、河北、山西等北方地区。产品大部分是碗盘等日用品。这件香炉为少有的大器，通体天蓝釉，口沿两侧有附耳，下接双鱼耳。颈部堆贴三个麒麟，正面中间有一块凸起的方形碑记，阴刻楷书款“己酉年九月十五小宋自造香炉一个”。整器釉质肥润，器形浑厚，气势非凡。

己酉年
九月十五
小宋自造
香炉一个

龙泉窑
Longquan Kiln

龙泉窑位于浙江龙泉，创烧于北宋早期，南宋晚期至元代达到鼎盛，明中期以后走向衰弱，是南方重要的青瓷体系。龙泉窑青瓷以釉色著称，南宋以后使用石灰碱釉，经过多次素烧多次上釉，使得釉层厚而不流，并在胎中掺入一定量的紫金土，降低白度，衬托出釉色的深沉、柔和、淡雅、莹润，创造出青玉般的效果。粉青、梅子青的烧制成功，成为青瓷釉色之美的典范。

The Longquan Kiln was located in Longquan, Zhejiang Province and started to produce ceramics during the early Northern Song dynasty, reached its most prosperous period in the Southern Song to Yuan dynasties, and declined after the mid-Ming dynasty. As was one of the important celadon centers of the south, the Longquan kiln was famed for its glaze color that after the Southern Song period was derived from an alkali lime glaze. Through a series of plain and glazed firings, the glaze layer became thick and firmly set. Longquan vessel bodies were composed of the highest quality clay. The white body provided an excellent base for the pale green glaze, producing vessels that had a jade like luster. The bluish green and plum green glazes that were Longquan specialties, when fired correctly, were hailed as perfect examples of the celadon color range.

龙泉窑青釉贴花葫芦瓶

元（公元1271－1368年）
高26.8、口径3.8cm
山西大同出土
大同市博物馆藏

Longquan Celadon Applique Gourd Vase

Yuan Dynasty (1271–1368 CE)
Height: 26.8cm, Diameter of mouth: 3.8cm
Excavated from Datong, Shanxi
Collection of the Datong Municipal Museum

葫芦瓶为龙泉窑的创新品种，形似上小下大的束腰葫芦，由上下两部分黏合而成。葫芦瓶与道教相关，其谐音为“福禄”，表达了人们美好的愿望。元代龙泉窑流行贴花装饰，将模印或者捏塑的泥质花片用泥浆粘贴在已成形的器物坯体表面，再施釉入窑焙烧。此瓶上半身贴朵云纹，下半身贴缠枝菊花纹。施釉肥厚，丰腴润泽，葱翠如玉，精巧又不失典雅。

龙泉窑青釉贯耳瓶

南宋（公元1127–1279年）
高31.1、口径4.9cm
四川遂宁金鱼村窖藏出土
遂宁市博物馆藏

Green Glazed Vase with Tube-shaped Vertical Handles from the Longquan Kiln

Southern Song Dynasty (1127–1279 CE)
Height: 31.1cm, Diameter of mouth: 4.9cm
Excavated from the Jinyu Village Kiln Site in Suining, Sichuan
Collection of the Suining Municipal Museum

贯耳瓶原为商周青铜礼器中"投礼"之用器，宋代崇尚商周礼制，遂成为官窑、龙泉窑中常见的器形。此瓶胎灰白致密，施豆青釉，肥厚润泽，制作精细，是南宋晚期龙泉窑中的珍品。

如银似雪·白瓷
Like Silver and Snow: White Porcelain

大邑烧瓷轻且坚，扣如哀玉锦城传。

——［唐］杜甫

青瓷之后，古代又使用高岭土和长石为原料，发明了白瓷。白瓷的出现，为后世各种颜色釉瓷、彩绘瓷提供了创造发展的基础。

白瓷创始于北方，河南、陕西等地北朝和隋代（公元6－7世纪）墓葬中皆有发现。白瓷的特征在于胎釉中铁含量少，当时工匠已经掌握了把原料中包括铁在内的杂质尽可能去除干净的技术，克服了铁元素的呈色干扰，白瓷得以脱离青瓷自成体系。

北齐起源、唐代成熟的白瓷，显示了烧造技术的巨大进步，是中国瓷器史上的一个新里程碑，奠定了彩瓷发展的基础，邢窑、定窑、景德镇窑和德化窑等窑口都曾闪耀过白瓷的辉煌。唐代邢窑的出现标志着白瓷烧造技术的成熟，“如银似雪”是最好的写照，它也开启了“南青北白”的瓷业格局。宋代定窑发明了支圈覆烧技术，白瓷胎体轻薄、器形规整。明永乐景德镇窑御器厂生产的甜白釉瓷器以见影的薄胎和肥腴的釉层成为白瓷中的极品。德化窑白瓷始于元，至明晚期以其光润如凝脂、微泛牙黄的釉成为流行欧洲的时尚，有“象牙白”、“鹅绒白”之美。

Dayi burns light but durable porcelain, it is like a sad piece of jade spreading around town.

——Du Fu, Tang Dynasty

After the emergence of celadon ceramics, potters began using kaolin and feldspar as raw materials, leading to the invention of true white porcelain. The appearance of this type of porcelain laid the foundation for the later development and creation of porcelains covered with glazes of all hues.

White porcelain originated in the north, and has been discovered in Northern Dynasties and Sui dynasty (6th - 7th century) burials in Henan, Shaanxi, and Anhui, etc. The characteristic of white porcelain is in the low iron content of its body glaze. Once the artisans mastered the technique of removing as much of the iron impurities as possible from the original material to achieve a greater purity, the problem of iron ingredients adding color was surmounted and white porcelain became separate from celadon.

White porcelain is one of the milestones of Chinese porcelain, from its origin in the Northern Qi dynasty to its maturity in the Tang dynasty. It is where the porcelain industry system of ‘Celadon in the South, White in the North’ comes from and also established the foundation for the development of painted pottery. White porcelain from the Tang dynasty Xing Kiln best shows the mature characteristic techniques, described as ‘like silver and snow’. In the Yuan dynasty the Dehua Kiln began to produce white porcelain, and was the representative variety through the Ming dynasty, including ‘lard white’, ‘ivory white’, and ‘goose down white’. The Xing Kiln, Ding Kiln, Jingdezhen Kiln and Dehua Kiln were all producers of the brilliant white porcelain. The lead white glaze porcelain that came out in the Yongle era of the Ming dynasty was the highest quality white porcelain.

早期白瓷
Early White Porcelain

白釉绿彩长颈瓶

北齐武平六年（公元575年）
高22、口径6.8cm
河南安阳北齐范粹墓出土
河南博物院藏

White Glazed Long Neck Vase with Green Designs

6th Year of Wuping Era, Northern Qi Dynasty, (575 CE)
Height: 22cm, Diameter of mouth: 6.8cm
Excavated from the Tomb of Fan Cui of the Northern Qi Dynasty, Anyang, Henan
Collection of Henan Museum

北朝范粹墓出土的几件白瓷器是早期白瓷的代表。胎体细白，釉层薄润。尽管与白瓷还有一定距离，却是有可靠纪年最早的标本。这件瓷瓶制作精美，全身施釉，釉色白中泛黄，腹部竖挂一片翠绿色斑纹，线条柔美，色彩协调。

白釉吏俑

隋开皇十四年（公元594年）
高72cm
河南安阳张盛墓出土
河南博物院藏

White Porcelain Figure of a Civil Official

4th Year of Kaihuang Era, Sui Dynasty, (594 CE)
Height: 72cm
Excavated from the Tomb of Zhangsheng, Anyang, Henan
Collection of the Henan Museum

俑是北朝至唐代墓葬中常见的陪葬品，显示着死者生前的显赫地位。一般为彩绘陶或者彩色釉陶，瓷俑少见。这件白瓷吏俑束发戴冠，浓眉大眼，络腮胡，身穿圆领广袖长袍，足登云头翘靴，双手拱袖，按剑直立于圆形莲座之上。俑身及莲座施灰白色釉，冠、履、剑鞘及领口、衣袖均以黑彩点染，形象生动。

白釉龙柄鸡首壶

隋大业四年（公元608年）
高27.4、口径7.1cm
陕西西安李静训墓出土
中国国家博物馆藏

White Glazed Chicken Head Ewer with a Dragon Handle

4th Year of Daye Era, Sui Dynasty, (608 CE)
Height: 27.4cm, Diameter of mouth: 7.1cm
Excavated from the Tomb of Li Jingxun in Xi'an, Shaanxi
Collection of the National Museum of China

两晋时期流行的鸡首壶，隋唐时造型上有了很大改变。鸡头由小变大，更为写实。壶身由矮变长，壶口变高，颈部更细长，颈中部以弦纹装饰，足部外撇，肩部双系也出现新的形式。这件白釉鸡首壶盘口外侈，竹节形颈，鼓腹下敛，底足外撇。肩部鸡首昂首挺胸，作啼鸣状。龙形长柄，肩部两侧各有一环耳状双系。体型修长，典雅端庄，是早期白瓷的典型代表。

邢窑
Xing Kiln

邢窑白釉穿带壶

五代（公元907−960年）
高29.5、口径7.3、足径13.5cm
上海博物馆藏

White Glazed Portable Teapot from the Xing Kiln

Five Dynasties (907−960 CE)
Height 29.5cm, Diameter of mouth: 7.3cm, Diameter of foot 13.5 cm
Collection of the Shanghai Museum

邢窑白瓷类银类雪，在唐代时期就名闻天下。这件穿带壶是邢窑精细白瓷的代表作。器身有四条瓜棱状凹线，两侧肩部和下腹部分别有四个对称的系，便于上下穿缚。胎质洁白细腻，釉色亦洁白匀净，光素无纹，淡雅大方。

定窑
Ding Kiln

定窑白釉刻花海波纹海螺

北宋（公元960−1127年）
高12.3、长19.3cm
河北定县出土
定州市博物馆藏

White Glazed Conch Shell from the Ding Kiln

Northern Song Dynasty (960−1127 CE)
Height: 12.3cm, Length: 19.3cm
Excavated from Dingxian County, Hebei
Collection of the Dingzhou Municipal Museum

1969年，河北定县静志寺与净众院两座宋代塔基中出土了100多件定窑白瓷，大部分为佛前供器。法螺为佛教八吉祥之一，是著名的法器。传说佛祖初传法轮时，帝释天曾送上右旋的白海螺。右旋的白海螺在佛教中象征的圆满吉祥。这件海螺出土于静志寺塔基地宫，釉色纯白透亮，遍体刻层层海浪纹，生动逼真，是定瓷中难得一见的珍品。

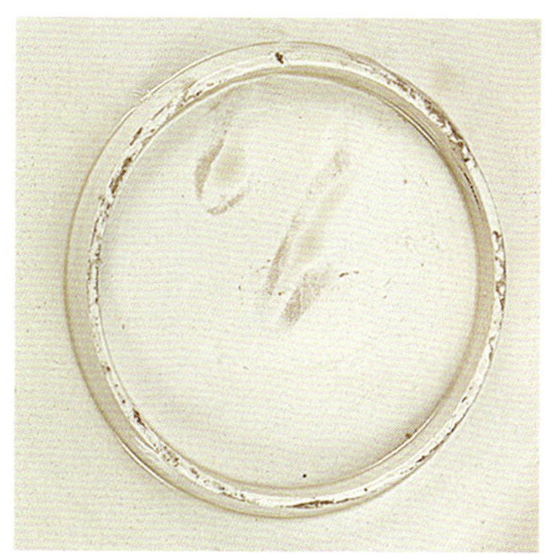

定窑白釉印花龙纹盘

金（公元1115－1234年）
高4.9、口径23.2cm
传河北曲阳出土
上海博物馆藏

White Porcelain Plate with Impressed Dragon Pattern from the Ding Kiln

Jin Dynasty (1115–1234 CE)
Height: 4.9cm, Diameter of mouth: 23.2cm
Excavated from Quyang, Hebei
Collection of the Shanghai Museum

定窑白瓷以胎体轻薄，印花繁密规整而著称，产品行销全国各地。定窑发明的覆烧技术，使产量大大提高，刺激了瓷业的发展。定窑印花云龙纹盘内壁盘心为缠绕的团龙，外圈围绕朵朵团云。外壁光素无纹，口沿镶铜。器形规整，布局错落有致，纹饰精致含蓄，十分美观。

景德镇窑
Jingdezhen Kiln

景德镇窑青白釉注子温碗

北宋（公元960–1127年）
通高21.6cm
上海博物馆藏

Pale Green Cup Warmer from the Jingdezhen Kiln

Northern Song Dynasty (960–1127 CE)
Height: 21.6cm
Collection of the Shanghai Museum

江西景德镇窑自宋代起仿制定窑白瓷，因其釉色微泛青色，被称为“饶玉”。古代人喜喝暖酒，注子、温碗就是温酒器。注子装上酒后，往温碗里注入温水，再将注子放在温碗里，以提高酒的温度。注子和温碗南方瓷窑烧制较多，以景德镇窑影青瓷最为精美。这件注子温碗保存完整，注子短颈，鼓腹，长曲流，弧柄。壶盖顶端有一蹲踞状的狮子。温碗为莲瓣形，下承圈足。釉色纯净，造型美观。

景德镇窑甜白釉锥花缠枝莲梅瓶

明永乐（公元1403－1424年）
高24.5、口径4.3、底径10.1cm
故宫博物院藏

White Glazed Plum Vase from the Jingdezhen Kiln

Yongle Period, Ming Dynasty, (1403－1424 CE)
Height: 24.5cm, Diameter of mouth: 4.3cm, Diameter of base: 10.1cm
Collection of the Palace Museum

明永乐白瓷以胎体轻薄见影、釉色温润肥腴、柔和甜美著称，被称为“甜白瓷”，是永乐朝创烧的新品种。器上多有暗花，含蓄雅致。梅瓶又称“经瓶”，是古代盛酒器，最早见于宋代。此瓶造型比例协调，挺拔秀美。釉色白净柔美，纹饰细腻典雅，为永乐甜白釉中的精品。

景德镇窑“太禧”款卵白釉印花龙纹盘

元（公元1271－1368年）
高3.2、口径18、足径11.4cm
故宫博物院藏

Egg-white Glazed Plate with ‘Taixi’ Mark from the Jingdezhen Kiln

Yuan Dynasty (1271－1368 CE)
Height: 3.2cm, Diameter of mouth: 18cm, Diameter of foot: 11.4cm
Collection of the Palace Museum

卵白釉瓷是元代景德镇窑在青白釉的基础上创烧的白釉瓷器，釉中含钙低，钾、钠成分增多，黏度较大，釉较厚，色白微青如鹅蛋色。器内多有印花，有的还印有“枢府”等字样，它是元代官府定烧的瓷器。卵白釉器形以碗、盘、高足杯居多，以印花为主要装饰技法，辅以刻划花。此盘敞口，圈足，内外施厚釉。盘心为印花龙戏珠，龙为五爪，张牙咧口，扭身翻舞，矫健凶猛。内壁一周为缠枝莲托八吉祥纹，花间对称印有“太禧”二字。

德化窑“何朝宗”款白釉达摩立像

明晚期（公元16世纪）
高43cm
故宫博物院藏

Bodhidharma (aka. Dharma) Porcelain Standing Figure in the Style of He Chaozong from the Dehua Kiln

Late Ming Dynasty (16th century CE)
Height: 43cm
Collection of the Palace Museum

始于宋代的德化窑，到了明代成为具有代表性的品种之一。瓷胎致密，含钾较高而具有较好的透光性，釉色纯白，色泽光润如凝脂，在光照下隐约呈现乳白或粉红，有“象牙白”、“鹅绒白”之称。德化窑以瓷塑见长，特别是有“何朝宗”款的更为难得。何朝宗为明代晚期著名瓷塑家，作品久负盛名。

达摩像是德化瓷塑的代表作。达摩出生于南天竺，是佛教禅宗的创始人，自古有达摩渡海的传说。这件达摩像身披袈裟，立于汹涌的波涛之上，前额宽阔，眉角紧锁，双目俯视，满脸虬须，双手合抱于袖中，衣褶旋回，线纹飘逸流畅。背部有“何朝宗”阴文葫芦形印款。刻划精细，雕工高超，神情兼备，栩栩如生。

文采飞扬·彩绘瓷
Painted Porcelains

彩笔为针，丹青作线，纵横交织针针见。何须锦缎绣春图，春花飞上银瓷面。

——佚名

彩绘瓷是融入色彩装饰的瓷器。六朝青瓷中出现的褐色点彩及釉下彩，是技术的突破，具有里程碑意义。彩绘技术在唐代长沙窑普遍运用，形成具有特殊艺术风格的外销瓷器。经唐宋时期诸多窑口的创造性发展，中国瓷器从元代开始逐渐进入彩绘时代，各种工艺、技法、纹饰和色彩的彩绘瓷争奇斗艳、异彩纷呈。

彩绘瓷将中国画的线条和图像融入到立体的器物表面，形成了双重的审美意趣。

彩瓷主要分为釉下彩和釉上彩两类。釉下彩是在胎体上进行彩绘，施透明釉后高温一次烧成。釉上彩则是在高温烧成的白瓷上用色料绘彩，再以低温烘烧而成。另外还有两者相结合的斗彩。青花和釉里红是釉下彩的代表，元代以后逐渐占据了瓷器生产的半壁江山。而明清各类釉上彩的发明与创新更是将彩瓷推向顶峰。

With a colored pen as a needle and ink as thread, every stroke can be seen clarly, Who needs embroidery on silks, when the spring flower is showing up on the face of silver porcelain.

——Anonymous Poet

Painted porcelain refers to ceramics decorated with colored patterns. During the Six Dynasties period celadon wares were produced that featured brown color dots that appeared beneath the glaze surface marking a technical breakthrough. Later, the Changsha Kiln during the Tang Dynasty frequently employed painted color techniques on their export porcelain wares. By the Ming Dynasty Chinese porcelain entered a period almost wholly devoted to painted porcelain and a large variety of techniques, designs and colors were used to create all sorts of ceramic wares.

Painted porcelain merged the arts of painting and ceramics to form an aesthetic category of unparalleled charm. There were two techniques for coloring this type of porcelain, underglazing and overglazing. After the underglaze color was applied to the body of a piece it was burned once in a high temperature to become a transparent glaze. Overglazing requires the application of color pigments directly onto the surface of white porcelain wares that had been burned at a high temperature. Next, the piece is burned a second time at a lower temperature. Particular techniques include doucai, a combination of underglaze and overglaze methods. Blue and white and underglaze red porcelain wares are representative of underglaze coloring and beginning in the Yuan Dynasty such pieces accounted for half of all porcelain production in China. Because of the various innovations in overglaze techniques during the Ming and Qing dynasties, the types and styles of colored glaze wares expanded greatly.

褐彩、绿彩
Green and Brown Color

青釉褐彩羽化升仙图盖壶

三国·吴（公元220–265年）
通高32.1、腹径31.2cm
南京南郊三国吴墓出土
南京市博物馆藏

Green Glazed Pot with Immortals and Animals

Wu of Three Kingdoms Period (220–265 CE)
Height: 32.1cm
Excavated from the Tomb of Wu, located to the south of Nanjing
Collection of the Nanjing Municipal Museum

中国彩绘瓷出现于公元3世纪，初期的彩绘只是简单的绘画、点彩或涂抹。将不同材料装饰于瓷器之上，这是技术和艺术的进步。

此壶盘口，盖钮为一鸾鸟，周围绘两柿蒂纹及四组人首、鸟、仙草纹，颈部绘异兽7只。肩部贴塑四铺首、两佛、两鸟，三者相间排列整齐有序。腹部分两层绘持节羽人21人，两两相对。盖内及盘口内外皆绘仙草、云气、连弧、弦纹等，图案充满神异气氛，反映了当时的社会思想和习俗。

越窑青釉点彩八系壶

东晋（公元317—420年）
高22.2、口径12.4、底径10.4cm
上海博物馆藏

Green Glazed Speckled *Hu* Vessel with Eight Handles from the Yue Kiln

Eastern Jin Dynasty (317–420 CE)
Height: 22.2cm, Diameter of mouth: 12.4cm, Diameter of base: 10.4cm
Collection of the Shanghai Museum

青釉点彩是在青釉器上不规则地加点褐色彩斑，它是南方瓷窑的一种高温点彩工艺，是早期越窑的创新。点彩始于西晋晚期，东晋、南朝浙江地区普遍流行。它打破了青釉单一的色调，使得瓷器更显活泼。此壶盘口，束颈，肩部八系，两个一组。口沿、系及肩部有酱褐色点彩，肩腹交界处刻划莲瓣纹。釉色青中泛黄，造型美观大方。

黄釉绿彩刻莲瓣纹四系罐

北齐（公元550—577年）
高24、口径8.7cm
河南濮阳李云墓出土
河南博物院藏

Yellow Glazed Jar with Four Handles and Incised Lotus Patterns

Northern Qi Dynasty (550–577 CE)
Height: 24cm, Diameter of mouth: 8.7cm
Excavated from the Tomb of Liyun at Puyang, Henan
Collection of the Henan Museum

这件黄釉绿彩罐是早期彩瓷的精品。直口微敛，鼓圆腹，平底。肩部有四个对称的方系，系下刻划一圈忍冬纹。腹部堆刻覆莲瓣，瓣尖肥厚翘起。器物施黄釉，从口沿到腹部垂挂六条绿色彩斑。下腹露胎。造型别致，典雅美观。

长沙窑黄釉褐绿彩云纹罐

唐中晚期（公元8-10世纪）
高29.8、口径16、底径19.5cm
扬州唐城遗址出土
扬州博物馆藏

Yellow Glazed Jar with a Cloud Decor from the Changsha Kiln

Middle to Late Tang Dynasty (8th–10th century CE)
Height: 29.8cm, Diameter of mouth: 16cm, Diameter at widest point: 19.5cm
Excavated from the Ruins of the Tangcheng Yangzhou
Collection of the Yangzhou Museum

公元8—10世纪，瓷器已经成为中国重要的贸易产品。湖南长沙窑为适应外销需要，创造出了以铁和铜为主要彩绘装饰，具有异域艺术风格的产品。褐绿彩是瓷器装饰彩之一，使用铁和铜在器物表面作画，呈现褐绿色花纹。此罐通体施黄釉，釉下用褐、绿两色的圆点排列出连珠状的涡云，间以莲花。绿色是铜的呈色，褐色是铁的呈色。色泽纯亮，花纹美观。

长沙窑青釉褐绿彩凤鸟纹壶

唐中晚期（公元8–10世纪）
高15.9、口径6.8、底径7.5cm
湖南省博物馆藏

Green Glazed Pot with Phoenix Decorations from the Changsha Kiln

Middle to Late Tang Dynasty (8th–10th century CE)
Height: 15.9cm, Diameter of mouth: 6.8cm, Diameter of base: 7.5cm
Collection of the Hunan Provincial Museum

褐绿彩用铁、铜色料绘画，在氧化气氛中烧成，花纹分别呈褐色和绿色。此壶肩部有多棱短流，腹为四瓣瓜棱，流下腹部用褐、绿彩描绘一振翅欲飞的凤鸟，构图简洁，用笔精准，造型优美。

磁州窑山水花鸟纹枕

元（公元1271—1368年）
高14.9、长44.4、宽17.7cm
上海博物馆藏

White and Black Pillow Decorated with Landscape, Foliage and Birds form the Cizhou Kiln

Yuan Dynasty (1217–1368 CE)
Height: 14.9cm, Length: 44.4cm, Width: 17.7cm
Collection of Shanghai Museum

元代瓷州窑常见长方形山水纹枕，这时的白地黑花已不像宋代那样黑白分明，一般白中泛黄，纹饰实际成为了褐色或酱色。

磁州窑白地黑花虎纹枕

北宋至金（公元960–1279年）
高9.4、长25.4、宽17.9cm
故宫博物院藏

White-glazed Porcelain Pillow with Black Floral and Tiger Designs form the Cizhou Kiln

Northern Song to Jin Dynasty (960–1279 CE)
Height: 9.4cm, Length: 25.4cm, Width: 17.9cm
Collection of the Palace Museum

公元11—14世纪磁州窑彩瓷以明快黑白色为主色调，其艺术风格具有浓郁生活气息，成为中国北方最大的民间瓷窑体系。其烧造的瓷枕纹饰笔法简练随性、生动活泼，极富情趣。

磁州窑白地黑花龙纹扁壶

元（公元1271-1368年）
高34、口径6.5、宽10cm
北京安定门出土
首都博物馆藏

Flask with a Dragon Pattern from the Cizhou Kiln

Yuan Dynasty (1127-1368 CE)
Height: 34cm, Diameter of mouth: 6.5cm, Width: 10cm
Excavated in Anding Men, Beijing
Collection of the Capital Museum

元代瓷器中，四系的小口方形扁壶具有时代特征，景德镇、龙泉、磁州诸窑都有烧造。此壶呈扁方形，肩有四系。全身白地黑彩，辅以刻划纹，正反两面分别绘龙纹和凤纹。两侧为缠枝花草。笔法遒劲，刀法熟练。

青花
Blue and White

青花标本

唐（公元618-907年）
扬州唐城遗址出土
扬州博物馆藏

Blue and White Floral Pattern Shard

Tang Dynasty (618-907 CE)
Excavated from the Ruins at Tangcheng, Yangzhou
Collection of the Yangzhou Museum

青花是在瓷坯上用钴料绘彩，施透明釉后入窑高温烧造而成的白地蓝花装饰的高温釉下彩瓷器。钴用于瓷器釉下装饰最早见于唐代。20世纪70年代江苏扬州唐城遗址出土了一批青花瓷片，所绘纹饰不再局限于点彩，出现了以线条描绘的各种花纹。唐代是青花瓷的滥觞期，为元代成熟青花的出现奠定了物质和技术基础。

景德镇窑青花萧何追韩信图梅瓶

元晚期（公元14世纪中期）
高44.1、口径5.5、底径13cm
江苏江宁明洪武二十五年（公元1392年）沐英墓出土
南京市博物馆藏

Blue and White Plum Vase from the Jingdezhen Kiln

Late Yuan Dynasty (mid14th century CE)
Height: 44.1cm, Diameter of mouth: 5.5cm, Diameter of base: 13cm
Excavated from the Tomb of Mu Ying, dated from the 25th Year of the Hongwu Era, Ming Dynasty (1392 CE), in Jiangning, Jiangsu
Collection of the Nanjing Municipal Museum

公元14世纪中期景德镇生产的元代青花成为中国青花瓷器成熟的标志。典型元代青花以造型硕大雄伟、青花鲜艳纯正、纹饰层次丰富、绘画细致工丽为特点。这件梅瓶胎体厚重，做工精致，使用进口青料，发色浓郁幽雅。肩部上下绘莲瓣杂宝纹和缠枝西番莲各一周。腹身主体纹饰为"萧何月下追韩信"图。胫部仰莲瓣中绘番莲纹。釉色白中泛青，肥厚滋润，青花发色稳定。

景德镇窑青花花卉纹八角烛台

明宣德（公元1426–1435年）
高29.8、口径8.7、底径21.8cm
上海博物馆藏

Blue and White Octagon Candleholder with Floral Design from the Jingdezhen Kiln

Xuande Period, Ming Dynasty，(1426–1435 CE)
Height: 29.8cm, Diameter of mouth: 8.7cm, Diameter of base: 21.8cm
Collection of the Shanghai Museum

宣德时期是青花瓷的黄金期，此时所用青料为苏麻离青，发色浓艳，胎釉精细，造型多样，纹饰优美。烛台呈八角形，上小下大为两层结构，底内凹，造型仿自西亚伊斯兰地区的铜质烛台。全身多重装饰，口部为仰覆莲瓣纹，颈部和腹部皆为缠枝花卉纹，疏密相间，优雅别致。

景德镇窑“癸巳秋月”款青花山水图瓶

清顺治十年（公元1653年）
高44.4、口径12、底径12cm
上海博物馆藏

Blue and White Vase with Landscape Scenes from the Jingdezhen Kiln

10th Year of the Shunzhi Era, Qing Dynasty，(1653 CE)
Height: 44.4cm, Diameter of mouth: 12cm, Diameter of base: 12cm
Collection of the Shanghai Museum

顺治青花用浙料绘彩，发色湛蓝，明亮幽雅。当时运用分水法，使得青花表现出浓淡不同的层次，效果如同中国传统水墨画。此瓶颈部绘折纸花草纹，瓶身用斧劈皴绘青花山水图，图的一侧有隶书题诗，以及“癸巳秋日写为西畴书院”纪年款，是顺治民窑青花的标准器。

景德镇窑青花山石花卉纹盖罐

明成化（公元1465－1487年）
通高11.3、口径7.9、足径10.3cm
故宫博物院藏

Blue and White Jar with Floral Designs from the Jingdezheng Kiln

Chenghua Period, Ming Dynasty (1465－1487 CE)
Height: 11.3cm, Diameter of mouth: 7.9cm, Diameter of foot: 10.3cm
Collection of the Palace Museum

成化青花的青料产自江西，发色稳定，色调清新淡雅。绘画上采用中国画的工笔画法，器身绘山石、蕉叶、花卉纹，盖面双圈内绘蕉叶山石，盖壁上下双圈内绘缠枝花，颈部和器底也各有一周双圈。釉色白中泛青，青花发色幽雅，是成化官窑青花的代表作品。

釉里红
Underglaze Red

景德镇窑釉里红龙纹盖罐

元晚期（公元14世纪中期）
通高28、口径12.8、腹径25.1cm
江苏吴县出土
苏州吴中区文物管理委员会藏

Vessel with an Underglaze Red Dragon Design from the Jingdezhen Kiln

Late Yuan Dynasty (mid 14th century CE)
Height: 28cm, Diameter of mouth: 12.8cm, Diameter of base: 25.1cm
Excavated from Wuxian, Jiangsu
Collection of the Suzhou Wuzhong District Cultural Relic Preservation Committee

元代景德镇窑真正开始生产釉里红瓷器，主要采用涂抹或填红的方法绘彩，呈色不稳，偏灰色，并有晕散。由于出土器物很少，江苏吴县、高安、保定等地发现的釉里红瓷器具有极高的研究价值，为了解元代釉里红的基本面貌提供了直接的证据。盖罐盖面模印对称葵花叶一周，肩部刻卷云纹，腹部浅刻两组云龙纹，胫部刻仰莲纹。盖、肩及腹部均以粗笔涂铜红色料，虽发色不很纯正，但仍是早期釉里红的珍品。

长沙窑青釉红褐彩花鸟纹壶

唐中晚期（公元8–10世纪）
残高17.5、底径9.8cm
长沙市博物馆藏

Green Glazed Pot with Red and Brown Floral and Bird Designs from the Changsha Kiln

Middle to Late Tang Dynasty (8th–10th century CE)
Height: 17.5cm, Diameter of base: 9.8cm
Collection of the Changsha Municipal Museum

釉里红是用铜在釉下绘彩，施透明釉后在高温还原气氛中烧成，花纹呈鲜亮的红色。公元9世纪长沙窑的高温釉下红彩是釉里红瓷器的先声，但多属偶然烧成。此壶的腹部用含铁色料在釉下勾勒了一只栖枝的飞鸟，再用铜料加以晕染，在还原气氛下烧成红褐彩器，生动活泼，十分难得。

景德镇窑
釉里红岁寒三友图梅瓶

明洪武（公元1368-1398年）
通高41.6、口径6.4cm
江苏江宁宋琥墓出土
南京博物院藏

Underglaze Red Plum Vase with the Three Friends of Winter from the Jingdezhen Kiln

Hongwu Period, Ming Dynasty, (1368-1398 CE)
Height: 41.6cm, Diameter of mouth: 6.4cm
Excavated from the Tomb of Song Hu in Jiangning, Jiangsu
Collection of the Nanjing Museum

明洪武时期釉里红盛行，与元代相比虽然发色仍然黯淡，但是出现如青花般的细致描绘，这件梅瓶是洪武釉里红的精美之作。肩部为缠枝菊花，腹部画松、竹、梅、芭蕉、山石。腹部下端为波涛纹，胫部画仰莲瓣。盖四周绘缠枝西番莲。纹饰繁而不乱，布局层次鲜明，是少见的佳作。

五彩
Polychorme

景德镇窑釉里红龙纹瓶

清康熙（公元1662–1722年）
高20.8、口径4.2、底径5.5 cm
上海博物院藏

Porcelain Vase with Underglaze Red Dragon Design, Jingdezhen Kiln

Kangxi Period, Qing Dynasty (1662–1722 CE)
Height: 20.8cm, Diameter of mouth: 4.2cm, Diameter of base :5.5cm
Collection of the Shanghai Museum

明朝中期以后釉里红衰微，至清康熙才恢复明前期的水准，发色更好，并创制了"釉里三彩"等新品种。釉色白中泛青，釉里红发色浓妍，绘图精细，是康熙釉里红的代表作。

景德镇窑青花五彩鸳鸯莲池纹高足碗

明宣德（公元1426–1435年）
高11.5、口径17cm
西藏萨迦寺藏

Blue and White Bowl with Five Colored Mandarin Ducks from the Jingdezhen Kiln

Xuande Period, Ming Dynasty, (1426–1435 CE)
Height: 11.5cm, Diameter of mouth: 17cm
Collection of the Sakya Monastry, Tibet

五彩瓷器源于明宣德而盛于嘉万。明天启《博物要览》中曾经提到"宣窑五彩，深厚堆垛"。宣德五彩始终不见踪影，后来发现在西藏萨迦寺收藏了全世界仅有的两件宣德五彩瓷器，其中一件就是这个高足碗。由此，五彩起源于宣德得到了证实。五彩使用透明彩，缺少层次的渲染，故又称"硬彩"。明代五彩还以釉下青花表现蓝色，至清康熙，随着釉上蓝彩的发明，五彩成为单纯的釉上彩。

这件青花五彩高足碗，口沿内侧书一周青花藏文吉祥经，外侧绘青花五爪云龙纹，腹部和足部以五彩绘鸳鸯莲池纹。圈足内有青花"宣德年制"四字楷书款。是明王朝赏赐萨迦寺的珍品。

➲ 景德镇窑五彩花鸟纹尊

清康熙（公元1662－1722年）
高44、口径22.4cm
故宫博物院藏

Zun **Vessel with Five Color Flower and Bird Designs from the Jingdezhen Kiln**

Kangxi Period, Qing Dynasty, (1662－1722 CE)
Height: 44cm, Diameter of mouth: 22.4cm
Collection of the Palace Museum

清康熙五彩瓷器上的蓝彩为釉上彩，并较多使用金彩。此尊造型典雅大方，通体绘荷池夏景，莲花盛开，彩蝶纷飞，翠鸟栖息于叶梗间，鹭鸶于水中觅食。整体图案蕴含了“一路荣华”之意。采用五彩加金的工艺，明艳丰富，绚烂多姿。

景德镇窑五彩花鸟纹瓶

清康熙（公元1662－1722年）
高48、口径13.6、足径15.1cm
故宫博物院藏

Polychrome Club-Shaped Vase with Birds and Flowers Design from the Jingdezhen Kiln

Kangxi Period, Qing Dynasty, (1662－1722 CE)
Height: 48cm, Diameter of mouth: 13.6cm, Diameter of foot: 15.1cm
Collection of the Palace Museum

此瓶在白地上绘制五彩纹饰，构图疏朗，色彩鲜艳，光泽明亮，体现了康熙时期五彩瓷的特色。

景德镇窑五彩龙凤纹笔盒

明万历（公元1573－1620年）
高8.9、口径29.9、宽11.1cm
上海博物馆藏

Five Color Dragon and Phoenix Brush Box from the Jingdezhen Kiln

Wanli Period, Ming Dynasty, (1573－1620 CE)
Height: 8.9cm, Diameter of mouth: 29.9cm, Width: 11.1cm
Collection of the Shanghai Museum

明代万历五彩以发色浓艳而著称。笔盒是古人装毛笔的文具，此盒为长方形，子母口，内分一大一小两格。器身和盖面均饰五彩图案。盖面中央为游龙戏凤，盖两端、侧面以及器身相应位置分别绘如意纹和龙凤戏珠纹，盖里和器里满绘如意云纹。色彩绚烂，纹饰繁密，制作精湛。

斗彩
Contrasted Colors

景德镇窑斗彩海水龙纹盖罐

明成化（公元1465－1487年）
高13.1、口径8.7、足径11.2cm
故宫博物院藏

Covered Pot Decorated with Dragons from the Jingdezhen Kiln

Chenghua Period, Ming Dynasty, (1465–1487 CE)
Height: 13.1cm, Diameter of mouth: 8.7cm, Diameter of foot: 11.2cm
Collection of the Palace Museum

斗彩是釉下青花和釉上彩绘的结合，用釉下青花勾勒纹饰轮廓，再填入釉上彩料，入窑烧成。明成化斗彩多为小型器物，制作最为精美，胎细腻、釉滋润、色彩典雅。这件盖罐的腹部和盖面均以黄、绿二色绘海水双云龙，肩部和近底部为红彩蕉叶纹。盖侧为绿彩海水波涛纹。图案皆以釉下青花勾边，釉上五彩填色的方法绘制。外底心书青花楷书“天”字款。

景德镇窑斗彩花卉纹尊

清雍正（公元1723－1735年）
高25.6、口径22.2cm、足径15.7cm
故宫博物院藏

***Zun* Vessel with a Floral Pattern from the Jingdezhen Kiln**

Yongzheng Period, Qing Dynasty, (1723–1735 CE)
Height: 25.6cm, Diameter of mouth: 22.2cm, Diameter of foot: 15.7cm
Collection of the Palace Museum

与明代相比，雍正斗彩将釉下青花与釉上粉彩相结合，使得色彩更为柔和秀丽。雍正斗彩纹饰规整，釉上彩色丰富，纹饰多以花鸟为主，风格淡雅。此尊通体作菊花瓣式，凸棱部位均饰斗彩枝花组成的直条花纹，纹饰描绘细腻。造型新颖，色彩丰富。底书“大清雍正年制”青花双圈楷书款。

珐琅彩
Enamel Colors

黄地珐琅彩花卉纹碗

清康熙（公元1662–1722年）
高7.6、口径15.6cm
中国国家博物馆藏

Yellow Ground Enamel Bowl with a Floral Design

Kangxi Period, Qing Dynasty, (1662–1722 CE)
Height: 7.6cm, Diameter of mouth: 15.6cm
Collection of the National Museum of China

珐琅彩是创造性地将以往装饰于铜胎上的珐琅彩施于瓷器之上，工艺开始于17世纪末，通常瓷器由景德镇御器厂制作，绘彩及烘烧由宫内造办处珐琅作承担。珐琅彩具有色彩浓厚、鲜艳、层次丰富的特点，有较强的立体感，具有油画的质感。此碗胎体较薄，外壁黄地上绘珐琅彩西番莲。外底书“康熙御制”宋体料款。

珐琅彩松竹梅纹瓶

清雍正（公元1723–1735年）
高16.9、口径3.9、足径4.8cm
故宫博物院藏

Vase with Enameled Pine, Bamboo, and Plum Design

Yongzheng Period, Qing Dynasty, (1723–1735 CE)
Height: 16.9cm, Diameter of mouth: 3.9cm, Diameter of foot: 4.8cm
Collection of the Palace Museum

雍正珐琅彩风格典雅，题材以花鸟为主，配上题诗、篆印，俨然是中国传统工笔画在瓷器上的再现。此瓶通体绘岁寒三友图，红、绿、赭、粉相互辉映。颈部墨书“上林苑里春长在”，引首和句尾有胭脂彩“翔采”、“多古”、“香清”三印章。瓶底书“大清雍正年制”青花楷书双圈款。造型优美，线条柔和，精巧雅致。

景德镇黄地珐琅彩云龙纹碗

清雍正（公元1723–1735年）
高5.5、口径10.2、足径4.2cm
故宫博物院藏

Bowl Decorated with Dragons Among Clouds Over a Yellow Ground in Cloisonne Enamel from the Jingdezhen Kiln

Yongzheng Period, Qing Dynasty, (1723 – 1735 CE)
Height: 5.5cm, Diameter of mouth: 10.2cm, Diameter of foot: 4.2cm
Collection of the Palace Museum

雍正时期珐琅彩色彩较前代增多，彩料一般娇艳华丽。此碗在黄色地上绘制云龙纹，地色娇嫩，纹饰沉着。

➲ 景德镇珐琅彩竹菊鹌鹑纹瓶

清乾隆（公元1736–1795年）
通高18.7、口径5.5、足径6.3cm
上海博物馆藏

Vase with Enameled Design of Bamboo, Chrysanthemum and Partridge from the Jingdezhen Kiln

Qianlong Period, Qing Dynasty (1736 – 1795 CE)
Height:18.7cm, Diameter of mouth5.5cm，Diameter of foot:6.3cm
Collection of the Shanghai Museum

此瓶在洁白的色地上饰山石、丛竹和菊花，几只充满意趣的鹌鹑正在嬉戏，色彩十分雅静。

珐琅彩芙蓉稚鸡图瓶

清乾隆（公元1736－1795年）
通高16.3、口径4cm
天津博物馆藏

Vase with Enameled Design of Hibiscus Flowers and Chickens from the Jingdezhen Kiln

Qianlong Period, Qing Dynasty, (1736－1795 CE)
Height: 16.3cm, Diameter of mouth: 4cm
Collection of the Tianjin Museum

乾隆珐琅彩风格繁华。此瓶主体纹饰底本出自花鸟画家蒋廷锡手笔，花朵娇艳欲滴，两只稚鸡并立于山石之上，神态亲昵。颈部用蓝彩绘蕉叶纹。釉色纯亮，色彩妍丽，纹饰细腻，十分美观。有行书诗句“青扶承露蕊，红妥出阑枝”，及朱文“春和”、“霞映”、白文“翠铺”印。底署“乾隆年制”楷书料款。

粉彩

Famille-rose

景德镇窑粉彩莲荷纹瓶

清雍正（公元1723－1735年）
高27.6、口径8.3、足径11.5cm
故宫博物院藏

Vase Decorated with Lotus from the Jingdezhen Kiln

Yongzheng Period, Qing Dynasty, (1723－1735 CE)
Height: 27.6cm, Diameter of mouth: 8.3cm, Diameter of foot:11.5cm
Collection of the Palace Museum

雍正瓷器瓷胎洁白轻薄，釉色莹润如雪，粉彩在制作精致、胎釉俱佳的瓷器上得到充分发展，充分运用没骨法等传统工笔画技法，层次清晰，极富立体感，终于登上釉上彩瓷器的巅峰。此瓶纹饰绘工精湛，风格写实。

景德镇窑粉彩镂空转心瓶

清乾隆（公元1736–1995年）
高40.2、口径19.2cm
故宫博物院藏

Revolving Vase from the Jingdezhen Kiln

Qianlong Period, Qing Dynasty, (1736–1795 CE)
Height: 40.2cm, Diameter of mouth: 19.2cm
Collection of the Palace Museum

乾隆粉彩瓷器以装饰繁华、造型奇巧著称。转心瓶是清代乾隆年间流行的一种样式，在瓶内套一个可以转动的内胆与颈部相连，转动颈部，透过瓶的镂空开光可以看到内胆的不同纹饰，设计精巧，十分别致。此瓶造型硕大，颈部堆塑两个象耳。口沿外侧饰胭脂地如意云肩纹，颈部和圈足外侧绘胭脂地西番莲，腹部为黄地轧花镂空开光四季花卉。口、颈、底、双耳和开光边缘均以金彩点缀。整器造型优美，设色艳丽，显得富丽堂皇。颈肩之间转动处上下分别书天干、地支，转动颈部，显示相对的干支，可以作日历使用。瓶底书“大清乾隆年制”青花篆书款。

景德镇窑粉彩花蝶纹盘

清康熙（公元1662–1722年）
高3.7、口径17.5、底径10.5cm
故宫博物院藏

Plate with Flower and Butterfly Design from the Jingdezhen Kiln

Kangxi Period, Qing Dynasty, (1662–1722 CE)
Height: 3.7cm, Diameter of mouth: 17.5cm, Diameter of base: 10.5cm
Collection of the Palace Museum

粉彩是清朝康熙后期在珐琅彩基础上创烧的一种低温釉上彩。在绘彩之前先施一层“玻璃白”，起乳浊剂作用，使色彩富有层次而柔和，具有更强的表现力。此盘内壁绘月季、玉兰、梅花合成的三组折枝花卉，以粉彩特有的胭脂红绘花朵。盘心青花双圈内绘折枝花蕾和飞舞的彩蝶。盘底书“大清康熙年制”青花楷款。五彩色泽淡雅，构图简洁、别致，是目前所见唯一的康熙粉彩器。

其他
Other Colors

卵白釉加彩戗金盘

元（公元1271–1368年）
高4.3、口径16.1cm
上海博物馆藏

Egg-White Glazed Plate with Gold Inlay

Yuan Dynasty (1271–1368 CE)
Height: 4.3cm, Diameter: 16.1cm
Collection of the Shanghai Museum

这是元代出现的新工艺，在烧成的景德镇卵白釉印花瓷器上加彩并戗金。戗金工艺是从金属器装饰借鉴而来。这类器物发现极少，主要在内蒙古出土，应该是专门为上层贵族制作的。此盘极为罕见，内壁有印花云龙纹，内壁口沿处为一周缠枝花，碗心花形开光内有一梵文“吽”。外壁为莲瓣纹内填杂宝纹，花卉边沿和内心采用戗金工艺。整器纹饰精美，金碧辉煌，是元代瓷器中难得的珍品。

扒村窑彩绘女坐像

金（公元1115–1234年）
高32.9cm
上海博物馆藏

Female Figure from the Bacun Kiln

Jin Dynasty (1115–1234 CE)
Height: 32.9cm
Collection of the Shanghai Museum

釉上彩是在烧成的瓷器表面绘彩，再经低温烧结。它诞生于公元13世纪的宋、金时期，最早见于中国北方简单的红绿彩。这件女俑是金代扒村窑釉上彩的代表作。女俑端坐，表情平和。双手相拱放于胸前。头戴凤冠，身着宽袖长衫，服饰上填红、绿、黄彩，色彩丰富。

流光溢彩·颜色釉瓷
Dazzling Colors and Varieties of Glaze

雨过天晴云破处，诸般颜色捉将来。

——［五代］柴荣

颜色釉有高、低温之分。高温釉的主要呈色元素有铜、钴、铁，烧成黑、红、蓝、酱等颜色釉；低温釉的呈色元素主要为铜、铁、锰，烧成红、绿、黄、紫等颜色釉。高温颜色釉源于公元2世纪初的黑釉，至公元14世纪成熟的铜红釉、钴蓝釉出现以后，得到较快发展。低温颜色釉源于公元14世纪景德镇窑的孔雀绿釉，明、清两代御器厂的设立，推动了低温釉的繁荣。特别是清代工匠们更是在继承传统工艺的基础上，吸收外国技术，增加了金、锑等釉料，创烧出浓淡深浅不一的釉色。

红色的浓烈奔放，黄色的雍容华贵、蓝色的恬和静谧，紫色的神秘典雅，千变万化，异彩纷呈。更有生动逼真的仿工艺釉，制造出青铜器、金银器、玉器、漆器以及竹刻等效果，显示了瓷器的高度表现力和工匠们的智慧。

After the rain clears and the clouds are broken, the colors of rainbow are what I need you to grab

——Chai Rong, Five Dynasties

Colored glazes can be divided into those fired at high or low temperatures. High temperature glazes include pigments derived from copper, cobalt, and iron, which, in turn, produce red, blue and brown glazed works. Low temperature glazes include those with elements of copper, iron, and magnesium, which when fired produce colors such as peacock green, yellow and purple. Vessels in all the above mentioned colors were produced at the Imperial Porcelain Kiln. Established during the Ming and Qing dynasties, the kiln produced large numbers of monochrome glazed porcelain. During the Qing dynasty artisans increasingly drew on their knowledge of traditional techniques, but also absorbed foreign techniques, such as the addition of gold and antimony glaze ingredients. Vibrant and deeply colored glazes of various types were produced through the careful control of quality and proportions of ingredients. The reds were intense and bold, yellows elegant and poised, blues refined and tranquil, and purples mysterious and alluring. Those glazes that imitated other substances were even more vivid, such as bronzes, gold and silvers, jades, and lacquer and demonstrated the keen abilities of porcelain artists.

黑釉
Black Glaze

黑釉罐

东汉永元十三年（公元101年）
高3.5、口径3.5、底径2.4cm
江苏丹阳东汉墓出土
镇江博物馆藏

Black Glaze Jar

13th year of the Yongyuan Reign, Eastern Han Dynasty, (101 CE)
Height: 3.5cm, Diameter of mouth: 3.5cm, Diameter of base: 2.4cm
Excavated from the Eastern Han Tombs at Danyang, Jiangsu Province
Collection of the Zhenjiang Museum

东汉中后期，黑瓷登上了历史舞台，成为瓷器生产的一大门类。黑瓷中呈色剂主要为氧化铁。与青瓷相比，黑瓷中含有更多的铁。这件黑瓷小罐是目前中国最早的黑瓷，距今约1900年。

德清窑黑釉四系壶

东晋（公元317–420年）
高24.9、口径11.4cm
上海博物馆藏

Deqing Kiln Black Glaze Teapot

Eastern Jin Dynasty (317–420 CE)
Height: 24.9cm, Diameter of mouth: 11.4cm
Collection of the Shanghai Museum

德清窑的兴起，标志着黑瓷烧造技术的成熟。浙江德清地区烧造黑瓷是在生产青瓷的基础上进行的，它依然以铁为着色剂，不同的只是在釉中增加了铁的含量到8%以上，同时增加釉的厚度，这样釉色更为纯正，滋润光亮，色黑如漆。

鲁山窑花釉腰鼓

唐（公元618-907年）
长58.9cm
故宫博物院藏

Glazed Drum from the Lushan Kiln

Tang Dynasty (618-907 CE)
Length: 58.9cm
Collection of the Palace Museum

黑色在装饰中可以对花纹作很好的衬托，唐代窑工开始利用这种优势，生产具有独特风格的装饰瓷器。山西鲁山花釉瓷器是在黑釉的表面加上挥洒自由的月白或天蓝色釉斑，它打破了黑色的沉闷，具有很强的装饰效果。

鲁山窑黑釉月白斑双系罐

唐（公元618－907年）
高11.3、口径7.6cm
上海博物馆藏

Black Glazed Teapot with Speckles from the Lushan Kiln

Tang Dynasty (618－907 CE)
Height: 11.3cm, Diameter of mouth: 7.6cm
Collection of the Shanghai Museum

鲁山窑始于唐代，终于元代，以烧造花瓷著称。花瓷是黑釉或者褐釉上带白色或月白色斑块的器物，器形有拍鼓、罐、壶等，对比鲜明，别有风味。此罐大唇口，圆腹，肩部两侧各有一系，黑釉，釉上装饰月白色斑，隐约透着蓝色。器形丰满圆厚，釉色搭配和谐，浑然一体。

吉州窑黑釉木叶纹碗

南宋（公元1127－1279年）
高5.5、口径14.8cm
江西省博物馆藏

Black Glazed Bowl with a Leaf Design from the Jizhou Kiln

Southern Song Dynasty (1127－1279 CE)
Height: 5.5cm, Diameter: 14.8cm
Collection of the Jiangxi Provincial Museum

吉州窑的复合釉是黑釉瓷器的突出代表，木叶纹是其独特的创造，也是典型的装饰纹样之一。它是以植物的叶片经过腐蚀处理后蘸上黄釉，贴在已施黑釉的碗坯上，入窑高温烧成，树叶的形状和脉络都清晰地留在器物上。黑釉的底色更好地衬托出木叶的效果，浑然天成。

吉州窑剪纸贴花三凤纹碗

南宋（公元1127－1279年）
高6.2、口径16cm
天津博物馆藏

Bowl with Three Paper-Cut Phoenixes Design from the Jizhou Kiln

Southern Song Dynasty (1127－1279 CE)
Height: 6.2cm, Diameter of mouth: 16cm
Collection of the Tianjin Museum

吉州窑黑釉继建窑而起又有创新，它以两种不同的色釉，通过剪纸、树叶等加以装饰，取得了与建窑结晶釉类似而又有区别的效果。剪纸贴花是将剪刻的纸花贴在已经施黑釉的坯体上，再施黄釉后将纸花剥去，然后入窑烧制，深色的剪纸花纹在棕黄色釉的衬托下分外醒目。此碗心用剪纸贴花印一花朵，周围围绕三只飞凤，生动活泼，极具情趣。

建窑黑釉兔毫盏

宋（公元960－1279年）
高7.5、口径18cm
故宫博物院藏

Black Glazed Hare's Hair Teacup from the Jian Kiln

Song Dynasty（960－1279 CE）
Height: 7.5cm, Diameter of mouth: 18cm
Collection of the Palace Museum

宋代风行斗茶，所用黑釉茶盏十分普及。建窑是生产黑釉茶盏的著名民间窑场之一，其胎、釉中都含有较高的铁，在高温中铁不能完全融于釉中，在釉的表面析出，在不同的烧成条件下形成不同形式的结晶斑，成为“兔毫”、“油滴”、“鹧鸪斑”等不同的品种。兔毫盏是其中最著名的品种之一，它的结晶斑呈细长的、黄棕色的兔毛状，时称“金褐兔毫”，是斗茶的上品。

➲ 景德镇窑

乌金釉开光岁寒三友图瓶

清康熙（公元1662–1722年）
高44.4、口径12.4、底径13.1cm
上海博物馆藏

Mirror-blaze-glazed Porcelain Vase with Medallion in which the Scene of "Three Friends of the Cold Months (Pine, Bamboo and Plum Blossom)" is Painted from the Jingdezhen Kiln

Kangxi Period, Qing Dynasty, (1662–1722 CE)
Height: 44.4cm, Diameter of mouth: 12.4cm
Diamater of base:13.1cm
Collection of the Shanghai Museum

清代康熙乌金釉的创烧，突破了黑釉以铁为主要呈色剂的传统，它以铁、钴、锰为呈色元素，取得了光润透亮、色黑如漆的效果。是景德镇创造的一种新的黑釉品种，代表了黑瓷烧造的最高水平。康熙乌金釉瓷器的表面常见金彩装饰，更显得富丽堂皇。

红釉
Red Glaze

长沙窑铜红变釉执壶

唐中晚期（公元8−10世纪）
高18.5、口径9.3、底径8.5cm
长沙市文物考古研究所藏

Pitcher with a Copper Red Glaze from the Changsha Kiln

Middle and Late Tang Dynasty (8th – 10th century CE)
Height: 18.5cm, Diameter of mouth: 9.3cm, Diameter of base: 8.5cm
Collection of the Changsha Municipal Institute of Cultural Relic and Archaeology

铜红釉以铜为呈色剂，在要求较高的高温还原气氛中烧成。它起源于唐代长沙窑，当时用氧化铜作绿釉的呈色剂，在偶然得到的高温还原气氛中烧成了红色。此壶釉色呈玫瑰紫红，红釉中微微泛绿。

钧窑玫瑰紫釉花盆

公元14世纪
高18.4、口径20.1cm
故宫博物院藏

Purple Glazed Flowerpot from the Jun Kiln

14th century CE
Height: 18.4cm, Diameter of mouth: 20.1cm
Collection of the Palace Museum

钧窑以色彩丰富的窑变釉著称。玫瑰紫是钧窑釉色的上乘之作，是在釉中掺入铜而形成。花盆一般与盆托一起使用，主要样式有葵瓣、海棠、长方、六方等。通体玫瑰红釉绚丽，器形凸出处“出筋”，现棕黄色。器底棕黄釉，釉下刻数码“四”。

➲ 景德镇窑红釉僧帽壶

明宣德（公元1426-1435年）
通高20、口径16.1cm
故宫博物院藏

Red Glazed Monk's Cap Jug from the Jingdezhen Kiln

Xuande Period, Ming Dynasty, (1426 – 1435 CE)
Height: 20cm, Diameter of mouth: 16.1cm
Collection of the Palace Museum

明代早期铜红釉趋于成熟，烧成了纯正的宝石红釉。僧帽壶因形似僧帽而得名，是模仿西藏的器型。这件宣德红釉僧帽壶极为精致，口沿至肩腹部设一曲柄，相对一侧有流，带盖。底书“大明宣德年制”青花楷书款。红釉光亮明艳，是明代红釉的代表。

➲ 景德镇窑红釉盘

明宣德（公元1426-1435年）
通高5.2、口径20.3、底径12.5cm
上海博物馆藏

Red Glazed Plate from the Jingdezhen Kiln

Xuande Period, Ming Dynasty, (1426 – 1435 CE)
Height: 5.2cm, Diameter of mouth: 20.31cm，Diameter of base:12.5cm
Collection of Shanghai Museum

盘的釉色明净，口沿和底足的白色边缘使器物显

景德镇窑豇豆红釉太白尊

清康熙(1662–1722年)
高8.7、口径3.5、底径12.5cm
上海博物馆藏

Cowpea Red *Zun* Vessel from the Jingdezhen Kiln

Kangxi Period, Qing Dynasty, (1662 – 1722 CE)
Height: 8.7cm, Diameter of mouth: 3.5cm, Diameter of bace:12.5cm
Collect of the Shanghai Museum

豇豆红是一种呈色多变的高温铜红釉，是康熙时期的名贵品种。其釉色淡雅，釉面局部氧化而呈绿色苔点。在浑然一体的红色中隐现点点绿斑，更显幽雅清淡、柔和悦目。豇豆红烧成难度极大。常见器形有印盒、水盂等文房用具。此尊小口微侈，短颈溜肩，腹部呈半球形，暗刻团螭纹。造型秀巧，釉层细腻，釉色淡雅。底施白釉，青花“大清康熙年制”楷书款。

景德镇窑郎窑红釉瓶

清康熙（公元1662–1722年）
高45.8、口径12.7cm
故宫博物院藏

Red Vase from the Lang Kiln at Jingdezhen

Kangxi Period, Qing Dynasty, (1662–1722 CE)
Height: 45.8cm, Diameter of mouth: 12.7cm
Collection of the Palace Museum

17世纪后期，铜红釉得到大发展，创造出郎窑红、豇豆红等新品种。郎窑红是以康熙督陶官郎廷极而命名的红釉器。其色泽浓艳，具有强烈的玻璃光泽。釉汁肥厚，釉面有大片裂纹和不规则的牛毛纹。在烧制过程中釉汁下垂，使口沿显露白色而器物底边釉汁凝聚呈黑红色。此瓶通身施红釉，色泽鲜亮。

红釉文吏俑

元至元四年（公元1338年）
高20.5cm
江西景德镇元墓出土
江西省博物馆藏

Red Glaze Tomb Figure of Civil Official

4th Year of the Zhiyuan Era, Yuan Dynasty, (1338 CE)
Height: 20.5cm
Excavated from a Yuan Period Tomb, Jingdezhen, Jiangxi
Collection of the Jiangxi Provincial Museum

真正的高温铜红釉出现于14世纪的元代，以铜为着色剂，在还原气氛中烧成。它为明清两代宝石红、祭红的创烧奠定了基础。这件文吏俑为实心模制，头戴官帽，身穿官服，双手执笏板于胸前。帽、服钧施红釉，呈色浓淡不均，人物神态生动。

景德镇窑蓝釉白龙纹瓶

元晚期（公元14世纪中期）
高43.8、腹径25.3cm
扬州博物馆藏

Blue Glazed Vase with a White Dragon from the Jingdezhen Kiln

Late Yuan Dynasty (mid 14th century CE)
Height: 43.8cm, Diameter at widest point: 25.3cm
Collection of the Yangzhou Museum

蓝釉瓷器是将钴料掺入釉料而烧成的高温颜色釉瓷。用钴着色的蓝釉陶器在公元7世纪的唐代已有，而蓝釉瓷器则由14世纪的景德镇窑创烧。此瓶先刻龙纹，然后施蓝釉，在施釉时在龙纹部位刻意留出白地，形成蓝釉白花。主体纹饰为三爪龙，昂首挺胸，张牙舞爪，凶猛矫健。

⬆ 景德镇窑洒蓝釉钵

明宣德（公元1426–1435年）
高11.5、口径25.3、底径11.8cm
首都博物馆藏

Speckle Blue Glazed Alms Bowl from the Jingdezhen Kiln

Xuande Period, Ming Dynasty, (1426–1435 CE)
Height: 11.5cm, Diameter of mouth: 25.3cm, Diameter of base: 11.8cm
Collection of the Capital Museum

洒蓝釉以吹釉法施釉，形成蓝中夹白、星星点点的效果，十分特别。明宣德时创烧，清康熙时发展成熟。此钵为目前仅存的宣德洒蓝器，外壁为洒蓝釉，内壁为白釉，底书“大明宣德年制”，十分珍贵。

➡ 景德镇窑天蓝釉琵琶式尊

清康熙（公元1662–1722年）
高18.7、口径6cm
故宫博物院藏

Sky Blue Glazed *Zun* Vessel in the Shape of a *Pipa* Lute from the Jingdezhen Kiln

Kangxi Period, Qing Dynasty, (1622 – 1722 CE)
Height: 18.7cm, Diameter of mouth: 6cm
Collection of the Palace Museum

天蓝釉是一种高温颜色釉，创烧于清康熙。在釉中加1%以下的钴料，在高温中可以烧成犹如天空一般的蓝色，因此得名。这件天蓝釉器形似弦乐器琵琶，造型柔美，釉色幽淡隽永，是一件精美的陈设器。

其他釉
Other Glaze

景德镇窑孔雀绿釉盒

元晚期（公元14世纪中期）
景德镇陶瓷考古研究所藏

Covered Case of Peacock Green Glaze Porcelain from the Jingdezhen Kiln

Late Yuan Dynasty (mid 14th century CE)
Collection of the Jingdezhen Porcelain Institute of Archaeology

孔雀绿釉又称“法翠”，是一种用氧化铅为助熔剂二次烧成的低温铅釉，创烧于公元14世纪的景德镇。明代成化时开始烧孔雀绿釉，正德时增多，清代康熙达到鼎盛。色调鲜艳青翠，十分美观。

景德镇窑黄釉盘

明成化（公元1465–1487年）
高4.3、口径21.2、足径13cm
故宫博物院藏

Yellow Glazed Plate from the Jingdezhen Kiln

Chenghua Period, Ming Dynasty, (1465–1487 CE)
Height: 4.3cm, Diameter mouth: 21.2cm, Diametr of foot:13cm
Collection of the Palace Museum

黄釉是低温铅釉，创烧于公元15世纪，明成化、弘治、正德时期最盛。尤其是弘治黄釉，娇嫩光亮，达到了历史上低温黄釉的最高水平。此盘敞口，浅腹，内外施黄釉，足内施白釉，书青花双圈“大明成化年制”六字双行楷书款。釉面匀净，呈色娇嫩。

景德镇窑法华釉描金云龙纹贯耳瓶

明嘉靖（公元1522-1566年）
高25.4、口径5.5cm
上海博物馆藏

Fahua Glazed Small Bottle with the Design of a Dragon from the Jingdezhen Kiln

Jiajing Period, Ming Dynasty, (1522-1566 CE)
Height: 25.4cm, Diameter of mouth: 5.5cm
Collect of the Shanghai Museum

法华器，通常在器物表面以"立粉"技法勾勒纹饰的轮廓，再以各种彩色填充。原在山西蒲州、泽州一带陶器上盛行，后被景德镇移植到瓷器装饰。法华瓷器盛行于明后期，器形以瓶、罐为主。该瓶全身施蓝釉，纹饰用金彩描绘。颈部为祥云，腹部五爪云龙纹。口沿和贯耳边沿均以金彩点缀，庄严而富丽。

景德镇窑胭脂红釉瓶

清雍正（公元1723–1735年）
高19.5、口径2.2、足径6.7cm
故宫博物院藏

Carmine Red Vase from the Jingdezhen Kiln

Yongzheng Period, Qing Dynasty, (1723–1735 CE)
Height: 19.5, Diameter of mouth: 2.2cm, Diameter of foot: 6.7cm
Collection of the Palace Museum

胭脂红以黄金作呈色剂，也称"金红"，是康熙年间从西方引进的一种低温釉。它在烧成的薄胎白瓷上施以含金万分之一、二的釉料，于彩炉中烘烤而成。釉汁细腻、光润、匀净，色如胭脂，故名。雍正、乾隆时期的胭脂红器非常精美，堪称典范。

景德镇窑金釉碗

清康熙（公元1662–1722年）
高4.8、口径15.4cm
上海博物馆藏

Gold Glazed Bowl from the Jingdezhen Kiln

Kangxi Period, Qing Dynasty (1662–1722 CE)
Height: 4.8cm, Diameter of mouth: 15.4cm
Collection of the Shanghai Museum

金釉是清康熙的创新品种，将金粉溶入胶水，加适量铅粉，涂抹在瓷器表面，经低温烘烤后，再用玛瑙棒或石英砂在表面碾磨抛光。此盘是康熙金釉器的经典之作，外壁施金釉至圈足，内壁施透明釉，碗心线刻一条捧寿五爪龙。底书"大清康熙年制"青花款。色如黄金，光亮璀璨。

景德镇窑古铜彩蕉叶纹觚

清乾隆（公元1736–1795年）
高29、口径15.8、底径8.3cm
上海博物馆藏

Imitation Bronze *Gu* Vessel with Banana Leaf Design, Jingdezhen Kiln

Qianlong Period, Qing Dynasty, (1736–1795CE)
Height: 29cm, Diameter of mouth15.8cm ,Diameter of foot: 8.3cm
Collection of the Shanghai Museum

此觚为仿早期铜器器形，用金彩模仿铜器的质地，以蓝彩模仿镶嵌纹饰，制作精细，其质感颇似铜器。

➲ 景德镇窑古铜彩牺耳尊

清乾隆（公元1736–1795年）
高21.8、口径13.2cm
故宫博物院藏

Imitation Bronze *Zun* Vessel from the Jingdezhen Kiln

Qianlong Period, Qing Dynasty, (1736–1795 CE)
Height: 21.8cm, Diameter of mouth: 13.2cm
Collection of the Palace Museum

古铜彩是模仿古代青铜器的一种装饰彩，是清乾隆时期制瓷工艺的特殊品种之一。它是在茶叶末釉上用红、绿、黑、蓝等低温彩仿青铜器的斑驳锈痕，或者用金彩摹绘错金银纹饰。足部多为黑、酱色，刻“大清乾隆年制”篆书款。

陶与瓷伴随着人类从古代走到了现在。
陶是世界性的，而瓷则是中国人的发明。
瓷器的烧造实践，深刻地影响了中国人的社会生活，
也广泛地影响了整个世界。
它的技术蕴涵着人文风采，显示了人类文明的发达程度，
也在传播中激励文明水准的提升。
精美的中国瓷器沿着唐代发端的“陶瓷之路”源源外输，
让世界人民分享了文明中国的创造，
也促进了国家和民族间的友好往来与经济、文化交流。

Ceramics are one of the earliest technical inventions seen in early societies across the world. The charm of these ancient pottery vessels is evident, but the invention of porcelain in China led to an entirely new and glorious chapter in the history of ceramic production. Porcelain and the various techniques for firing porcelain have deeply influenced the society and lives of the Chinese people. Innovations and developments in crafting porcelain wares attest to the scientific and aesthetic peaks scaled by ceramic artisans. As ever more elegant porcelain wares were produced they seemed to mirror the increasing elegance of human civilization. Thc lustrous, finely crafted vessels not only changed the very nature of China but also touched those in other countries. From the Tang Dynasty Chinese porcelains were exported to every corner of the globe and the exquisiteness of these porcelain wares have played a large role in promoting friendship, economy, and cultural exchange between nations and people.

结束语

历史这样一页一页地翻过，那些逝去的岁月里原来有如此灿烂的篇章。

是巧思为岁月增添着点点缤纷的色彩，是神工一天天为世界改变着模样。

火药，指南针，造纸和印刷术，写入史册的古代中国的原创发明，不仅改变了古代中国的历史面貌，也改变了世界历史前行的速度。

这些发明是科学复兴的手段，是历史发展强大的杠杆。

数不清的发明也改变了历史的细节，许多的创造都提升了人类的生活质量。一枚衣针，一双筷子，一孔窑洞，一个马镫……，这曾经是千年万年前的发明，一点一滴改变着人类的衣食住行，一步一步推动着历史前行。

本次展出的都是基于自然的古代发明创造，矿石、泥土、平常的动植物在创造中发生了这样多的神奇变化。这些发明伟大而平凡，数千年的时光过去，我们至今仍然在享用历史奇迹所成就的果实，先祖们创建的技术与科学体系为全人类带来了福祉。

往古来今，历史就这样在科学杠杆的助力下加速前行。科技也在不断进步，不断创新，看到这些珍藏的历史文物，我们可以体悟出科技演进的历史轨迹。

在各地的博物馆里，珍藏着许多的古代奇迹，这些奇迹将会陆续展示，让我们共同期待。

CONCLUSION

History is an ever-changing entity, constantly turning over a new page. Some of these developments are particularly magnificent, representing great epochs in the human achievement. Succeeding eras sought to build on these triumphs and push culture, society, and knowledge to even greater heights. The inventions of the compass, gunpowder, papermaking, and printing are noteworthy entries in ancient Chinese historical records. These discoveries not only changed the very face of ancient Chinese society, they also g reatly contributed to the overall development of world history. They revived interest in scientific inventions and engineering within China, thereby spurring progress in traditional China to dizzying speeds.

Countless other inventions have changed the course of China's development and these creations continue to improve the lives of the people. A cave dwelling, a needle, a pair of chopsticks, a stirrup, although invented thousands of years ago, these seemingly simple discoveries have greatly improved the quality of life in China.

This exhibition demonstrates that the foundation for China's various inventions lay in the ability to manipulate natural resources such as metal ores, clay, animal, and plant byproducts. Although centuries have passed by since some of these magnificent or simple inventions were created, we still benefit from these achievements today, since they are the part of the groundwork that forms our own society and culture.

Now, as in ancient times, the continued evolution of human society remains heavily dependent on scientific inventions and advancements. These unceasing technical improvements and innovative creations are put on display in this exhibition. Their aesthetic magnificence is second only to the role they played in improving the existence of humankind. In exhibiting their works of art, museums throughout the world seek to showcase the glory of human accomplishments and irrefutably link us to our ancient ancestors.

总　　撰　王仁湘

大纲设计　徐艺乙　苏荣誉
　　　　　　杭　侃　吕品田

古代丝绸染织术

撰　稿　赵　丰　徐　铮

古代青铜铸造术

撰　稿　吴来明　周　亚
　　　　廉海萍　丁忠明

古代造纸印刷术

撰　稿　董　琦　王永红
　　　　佟春燕

古代瓷器制作术

撰　稿　陈克伦　罗宏杰
　　　　陆明华　叶　倩
　　　　徐霁明　张　东

翻　译　丁晓雷　郭爽怡〔美国〕
　　　　北京译祚翻译有限公司

摄　影　孙之常　刘小放
　　　　郑　华　严钟义
　　　　董　清　薛皓冰
　　　　田明洁　冯　辉
　　　　王　泉　赵　山
　　　　胡　锤　刘志岗

奇迹天工——中国古代发明创造文物展

支持单位

北京市文物局、上海市文物管理委员会、天津市文物局、河北省文物局、山西省文物局、内蒙古自治区文物局、辽宁省文物局、黑龙江省文物局、江苏省文物局、浙江省文物局、安徽省文物局、江西省文物局、山东省文化厅、河南省文物管理局、湖北省文物局、湖南省文物局、广东省文物局、四川省文物局、陕西省文物局、甘肃省文物局、宁夏回族自治区文物局、青海省文物局、新疆维吾尔自治区文物局、西藏自治区文物局、西藏日喀则地区文物局

故宫博物院、中国国家图书馆、中国社会科学院考古研究所

参展单位

首都博物馆、北京大学图书馆、天津博物馆、河北省博物馆、河北省文物研究所、河北省文物保护中心、定州市博物馆、山西博物院、山西省考古研究所、应县木塔文管所、大同市博物馆、内蒙古博物馆、巴林右旗博物馆、辽宁省博物馆、旅顺博物馆、黑龙江省博物馆、南京博物院、南京市博物馆、淮安市博物馆、镇江博物馆、苏州博物馆、扬州博物馆、浙江省博物馆、浙江省文物考古研究所、良渚文化博物馆、奉化县文管委、上虞文管所、慈溪市博物馆、安徽省博物馆、南陵县文物管理所、江西省博物馆、丰城市博物馆、景德镇陶瓷考古研究所、曲阜市文物局、河南博物院、河南省文物考古研究所、郑州市文物考古研究所、洛阳市博物馆、三门峡市虢国墓博物馆、叶县文化局、新郑市博物馆、湖北省博物馆、湖北省文物考古研究所、荆州博物馆、随州市博物馆、黄石市博物馆、湖南省博物馆、长沙市博物馆、长沙市文物考古研究所、岳阳市博物馆、益阳市博物馆、西汉南越王博物馆、四川省博物馆、遂宁市博物馆、西安博物院、宝鸡市青铜器博物馆、法门寺博物馆、耀州窑博物馆、甘肃省博物馆、甘肃省文物考古研究所、敦煌研究院、兰州市博物馆、成县文化馆、武威市博物馆、宁夏回族自治区博物馆、青海省文物考古研究所、新疆维吾尔自治区博物馆、新疆文物考古研究所、和田地区博物馆、吐鲁番市博物馆、西藏萨迦寺

封面设计　敬人设计工作室
　　　　　吕敬人+吕旻
版式设计　李　红
设计制作　北京雅昌视觉艺术中心
责任印制　陈　杰
责任校对　周兰英　安倩敏
　　　　　孙　蕾　赵　宁
　　　　　李　薇　陈　婧
责任编辑　张征雁　李　红

图书在版编目（CIP）数据
奇迹天工：中国古代发明创造文物展／国家文物局，中国科学技术协会编.—北京：文物出版社，2008.7（2011.10重印）

ISBN 978-7-5010-2468-1
Ⅰ.奇… Ⅱ.①国… ②中… Ⅲ.创造发明—文物—中国—古代—图录 Ⅳ.K873

中国版本图书馆CIP数据核字（2008）第053690号

奇迹天工——中国古代发明创造文物展
编　　者　国家文物局　中国科学技术协会
出版发行　文物出版社
社　　址　北京东直门内北小街2号楼
邮　　编　100007
网　　址　http://www.wenwu.com
邮　　箱　web@wenwu.com
经　　销　新华书店
制版印刷　北京雅昌彩色印刷有限公司
开　　本　889×1194毫米　1/16
印　　张　21
版　　次　2008年7月第1版
印　　次　2011年10月第二次印刷
书　　号　ISBN 978-7-5010-2468-1
定　　价　420.00元